PERGAMON INTERNATIONAL LIBRARY
of Science, Technology, Engineering and Social Studies

*The 1000-volume original paperback library in aid of education,
industrial training and the enjoyment of leisure*

Publisher: Robert Maxwell, M.C.

*Policy Sciences:
Methodologies and Cases*

─────── **Publisher's Notice to Educators** ───────

THE PERGAMON TEXTBOOK
INSPECTION COPY SERVICE

An inspection copy of any book published in the Pergamon
International Library will gladly be sent without obligation for
consideration for course adoption or recommendation. Copies may
be retained for a period of 60 days from receipt and returned if not
suitable. When a particular title is adopted or recommended for
adoption for class use and the recommendation results in a sale of
12 or more copies, the inspection copy may be retained with our
compliments. If after examination the lecturer decides that the
book is not suitable for adoption but would like to retain it for his
personal library, then our Educators' Discount of 10% is allowed on
the invoiced price. The Publishers will be pleased to receive
suggestions for revised editions and new titles to be published in this
important International Library.

Other Books of Interest

Belshaw — *The Sorcerer's Apprentice — An Anthropology of Public Policy*

Frost — *The Impact of Regional Policy*

Gooberman — *Operation Intercept — The Multiple Consequences of Public Policy*

Tropman et al. — *Strategic Perspectives on Social Policy*

The terms of our inspection copy service apply to all the above books. A complete catalogue of all books in the Pergamon International Library is available on request.

The Publisher will be pleased to receive suggestions for revised editions and new titles.

Policy Sciences:
Methodologies and Cases

By

Arie Y. Lewin
Duke University

and

Melvin F. Shakun
New York University

PERGAMON PRESS INC.

New York / Toronto / Oxford / Sydney / Frankfurt / Paris

Pergamon Press Offices:

U.S.A.	Pergamon Press Inc., Maxwell House, Fairview Park, Elmsford, New York 10523, U.S.A.
U.K.	Pergamon Press Ltd., Headington Hill Hall, Oxford OX3 OBW, England
CANADA	Pergamon of Canada, Ltd., 207 Queen's Quay West, Toronto 1, Canada
AUSTRALIA	Pergamon Press (Aust.) Pty. Ltd., 19a Boundary Street, Rushcutters Bay, N.S.W. 2011, Australia
FRANCE	Pergamon Press SARL, 24 rue des Ecoles, 75240 Paris, Cedex 05, France
WEST GERMANY	Pergamon Press GmbH, 6242 Kromberg/TS, West Germany

Library of Congress Cataloging in Publication Data

Lewin, Arie Y   1935-
        Policy sciences.

        Bibliography: p.
        1.   Policy sciences.   2.   Policy sciences—Case
studies.   I.   Shakun, Melvin F., 1928-   joint author.
II.   Title.
H61.L477   1975   300'.1'8   75-23356
ISBN 0-08-019601-2
ISBN 0-08-019600-4 pbk.

Printed in the United States of America

To Anita and Norma

Contents

PART III
Cases

Preface

Recently there has been an intensification of efforts to improve policy making by integrating and developing the management sciences into an evolving field which has been termed "policy sciences." The objective of this book is to present an integrated and unique approach—situational normativism—to policy sciences. The uniqueness derives from the integration of behavioral, political, and social considerations with a broad range of systems and quantitative methodologies. Furthermore, this approach encompasses specific considerations of implementation, political feasibility, and organization redesign.

The book is conceived of as a combination of original text material developing the authors' framework (situational normativism) for policy sciences and cases that are related to this framework. Each case was selected either for the real policy problem being analyzed, the approach to the problem, or the specific methodology being applied.

The material is based on the authors' research and joint teaching of a graduate-level course in policy sciences and interorganizational decision making during the past five years at The Graduate School of Business Administration, New York University.* The book is designed as a text for such a course and for similar courses which are increasingly being offered by schools of business, public administration, public affairs and engineering, in addition to departments of economics, management science, and political science. It can be used as a primary or supplementary text at either of two levels—as an

---

*For a discussion of early teaching experiences in this course, see Lewin and Shakun (1971).

introductory overview or as an in-depth conceptual and methodological treatment of policy sciences. Thus, the book can be used both for senior undergraduate and graduate-level courses.

The book is also designed as a basic reference for practicing policy scientists and policy makers. The situational normativism approach developed here provides an encompassing framework for policy making and for utilizing the management sciences in the analysis and solution of policy problems.

We wish to acknowledge the assistance of Mr. Hershy Stern, our research assistant, and Ms. Floydstyne Williams and Ms. Marilyn Eichelberger, our secretaries, who took care of the necessary typing and administrative details. We also wish to express our appreciation to Mrs. Sylvia M. Halpern of Pergamon Press, Inc. for her editorial assistance.

Most important, we wish to thank our wives, Anita Lewin and Norma Shakun, and our children, Oren and Tal Lewin and David and Laura Shakun, for their love—a value with which all policy-making systems should be consonant. We hope the ideas in this book will contribute to better policy making, especially for the sake of our children and all children whose world it will be.

Arie Y. Lewin
Melvin F. Shakun

New York, N.Y.

PART I
INTRODUCTION

Overview of Policy Sciences

The past two decades have witnessed a rapid increase in the number and complexity of policy issues facing policy makers in all branches of government and business. As the magnitude and complexity of problems have increased, policy makers have turned to professionals in the sciences—social sciences and decision sciences—for scientific support in policy analysis and policy formulation. Thus, the military establishment pioneered and institutionalized the involvement of think-tank organizations in policy analysis and formulation of solutions pertaining to defense. The RAND Corporation is perhaps the best-known example of such an organization.

Laswell (Leanner and Laswell, 1951) was the first to observe that the analysis and resolution of policy issues would require a new scientific discipline. He called this discipline "policy sciences," and saw it as an integrated, multidisciplinary approach to policy analysis and policy making.

Dror (1971), in presenting his design for policy sciences, describes current policy-making practices and identifies weaknesses therein, which he traces to the lack of a well-defined operational discipline such as policy sciences. According to Dror, the major problem in most policy analysis and policy making occurs as a result of disciplinary blindfolds. Thus, scientists trained in a specific discipline tend to formulate all problems in the narrow terms of their discipline. Furthermore, the theories used as a basis for analysis reflect their disciplinary origin without regard to the applicability of the theory to the problem being analyzed.

Other weaknesses which Dror observes in existing policy-analysis approaches are the imposition of value judgments, the neglect of critical variables, the absence of political feasibility considerations, and the lack of performance evaluation criteria for specific policy solutions.

These weaknesses point to the need for a multidisciplinary approach to policy sciences and for a new type of policy analyst, one who can combine both a multidisciplinary breadth and depth in the application of these disciplines.

Policy analysis and policy making focus on real-world problems and require application of both normative and behavioral sciences. The underlying disciplines of the policy sciences are the management sciences (operations research, cost-effectiveness analysis, systems analysis, economics, etc.) and the behavioral sciences (political science, sociology, social psychology, organization theory, behavioral theory of the firm, psychology of judgment, etc.). The management sciences can be viewed as sciences of normative knowledge—what one should do—with the application of their methodologies involving optimization of some objective function. Normative analysis, however, begins with a description of or assumptions about the problem situation being analyzed. A complete descriptive model requires behavioral inputs derived from knowledge about organizations, goals, organizational decision making, individual behavior, political systems, etc. In the domain of policy sciences, behavioral inputs regarding system constraints on implementation and political and organizational feasibility are most critical.

The objective of policy sciences is improved policy making through the integration and application of the various underlying disciplines. This book presents a pragmatic descriptive-normative methodology for policy analysis within which normative and behavioral disciplines can be integrated for the purpose of policy analysis and policy formulation.

ORGANIZATION OF THE BOOK

The basic plan of this book is to present the framework of situational normativism—a descriptive-normative methodology for policy sciences. Situational normativism is an approach by which the components of policy sciences may be pragmatically integrated and applied to real decision problems. The approach is situational in that each problem must be analyzed individually; yet, the methodology can be viewed as a general heuristic procedure.

Part II develops our view of policy-making systems and presents the adaptive analytical framework of situational normativism. The framework involves obtaining descriptive models of problem situations, using optimizing techniques or other normative methods in the evolution of constraints and the selection of alternatives, and effecting implementation. Thus, Part II focuses on methodologies by which descriptive models are obtained, normative methodologies applied, and organization redesign and political feasibility analysis undertaken.

Part III consists of original cases which demonstrate the application of the specific methodologies presented in Part II to real-world problems. An introduction to Part III sets the problem for each case and discusses the specific methodologies being applied within the framework of situational normativism.

PART II
METHODOLOGIES

1

A View of Policy-Making Systems

We shall consider policy making as a process of adaptation and shall view a policy-making system as being generally composed of two or more coupled policy makers, each of whom is viewed as an adaptive purposeful system. In doing this, we shall draw on research on situational normativism, values, and adaptive purposeful systems.

SITUATIONAL NORMATIVISM

Discussed further in Chapter 2, some key aspects of situational normativism will be presented here for the purposes of developing a view of policy-making systems. Under situational normativism, policy-making systems are regarded situationally—i.e., they are considered in terms of a decision situation problem involving participants, their goals, and current decision rules. A decision process model—i.e., a behavioral model of the decision process in computer program form—can serve to model a policy-making system. A mathematical model of a policy-making system might be represented by

$$g_i \, (x_1, \, x_2, \, ..., \, x_n) \geqslant b_i, \text{ for } i = 1, 2, \, ..., m, \tag{1}$$

where $x_1, x_2, ..., x_n$ are decision variables controlled by various policy makers. The functional forms g_i in general may be controlled by various groups of policy makers. The set of n strategy variables $x_1, x_2, ..., x_n$ is not fixed (e.g., some new strategy variables $x_{n+1}, x_{n+2}, ...$ may be added). The number of constraints is not fixed (e.g., $g_{m+1}, g_{m+2} ...$ may be added). Some

9

of the constraints are aspiration-level constraints—i.e., the function $g_i(x_1, x_2, ..., x_n)$ must be greater than or equal to aspiration level b_i—and the other constraints involve technological, resource, etc. limitations. The b_i are subject to change. We consider the existing system goals (including the goals of all policy makers in the existing system) to be contained in the whole set of constraints (1) to be satisfied. The left-hand side of (1) corresponds to the means available to achieve the right-hand side—the ends. Thus, goals are viewed in terms of the whole set of means-ends relationships which solutions must satisfy—i.e., in terms of the whole set of constraints. In general, the policy-making system of relationships (1) as seen by the various policy makers may be different. Their respective models (1) may be incompatible in the sense that no solution $(x_1, x_2..., x_n)$ may satisfy these models (the joint solution space may be empty). However, these models are not viewed as fixed. The solution process involves a search for change in the constraints (goals, means-ends) represented by policy makers' models (1) as well as a search for solutions satisfying the changed constraints. In this, implementation constraints (e.g., cognitive style and political constraints) should be explicitly considered (Shakun, 1972).

Thus, we have a problem in adaptation in which the structures (1) as seen by the various policy makers change. Using appropriate behavioral assumptions and mathematical structures, one may study the adaptive process by which various policy makers can arrive at solutions in (1).

An example is the negotiation model by Rao and Shakun (1974), which is a special case of the general situational normativism system (1). In the Rao-Shakun model of negotiation, various behavior concepts guide the search of the negotiators for a solution—an agreed-upon point—in a non-empty joint solution space. The approach employs player 1's subjective probabilities of future concession making by player 2, conditional on the last concession made by player 2 and player 1's current concession decision (and vice versa for player 2). A dynamic programming model is developed to yield normative recommendations as to concession making.

In cases where the joint solution space comprising values $(x_1, x_2, ..., x_n)$ which satisfy (1) is empty, behavior concepts which guide changes in constraints (so that the joint solution space becomes non-empty) as well as guide the search for solutions satisfying the constraints are needed. (See Shakun, 1975.)

POLICIES, STRATEGIES, AND TACTICS:
SYSTEM DESIGN AND PLANNING

We may relate the constraint system (1) to concepts of policies, strategies, and tactics, and to system design and planning (Shakun, 1975). At the *tactical* (operational) level, we are given a particular system (1) and must find solutions $(x_1, x_2, ..., x_n)$ which satisfy that system—that is, satisfactorily relate the means (left-hand side) to the ends (right-hand side). At the *strategic* level, we must choose the ends (b_i values) and the set of strategic variables $(x_1, x_2, ..., x_n, x_{n+1}, x_{n+2}, ...)$. At the *policy* level, we must choose the set of goal variables $(g_1, g_2, ..., g_m, g_{m+1}, g_{m+2}, ...)$ and choose the functional forms of the g_i (the problem of *system design*). Hence, at the policy level, we must design the system's "culture" or capability with respect to its goals (and underlying values), structure, technology, information processing, and the perceptions, attitudes, and skills of its people.*

In situational normativism *planning* is the process of designing and bringing about a desired future for the system (1). It involves making and evaluating interrelated decisions before action is required. Planning occurs at the three levels of policy, strategy, and tactics (see Ackoff, 1970; Jantsch, 1972, 1973; Shakun, 1975).

VALUES, NORMS, AND GOALS

Under situational normativism, operational goals are viewed as the whole set of non-fixed constraints (1) (means-ends relationships) which solutions must satisfy. But what is behind the choice of these goals? A general answer is values and norms.

Norms, as defined by Vickers (1973a), are specific and tacit standards of what is acceptable. (However, Vickers notes that norms may be made explicit—for example, as expressed in a building code.) Tacit norms reveal themselves by match or mismatch signals between the standards and hypothetical or actual events. Values, in Vicker's terms, are general and explicit concepts (such as freedom and order, independence and interdependence, justice and mercy, etc.) coming in inconsistent pairs which fuel ethical debate about them. Norms and values affect each other, and each affects and is affected by policy. Vickers views the role of the policy maker as "devising one among many possible but always partial realizations of contemporary norms and values, and as a partially conscious agent in reshaping the norms and values of his time" (Vickers, 1973a).

Shakun (1975) outlines a referral process between operational goals g_i in (1) and nonoperational goals (values) and norms, which provides a search mechanism whereby the goals g_i in (1) can be changed. This *referral process* goes (Fig. 1): (1) from nonoperational goal I to operational goal A, which subjectively satisfies it (or the process may begin with operational goal A, with nonoperational goal I implicit—represented by dotted (1) in Fig. 1); (2) from operational goal A, which is no longer being satisfied, back to

---

*Thus, *policies* are largely concerned with *what we ought to do* and with *design; strategies* with *what we can do* and with *analysis; tactics* with *what will happen if we do it* and with *operation* (Jantsch, 1972, Chapter 2).

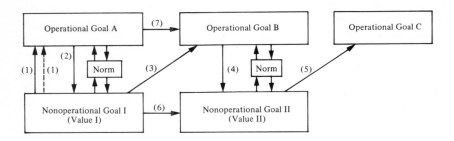

Fig. 1. Purposeful Search and Adaptation by Referral to Norms and Values

nonoperational goal I; (3) then from nonoperational goal I to new operational goal B, which now satisfies nonoperational goal I. Failure to satisfice on goal B can lead to referral (4) to nonoperational goal II and then (5) to operational goal C. The path (6) from nonoperational goal I and II and then to C is also possible, as are others, e.g. (7).

A policy maker may try to change the set of operational goals g_i in system (1) by directing the referral process. Since agreement at the nonoperational level is easier than at the operational level, a policy maker can try to use such nonoperational agreement as a negotiation argument for gaining acceptance of an existing operational goal or a different one which he now wants.

In addition to nonoperational goals (values), which are general and explicit, there are norms that are specific and tacit. In revealing the latter by noting mismatch between current operational goals in system (1) and standards of acceptability, a policy maker can further try to direct the search process in a way he desires. A norm made explicit can strongly influence operational goals g_i in (1) as well as aspiration levels b_i.

Thus, the referral process between operational goals g in (1) and non-operational goals (values) and norms provides a search mechanism whereby the goals g in (1) can be changed. Clearly, the nonoperational goals and norms are also subject to change by referral to the operational goals in (1) as well as to other outside influences. The value impact of technology concept discussed by Baier and Rescher (1969) exemplifies the influence of operational goals on norms and values. This reference also discusses possibilities for prediction of future norms and values using combinations of Delphi, simulation, and forecasting techniques.

Adaptation in policy-making systems is evidenced by match signals between standards (normative values,* mutual expectations or norms) and

---

*Laszlo (1973) views normative values as states of adaptation of the human being to his biological and sociocultural environment. While systems value theory has a long way to go, he feels we may eventually be able to model man in his environment well enough to identify adapted states (standards) for him—i.e., normative values.

hypothetical or actual events. (Nonadaptation is evidenced by mismatch signals.) A nonadapted system is "motivated" to reduce mismatch signals by modification of standards and/or actual events (see Vickers, 1973b). Shakun (1966) suggests that, given existence, a primary value is the overcoming of separateness inherent in human existence. In cybernetic terms, the over-coming of separateness involves adaptation as evidenced by match signals between standards and hypothetical or actual events.

ADAPTIVE PURPOSEFUL SYSTEMS

As noted, policy making may be viewed as a process of adaptation. Prior to discussing this further, we shall develop some fundamentals of adaptive systems applicable to policy making. Such systems will be considered "open systems"—i.e., open to energy exchanges with an environment (Emery, 1969).

A *system* is "a set of interrelated elements each of which is related directly or indirectly to every other element, and no subset of which is unrelated to any other subset" (Ackoff and Emery, 1972, p. 18). The *environment* of a system consists of elements that are not part of the system but can affect it.

An *adaptive* system is one which *reacts* or *responds* to *change* to attain goals. Thus, an adaptive system uses change (i.e., the reaction or response is the use of change) to cope with change. The *change* may be *internal* (within the system) or *external* (in its environment). The *reaction* or *response* may be *passive* (the system changes itself—i.e., how it behaves) or *active* (the system changes its environment—i.e., how the environment behaves).

A *reactive* system can exhibit only one structural behavior in any one environment (e.g., a thermostatically controlled heating system). A *responsive* system can do more—it can learn from its performance, and can choose its means and increase its efficiency. Both are adaptive systems. However, an *adaptive system in policy making* can do still more—it can also choose its goals and is thus *purposeful* (see Ackoff and Emery, 1972). Thus, the adaptive systems with which we shall deal are purposeful.

For such a system, feedback control involves (1) specifying (predicting) outcomes of decisions in terms of performance measures related to goals, (2) obtaining information on actual performance, (3) comparing actual with specified (predicted performance) and taking corrective action as needed. Thus, the feedback process may be viewed as a three-step cybernetic cycle (see Shakun, 1960):

1) *Specification* of goals and performance measures influenced by feed-back from Step 3,

2) *Operation* in pursuit of the goals through execution of a course of action selected in Step 3,

3) *Evaluation* of performance resulting in respecification of goals and reselection of a course of action for further operation.

The essentials of a cybernetic system are readily describable in terms of the diagram in Fig. 2, an adaptation of one given by W.R. Ashby (1956).

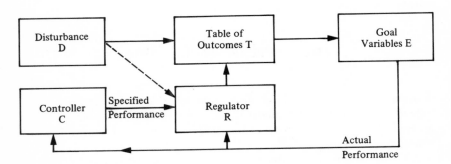

Fig. 2. An Adaptive Purposeful System

The Controller C of the system (policy maker) specifies desirable values for Goal Variables E. Disturbance D represents a set of disturbances which may interfere with the achievement of goals. D may include one or more competitive players in the game theory sense. (C may also be viewed as such a player.) The Table of Outcomes T represents the payoff matrix or structure yielding payoffs to the system (policy maker), expressed as values of the Goal Variables E. The function of the Regulator R is to maintain the output (Actual Performance) in accordance with the controller's specification of goals (Specified Performance)—i.e., R coupled to T acts to keep E within specified limits in the face of Disturbance D.

The solid lines with arrows in Fig. 2 indicate the flow of information in feedback control. The Regulator R is error controlled, error being the difference between specified and actual performance. With feedback control, R's information regarding D is received indirectly via the output E (i.e., there is no direct channel between D and R). *Feedback* control regulation by error may be contrasted with *feedforward* control, which is possible when direct information flow from D to R exists (represented by the dotted line and arrow). When the channel D to R exists, more perfect regulation may be achievable than in regulation through feedback. Hence, we should be alert to the use of direct channel capability between D and R. (Use of the so-called lookout organization and, in general, forecasting efforts may be viewed as attempts to establish such a channel in policy-making systems.) However, in may practical situations this channel is missing or limited. In such cases, we resort to feedback, which often provides regulation that is good enough.

The prime function of feedback or feedforward is to provide R with information regarding Disturbance D. Given this information and provided that it has sufficient *variety* (alternative choices), R can effectively regulate output E. Ashby's Law of Requisite Variety reveals this fundamental requirement of a good regulator: A regulator should have sufficient variety to deal with the disturbances it may encounter or, equivalently, it should have sufficient information capacity.

The success of the regulator depends first on the extent of its variety (entropy) and second on its ability to properly choose among the alternatives available to it (decision making). The latter ability is highly dependent on the intelligence (usable information) which it receives concerning the disturbances. The controller functions to set goals, to increase the variety available to the regulator, to provide solution or behavior concepts for use by the regulator in selecting among alternatives, and to provide means for information transfer. We note that other information flows can exist in Fig. 2—for example, from R to D as well as D to R, E to D, etc.

From an overall view, the behavior of adaptive systems may be viewed as stability seeking. This tendency toward a steady state in its simplest form is homeostatic, as in the maintenance of a constant body temperature. At more complex levels, the basic stability-seeking principle is the preservation of the character of the system, not infrequently through growth and expansion (Katz and Kahn, 1966, Chapter 2). Thus, an organization may attempt to insulate itself from its environment, may negotiate with its environment, and may attempt to incorporate part of the environment within itself, thus controlling it and expanding the system. This is not to say that systems never change but, rather, that stability seeking is operative and much apparent change (including goal evolution) can be interpreted in terms of the preservation-of-character principle.

POLICY MAKING AS A PROCESS OF ADAPTATION

We shall now extend the foregoing discussion on adaptive systems and consider policy making as a process of adaptation. Policy makers may each be viewed as adaptive purposeful systems that are coupled to form a supra-system—the policy-making system. Suppose we have two policy makers, 1 and 2. Viewed as two adaptive systems, policy makers 1 and 2 are coupled to form the policy-making system as shown in Fig. 3.

Figure 3 is an elaboration of Fig. 2. If we view Fig. 2 as representing policy maker 1, then we note that in Fig. 3 we have elaborated on the Disturbance D of Fig. 2. In particular, we have broken out one possible component of Disturbance D in Fig. 2 (namely, a policy maker 2) and represented the latter as an adaptive system in Fig. 3. The other components of disturbance affecting policy maker 1 (e.g., random effects in the environment) remain as

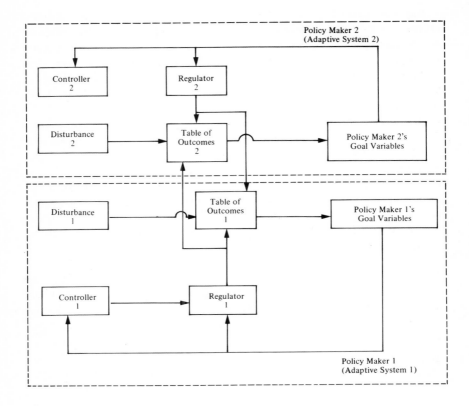

Fig. 3. A Policy-Making System

Disturbance 1 in Fig. 3. Thus, the environment of player 1 includes player 2 and vice versa. The couplings between systems 1 and 2 shown in Fig. 3 are via the information channels between the Regulator R of one system and Table of Outcomes of the other system. Couplings via other channels are, of course, possible (e.g., between regulators).

The two coupled adaptive systems in Fig. 3 represent collectively a suprasystem—a policy-making system in which there are two policy makers. The goals of this policy-making system are the collective goals of two policy makers. Sometimes, as discussed under situational normativism above, the goals of a policy-making system at a particular time are not realizable, but they may become so through a process of adaptation.

For example, we consider a situation in which the process of adaptation involves negotiation between the policy makers. As a simple case, consider that two policy makers each have one goal variable. Each goal variable (say,

g_1 for policy maker 1 and g_2 for policy maker 2) is a function of the quantity (say q_1 and q_2 for policy makers 1 and 2, respectively) of a good that each policy maker demands and gets and the time in the future at which he gets it (say t_1 and t_2, respectively). The negotiation problem is that there is a total M of the good available and the two policy makers must agree on how to divide M into q_1 and q_2, such that q_1 and $q_2 = M$.

In terms of situational normativism, the mathematical representation (1) above of the policy-making system in this situation simplifies to:

$$g_1 (q_1, t_1 \overset{\geq}{} b_1; \tag{2}$$

$$g_2 (q_2, t_2) \geq b_2; \tag{3}$$

$$q_1 + q_2 = M; \tag{4}$$

$$t_1 = t_2. \tag{5}$$

Inequality (2) represents policy maker 1's goal—he wishes goal variable g_1 (which is a function of q_1 and t_1) to be greater than or equal to an aspiration level b_1. Similarly, (3) represents policy maker 2's goal. Equation (4) is simply the constraint that, at agreement, q_1 plus q_2 must equal the total amount M of the good available for division. Equation (5) states that each policy maker gets his agreed-to share of the good at the time of agreement, $t_1 = t_2$. If policy makers 1 and 2 think, not in terms of aspiration levels, b_1 and b_2, respectively, but in terms of making g_1 and g_2 as large as possible, then the mathematical representation of the policy-making system becomes:

$$\max g_1 (q_1, t_1), \tag{6}$$

$$\max g_2 (q_2, t_2), \tag{7}$$

$$q_1 + q_2 = M; \tag{8}$$

$$t_1 = t_2. \tag{9}$$

The sense in which these maximizations take place requires discussion of the negotiation model to be employed.

The negotiation model we shall use for illustration (without necessarily recommending the resulting design) employs (6), (7), (8), and (9) and is based on the work of Coddington (1968). First, some discussion of notation is necessary. Present time is denoted by T and is measured from a moment which is fixed in history. Future time is denoted by t and is measured from the present moment. Demands of bargainers (policy makers) are represented by q_1 and q_2 with q_1 (T) and q_2(T) representing present demands; $q_{1(t)}$ and

$q_2(t)$ representing future demands. E represents expectation in the following sense—namely, that $E_r(T)[q_s(t)]$ represents bargainer r's current (i.e., at present time T) expectation of bargainer s's demand at future time t (here r = 1, 2; s = 1, 2; $r \neq s$).

The expectations of each bargainer regarding the other bargainer's behavior is a function F_r of t, $q_r(T)$, $q_s(T)$, and $V_{rs}(T)$. The latter is an adjustment variable which serves to determine r's expectations of s's future behavior in making concessions. Thus, we may write

$$E_r(T)[q_s(t)] = F_r[t, q_r(T), q_s(T), V_{rs}(T)]. \qquad (10)$$

Bargainer r modifies (corrects) $V_{rs}(T)$ according to

$$\frac{d\,V_{rs}(T)}{dt} = \gamma_r \left\{ - \frac{d\,F_r}{dt}\left[t, q_r(T), q_s(T), V_{rs}(T)\right] + \frac{dq_s(T)}{dt}\bigg|_{t=0} \right\}. \quad (11)$$

Thus, the rate at which bargainer r corrects $V_{rs}(T)$ is proportional to the difference or error between the expected and actual concession rates. Parameter γ_r is a measure of how sensitively bargainer r's expectations react to error.

The expectation of each bargainer regarding his own future behavior is given by the function G_r:

$$E_r(T)[q_r(t)] = G_r[t, q_r(T), q_s(T), V_{rr}(T)], \qquad (12)$$

when $V_{rr}(T)$ is an adjustment variable which serves to determine r's expectations of his own future behavior in making concessions. While $V_{rr}(T)$ may change, it is known by bargainer r. It follows that bargainer r expects agreement to occur at that future time $t = t_r^*$, which is given by

$$E_r(T)[q_s(t)] + E_r(T)[q_r(t)] = M. \qquad (13)$$

Further, at time T, bargainer r expects to obtain agreement at the outcome $q_r = q_r^*$, which is given by

$$E_r(T)[q_r^*] = G_r[t_r^*, q_r(T), q_s(T), V_{rr}(T)]. \qquad (14)$$

In other words, at any present time T, bargainer r expects the outcome q_r^* at time t_r^* in the future, and the goal variable g_r to have a value $g_r(q_r^*, t_r^*)$. Then, following (6) and (7), bargainer r would at every time T make that demand $q_r(T)$ which satisfies

$$\max_{q_r(T)} \quad g_r(q_r^*, t_r^*). \qquad (15)$$

Expressions (10) through (15) represent the basic Coddington negotiation model.

The above negotiation situation is an example of a policy-making system composed of two coupled adaptive systems. Thus, the design of the regulators in Fig. 3 would follow equations (10) through (15).

As mentioned above, Rao and Shakun (1974) have developed a more comprehensive negotiation model which is also a special case of the general situational normativism system (1).

SYSTEM HIERARCHY

We have developed the concept of a policy-making system composed of two or more coupled policy makers, each of whom is viewed as an adaptive system. This policy-making system itself may be controlled by an adaptive system one level higher than the level of the individual component adaptive systems. Thus, we have a hierarchy of adaptive systems. At one level, we have adaptive systems 1 and 2 as shown in Fig. 3. If we add the next higher order level, we have adaptive system I—the policy-making system shown in Fig. 4. Figure 4, representing system I, is an elaboration of Fig. 2. With respect to the latter, we have broken out and drawn in Fig. 4 one part of Disturbance D—namely, the two coupled systems of Fig. 3. Other components of disturbance affecting system I remain as Disturbance I in Fig. 4. We note that in the absence of a system I, systems 1 and 2 nonetheless constitute a policy-making system which is uncontrolled from above. Some examples illustrating system hierarchy are:

Level of Systems 1 and 2	Level of System I
1. Labor unions and company management	1. National government
2. Multinational corporation and host government	2. Largely uncontrolled from above (some control from the home country of the multinational corporation)
3. Securities firms	3. Securities and Exchange Commission
4. Municipal departments	4. Mayor
5. Electric utility and conservationist organization	5. Federal Power Commission

6. Federal Power Commission, electric utility and conservationist organization

6. Judicial system

7. United States and Soviet Union

7. Uncontrolled from above (in principle, system I could be some organization such as the United Nations)

The foregoing constitutes a view of policy-making systems underlying situational normativism. We now turn to a more detailed treatment of this methodology.

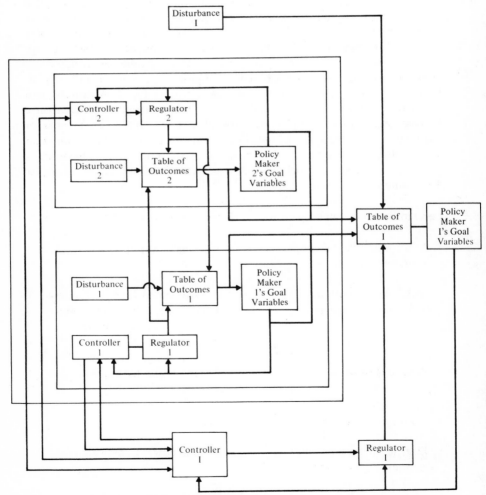

Fig. 4. A Hierarchical Policy-Making System

2

Situational Normativism—
A Descriptive-Normative
Methodology for Policy Sciences

It is almost axiomatic that any problem-solving process must begin with the recognition of a problem. The policy sciences aim at the analysis and solution of complex real-world situations which may face one or more primary active policy makers and one or more secondary policy makers who impose constraints on the feasible policy solution set which must be satisfied. Thus, we view the process as being motivated by the awareness of a policy problem situation on the part of a policy maker. He is treated as the primary policy maker because of his recognition of the problem and because of his motivation to obtain a resolution of the problem. Other participants, or policy makers, become part of the policy analysis process because the final problem definition and the solution affect other participants.

In other words, the problems we wish to consider here are such that both their formulation and their solutions involve many policy makers and these policy makers can be viewed as active and inactive.* Such problems are usually found in the interface between organizations that is the domain of interorganizational decision making. They also occur within an organization when the problem occurs between departments.

As an example of the class of problems and the nature of the process consider an electric power utility. As part of its long-range plan, the utility company concludes that it will need to increase its power-generating capacity. Thus, the awareness of a future need for power-generating capacity initiates the process with the utility as the primary active policy maker. In its analysis the utility will consider technological, economic, regulatory, and environ-

---

*It should be noted that although we began by postulating at least one active policy maker, this does not preclude inactive policy makers becoming active or new active policy makers joining as the solution process proceeds.

mental factors. These all impose constraints on the range of reasonable solutions and thus are being considered as inactive participants in the process. As specific solutions are being developed, additional inactive or active participants and their constraints may be added to the process. For example, the consideration of a nuclear power plant would involve the Atomic Energy Commission and possibly local and national civic action and environmental groups. The AEC usually would be considered an inactive participant with a well-defined set of constraints to be satisfied. The various environmental groups could be both active and inactive. Similar examples can be demonstrated for almost any interorganizational problem and for a subset of intraorganizational problems which cross departmental boundary lines and usually involve the firm's policies or strategic posture.

In summary, the domain of problems to be considered may arise in the environment of the firm, between one firm and another, between departments within the firm, between citizens groups and their governments, and between governmental units (e.g., between state and federal agencies).

Situational normativism is an iterative problem-solving framework for the type of real-world complex problems mentioned above. The approach is situational in that each problem must be approached individually, although the methodology can be viewed as a general heuristic. The methodology of situational normativism involves a synthesis of descriptive (behavioral) and normative approaches. It begins with the formulation of a descriptive model of the real-world situation in terms of the known active and inactive participants, their goals, and estimates of the desired levels of attainment (aspiration levels). Given such a descriptive model, the analysis becomes normative in the sense of generating prescriptive solution alternatives within the identified constraints. The process is iterative as alternative solutions are tested for implementation and political (also organizational) feasibility and as constraints on the process become better defined. Solutions obtained are not "optimal" as such (although mathematical optimizing techniques may be employed) but are satisfactorily prescriptive (preferable) in the sense that they better solve the original problem or a redefined one which emerges in the process. Thus, situational normativism begins with the development of a descriptive model for a specific policy issue which can serve as the input to the normative analysis phase.

In problem solving, a problem can be described as simple or complex or as structured or unstructured. A structured problem is generally one that is well defined and to which a solution may be found by adapting or modifying existing solutions to similar problems or, more generally, by applying known analytical structures applicable to that class of problems.

Unstructured problems, which characterize the problem set in the domain of policy sciences, are poorly defined both in terms of the nature of the exact problem and the class of solutions that might be applicable. Unstructured problem solving consists of a number of phases—problem definition, search and design of solutions, testing of the solution, and implementation.

In the situational normativism framework the formulation of the descriptive model is analogous to the problem definition phase, and the normative analysis includes the search for and design of policy solutions. Although the following two sections treat the descriptive and normative phase independently, the reader should note that this is an iterative policy design process where the problem definition may change as successive solutions are designed and tested against the problem definition and against criteria of implementation and organization feasibility.

A major feature of the situational normativism approach is the implicit consideration of change, implementation (organization redesign), and political feasibility.* There have been many instances where prescriptive policy recommendations (solutions) obtained after accepted rational analysis could not be implemented. Generally, implementation failures have resulted where analysts did not adequately consider the total implementation process—that is, the political feasibility of the solution and the factors involved in organization redesign: changes in structure, technology, people, and goals. **

While some constraints arising from considerations of change, implementation, and political feasibility can be explicitly incorporated in the descriptive model and the normative analysis, by and large these considerations must be handled by judgment at present. However, judgments made in conjunction with a descriptive model can be more rational. Hence, in situational normativism proposed solutions arising from the normative analysis are examined with reference to the descriptive model. This type of analysis often can serve as a basis for modifying the solution that was being considered and also can result in modifications of the basic initial model. Thus, the process may be revised making it possible to reexamine previously rejected solutions and to generate additional new ones via another iteration of the normative analysis.

---

*See also Dror (1970).
**See the discussion in Leavitt (1965).

3
Situational Normativism—Descriptive Models

The problem identification phase—the formulation of the descriptive model—basically requires the identification of the participants affected by the problem situation and the constraints which they place on the design and implementation of an ultimate solution.

The identification of participants is an iterative process by itself. It is not unusual to discover additional participants and therefore new constraints even during the stage of solution design and testing. Companies or public agencies often discover, upon announcement of a plan or policy decision, additional affected participants not previously considered or not explicitly recognized in the proposed plan or policy decision.

Once participants and their goal dimensions have been identified, it is necessary to determine desired levels of attainment (aspiration levels). Although under some circumstances the aspiration level for a specific goal dimension can be established before the solution design phase, such values typically are redetermined in the context of designing and testing the solutions.* This is typically the case because judgmental and bargaining processes are often involved in determining specific goal levels. This is a characteristic of the iterative process embodied in the methodology and is a recognition of the interaction of goals and solutions as the process of policy analysis progresses.**

In the methodology of situational normativism the process of identifying the goals of the participants is analogous to writing the constraint inequalities in a mathematical programming formulation. In situational normativism, however, the specification of the goal constraints may range from nonopera-

*See, for example, Soelberg (1967).
**See, for example, Mintzberg (1973), Weber (1965), and Whitehead (1967).

tional to operational, whereas the inequality constraints in mathematical programming are a strict representation of operational goals only. Operational goals can be stated in a level of aspiration form:

$$g_i \geq b_i,$$

where g_i = measure of performance for i^{th} goal variable, and
b_i = aspiration level for goal i.

Nonoperational goals have no specific measure of performance attached to them. In general, these are policy (value) statements without a specification of the means-end chain which presumably will attain these goals. Organizational nonoperational goals can be regarded as policy statements without the accompanying resource allocation plan. In policy analysis a nonoperational goal is a constraint without a specific measure. For example, the statement "It is our objective to be environmentally socially responsible" is nonoperational. It lacks specific definitions of environmental social responsibility and it lacks performance measures of environmental social responsibility. However, the same nonoperational goal could be transformed into a set of specific operational goals for a particular situation. For example, in the case of a nuclear power facility discharging its coolant water into a river the set of operational environmental goals could include the following: "The temperature of the coolant water when entering the river must not exceed that of the river water." The constraint could be expressed as follows:

$$\text{Temp. (coolant water)} \leq \text{Temp. (river).}$$

In general, unstructured problem solving involves an iterative process between the definition of the problem parameters and the solution. In situational normativism the policy maker/analyst most likely begins with a mixed set of operational and nonoperational goals for his own goal set and for each participant. Simon (1964) noted that goals (constraints) guide the synthesis of proposed solutions and are also used as constraints for evaluating the feasibility of proposed solutions. Thus, the constraints of the problem (whether real or perceived, operational or nonoperational) can serve as stimuli to the design of alternative solutions.

The solution design process includes the transformation of nonoperational goals into operational constraints. In situational normativism the process of operationalizing nonoperational goals is both objective and political (the outcome of bargaining). In many instances operational constraints can be estimated or obtained directly. For example, a power utility considering the building of a nuclear power plant knows that it must satisfy a series of Atomic Energy Commission regulations and acceptance tests, which if not explicitly specified at the outset can be so stated as a result of interaction with the staff at the AEC. The same utility may be aware of the possibility of environmental objections from civic action groups to the same proposal and may not be able to proceed directly to operationalize these objections. This could happen when the specific environmental civic action groups cannot be identified but the recognition of their potential emergence creates a nonoperational goal (constraint).*

It should be noted that the process of identifying the system goals does not necessarily lead to a set of consistent nonoperational and operational goals. In a mathematical programming formulation no feasible solution would be found if the constraint system were internally inconsistent. However, through a process of search and adaptation, the constraint system may be modified so that a feasible solution then exists. If not, other means to a solution must be found. Cyert and March (1963) observe that organizations resolve policy conflict situations through agreement on superordinate goals, sequential attention to problems, and delegation of problem solution and implementation to different subunits or levels in the organization. The policy maker/analyst will also find it necessary to design policy solutions which satisfy conflicting nonoperational goals and which can be implemented operationally through time and spatial separation. Thus, for example, the implementation of a social responsibility policy statement (a broad nonoperational goal) of a large multibranch bank might be left up to the various local branch managers who will fashion local solutions reflecting their particular branch operating environment and their own values (nonoperational goals).

It is conceivable that no feasible solutions can be found for a particular set of problem constraints (i.e., the joint solution space is empty). In practice this can lead to a reexamination of the means-ends transformation of nonoperational goals into operational goal constraints. The objective would be to identify some other operational goal which is perceived to achieve the nonoperational goal and which would permit at least one feasible solution (Shakun, 1974). Which specific nonoperational goals and operational goal constraints (means-ends chains) to examine generally becomes evident during the analysis process. It is, however, related to the perceived ease of change and substitution in a particular means-ends chain and the perceived power of a specific participant. The less the attributed power of a problem-definition participant the more likely that his goals will be subject to change.

The methodology of situational normativism through the formulation of the descriptive model aims at obtaining as complete an initial description of the problem as is feasible. The following two sections detail the application of

*A vivid description of just such a process can be found in a recent report on floating nuclear plants (FNP) in *Science* (March 15, 1974. Vol. 183. No. 4129. pp. 1063-1065). The report describes the evolution of the concept of FNP as a response to the spector of nuclear accident on land, the adoption of FNP by the Public Service Electric and Gas Company of New Jersey (PSE&G) as a technologically and environmentally feasible solution to its long-term power requirements, the negotiations between PSE&G and the Atomic Energy Commission (AEC) regarding licensing of FNP, and the unexpected emergence of several new environmental groups concerned with a potential poisoning of the sea.

two approaches to identifying the system goals—the Delphi method and Decision Process Models.

Although the two methods are presented separately, they can be complimentary and used in conjunction with one another. In addition other methods can be employed—in particular, survey and questionnaire techniques.

THE DELPHI APPROACH

In the early 1960s Helmer, Dalkey, and their associates at the RAND Corporation introduced the Delphi technique for technological forecasting. The objective of the Delphi approach was to improve the use of expert opinion through a polling procedure which required anonymity of experts, statistical feedback of results, and feedback of experts' opinions and reasoning.

The experts on the panel usually do not know one another or, at the very least, must not associate predictions or critiques with an individual. The forecasts are structured in such a way that the median and interquartile range (IQR) can be computed and reported back to the panel. After receiving the summation feedback, the panel members are urged to challenge or support predictions that fall outside the IQR and to make new forecasts. The procedure is repeated until (usually within three to five rounds) the panel converges on a forecast.

Anonymity of the experts on the panel can be achieved through the use of questionnaires or other formal information-gathering procedures. Anonymity serves to eliminate problems, inherent in interpersonal interactions (such as problems related to authority figures, persuasiveness, bandwagon effects, and unwillingness to change previously publicly stated opinions). The use of statistical feedback quantifies the panel responses, minimizes extreme variations, and reduces felt pressure for conformity. The controlled feedback of responses, critiques, and rationales serves to influence participants to consider factors they may have neglected or considered unimportant and promotes a reliable consensus by facilitating rethinking.

According to Bright (1972), the Delphi technique for technological forecasting was widely accepted around the world; by 1972, over 1000 studies had been conducted.

Although the Delphi technique has been used primarily for technological forecasting, it may also be used in situational normativism in the identification of system participants and their goal dimensions and in obtaining initial estimates for aspiration levels.

In the past few years there has been a large increase in the variety and number of Delphi applications, including the analysis and definition of organizational goals and political feasibility analysis in public policy for education, transportation, and health.* A variation of the procedure, which calls for making a forecast, then proposing the extreme opposite and exposing both to strong critical arguments, is presented by Mason (1969) in his description of a strategic planning application in industry.

Of central importance within the situational normativism framework is the formulation of a descriptive model for the problem situation. The concern of the active policy maker is to define the problem situation by identifying and stating the constraints of the problem. For the class of unstructured complex problems considered here, the Delphi approach offers a relatively fast, valid, and simple procedure for identifying inactive or additional active policy makers and their goals.

Although the general Delphi methodology is quite standardized in terms of the need for a panel of experts and the use of some polling procedure and controlled feedback, it must be uniquely designed for each task. The panel of participants must be carefully selected. They should be experts for the perceived problem situation. The polling instrument and the feedback procedure must be carefully designed and objectively implemented. Often the procedure is best implemented by retaining an outside consultant to design and implement the Delphi study for the active decision maker. It should be noted that within the framework of situational normativism it may be necessary to conduct a series of Delphi studies as the analysis iterates from problem definition to solution design, etc.

A case example of a Delphi study to determine organizational goals is described in Part III of this book. The procedure seems to have significant potential for obtaining simple descriptive models of a policy problem situation. It is simple to administer and will obtain valid results. It seems particularly useful for seeking and defining constraints for interorganizational problems.

DECISION PROCESS MODELS

In recent years certain organization theories have emerged which describe organization processes in terms of the problem solving, information processing, and decision making used by their participants. March and Simon (1958) have argued that humans make satisfactory rather than optimal choices in problem-solving and decision-making situations. Furthermore, these problem-solving behavior routines are based on past experience and thus reflect gradual learning as the result of feedback. Within organizations, March and Simon observe that the organization member will aspire to achieve two sets of goals—personal and organizational—and it is not necessary for the two sets of goals to be internally consistent. Cyert and March (1963) extended this

*See, for example, Q. North Harper, "Technology, the Chicken—Corporate Goals, the Eggs," in Bright (1968).

concept by describing organizations as being continually in a latent state of conflict regarding resource allocations. Quasi-resolution of the conflict is achieved through internal bargaining about goals or their redefinition and about the means to achieve these goals. An important characteristic of this process is its dependence on past precedents and standard operating procedures which have been developed from previous experience and trial-and-error learning. The result is an apparent stability of the organization and an ability to predict changes based on knowledge of the goals and the decision rules.

In addition to being the outcome of a bargaining process, the goal set of the organization also has the characteristic of not being internally consistent. According to Cyert and March (1963) and Simon (1964), organizations are able to function within such a conflict situation because (a) localized attention to goals permits many goals to be pursued by decentralized independent units of the organization and (b) sequential attention to goals enables the achievement of conflicting goals at different time periods.

Standard operating procedures or decision rules are developed over time to cope with recurring problem situations. Standard operating procedures (formal or informal) are used for classifying problems, searching for solutions, and for the solutions themselves. Thus, the decision processes most often used in organizations involve (a) information simplification via classification systems, stereotyping, and summarizing information in the form of inferences, (b) factorization of the problem by suboptimizing smaller segments, and (c) adaptive rationality whereby short-run trial-and-error learning is substituted for analysis and calculation.

To the extent that organizations can be described in terms of stable conflict systems by identifying their various member groups, their goals, and the network of decision-making procedures, a viable descriptive model should obtain. The Cyert and March (1963) theory should hold for organizations other than business firms. Thus, for example, Wildavsky (1964) reports similar observations regarding the use of standard operating procedures in the appropriation process of the federal government. Davis, Dempster, and Wildavsky (1966) describe the use of simple decision rules in the federal budget process, supporting the point made earlier on the importance of the network of standard operating procedures in predicting organizational decision making. The foregoing discussion summarizes the behavioral foundations underlying the development of behavioral decision (in formation) process models.

Behavioral models of decision processes in computer program form have been developed by a number of researchers. An early example of a process model in an organizational setting describing the decision-making behavior of a bank investment trust officer was reported by Clarkson (1962). Crecine (1967) developed a process model of the municipal budgeting process. The model was stated as a computer program and tested for the cities of

Cleveland, Detroit, and Pittsburgh. Gerwin (1969a) developed a similar process model of budgeting in a public school system. Based on this model, Gerwin (1969b) then outlined a positive theory of public budgetary decision making. Other examples of decision-making process models of sales planning, purchase planning, administrative budgeting, and search processes are described by Weber and Peters (1969).

In a number of instances process models have been used to guide normative analysis in the sense that they served as the basis for making changes either in the decision rules used in their network of relationships or for a broader redefinition of the problem. A process model, however, can provide the basis for a formulation of the decision situation in mathematical model form to permit a systematic search in normative analysis for improved solutions within a search for improved decision-making structures. (See the section on *Normative Satisficing* in Chapter 4.) Furthermore, the process model also can provide a basis for judging whether the changes implied by a new normative solution are politically feasible. (See the section on *Organization Redesign* in Chapter 5.)

In the following section, Gerwin discusses the concept, methodology, and application of information (decision) processing models to policy analysis.

INFORMATION-PROCESSING MODELS FOR POLICY ANALYSIS

DONALD GERWIN*

In *The Structure of Scientific Revolutions*, Kuhn (1970) argues that science develops as the result of a competition between "paradigms" or "schools of thought." Further, it is his contention that advocates of competing paradigms usually practice science in different worlds—they perceive the same concepts and data in different ways, attack different problems (or separate levels of the same problem), employ different methods and techniques, and use different standards in gauging the acceptability of solutions. It is these unlike values and perceptions which hinder communication between competing viewpoints and reduce the importance of intellectual argument in resolving issues. It seems to me that conflicts over the various approaches to the study of public policy involve aspects of this dilemma and therefore it is necessary to furnish policy scientists with a comprehensive account of a new paradigm based on research in the fields of computer science and administrative theory.

Information-Processing Models
Computer simulation is a broad term which may apply to monte carlo,

*University of Wisconsin-Milwaukee.

industrial dynamics, and certain types of economic and heuristic models. My purpose is to concentrate on the use of heuristic or information-processing (I.P.) approaches to the study of public policy. I.P. models have their roots in two related aspects of empirical science: the study of individual problem solving in laboratory situations by Newell and Simon (1972) and research into administrative decision making in the private sector by Cyert and March (1963). Newell and Simon have dealt with problems characterized by well-defined finite problem spaces such as occur in symbolic logic and chess. A problem space consists of an initial existing state, a set of final states (some of them desired), alternative sets of intermediary states, and operators allowing movement from state to state. Problem solving involves a search in this space until either a path from the initial to a desired position is found or search is discontinued. A crucial aspect of the process is that search is not exhaustive. Instead, it is guided by heuristics, which allow concentration on promising routes but do not guarantee that a solution will be found. Examples of some general heuristics include means-end analysis, factoring into subproblems, and abstracting out the most essential characteristics to work upon.

The Cyert and March research is in part based on the individual problem-solving theories. However, it has been concerned with middle-management types of decisions, such as those involving pricing and output. Here, problem spaces tend to be ill defined or not capable of being specified in advance. Cyert and March have indicated that organizational decisions are made by comparing feedback on performance (initial state) to a goal in the form of an aspiration level (desired state). If the feedback value falls short of aspirations, search processes consisting of fairly stable standard operating rules are triggered in an effort to reduce the difference. There also exist learning rules for revising goals and search rules depending upon whether or not the goals have been attained or the search successful. The incorporation of learning mechanisms is another factor which distinguishes the organizational research from Newell and Simon's.

These works, however, share the general view that problem solving and decision making are closely related, and that in both cases individuals engage in a "selective trial-and-error search" aided by rules which narrow down alternatives. Of what value can such research be to the student of public policy? It is true that it offers little in the way of general premises from which theories can be directly derived. On the other hand, it has supplied a conceptual framework or a way of analyzing governmental issues. For example, consider some governmental unit's annual problem of preparing a budget. It involves an initial state, represented by the value of this year's budget plus new uncontrollable spending for next year, and a desired state, represented by the value of revenue forecasts for the coming year. To balance the budget either by reducing the deficit or eliminating the surplus, we can think in terms of two fairly well-elaborated sets of search rules. The most abstract rule in each set might be a factoring heuristic which considers decisions on the various departmental requests, salary raises, fringe benefits, etc., as independent subproblems. Specific standard operating rules would determine the amounts to be allocated to or from each area. This would be done by a comparison of aspiration level goals and actual performance. The I.P. budgeting models to be discussed later do in fact exhibit these and other information-processing characteristics. Crecine (1969), for example, has indicated the relationships between his budgeting model and Newell and Simon's General Problem Solver.

The example above illustrates the utility of the I.P. view as a conceptual framework but it is characterized by an *ad hoc* approach. We need a more general and systematic statement in order to have a guide for policy analysis. In sketching such a framework below I have made use of not only the I.P. concepts already discussed but others as well, especially those of Feigenbaum (1963).

As shown in Fig. 5a, a governmental unit's decision process in any time interval is viewed as consisting of inputs of information (performance feedback, previous decisions, communicated demands), a transformation represented by the unit's policy, and a specific choice as the output. The last has effects on the organization's environment because it serves as an input for the making of decisions elsewhere. These, in turn, act as inputs in the succeeding time period to the governmental unit in question (along with its own latest choice), and the cycle is repeated.

More needs to be said about the conversion of inputs into outputs. An organization's policy is viewed as consisting of more or less standard rules developed by decision makers on the basis of personal values, past experience, and information stored in memory. These rules involve comparisons of feedback and objectives, search processes, and learning routines. Operationally, they are represented by a discrimination net consisting of test nodes, operations nodes, terminal nodes, and the pathways between them. At a test node, a question is asked about the input data. Depending upon the answer (which is always of the binary variety), we are led down one of two paths, each of which leads either to another test node, an operations node where calculations are made using the data, or a terminal node which stores an outcome. The outcome may be either a numerical value or a function which computes a value.

Solely as an example, consider the following rather naive policy which a hypothetical school district employs to set teachers' salaries (Fig. 5b):

1. Gather data on the current salaries of neighboring districts.
2. *Operations Node:* Compute the average of these salaries.
3. *Test Node:* Is our current salary $<$ the average?
4. *Terminal Nodes:* If the answer to the above question is yes, set our new salary equal to the average; if the answer is no, set our our new salary equal to the current value.

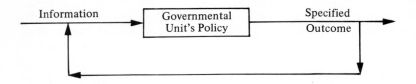

Fig. 5a. Information Processing Framework

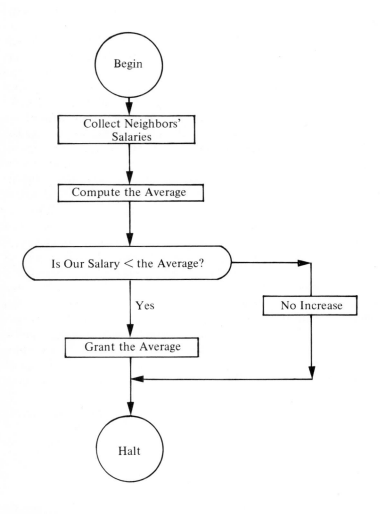

Fig. 5b. Example of a Discrimination Net

Thus, information is processed along a path through the net until ultimately a choice is reached.

It should be readily apparent from Fig. 5b that a discrimination net has a representation similar to that of a computer flowchart. This has an important implication for it means that one can develop a computer simulation model from the net, provided the nodes can be given operational meaning (e.g., what is meant by the term "neighboring" in Fig. 5b). The most exciting consequence of the I.P. paradigm is the opportunity to explicitly formulate and rigorously analyze public policies.

At least four studies have utilized the I.P. methodology to describe and analyze public decisions. Each of them involves a model consisting of discrimination nets connected in a definite sequence so that the output of one is part of the input to the next. Two of the models concentrate on financial resource allocation. Crecine (1969) has developed a model of the municipal budgetary process based on data from Detroit, Cleveland, and Pittsburgh. It consists of nets for requests, the mayors' decisions, and the city councils' review. Inputs are mainly current and past requests, spending and appropriations data, while the outputs are departmental allocations. The most crucial part of the model represents the mayors' decisions. It makes a preliminary expenditure determination for each account which is a function of historical data. Then, after a comparison of total preliminary spending and forecasted revenues, priority systems based on account classifications (maintenance, equipment, salaries, etc.) cut the deficit or distribute the surplus.

Gerwin's (1969a) model of budgeting in the Pittsburgh School District is similar. It involves administrative decisions and the school board's review. Outputs include departmental allocations, salary raises, and other items. Each type of output has its own appropriate informational input. The rules for preliminary departmental spending are based upon the interaction of a priority system and revenue expectations. The most important salary heuristic grants an increase to all employees only when no other comparable system has a lower starting salary for teachers. Deficit elimination rules are designed to affect existing expenditure agreements as little as possible (e.g., raise forecasted revenues or transfer capital outlay appropriations to the bond fund). Surplus reduction heuristics allocate funds to areas of potential conflict so that, for example, teachers receive fringe benefits in the years between salary increases.

A study that may be classified into either the resource allocation or wage determination category is Gerwin's (1971) model of teachers' salary increases in six suburban Milwaukee County school districts. These systems form a "cluster" in the sense that their decision making is interdependent. Each is considered a unit by the model with input information being mainly neighboring salaries and the output being a salary decision. Some decision rules reflect pressures from teachers, citizens, and other school boards, and their effect is to keep any one system within range of the others. Others rules are determined by unique local issues or the personal values of board members, and these rules control where within the range a district will settle. For example, one suburb for a time maintained a small increment over Milwaukee's salary because its board members felt it incongruent to do otherwise.

Recently, Davis and Rueter have applied the I.P. framework to municipal zoning decisions.* The governmental units involved are the City Council and City Planning Commission of Pittsburgh. Each net consists of subnets to handle the problems considered when evaluating a proposal for a change in zoning. The specified outcome is whether or not a proposal is approved while the inputs are mainly the proposal's characteristics and implications. The model contains various heuristics which search for modifications to avoid undesirable zoning map configurations, test for consistency with past decisions, examine compatibility with existing facilities, and investigate the effects upon tax revenues. It also handles a number of other issues.

Constructing I.P. Models

There is no well-formulated strategy for conducting I.P. research on public policy. However, enough experience has been accumulated to report something about the utility of existing methods. To do this, let us think in terms of a two-stage strategy—a preliminary phase in which the researcher familiarizes himself with the system to be studied and a final one in which emphasis is placed on uncovering discrimination nets.

In the preliminary stage the researcher seeks to answer at least three basic questions: Who are the participants in decision making? What is the description of the process? What information is used in making choices? The first question is difficult to answer because there are no objective criteria for determining who is responsible for governmental decisions. Frequently, the formally designated officials are not the only ones and may be reluctant to divulge the other participants. Political scientists who have been interested in this question have developed some techniques (e.g., positional, reputational, decisional) which unfortunately lead to lengthy studies in themselves.** I.P. research has for the most part concentrated on formal leaders, which may be quite reasonable for the types of decisions studied. Since these individuals are relatively easy to find, no special methods have been employed. I think it is reasonable that an explicit determination of the steps in decision making and of the sources and content of information (to be discussed below) may reveal hidden participants.

A description of the choice process means an explanation of the steps in making decisions. For example, budgeting in a hypothetical school district

*See Otto A. Davis and Frederick H. Rueter, "An Information Processing Simulation of Zoning Decisions" in Part III of this volume.
**See, for example, Bonjean and Olson (1964).

may involve the superintendent notifying department heads to send in requests, their complying with his order, an administrative meeting to determine expenditure levels, and the school board's review. Outlining these steps, which can be done explicitly in flowchart form, provides an understanding of who is involved, their functions, and the timing of decisions. One drawback, however, is that there is a tendency to learn mainly about the more formal aspects of the process.

According to our theoretical framework, information is the key input to decisions. Consequently, the preliminary stage should also include a familiarization with the sources and content of information. Typically, this has been done by asking respondents who receives what data. A more systematic method is to incorporate information flows at the appropriate steps in the flowchart just described. Another approach, which should be applicable to many different types of decisions, has been used in the context of teachers' salary increases.* A typology of information was constructed using three basic dimensions. The first classifies communications according to 11 general types such as recruiting, costs, salary structure, etc. The second classifies sources of information according to their location—i.e., the negotiations site, the school district, the metropolitan area, etc. The third classifies sources according to who receives their outputs—i.e., the school board, the teachers' association, or both. As a result of this analysis, individuals such as business managers (who were observed to act as channels for a number of different types of data) were pinpointed as being influential. It is not feasible, however, to learn from the typology which information is most crucial. Clues can be obtained from interviews of the participants and checked out using sensitivi analysis on the computer model.

The final stage of uncovering discrimination nets is complicated by fact that the types of choices investigated are made relatively infreque over a period of months by a group whose membership is subject to ch As a result, the use of direct observation is not usually feasible. Only and Rueter have made some use of it. Instead, the researcher depends upon unstructured interviews in which previous decisions and hyp choices are discussed. A second source is various written docume cially minutes of meetings closed to the public. However, un interviews suffer from respondents not accurately remembering th written documents are not prepared with the researcher's intere An alternative technique based on direct observation in a simula has been tried by Gerwin (1969a). In a preliminary interview t was asked to identify the types of information which had bee in the school board's salary decision. Later, he was prese information for each time in the past he had been involved in was then asked to remake the decision year by year usin verbalize his thinking. Any discrepancy between his ansv

*See, for example, Gerwin (1969a).

value was also discussed. While this technique led to some valuable insights, it suffered from the fact that ideally the entire school board should have been interviewed simultaneously. On the other hand, use of an actual (although simulated) situation mitigates the effect of retrospective bias and exerts a motivating influence upon the respondent.

Next, flowcharts of discrimination nets need to be developed from the tape-recorded interviews. It is not feasible, given the state of the art, to perform a formalized content analysis.* Essentially, clues about rules are gleaned from the tape recordings and then tried out on the numerical data (e.g., actual budgetary allocations) to see the extent to which the latter are explained. Patterns existent in the numerical data also influence hypothesis generation.

One final point about the construction of these models needs to be made. The steps outlined above are not to be interpreted as being strictly sequential in nature. On the contrary, they form a rather complex iterative process. Thus, the unstructured interviews may reveal new information sources and, consequently, additional participants who must be interviewed. Likewise, the inability to explain aspects of the numerical data will lead to a need for more interviews. Ideally, the process should stop only after one is ready to test the model against data not used in hypothesis development.

Limitations of the I.P. Paradigm

Having discussed the I.P. framework, it is now possible to analyze it a bit more critically. For what types of governmental decisions is it most suited? First of all, it is designed to handle routine, repetitive types of choices and in general these are not the most crucial ones. The limitation stems from the fact that only fairly standardized administrative responses can be easily uncovered and programed by the researcher. Thus, Gerwin's budgetary model contains a routine for selecting the year of a salary increase which is highly accurate since the issue comes up every year, but his rules for allocating a surplus are less valid since this opportunity occurs infrequently. Second, in order for the model to be operational, the decisions studied must rely upon information that is quantifiable. Two general types of information seem appropriate—that which is usually termed "numerical data" needed for realistic judgment (requests, revenue forecasts) and that which can be made to represent certain kinds of interest group pressures (salary comparisons as a measure of teachers' dissatisfaction, the proportion of individuals responding negatively to a zoning change on zoning commitment forms). There remains a wide range of unquantifiable data that cannot be represented in a computer model. Davis and Rueter have dealt with this problem by developing a flowchart of the entire zoning decision process and explicitly indicating which aspects could not be programed.

A third limitation stems from the reliance on an *individual* problem-solving

owever, research in this area is beginning. See Waterman and Newell (1971).

view when in fact the decisions being studied are made by groups. It is appropriate to examine situations in which there is usually common agreement or where the members will defer to the judgment of a single person so that a standardized response emerges over time. However, what about groups in which genuine differences of opinion constantly appear or in which the membership is constantly changing so that the decision is not always made in a uniform manner? Here the members will pay attention to different types of information, perceive the same data in different ways, advocate different policy positions, and have different ranges for acceptable solutions. In short, there may be as many discrimination nets as members, and there is no information processing theory of *group* problem solving to help us understand how a collective decision emerges.*

Typically, economic models of public choice exemplify hypothetico-deductive reasoning.** They start from premises which in themselves are not expected to be subject to tests. However, implications are drawn from these assumptions which are meant to be at least conceptually testable. I.P. models are based on a different style of reasoning, which can be termed retroduction, abduction, or hypothesis. Retroduction has been the source of many important scientific discoveries including Kepler's finding of the elliptical orbit of Mars from the data of Tycho Brahe and Watson and Crick's uncovering of the structure of the DNA molecule using a tinker-toy type model to fit existing laws and x-ray diffraction data (Watson 1968). It depends upon the ability of the researcher starting from his observations (numerical data, interviews, etc.) to develop hypotheses which explain them (the computer model), and then to fit his hypotheses into an organized theoretical system (the level of generalizable theory). In short, hypothetico-deductive reasoning proceeds from assumptions to empirical propositions to data, while retroduction moves in exactly the reverse order. Thus, to an economist a hypothesis is a consequence of a given set of premises, while to the information processor it consists of a pattern in a given set of data.

There is at least one crucial difference between retroduction in the physical and biological sciences versus the social sciences. Researchers in the first two areas can often be reasonably certain that the specific units from which data are being collected will either maintain the same pattern over time or have the same pattern as other similar units. For example, Kepler did not have to concern himself with the possibility that Mar's orbit might change significantly over time. Watson and Crick could be assured that all DNA molecules would have the double helix structure. On the other hand, the fact that I.P. models of public policy are based on data from specific cases (three for Crecine and one for each of the others) does raise the issue of their generalizability. It is not to be expected that the details of these models will necessarily be generalizable. However, the basic strategies that have been

*Some promising work, however, has been conducted in this area. See Clarkson and Tuggle (1966) and Clarkson (1968).
**See, for example, Popper (1965).

uncovered serve as plausible hypotheses about the decision-making behavior of other, similar, local governmental units. These may be tested and refined in at least three ways. The model may be adjusted on the basis of additional data as is done in problem-solving simulations, the same type of model may be developed elsewhere and comparisons made with the original one, or verbal hypotheses may be drawn from the model and tested using conventional hypothesis-testing techniques on new data. Gerwin (1969b) has made a start in the direction of generality for the budgeting models utilizing the third approach but without testing against new data. Crecine has been working on the first approach.

The generality of one's findings can also be evaluated in a fourth way—by comparing them to the literature. In this way Gerwin demonstrated that incremental budgeting, priority systems, salary decisions based on comparisons, the cutting of vulnerable areas, etc. were in wider use than just in his school district. In particular, the basic structure of Crecine's mayors' model and Gerwin's model are the same. They both involve a preliminary stage of making expenditure decisions, a comparison of total preliminary spending to total forecasted revenues, and a revision stage in which either the deficit is eliminated or the surplus is distributed to balance the budget. Other more detailed similarities include a reluctance to reduce personnel expenditures and the preliminary approval of requests less than current appropriations. While these results are encouraging, the fact remains that not enough has yet been done to carry out the latter part of the retroductive plan.

Significance of the I.P. Paradigm

What are some of the reasons for employing the I.P. framework in the study of public policy? This question can be explored from two vantage points. We will want to examine the contributions that are being made toward developing more realistic theories of the way governmental decisions are made (theory building) and also toward improving policy formulation (normative analysis).

There are at least two methodological indications of the significance of I.P. models for theory building. First, in contrast to economic theories, the assumptions of I.P. models can be directly tested. The resource allocation studies, for example, are in part based on the incremental budgeting concept for which there exists a great deal of verification in the political science literature. The salary study is based on the wage comparison principle, which receives considerable support in the industrial relations and labor economics literature. Secondly, the several viewpoints developed by economists have utilized comparative statistics as the main analytical tool. The information processor, on the other hand, is capable of producing operational dynamic models of decision making—that is, models in which the values of lagged endogenous variables are predicted rather than being exogenous. Consequently, it becomes possible to trace the time path of the values of those variables which are of interest.

The most significant implication for theory building, however, is the fact that I.P. studies are based on models of specific cases. This allows a perspective on inter- and intraorganizational issues that alternative approaches cannot match. Political scientists, especially those interested in public administration, have made contributions to our understanding of resource allocation at the organizational level, but without being able to operationalize their ideas in general. Economists, while being rigorous enough in their modeling, have been chiefly concerned with more aggregative units and consequently have tended to ignore the bureaucracy mediating between the demands of citizens for public goods and governmental officials' supply of these goods. A good example is Tullock's criticism that the decision makers in Gerwin's theories ignore the demand for education by not considering enrollment increases.* He fails, however, to realize that departmental requests represent much of the demand information in a bureaucratic setting and that these do reflect enrollment increases.

The situation is not much different in the area of wage determination with the exception that much less has been learned about the public sector. Studies in industrial relations, for example Levinson's (1966) case analyses of six Pacific Coast industries, provide considerable detail on wage setting at the interfirm level but do not typically develop formal models capable of being tested. On the other hand, labor economists such as Eckstein and Wilson (1962) indicate the presence of wage spillovers at the interindustry level using regression analysis, but from a highly aggregative viewpoint.

What are some of the findings developing from the new perspective? The budgeting studies have in particular stressed the importance of institutional constraints and intraorganizational conflict. They have demonstrated the specific manner in which the requirement of a balanced budget, a biennial distribution of state funds and other regulations influence the basic structural characteristics of the process. For example, the balanced budget calls for deficit removal and surplus reduction processes, while a biennial distribution leads to a two-year planning horizon. In addition, it has been shown how administrators' attempts to mitigate conflict affect the biasing of revenue forecasts (initially downward in order to avoid making commitments that can't be kept), the determination of priority systems (rules for who gets how much when revenues are scarce), and the timing of salary increases (all employees tend to get raises at the same time). The research on teachers' salaries has highlighted interorganizational effects on decision making by studying the way inflationary tendencies spill over from one school district to another. It has shown that suburbs in the metropolitan areas of large cities form salary comparison clusters based on similar geographical and socio-

*See Gordon Tullock's book review of Crecine (1969) and Gerwin (1969a) in *The Journal of Finance*, Vol. XXIV, December 1969, pp. 1026-1031.

economic characteristics. Once more, each district, at least in the cluster studied, used salary comparison data to first calculate an allowable range and then to choose a definite salary within the range. Other factors such as the cost of living and fringe benefit trade-offs were relatively uninfluential.

Most significantly, the I.P. studies indicate that citizens' preferences have much less direct influence on local governmental decision making than had been previously thought, and that bureaucratic rules, which introduce considerable stability into decision making, are much more important than previously thought. This is most apparent in the large bureaucracies of the budgeting studies where rules are mainly designed to mitigate internal conflict rather than external pressures. In the salary research, which involves small bureaucracies, there is more of a tendency for rules to handle environmental demands from citizens, teachers, and other school boards. Some examples, all of which keep a district from going too high or too low with respect to its neighbors, include the tendency to average available salary data and to have upper and lower limits on raises.

There are also a number of ways in which the I.P. framework contributes to the normative analysis of public policy. An explicit record of the sources and content of information and current heuristics indicates the presence of logical inconsistencies in thinking and areas where choice is largely intuitive (where rules do not exist). The explicit formulation of rules also represents an inventory of the organization's strategies which can be used for the transfer of knowledge to new administrators and as a source of ideas when handling exigencies. For example, a record of rules used previously in balancing projected deficits can be helpful when the need arises again. Because of the dynamic capabilities of I.P. models, predictions can be made for more than one year ahead. This is crucial in financial resource allocation, for example, since current decisions may have future cost implications.

It is also possible to study hypothetical changes in policy by noting the effects on decisions of changes in rules and their parameters. In this way administrators may be forewarned of the implications of impending changes in external constraints, such as state regulations, and be better able to determine whether or not to put changes in internal policy into effect. For example, in Gerwin's budgetary model the school district's policy was to give a salary raise when and only when no comparable system had a lower starting salary for teachers with a Bachelor's degree. The model investigated a policy of aspiring to more of a position of leadership by granting raises when four and then eight comparable systems had lower salaries. In both cases the resulting budgetary reallocation was determined, but of course nothing could be said about the benefits side.

It is no secret that normative techniques for making operations more efficient in the public sector (such as PPBS) have had difficulties in being applied at all levels of government. One reason is that problem formulation and solution have concentrated on efficiency aspects and tended to disregard bureaucratic influences. The reluctance to deal with the latter issues has produced solutions which, from the administrative viewpoint, are narrow in scope and utility. It has also led to implementation difficulties characterized by a lack of acceptance on the part of those who are to use the new systems. The traditional answer to the implementation aspect has been to take the narrow solution as given and to utilize behavioral science principles to overcome resistance to change.

The I.P. paradigm can contribute to the incorporation of bureaucratic factors into normative techniques. It thus works *directly* on the twin problems of narrowness and implementation. This contribution can be made at two different levels, which I have termed the problematic and the strategic. At the problematic level, I.P. *findings* indicate which assumptions of normative techniques are in need of revision. Consider the following implications of Gerwin's budgetary study for PPBS. Starting from the assumption that the individuals in the decision process have different values and therefore that allocations are subject to intraorganizational conflict, it can be concluded that:

1. an important use of surplus funds is to mitigate conflict, a factor not easily incorporated into cost-benefit calculations;
2. there is an inevitable tendency to bias information needed for allocation decisions in directions that will lead to favorable consequences for the estimator;
3. the requirement that all programs be reevaluated each year will lead to heightened tensions, the effects of which are not easily measured.

The strategic level involves the incorporation of information processing *strategies* into the design of new methods for improving efficiency, which is the basis of the situational normativism methodology developed in this book. Actual decision-making models can be used to identify participants, goals, and standard rules in the existing situation. Then, for normative purposes, a mathematical model based on this information is designed. The model should generate satisfactory solutions that are better than the existing one using a search process in which goals and constraints are modified.

Conclusions

Information-processing models of governmental choice have their origins in psychological studies of individual problem solving and research into the behavioral theory of the firm. This background has supplied more in the way of a conceptual framework than a set of assumptions from which propositions can be developed. The framework focuses on the decision process, which is looked at as consisting of informational inputs that are transformed into specified outcomes by means of organizational policy. Policy is represented by a set of heuristics, which in turn are formalized into a computer simulation model. This is as operational a definition of policy as anyone has ever supplied.

The I.P. paradigm is best suited for research into fairly structured types of governmental choices. Up to the present, these have included budgetary allocations, salary increases, and zoning changes—decisions which are characterized by standardized administrative responses and quantifiable informational inputs. There are empirical difficulties in identifying the participants in the decision process and in uncovering policy rules, but new techniques currently being implemented should reduce them. I.P. models are based on the retroductive style of reasoning, which moves from observations to empirical hypotheses to general explanatory systems. However, so far there has not been enough emphasis on carrying out the last part of the retroductive scheme.

The information-processing framework should lead to more realistic theories of governmental choice because it allows a depth of rigorous analysis that other methods do not. It is possible, for example, to study organizational influences on decision making. Once more, an I.P. model has assumptions that can readily be tested, yields quantitative predictions, and can indicate the time path of the values of endogenous variables. The main implication for normative analysis is in suggesting ways in which techniques for improving decision making can be made more practical. This can be done by incorporating I.P. findings into existing normative models and by designing new normative strategies which include I.P. approaches. There are also benefits in the facilitation of information evaluation, the transfer of learning, and the study of hypothetical changes affecting outcomes before they occur.

4
Situational Normativism—Normative Analysis

In normative analysis, we are concerned with what ought to or should be done in a decision situation. In situational normativism, normative analysis begins with a descriptive model of the policy-making system. Then, the normative phase involves a search for satisfactorily prescriptive solutions satisfying original goals or goals that have evolved in the process of analysis. We call this phase *normative satisficing.*

In normative satisficing, we can make use of mathematical programming, simulation, econometric models, accounting methods, even implicit models— any technique that will generate satisfactorily prescriptive solutions. Here we shall focus on the mathematical programming approach to normative satisficing.

The general nonlinear mathematical programming problem (Hillier and Lieberman, 1967; Zangwill, 1969) is to find $(x_1, x_2, ..., x_n)$ so as to maximize

$$f(x_1, x_2, ..., x_n)$$

subject to

$$g_i(x_1, x_2, ..., x_n) \leq b_i, \quad \text{for } i = 1, 2, ..., m;$$

$$x_j \geq 0, \qquad \text{for } j = 1, 2, ..., n,$$

where f and g_i are functions of $(x_1, x_2, ..., x_n)$. In the traditional problem, the values of b_i and the functions f and g_i are given.

Traditionally, optimizing (associated with normative theory) takes place within given constraints, whereas under satisficing (associated with behavioral theory) the evolution and definition of constraints occur simultaneously with the search for solutions. However, under the situational normativism viewpoint, mathematical optimizing algorithms (or heuristic solution techniques or simulation)* may be used in searching for solutions within the search for goals (constraints). The result is mathematical *normative satisficing* in the sense of generating satisfactorily prescriptive solutions which satisfy evolved-in-the-process constraint (goal) sets. We shall illustrate the idea of normative satisficing using a mathematical programming conceptual framework.

SITUATIONAL NORMATIVISM: NORMATIVE SATISFICING

In situational normativism, normative analysis begins with a descriptive process model of the policy-making system in which the participants, their goals, and the decision rules which determine existing outcomes are identified. Assume the policy scientist has identified m goal variables $\beta_1, \beta_2,$ ..., β_m and levels of aspiration $b_1, b_2, ..., b_m$ in the system, so that there are constraints $\beta_i \geq b_i$ (i = 1, 2, ..., m). Based also on the process model, he recognizes n strategy or decision variables $x_1, x_2, ..., x_n$ whose values in general controlled by various different policy makers in the system, affect the achievement of the levels of aspiration. If we write $\beta_i = g_i (x_1, x_2, ... x_n)$, that is, if β_i is in general a function of the n strategy variables, then we have $g_i (x_1, x_2, ..., x_n) \geq b_i$.

Extending the notion of Simon (1964), who illustrates the concept in terms of the diet problem in linear programming, we shall consider the system goals (i.e., the goals of all policy makers in the system) to be that the whole set of constraints $g_i (x_1, x_2, ..., x_n) \geq b_i$ are satisfied. If, as is frequently the case, the x values are non-negative, the system goals or set of constraints can be represented by:

$$g_i (x_1, x_2, ..., x_n) \geq b_i, \quad \text{for } i = 1, 2, ..., m; \tag{1}$$

$$x_j \geq 0, \quad \text{for } j = 1, 2, ..., n. \tag{2}$$

*Heuristics are rules of thumb for searching for solutions (see Meier, Newell, and Pazor, 1969, Chapter 5). With simulation, we describe the operation of the system in terms of the behavior of the individual elements and their interactions. By generating input data, we can simulate the operation of the system and determine its overall behavior. Simulation may thus be viewed as carrying out statistical sampling experiments on the model of the system. By varying the controllable variables in the model and comparing performances, we can identify satisfactorily prescriptive solutions (Guetzkow, Kotler, and Schultz, 1972; Hillier and Lieberman, 1967, Chapter 14; Meier, Newell, and Pazor 1969; Naylor, Balintfy, *et al.*, 1966). For a recent interesting example of the possibilities of using simulation in world policy problems, see Mesarovic and Pestel (1974).

In effect, equations (1) and (2) constitute a set of means-ends relationships, a mathematical model of the decision situation. In practice, of course, other constraints—technological, resource limitation, etc.—would be added to the aspiration level constraints in (1). Based on the process model, the policy scientist attempts to state this mathematical model explicitly. Even if an explicit mathematical model is not stated, a model relating the decision variables x_j to the levels of aspiration b_i exists in the mind of a given policy maker. We are, however, particularly interested in using explicit mathematical models with available search and optimizing techniques to generate prescriptive alternatives. We use the descriptive process model as the basis for constructing the explicit mathematical model.

Suppose that for a particular value of i the left side of (1) is made an objective function. This results in the following mathematical programming problem: Choose $x = (x_1, x_2, ..., x_n)$ to maximize

$$g_i (x_1, x_2, ..., x_n) \tag{3}$$

subject to

$$g_k (x_1, x_2, ..., x_n) \geq b_k, \quad k = 1, 2, ..., m; k \neq i; \tag{4}$$

$$x_j \geq 0, \qquad j = 1, 2, ..., n. \tag{5}$$

We note that sometimes the objective function could be a function of more than one g_i.

For purposes of generating prescriptive alternatives, we treat the maximization of (3) subject to (4) and (5) as a mathematical programming problem, even though we know that the components of x are not in general all controlled by the same policy maker. Further, we do not view the system constraints (1) and (2) nor the associated mathematical programming problem (3), (4), (5) as fixed. Rather we view them in terms of an iterative and adaptive search for a set of means-ends (goals, constraints) relationships within which a search for solutions may be undertaken. Thus, we have a search within a search. Through a process of change and exploration using the mathematical programming framework, various prescriptive alternatives satisfying evolved-in-the-process constraint (goal) sets may be systematically generated. We shall clarify this concept below. Further, while search begins with the existing system, search may end with radical adaptive system redesign in which case the mathematical structures (1), (3) and (4) would change radically.

Simon (1964) distinguishes between goals (constraints) which guide synthesis or generation of proposed solutions (alternative generation) and constraints (goals) which test whether alternatives generated are in fact feasible (alternative testing). For example, in the mathematical programming problem, goal i stated by (3) is being focused on to guide the generation of solutions, and constraints (4) and (5) to test whether solutions are feasible. As a familiar illustration, focusing on (3) using linear programming we might employ either the simplex method of solution which deals with feasible but non-optimal solutions and works toward optimality or the dual simplex method which deals with infeasible but "better-than-optimal" solutions and works toward feasibility. In both cases the focus is on goal i and a sequence of alternatives is generated. In the first case all (but the last) of these are "less than optimal" in terms of the distinguished goal, while in the second case all (but the last) are optimal relative to a specified revision (relaxation) of the current aspiration levels for the other goals.

We note that at the present stage of development the path of the search process is not specified by the methodology and in fact is likely to be different for different policy makers. Different policy makers are likely to divide the constraints (i.e., the system goals) differently—that is, they are likely to have different goal generators and tests and different levels of aspiration. Further, a key aspect of the search path problem is the bargaining problem. Principles from research in bargaining, game theory, values, relevant behavior theory and experiments, and adaptive system design can be suggestive as to search path. Although Shakun (1975) has developed a behavioral model for search and adaptation in (1), as presently formulated the general methodology itself does not give specific normative recommendations as to which path in the search process a given policy maker should follow. However, as search occurs, the methodology does generate prescriptive (normative) solutions which satisfy evolved-in-the-process constraint (goal) sets.

As an example of using the mathematical programming problem to generate solutions, suppose we have an ongoing situation in which a solution $x^\circ = (x_1^\circ, x_2^\circ, ..., x_n^\circ)$ satisfying (1) and (2) is being used at present. One policy maker in the system feels that there is currently pressure on him to make his goal variable β_i as large as possible (his existing aspiration level b_i which is barely being exceeded is too low in light of current circumstances). Focusing on goal variable $\beta_i = g_i(x_1, ..., x_n)$ as an alternative generator. the mathematical programming problem—maximize (3) subject to (4) and (5)—is solved yielding $x = x^*$ and max $g_i(x) = g_i(x^*) = b_i^*$. First, suppose b_i^* is too small in the policy maker's view. If $g_i(x)$ is to be increased further, at least one of the levels of aspiration b_k must be lowered. Exploration of the effect of changing b_k may be facilitated by appropriate post-optimality techniques (e.g., see Dantzig, 1963). Second, assume b_i^* is not only large enough in the policy maker's view but perhaps larger than necessary. In other words, in the programming model the policy maker has a new aspiration level b_i' where $b_i < b_i' < b_i^*$. He would like to have $g_i(x) \geq b_i'$ and increase some $g_k(x)$, say

$g_K(x)$ where K is a particular value of k. In the mathematical programming model $x = (x_1, x_2, ..., x_n)$ is now to be chosen to maximize

$g_K(x)$ subject to

$$g_k(x) \geq b_k \qquad \text{for } k \neq K$$
$$g_i(x) \geq b_i'$$
$$x_j \geq 0.$$

As a concrete example of how feedback to the policy maker of the solution to the mathematical programming problem may result in a modification of goals (constraints), consider the familiar diet problem in linear programming. If this problem were formulated to maximize bulk per calorie (instead of the usual objective which is to minimize cost) and if the optimal solution involved eating 80 pounds of vinegar per day, then a modification of goals (constraints) would be undertaken by the policy maker.

Of course, if no feasible solution—no solution satisfying (1) and (2)—can be found, then one or more of the levels of aspiration b_i will have to be lowered (assuming other quantities fixed).

As additional illustrations, some other situations which may be encountered are

1. The technology changes unfavorably—i.e., one or more of the parameters in the $g_i(x)$ change with the result that one or more of the constraints $g_i(x) \geq b_i$ is not being met. Focusing on those goals which are not being met, the effort will be made to generate new alternatives satisfying the current levels of aspiration; if none is available, these levels will have to be lowered (unless other quantities can be changed).

2. A new constraint (goal) is added.

3. A new decision variable, say x_{n+1}, is added.

In the mathematical programming problem, study of the effect of these changes on solutions may be facilitated by "post-optimality techniques." As mentioned above, radical change in system design could radically change the basic structure of the mathematical programming problem. Thus, the functional forms of the g_i may be subject to change. In some instances the above changes may result from a change in the set of policy makers in the system.

In summary, then, the normative phase of situational normativism involves *normative satisficing* in the sense of generating satisfactorily prescriptive solutions which satisfy evolved-in-the-process constraint (goal) sets.

5
Situational Normativism—Implementation

The methodology of situational normativism incorporates specific consideration of constraints associated with the process of policy implementation. To the extent that problem definition and normative analysis has been a joint decision-making process, consideration of implementation will already have been incorporated into the normative solution. However, in practice such joint decision making is often limited.

The failure of public and business policy proposals to be implemented can be traced to the failure of their proponents (or of the policy analysts) to consider the political and organizational feasibility of their proposals (Rogers, 1971). The implementation of a policy decision implies the creation of a political coalition necessary for the implementation of a change and the introduction of the change through organization redesign. Generally, implementation failures here resulted where analysts did not adequately consider what political constraints were involved and what organizational changes—in structure, technology, people, and goals (see Leavitt, 1965)—would be required.

While at times they may be incorporated as mathematical constraints, at present consideration of political feasibility and organizational change (organizational redesign) involves, in the main, judgmental processes. However, judgments made in the context of the previously developed descriptive model can be more rational in that proposed solutions arising from the normative analysis can be examined with reference to it, thus making the judgments more systematic.

In other words, the analysis of change, implementation, and political feasibility involves the risks of errors in judgment. However, when based upon the type of micro-description of behavior implied in a detailed descriptive model, the occurrence of such errors can be reduced. Furthermore, this type of analysis can serve as a basis for modifying the normative solution and can result in reformulation of the initial descriptive model so as to accommodate the solution. Where the descriptive model is revised, one may reexamine previously rejected solutions and perhaps generate additional new ones via another iteration of the normative analysis.

POLITICAL FEASIBILITY

Since most policy solutions affect the participants in some way, the implementing policy maker must evaluate the effect of political constraints on their implementation. As noted, at present the evaluation of political feasibility is largely a judgmental process. We have suggested above that such judgments can be made more rational by examining solutions with reference to the descriptive model. When such examination reveals an operating political constraint, the solution being considered can be modified, or a modification of the descriptive model may serve to relax the constraint so that the proposed solution can be implemented.

In developing the descriptive model, the policy analyst has identified the affected participants and has formed estimates of their relative power and of the degree to which the problem situation is important to them. By the time a normative solution is developed, by definition, it satisfies the goal sets (payoff structures) of the various participants in the context of the problem situation, as estimated by those doing the analysis. This amounts to conceptually having identified a potential coalition in the sense discussed by Cyert and March (1963). However, it remains to test the political feasibility of the evolved policy in the context of the real world. The policy analyst should play the role of political scientist in analyzing the political realities. These political realities should be made explicit as far as possible. Operationally, political feasibility means trying out the solution on the various participants to ascertain its feasibility with respect to the totality of their real-world constraints (over and above those identified in arriving at the solution). This may result in a negotiation process whereby the solution may be modified—where there has been inaccurate estimation of aspiration levels by those doing the analysis or where newly identified constraints need to be incorporated. Ultimately, the implementing policy maker will have formed a coalition capable of implementing the proposed policy.

At times, the implementing policy maker must be concerned with influencing the political process itself. For example, the political feasibility analysis may point to the need to co-opt new participants critical to achieving political acceptance of the solution. This latter point is illustrated by Lewin and Blanning (1974). Their study proposes that municipal governments be required to publish annually detailed financial and performance reports of their operations to their electorate. Lewin and Blanning include a political feasibility analysis as part of their study. Their analysis shows that the greatest resistance to the idea of an annual municipal report would originate at the municipal government level. They conclude that wide, uniform acceptance of municipal annual reporting could most likely be achieved if it were introduced through legislation either at the state or federal level, and that such legislation would have to be accompanied by the creation of an independent agency similar to the Securities and Exchange Commission (SEC) to monitor and regulate such disclosures. Thus, in general, implementation of municipal annual reporting seems to require the involvement of new participants at the state or federal level. However, in special cases the analysis also noted that local political considerations may be favorable to such implementation by a particular municipality without state or federal participation. At the present time there are few instances where the local political climate has been such that the concept of an annual municipal financial and performance report has been adopted.*

ORGANIZATION REDESIGN

Implementation of policy decisions in some form affects all participants to the problem situation. It may entail the design of new organizational units or the redesign of existing organizational relations. Within an organization, it often requires the co-opting of the participants to accept the new policy solution.

At the national level, for example, the implementation of Congressional legislation almost always requires organization redesign on the part of the executive branch. Generally, the enactment of legislation requires the creation of a department within a government agency to implement the legislation and to be accountable to the Congress on achieving the intent of it. Occasionally, the implementation of a Congressional act (which is equivalent to having developed a policy solution to a problem) results in the creation of an entirely new organization. Examples are the creation of various quasi-independent regulatory agencies such as the ICC, SEC, FPC, AEC, etc., and other special governmental agencies such as the TVA, NSF, NIH, GAO, etc. It is clear that as part of the legislative process Congress is always concerned with specifying or creating the agency which is given the task of implementation and is made accountable to it.

The process of implementation is itself iterative. Congress, for example, may specify the organizational unit responsible for implementing an act. The process of organization design (or redesign) which follows to achieve implementation is an evolutionary one. A classical example of this process is

*A notable example is the report published by the city of Sunnyvale, California.

provided in the study by Selznick (1949) of the Tennessee Valley Authority (TVA) during its formative years. The TVA Act, which was passed by the U.S. Congress in 1933, envisioned the creation of public power utility as a by-product of a comprehensive flood control and navigation system on the Tennessee River and its tributaries. This Act gave effect to a new regional concept for which a special governmental agency was created. Selznick's study vividly describes how the organization and goals of the TVA evolved as it proceeded to implement (define for itself) the "intent" of the Congress and as it responded to evolving situations and demands from new participants in its environment.

Within situational normativism, the descriptive model of the problem situation provides the basis for the initial consideration of the change factors affecting implementation. As in the TVA example, neither the descriptive nor the normative analysis can be expected to completely specify the course of actual implementation. Indeed, the policy being implemented will be adapted and modified in response to problem-specific feedback and the discovery of new, unanticipated factors.

By reference to the descriptive model, the policy maker can determine the strategy of the change process. Knowledge of the participants, their relative power, the interrelationships of the affected organizational units and the network of administrative decision rules provide the basis for evaluating the source and extent of the resistance to the new policy and for selecting the organization redesign strategy.

As the approach to organization design is chosen by the implementing policy maker, it is best analyzed from his point of view. His choice of an implementation structure depends on which of the constraining factors—time, availability of resources, information overload at the policy-making level, and implementation uncertainty—are viewed as being critical in the particular situation.* The more time constrained the implementation of a solution is and/or the more resources are limited the greater the need to plan the implementation process. This will require the development of specific objectives, administrative rules and programs, and a hierarchical referral system for coordination of the project and deciding non-routine problems. Such pre-planning can be achieved through such techniques as PERT and PPB, which can be applied to the identification of sequence of project objectives and the planning of their implementation within predetermined time and budgetary constraints. Pre-planning requires a heavy investment in a control structure and a vertical information-processing system. It also requires the policy maker to make a large initial investment in anticipating non-routine implementation problems and structuring their solutions. Pre-planning will minimize information overload at the policy-making level during

---

*This contingency approach to organization design, particularly as it relates to the predictability of the environment, is discussed by Lawrence and Lorsch (1967).

implementation, but it does require detailed specification of the implementation process.

The development of such a detailed implementation plan may not always be feasible and, under some conditions, may not be desirable. Specifically, where high implementation uncertainty is unavoidable, a preferable approach might be one which facilitates adaptation at the lowest level of the organization or establishes an independent organizational unit responsible for implementation.

The establishment of an independent organizational task unit responsible for implementation requires the identification and inclusion in this unit of major participants and organization groups which will be involved in the implementation of the solution. Once such a task group has been identified and formally structured, its problem (the implementation of the solution) is largely self-contained. The result is a shift in responsibility and authority for the implementation phase from the policy maker to this group. This also reduces the need for creating a complex administrative control structure and for an extensive pre-planning effort on the part of the policy maker.

Self-containment of the implementation task, however, dilutes the control of the policy maker. It may also result in losing the advantages of specialization by having to duplicate at a lower level of capability within the task group many technical and service functions which already exist in the organization but are not sufficiently available to this group; or the task group may have to do without such services. For example, depending on how computer support is available within the organization, the task group may be able to share this resource fully or, as often happens, may have to make do with a lower level of support (unless the task is large enough to justify its own specialized computer support group). In general, the larger the scope of the task and the greater the uncertainty associated with implementation, the greater the likelihood of assigning the task to a formally designated task group.

Another approach for the implementation-organization redesign-problem is to rely on or foster an informal implementation of the solution at the level of the participants and organizational subunits directly affected by the proposed policy. The informal approach relies on voluntary cooperation by the involved participants as they become aware of the task and the need for their cooperation in achieving it. Voluntary cooperation, however, may not always occur. To the extent that the problem is interorganizational (in contrast to intraorganizational), and the more the implementation of the solution depends on participants external to the implementing policy maker, the more it becomes necessary to structure the informal process. Galbraith (1973) describes this as selectively designing lateral relationships. Depending on the magnitude of the task situation and the degree of implementation uncertainty, the policy maker can effect implementation through different options. Galbraith has described these options as creating direct contact between the participants involved, instituting liaison roles, establishing temporary task forces, and/or creating formal project teams.

Except for the concept of the formal project team, which approaches the idea of structuring a self-contained task group, the options discussed by Galbraith are informal, transient approaches to organization redesign. These will work best on relatively simple problems where close monitoring is not necessary. In general the nature of such problems is that their solution at the informal level of the organization is feasible, but it is necessary to create the facilitating transient structure. In such a situation, higher level management can be the catalyst in the process.

In summary, the characteristics of the problem situation—complexity of problem, number and location of participants, information overload at policy-making level, and implementation uncertainty—are parameters in the choice of an approach to organization design. The descriptive model can provide the information about the number and location of the participants, information overload of the decision-making system, and the complexity of the policy to be implemented. The implementing policy maker must evaluate implementation uncertainty and then apply his own values in selecting the organization design approach.

PART III
CASES

Introduction

Part III consists of nine cases which demonstrate the application of situational normativism and its underlying methodologies to real problems. Each case was selected either for the real policy problem being analyzed, the approach to the problem, or the specific methodology being applied. In the following paragraphs, the cases are introduced by posing the problem of each case and relating the specific methodology being applied to the framework of situational normativism.

Case 1. "An Information-Processing Simulation of Zoning Decisions."
This paper by Davis and Rueter was chosen because it represents one of the most recent examples of applying the decision process methodology. Earlier models were developed by Crecine (1969) to municipal budgeting and Gerwin (1969a) to the budgeting process of a school district.

This paper develops a descriptive process model of the zoning decision process in the city of Pittsburgh. It describes the authors' observations of the decision-making process by the City Planning Commission and the City Council. It identifies the three major bodies involved in zoning decisions and the decision-making procedure. Davis and Rueter then proceed to develop the decision process model, which is composed of a series of separate sub-process models each of which was related to a particular problem of concern to either the Planning Commission, the City Council, or both. The paper also includes a simulation of the model to test its validity. The simulation correctly predicted 93.6 percent of both the City Planning Commission and City Council decisions. The results are even better when the City Planning Commission and the City Council decisions are taken separately.

The model is an excellent example of the power of the information-processing approach as applied to an essentially political problem situation.

Case 2."Goal Definition and Influence: A Delphi Case Study."

This case by Cutuly demonstrates the application of the Delphi procedure to the identification of organizational goals. The study was done in the Information Systems Division (ISD) of one of the largest manufacturing companies of the Fortune 500. The study was undertaken with the approval of the division general manager, and its stated intent was the identification of the operational goals of the division at the operating manager level. The panel, therefore, consisted of the nine operating managers reporting to the general manager.

The case describes the step-by-step procedure followed by the author. The goal questionnaire was administered four times. The first questionnaire obtains a goal listing for ISD. The subsequent questionnaires are used to derive successive operational goal definitions.

The case clearly shows the usefulness of the Delphi procedure for obtaining converging estimates, in this instance of the Information Systems Division operational goals. Moreover, it demonstrates the applicability and procedural simplicity of the Delphi method for identifying the participants and their goals as part of the descriptive phase of policy analysis.

Case 3."The Fourth Jetport for Metropolitan New York: A Case Study."

Beginning in 1957, the Port of New York Authority made periodic forecasts of air travel which indicated a substantial increase in passenger traffic utilizing the three New York area jetports. In 1959, the Port Authority recommended that an additional major airport be constructed. It evaluated 15 possible sites and concluded that the fourth jetport should be located at the Great Swamp site in Morris County, New Jersey. The recommendation was greeted with immediate and continuing opposition by local groups, conservationists, and various government officials. It could not be implemented. Following additional studies of 23 sites, a subsequent proposal by the Port Authority for a Solberg location (Hunterdon County, New Jersey) was also opposed, as were sites suggested by other participants.

As of 1970, the situation was deadlocked. In that year a study team at the Graduate School of Business Administration of New York University undertook research on the problem and prepared "The Fourth Jetport for Metropolitan New York: A Case Study." Following the situational normativism framework, the team identified the participants—the governors and legislatures of the States of New York and New Jersey, Port of New York Authority, Federal Aviation Agency, Federal Department of Transportation, airlines, general aviation, local communities, conservationists, Congress, etc. Participant goals and interrelationships were described. Preferences of 16 key participants for various possible outcomes were scaled, and participant relative power was estimated subjectively. Preference coefficients taken as a measure of the likelihood of occurrence of various outcomes were computed. These indicated that expansion of existing jetports and diversion of general aviation from these to smaller airports were favored and likely possibilities. A weakly favored outcome was for a separate central New Jersey airport.

Following the descriptive phase, two normative solutions to the problem—supported by the preference coefficient analysis—were developed. One of these involved three alternatives for resolving the problem without a fourth major jetport—by further expansion of Kennedy International Airport, by construction of a system of general aviation airports to draw that traffic away from the commercial jetports, and by development of an advanced air traffic control system to increase the capacity of the existing facilities. The other normative solution discussed by the team was that New Jersey, on its own, build a jetport at the McGuire/Lakehurst site. Implementation of these solutions was judged to be feasible.

Subsequent to this 1970 case study, the participants in the jetport controversy agreed to select Stewart Air Force Base in New York as the site of a fourth jetport. However, in 1974 the Port Authority questioned the need to build a fourth jetport largely on grounds given in the case study for resolving the problem without such a facility.

Case 4. "National Policies Toward Foreign Private Investment."

In the paper by Tsaklanganos and Rao, the policy problem is a generic one, concerning the policies of host countries toward foreign private investment. The problem is formulated from the point of view of the host country, which wishes to achieve its economic goals, such as growth in gross national product, reduction in unemployment, etc. It is assumed that the foreign investor has as a goal the achievement of a satisfactory rate of return with a preference for repatriating profits rather than reinvesting them (this preference is reflected by discounting the latter). The question is what the national policy should be toward the foreign investor; in particular what incentives (controllable variables) in tax rates, repatriation of profits, etc. should the host country offer to attract foreign investment in order to achieve its economic goals. The problem was formulated as a dynamic goal programming model wherein the trade-offs between incentive levels, investment levels, and achievement of economic goals can be studied by the host country as a basis for policy formation as to incentives. The paper illustrates the use of mathematical programming in the normative phase of situational normativism, although iterative aspects with respect to goals are only implicit.

Case 5. "Effecting Change in Public Policy: Financing Urban Transportation in the New York, New Jersey, and Connecticut Region."

In this case, the authors were charged by the Tri-State Transportation Commission with studying the policy problem of financing transportation services in the New York Metropolitan Region. In the descriptive phase, the authors use an "enterprise" accounting approach in which a financial study is made of the overall transportation system in the New York Metropolitan

Region, involving the various forms of transportation. The sources and expenditures of transportation funds are analyzed and a transportation surplus is calculated. This provides the basis for making normative recommendations with regard to organizational arrangements and the flow of funds (sources and uses). Considering implementation, the authors do not propose an overall regional transportation agency because of the legal difficulties in creating an interstate arrangement among the three states and the opposition of existing state and local organizations. Instead, the following organizational changes are recommended and have been implemented: The establishment of a federal Department of Transportation; the coordination in each of the three states of the administration of all modes of transportation in one department; the organization in each state of a commuter transportation agency with overall responsibility for mass transit facility operations. Although there have been some encouraging signs recently, the recommendations on flow of funds have as yet not been implemented—showing that when it comes to generation and allocation of resources, compared to establishing organizational structural arrangements, the political constraints operate even more severely.

Case 6. "Statement by Texaco, Inc., to the Air and Water Pollution Subcommittee of the Senate Public Works Committee, June 26, 1973."
On June 26, 1973, Mr. John K. McKinley, President of Texaco, Inc., accompanied by Dr. W.J. Coppoc, Vice President of Texaco's Environmental Protection Department, presented a statement to the Air and Water Pollution Subcommittee of the Senate Public Works Committee. It covered Texaco's views on the recent decision of the Administrator of the Environmental Protection Agency to suspend for one year the 1975 automobile emission standards.
The statement together with detailed supporting analysis was made part of the record. It was chosen as a case for this book because it highlights one mechanism by which business can influence public policy and because of the analyses contained in the attachments.
From a policy analysis point of view, the case is of particular interest in terms of the position taken by Texaco, Inc., and the descriptive and normative supporting analyses presented. In essence Texaco, Inc., is asking the Air and Water Pollution Subcommittee of the Senate to consider four changes to The Clean Air Act of 1970. The effect of proposed normative changes would be to establish auto emission standards over the 1975-1980 time period at the pre-1971 level. This would eliminate the need for catalytic exhaust devices, would permit burning of leaded gasoline, would improve the efficiency of the gasoline engine, would arrest the increased dependence on imported petroleum, and would free capital for expansion of refinery capacity. Regardless of the merits of this position, it seems valid to ask why was not the same basic analysis presented to the Senate Public Works Committee when it was considering the 1970 Amendments to The Clean Air

Act. The authors wish to leave it up to the reader to determine to what extent it was feasible for Texaco, Inc., to have made its case, supported by essentially the same analyses, in 1970 when it could have had a major impact on what turned out to be a very significant policy issue.

Case 7."Some Experiences with Guaranteed Incomes and Lump Sum Payments: The Case of the Klamath Indians."

At times, before a national policy is implemented it may be desirable to test it on a limited scale in the real world. This paper by Bunting and Trulove is an example of what results and policy implications such an experiment might yield.

As a means to "eliminate" poverty, recent proposals have suggested some form of guaranteed income or lump sum cash payment. Because these proposals are as yet untried, little information exists indicating their probable consequences for policy making. In this case, Bunting and Trulove examine the experience of a minority group that first received a guaranteed income and later received a large cash payment.

Specifically, for about 40 years, members of the Klamath Indian tribe of Southern Oregon each received a yearly per capita cash payment from the cutting of reservation timber. At times, for a family of five, this payment generated an income approximating the median regional family income. In 1961 federal supervision was terminated and each Klamath received about $43,000 in cash or under trust as his pro-rata share of tribal assets.

The policy goal presumed by Bunting and Trulove is the achievement of economic self-sufficiency by the Klamath. In the descriptive phase, the authors use various data on the Klamath—size of per capita payments relative to the income of other groups, extent of self-support among able-bodied adults, use and remaining balance of pro-rata lump sum payments, earned and unearned incomes, employment—to assess the effectiveness of guaranteed incomes and lump sum payments in promoting economic self-sufficiency. Generally, the authors find the per capita/guaranteed income situation debilitating. The Klamath adjusted their lifestyles downward and ceased to be economically active. When per capitas ended, the Klamath utilized their $43,000 ambiguously—some wisely, some foolishly—but little overall improvement in their economic circumstances is evident.

Based on their descriptive analysis, the authors conclude that for the Klamath, low skills, poor education, and current needs offset positive influences of cash payments. Their normative recommendations follow: Retraining, education, and viable employment are more important than mere cash; further, without incentives, such payments have detrimental effects by encouraging reduced economic activity, by diminishing parental controls, and by discouraging educational attainment.

Case 8. "Annual Reporting by Municipal Governments: An Extension of the Corporate Annual Report."

In this case by Lewin and Cahill the policy issue is a generic one, concerning the need for and the feasibility of requiring municipal governments to publish an annual report for their residents similar to the annual report published by corporations for their stockholders. In the descriptive phase the authors identify the seven major groups that would be affected by such a report. These are the city residents; special interest groups; the city council; county, state, and federal agencies; public media; elected officials; and city government officials. The authors conclude that although the public, through its exercise of the ballot, is called upon to evaluate the performance of the mayor and the city council and to decide whether to keep them in office or to replace them, in reality it does not have sufficient information on the basis of which to make such a judgment.

In the normative phase the authors note that at present the citizen faces a dilemma similar to that which confronted the investor in 1929 and which led to the Securities Act of 1933 and the Securities and Exchange Act of 1934. Among other provisions, these acts established the rules setting the disclosure requirements of corporations to their stockholders. The case therefore proceeds with an evaluation of the applicability of the concept of the corporate annual report to stockholders to the problem of increasing the accountability of local governments to their residents. The normative phase includes the specification of the makeup and content of the municipal report and an extensive analysis of its accounting and organizational feasibility. It includes an illustrative application to several municipalities and concludes with an evaluation of the political feasibility of implementing municipal annual reporting.

Case 9. "The Politics of Manpower Delivery Systems."

This paper by Rogers was chosen for its comparative analysis of the politics affecting the design and implementation of manpower delivery systems in big cities. The three cities studied by Rogers were Cleveland, New York, and Philadelphia. The issue of manpower policy and the design of effective delivery systems has become a major policy problem at the national level, and a political and organization design problem at the local and state level. As Rogers points out, the political issues involve who will control the various manpower programs and how to resolve conflicts between various parties—county, city, state, new and old line agencies, commissioners, program administrators, and various client groups with competing claims for services. The organizational design issues include who should do what, to what extent should the various components of the manpower system (policy, planning, and operations) be centralized or decentralized, and what administrative, research, and programmatic services should be provided.

In his comparative analysis, Rogers clearly develops the situational aspects of the politics surrounding the design and implementation of manpower delivery systems in the three cities. For each city, Rogers analyzes the structure of the manpower delivery system and evaluates its effectiveness. He also relates the structure to the local political situation by identifying and describing the goals of the various political units and their interaction with the system. It is noteworthy that each city implemented, with varying degrees of success, its own particular manpower delivery system which reflected the political power structure of that city. The case concludes with some normative guidelines for developing local manpower delivery systems.

Case 1
An Information-Processing Simulation of Zoning Decisions *

OTTO A. DAVIS[†] and FREDERICK H. RUETER[‡]

AN EMPIRICAL APPROACH TO MUNICIPAL ZONING PROBLEMS

The objective of this study is to develop and then verify a simulation model of the decision process by which zoning ordinances are altered and adapted to the changing conditions of a city. Historically, while many studies by political scientists, economists, planners, and lawyers[1] have also been interested in the so-called "politics of zoning," most of them have continued to utilize the traditional methodologies of analysis. This study, however, applies the Information-Processing Model to (1) simulate the actual decision roles described in the political zoning process, and (2) determine if a computer program (using these rules) can then produce decisions similar to those made by the human participants.

THE PROBLEM IN PERSPECTIVE

The basic methodology of zoning is to divide the geographic area under consideration into a set of mutually exclusive and exhaustive area districts. When these are cross-referenced to the categories specified within the ordinance, they determine the uses for which physical structures may be employed in each zone, such as minimum lot sizes, minimum distances of

*Adapted by permission from Davis, O.A. and Reuter, F.H., "A Simulation of Municipal Zoning Decision," *Management Science,* Vol. 19, No. 4, Part II, December 1972, pp 39-77.

[†] Carnegie-Mellon University

[‡] Clemson University

structures from boundary lines, maximum building heights, etc. These restrictions are imposed in order to eliminate any negative externalities[2] that may develop within each area. Hence, given a complete listing of the categories and their specifications, a static zoning ordinance is completely described, for all practical purposes, by a map which indicates the division of the urban area into distinct and separate districts.

The story would end at this point and certainly be of little interest to us were it not for the inherently dynamic nature of modern-day urban centers. The potential for conflict is obvious when the change of a zoning ordinance is at issue. Areas once assigned for single family residences, for example, may become suitable for high rise apartments. Land developers may see an opportunity for quick profit, if the zoning assignment can be changed successfully. Residents, however, may or may not be willing to sell and move out for the values appraised and offered on their properties. Municipal decision makers, therefore, must necessarily tread a very thin line in keeping the city's separate zoning issues from becoming a chaotic or inequitable experience. Obviously, the municipal zoning problem is a highly volatile, political affair.

Beginning with the requests for change, our objective here is to construct and test a simulation model of this decision process. Part of this task is to define the formal and informal procedures to which such requests are submitted. Another would be to discover and specify the varying decision rules employed by the different participants at the appropriate stages in the process. Lastly, our computer program, which is descriptive of the decision-making process and capable of transforming input information into initial and final decisions on actual case studies must give outputs that correspond to the actual decisions reached by those who participated in the historical zoning proceedings.

Those research objectives, when completed, place this study within an intellectual framework initiated by Simon,[3] elaborated on by Cyert and March,[4] and continued in the context of budgeting by Crecine[5] and Gerwin.[6]

DEVELOPMENT OF THE SIMULATION MODEL

Observation of the decision-making process for zoning in the city of Pittsburgh took place during a six-month period (February through August) in 1968. City Planning Commission meetings were attended by the authors during the entire period as were the City Council hearings that were concerned with decisions on zoning. Formal meetings of the City Council were not visited very often because, as will soon become apparent, the decision procedure is, for all practical purposes, completed prior to the formal meetings. Incidentally, after the participants had developed some confidence in the investigators, attendance was even permitted at the closed meetings of the City Council Committee. For the most part, the municipal decision makers were willing to openly discuss their understanding and views on the zoning process with the research investigators.

These discussions, the observations indicated above, and a thorough examination of many city and news-reporting records gave the insight from which developed certain procedural zoning flowcharts described in the next section.

Decision-Making Procedures

There were three separate bodies that participated directly in the zoning change process: the City Council, the City Planning Commission, and the City Planning Department. The City Council is the legislative branch of urban government. It was composed of nine members, each having been elected by the voters at large. In the map-changing process, the City Council always had the final power of approval after all the deliberations were finished.

The City Planning Commission was composed of nine private citizens (traditionally, architects, educators, lawyers, executives, and government administrators) who were appointed by the City Council to provide them with an impartial, non-political recommendation on every proposal. The powers of the Commission, outlined below, depend strongly on the way a proposal was originally introduced into conference. The Commission usually had only an all-or-nothing say on each zoning matter. The City Planning Department was comprised of a staff of city-employed, professional land-use experts, who served as the advisory body that investigated all map changes and then made their recommendations to both the Commission and the Council. The general procedure for introduction through determination of any zoning proposal is outlined below in Fig. 1.1.

A proposal for change in the zoning map may be introduced into the decision process either as a petition or as a Council bill. A petition is filed with the City Planning Department, which examines the proposal in depth and makes a recommendation to the City Planning Commission. The Commission considers the advice of the Department plus any arguments which might be advanced by either the proposed developer or other property owners or residents in the neighborhood of the proposed map change. It then decides whether to approve or deny the petition. If the Commission chooses denial, the decision process terminates; if it recommends approval, the proposal is transmitted to the City Council for final action. The Council convenes a public hearing at which the City Planning Department presents the position of the Commission, the proposed developer promotes his request, and all other proponents and opponents of the proposal state their opinions. On the basis of this information, the Council either approves or tables the petition. It never formally disapproves a request since such action would make it impossible to initiate any other zoning action on the property in question until a new Council convenes, which could cause a delay of up to two years.

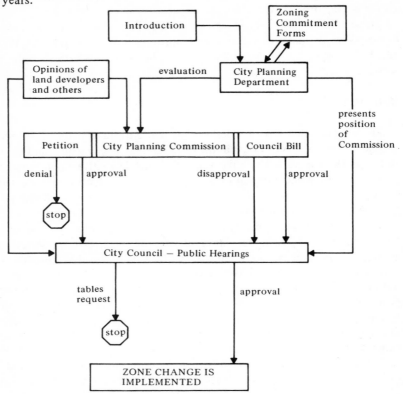

Fig. 1.1. General Decision-Making Procedure.

Alternatively, a proposal can originate in the City Council as a Council bill. It is then forwarded to the City Planning Department, where it enters into a decision process which is identical to the procedure for petitions with one exception—the City Planning Commission no longer has the power of denial. The Commission merely can recommend approval or disapproval to the Council, but in either event the proposal is returned to the City Council for final action. A recommendation of disapproval does have one major consequence, however. It necessitates an affirmative vote by seven of the nine Councilmen for final approval instead of just a simple majority.

The City Council vote may also be restrained or "qualified" by adverse public opinion. The City Planning Department is required by the Zoning Ordinance to send Zoning Commitment Forms (questionnaires requesting statements in support of or in opposition to the proposal) to all property owners within the area included in the proposed map change or within 150 feet of that area. If these property owners comprising 20 percent of any one of four well-defined regions within the total area receiving questionnaires are opposed to the proposal, a seven-ninths or "qualified" majority in Council is required for approval. In addition, a summary of the number of questionnaires mailed, the number of property owners favoring the proposal, and the number of property owners opposing the proposal is likewise reported to both the City Planning Commission and the City Council.

A Decision Process Model

The roles of the City Planning Commission and the City Council in approving a zoning map change have been outlined in the above discussion on general procedure. In this section, we turn to an analysis of the individual behavioral distinctions that determine the final outcome in the two departmental decisions. This processing model, presented below in schematic flowcharts, also formed the basis of our computer programs used to simulate the input-output results of the historical zoning decisions.

Since our perception of the overall process was that it is composed of a series of conceptually separate sub-processes, each of which was related to a particular problem that may be of concern to either the Commission, the Council, or both, and that the sub-processes are identical when they are common between the two agents, the flowcharts are presented as integrated decision procedures for either unit. (Eds. note: For a more detailed listing and description of all the flow charts used in the computer simulation, see Davis and Rueter, 1972.)

Figure 1.2 presents a test of consistency for a change in the zoning classification suggested in the present proposal, with the decisions taken by the zoning units on previous proposals for changes in either the area involved in the present proposal (the "concerned area" in the parlance of the City Planning Department, Fig. 1.2, Item 2) or the region in the neighborhood of that area (Fig. 1.2, Item 4). If any inconsistency is discovered, an attempt is made to determine whether underlying land-use conditions have changed sufficiently to justify reversing these previous decisions (Fig. 1.2, Items 3 and 5).

The incremental demands which the proposed development will place upon the existing public facilities in its neighborhood and the ability of these facilities (and any presently planned expansions of these services) to accommodate these increases in demand are considered in Figs. 1.3, 1.4, and 1.5. In addition, Fig. 1.5 evaluates the potential positive or negative contribution of the proposed development to the solution of the city's perceived housing, employment, and structure abandonment problems.

Finally, in Fig. 1.6, the zoning process takes account of the stated opinions of all private individuals who perceive themselves to be affected by the proposal; it attempts to reconcile these public opinion considerations with the technical and procedural considerations examined previously.

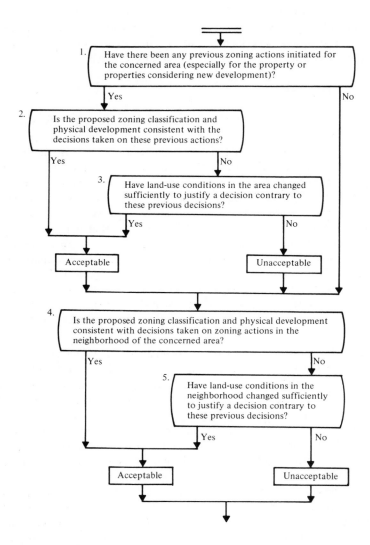

Fig. 1.2. Consistency with Previous Zoning Actions

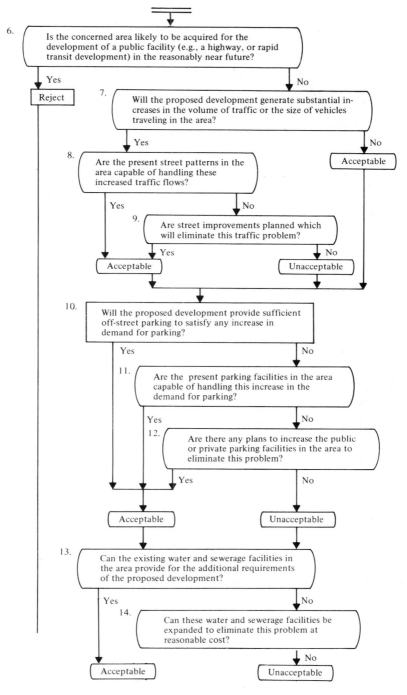

Fig. 1.3. Public Facilities Problems—Traffic, Parking, Water, and Sewerage

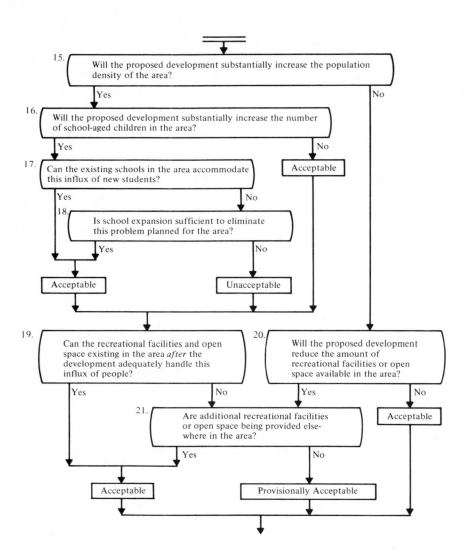

Fig. 1.4. Public Facilities Problems—Schools, Recreation, and Open Space

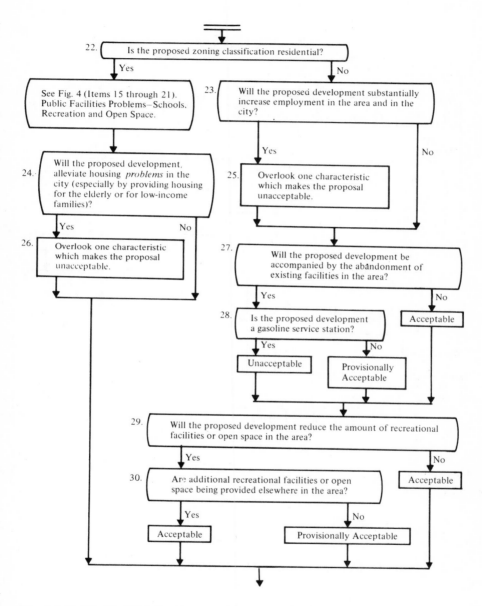

Fig. 1.5 Public Facilities Problems—Schools, Recreation, and Open Spaces. Employment Effects and Abandonment Problems

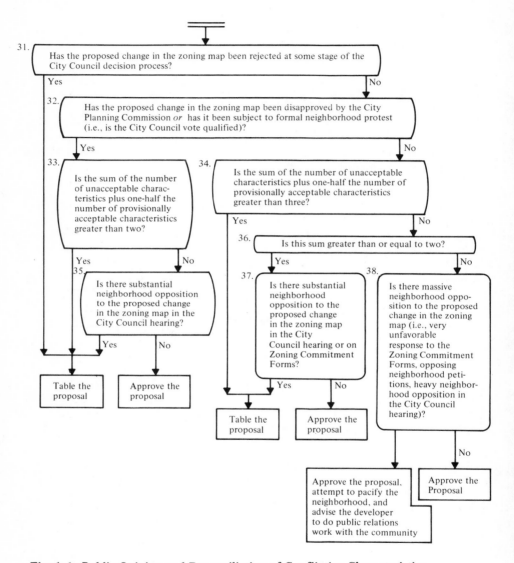

Fig. 1.6. Public Opinion and Reconciliation of Conflicting Characteristics

These five decision blocks may now be combined (with the other figures in the original study) to form the integrated decision processes of both the City Planning Commission and the City Council.

Before discussing the actual simulation, it is appropriate to mention that one of the major problems in the exercise involved the assignment of weights to characteristics which were regarded as undesirable ("unacceptable" and "provisionally acceptable") or as especially desirable and having the power to offset the undesirable features of any given proposal. As can be seen in Fig. 1.6, the weighted sum of these characteristics leads to the decision to accept or reject any given proposal. One might note in this diagram the somewhat magical appearance of the number three (Fig. 1.6, Item 34). Any (weighted) sum of desirable and undesirable features exceeding three means automatic disapproval, whereas a smaller number can lead to disapproval only if there is neighborhood opposition to a given proposal. The number three was chosen to be the cut-off point because it was the smallest number of official reasons given for the disapproval of a petition during the period under consideration by the City Planning Commission. Hence, if reasons were weighted equally, there would be a strong argument for the use of that number. While the program was run with this egalitarian assignment of weights (as will soon be evident), all of the people associated with the decision process will inform one that "some things are more important than others," so that the use of differential weights is obviously necessary. Hence, the magical number three is really a function of the weighting scheme and any number would serve equally well if the weights were properly adjusted.

Our approach to the assignment of weights was essentially pragmatic. Starting with the egalitarian assumption, weights were adjusted according to our intuition which, in turn, was developed from the variety of ways in which the process was observed. In some sense, these weights can be viewed as non-rigorous tests of hypotheses concerning the relative importance of various portions of this observed process. While the parameters of the structure probably are not identified according to traditional econometric criteria, our procedure may be vindicated by an acceptance of the *a priori* belief in what may be euphemistically termed the "principle of cognitive egalitarianism." According to this view, even admitting that some things are more important than others, most characteristics must be weighted equally because humans try to reduce their cognitive load and insist upon isolating only a few items for special consideration. Whether or not one accepts this argument, careful iterative steps were followed in attempting to find the "best" assignment of weights and specification of parameters. Best is defined here in terms of goodness of fit—the percentage of decisions "predicted" by the simulation which agreed with those made by the actual human participants. Sensitivity tests were conducted as an additional precaution. Aside from some unavoidable indeterminacy and a certain amount of arbitrariness, the weights which are reported for these particular results may be viewed as the "best estimate" of the "true" weights. But no matter what the principle of estimation, the authors hold that "the proof of the pudding must lie in the eating," and it is in this spirit that they present the results.

THE SIMULATION EXERCISE

After reducing the flowcharts into a computer program, data concerning actual cases were fed into the system so that they might decide the cases according to the decision procedure outlined above. The data concerned 125 proposed changes in the zoning map of the City of Pittsburgh, which included the entire set of such cases considered during the period 1963 to 1965 inclusive. The data were gathered from the following primary sources:

1) *The Zoning Report of the City Planning Department* to the City Planning Commission and the City Council, presenting background material concerning the area affected by the proposal, a zoning map of the area, the Department's recommendation on the proposal, and its stated reasons for this recommendation;

2) *The Minutes of the City Planning Commission,* specifying its action upon the recommendation of the Department, including amendments and modifications, if any;

3) *The responses of property owners to the questionnaires* distributed by the City Planning Department as a part of its notification process;

4) *The Minutes of the public hearings* conducted by the City Council on all proposals which are not denied by the City Planning Commission *and* newspaper reports of all of those hearings attended by representatives of *The Pittsburgh Press* or *The Pittsburgh Post Gazette;*[7]

5) *The Municipal Record* (the summarized minutes of the City Council), stating the decision of the City Council and the voting pattern of the Council members;

6) *Voluntary petitions or letters* submitted by concerned individuals or civic organizations to either the City Planning Department or the City Council;

7) *Land-use maps of the City of Pittsburgh,* specifying the physical development of all properties in the city as of December 1967; and

8) *Polk's Pittsburgh City Directory 1965,* detailing the land use of each street address in the city as of December 1965.

Quantitative measures of the information gathered from these sources were generated for inclusion into the computer program. Much of this data was transformed into continuous measures of the intensity of various phenomena (e.g., the percentage of the adjacent area included in each of the 24 zoning classifications; the percentage of that area developed in each of 11 land-use classifications; the frontage, slope, and area of the properties involved in the proposal; the number of nonconforming uses created or eliminated by the proposed map changes; and all of the public variables), while other data has been included as dummy variables (e.g., the existence of school, recreation, traffic, parking, water, or sewerage problems; consistency with adopted area land-use plans; and the existence of taxation effects).

Intermediate Results

Before presenting the final outcome of the simulation, it is appropriate to review some intermediate results which were actually used in the simulation but which may be of independent interest. These results are the estimated effects of public opinion upon the City Planning Commission and the City Council. By using standard least-squares estimation techniques in a situation where they are not fully appropriate, taking the decision of the two decision units as dependent variables, and utilizing various measures of public opinion, it is possible to get some idea of the responsiveness of these bodies to pressures from the public. Final forms of the public opinion decision rules which were incorporated into the computer program as the operational representation of the appropriate parts of Fig. 1.6 are presented below.

A. *City Planning Commission actions:*

$$Y = 0.64218 + 0.01528\ X_1 + 0.01261\ X_2 - 0.00811\ X_3$$
$$(0.05689)\ (0.00425) \qquad (0.00411) \qquad (0.00270)$$
$$- 0.00245\ X_4 - 0.02916\ X_5 + E,\ R^2 = 0.3439$$
$$(0.00155) \qquad (0.01752)$$

where Y = the decision of the City Planning Commission
  (1 for approval, 0 otherwise);
and X_1 = the proportion of the property area included in the
  proposed map change whose owners oppose the change;
  X_2 = the proportion of the property area within 150 feet of
  the area proposed to be changed whose owners are
  opposed to the change;
  X_3 = the proportion of the individuals *receiving*
  questionnaires who are opposed to the change;
  X_4 = the proportion of the individuals *responding* to the
  questionnaires who are opposed to the change; and
  X_5 = the number of letters received opposing the proposal.

B.   *City Council actions:*

1. Proposals for which hearing records are available:

$$Y = 0.89512 + 0.36589\ X_1 - 0.00396\ X_2$$

    (0.06448) (0.11063)   (0.00152)

$$- 0.00608\ X_3 - 0.04631\ X_4 + E,\ R^2 = 0.3985$$

    (0.00179)   (0.01841)

where Y = the decision of the City Council
(1 for approval, 0 for denial);

and X_1 = vote qualification due to adverse public opinion
(1 if qualified, 0 otherwise);

    X_2 = the proportion of the individuals *responding* to the
questionnaires who are opposed to the change;

    X_3 = the number of signatures appearing on petitions
submitted in opposition to the proposal; and

    X_4 = the number of civic organizations opposed to
the change.

2. Proposals for which *no* hearing records are available:

$$Y = 0.72194 + 0.18926\ X_1 + 0.00708\ X_2$$

    (0.13136) (0.13412)   (0.00507)

$$- 0.01303\ X_3 + 0.03165\ X_4 + E,\ R^2 = 0.5182$$

    (0.00250)   (0.02458)

where Y = the decision of the City Council;

and X_1 = vote qualification due to adverse public
opinion;

    X_2 = the proportion of the individuals *receiving*
questionnaires who favor the change;

    X_3 = the proportion of the individuals *receiving*
questionnaires who oppose the change; and

    X_4 = the number of articles about the proposal
appearing in *The Pittsburgh Press.*

One rather surprising result of these regression estimates merits special consideration. Those variables which are formally required by law to be a part of the decision process (X_1 and X_2 in the City Planning Commission decision rule, and X_1 in each of the City Council's estimated decision rules) appear in these estimations with a positive sign. While this result was not expected *a priori* (and, indeed, the opposite was anticipated), in retrospect a rationalization is easily supplied. The City Planning Department attempts to influence potential developers to withdraw proposals which the Department regards as undesirable from either a technical or a political viewpoint. Whenever such an attempt is successful, the instance cannot appear with the set of cases under consideration here. In other words, this informal activity of the City Planning Department means that it is extremely unlikely that any proposal which is both technically weak and politically unpopular will be a part of the formal zoning process.

The remainder of the variables, on the other hand, do have estimated coefficients whose signs are those that were anticipated. These latter results, even in light of the above argument, do suggest that both the Planning Commission and the City Council respond to public opinion. In fact, this latter set of variables might tend to indicate that both decision-making units respond more to democratic nose counts of those for and against specific proposals than they do to the less egalitarian concept of considering only those with a direct financial interest.

Final Simulation Results

For any given set of weights, the computer simulation took the indicated data as inputs and produced decisions on each of the 125 proposed changes in the zoning map of the City of Pittsburgh which occurred during the period 1963 to 1965 inclusive. The best results, after all adjustments for parameters and weights were made, are reported below in Table 1.1. "Predicted correctly" for both decision-making units means that the actions of both must have been decided as that unit actually determined the case.

Table 1.1

	Both City Planning Commission and City Council Decisions	City Planning Commission Decisions Alone	City Council Decisions Alone
Total Cases	125	125	86
Predicted Correctly	117	121	81
Predicted Incorrectly	8	4	5
Percent Correct	93.6	96.8	94.2

While the simulation clearly is not perfect, since the program decides some cases differently from the decisions of the actual participants, the correspondence appears to be rather good and the authors judged the exercise to be a success.

The standard practice of the City Planning Commission in Pittsburgh, as in most other cities, is to list a number of reasons for either a denial or an approval on the official form relating to each case. While there is a noticeable tendency for the Commission to be more brief in explaining approvals than denials, it is possible to divide both sets of reasons into standard categories.

Hence, at least for the final run with the "best" assignment of weights, the authors thought that it might be of special interest to see how closely the reasons listed by the Planning Commission corresponded to the set produced by the simulation as an explanation for acceptance or denial.

For the 125 cases which occurred during the period 1963 through 1965, the City Planning Commission listed a total of 384 reasons for its decisions. On a case-by-case basis, the machine duplicated 293 of those reasons, leaving 91 reasons listed by the humans which the computer did not consider. In all fairness to the machine, one should also report that it noticed 80 reasons which, apparently, escaped the consideration of the human participants. These 80 reasons were associated with 57 of the cases.

When viewed in a slightly different manner, however, these statistics do not seem quite so impressive. There were only 49 cases in which the simulation produced all of the reasons listed by the City Planning Commission, and in some of these it added additional reasons of its own. In fact, in merely 26 cases did the machine produce the exact set of reasons, no more and no less, that were listed by the human participants. On the other hand, there was only one case in which the computer had totally failed to list even one of the reasons given by the Commission, and in 61 of the cases, it did manage to produce all save one of the reasons given by the Commission. Thus, in 110 (49 + 61) of the 125 cases the simulation was able to produce all and all less one of the official reasons given by the Planning Commission for its own zoning decisions.

Tests Against Alternative Models

One standard method for testing simulation results with results of other estimation models is a comparison of their predictability. Since 71 of the 125 cases in our selection were approved, the probability for an approval of a randomly drawn case is $71/125$. Likewise, the probability of disapproval is $54/125$.

Combining these two ratios for the expected number of correct classifications (assuming replacement) we get

$$71(71/125) + 54(54/125) = 63.66$$

cases that should, on repeated trials be correctly classified. This represents 50.9 percent ($63.66/125$) of the total group of cases observed in our simulation. Clearly, Table 1 above indicated that our model performed much better than this random process.

Actually, this probability model, although instructive for overall comparison, does not really do justice to the details of the simulation since the latter also made separate predictions for both the City Planning Commission and the City Council. Hence, it may be useful to compare outcomes with more detailed models of the same type.

As a preparation for such models, it may be useful to cross reference the outcomes for the cases which were studied so that the issues may be more easily comprehended. Table 1.2 presents this cross reference along with row and column totals.

Table 1.2   City Council

	Outcomes	Approval	Table	No Action	Totals
City Planning Commission	Approval	66	5	0	71
	Disapproval	5	10	39	54
	Totals	71	15	39	125

The entries mean, for example, that the City Council approved five cases that the Planning Commission had disapproved, tabled five that the Commission had approved, and took no action on 39 instances in which the Commission had also disapproved.

Consider the City Council first. Since we are concerned with the final outcomes in the simulation compared to the results in a probabilistic model, we account for only those cases brought before the Council chambers. Of the 125 decisions, only 86–71 Commission approvals and 15 Commission disapprovals—were reviewed by the City Council. Again, of these 86 cases, the expectation of correct classification was broken down into four states:

66(66/71) + 5(5/71) represents the Council Approvals and Tables, respectively, of the Commission approvals, and 5(5/15) + 10(10/15) for the breakdown between the Council Approvals and Tables, respectively, of the Commission disapprovals.

The total expectation of correct cases, by the probabilistic model, is 70.03 or 81.4 percent compared to 81 cases or 94.2 percent in the simulation.

The City Planning Commission is somewhat simpler since it only approves or disapproves from one pool of cases (at least in this model). Without repeating the story, the proper calculations are:

$$71(71/125) + 54(54/125) = 63.66$$

which is the expected number of correct classifications and

$$63.33/125 = 50.9$$

which is the percentage expected to be correct on the basis of this random model. From Table 1.1, we may determine that the simulation model predicted 121 cases, or 96.8 percent, correctly, which appears to be substantially better than this random model.

Finally, the simulation model itself produces results which can be classified according to the matrix representation of Table 1.2 so that the proper overall comparison is against a random model based upon this kind of information. Without repeating the now familiar imaginary experiment, the appropriate calculations are:

$$66(66/125) + 5(5/125) + 5(5/125) + 10(10/125) + 39(39/125) = 48.22$$

cases which one should expect to be correctly classified according to this cross classification. In percentage terms,

$$48.22/125 = 38.6$$

percent of the cases should be correctly accounted for on the basis of this random model. From Table 1.1, we find that the appropriate comparative number for the simulation model is 93.6 percent, which would appear to be substantially better than can be expected on a random basis.

Given the above, it would appear that the simulation does perform better than alternative random models, which is encouraging in view of the fact that the random models had the advantage of being given the appropriate probabilities whereas the simulation operated without recourse to such information. On the other hand, it may be appropriate, especially in view of the political and economic nature of the basic subject matter, to compare the performance of the simulation to alternative "political" and "economic" models. Comparisons with several such naive models are offered below.

The series of the simple "political" models that will be examined here takes advantage of the fact that enabling legislation requires "affected" property owners to be notified by mail that a proposal is in process. These property owners—those owning property in the concerned area plus those whose property lies within 150 feet of the boundary of that area—are sent questionnaires upon which they can respond favorably or unfavorably to any given proposal. These naive political models assume that the entire decision-making process responds "democratically" to public opinion as it is registered on these questionnaires.

The first four models assumed that the participants acted with respect to the percentage of the *total number of forms which were mailed*. Thus, the two most obvious rules, given the majority rule bias of our culture, are the following: (1) Approve only petitions or bills for which a simple majority of the mailed questionnaires records a favorable response. (2) Reject only petitions or bills in which a simple majority of the mailed questionnaires records an unfavorable response. Note that these two rules are not symmetric due to the fact of the existence of non-respondents. For the 125 cases that were studied here, the application of these simple rules produces the results reported in Table 1.3.

Table 1.3 Rules for the Percent of Forms Mailed

	Pass if 50 percent or more favor	Reject if 50 percent or more oppose
Predicted Correctly	56	82
Predicted Incorrectly	69	43
Percent Correct	44.8	65.6

Clearly, neither of these "majority rule" decision procedures produces results that are nearly as good as those produced by the simulation.

Given the above results, it is only natural to wonder whether something different from majority rule might perform in an improved manner. Thus, the following may be considered: (3) Approve only those petitions or bills for which an 80 percent or larger majority of the mailed questionnaires records a favorable response. (4) Reject only those petitions or bills for which 20 percent or more of the mailed questionnaires records an unfavorable response. The selection of a critical value of 20 percent is suggested by its appearance in the formal decision rule for City Council vote qualification due to adverse public opinion. Again, note that these are not the reciprocal of each other due to non-response. The results of the application of these simple rules are reported in Table 1.4.

Table 1.4 Rules for the Percent of Forms Mailed

	Pass if 80 percent or more favor	Reject if 20 percent or more oppose
Predicted Correctly	54	92
Predicted Incorrectly	71	33
Percent Correct	43.2	73.6

Thus, these rules, too, do not produce results that are as good as those of the simulation model.

An alternative way of utilizing this data is to presume that the decision makers look upon those who do not bother to return questionnaires as being indifferent to a given proposal and thus not worthy of consideration. This thought leads one to look at rules relating to the percentage of forms that were *returned*. Using this notion, the above rules may be reformulated as follows: (5) Approve only those petitions or bills which 80 percent or greater majority of the respondents favor. The application of these simple rules provides the results reported in Table 1.5.

Table 1.5 Rules for the Percent of Forms Mailed

	Pass if 50 percent or more favor	Reject if 20 percent or more oppose
Predicted Correctly	83	81
Predicted Incorrectly	42	44
Percentage Correct	66.4	64.8

Again, these rules do not produce results that are as good as those of the simulation model.

A quite different notion is that the decision makers eschew politics and the pressures of public opinion, and abide by essentially "economic" criteria. Two alternative criteria are used here. The first is based upon the notion that the decision makers desire to see the city develop physically, that the market test of profitability is the proper criterion, and that (aside from development) the purpose of zoning is to protect existing property. When the notions that developers will propose investment only when they expect a profit, and that the decision makers are willing to believe that these expectations are accurate are added to the other considerations, then the following rule can be stated: (7) Approve only those petitions or bills associated with and necessary for specific physical development proposals. A somewhat altered version of this rule may also be interesting. Presume that the decision makers add to the above considerations the notion that physical development is fine except when it adds to problems associated with existing public facilities such as streets, schools, playgrounds, etc. The following are the results: (8) Approve only those petitions or bills associated with and necessary for specific physical development proposals and only in the event the construction of the proposed project will not create problems for existing public facilities. The application of these two rules to the 125 cases under consideration provides the results reported in Table 1.6. Clearly, these rules do not produce results that are as good as those of the simulation model.

It was not surprising, of course, that the simulation was able to outperform these alternative models, although from a scientific view this performance factor is very important. In a sense, these non-random alternatives can be considered as crude subparts of the simulation model. Pragmatically speaking, it is important to know that even crude representations of the subparts do not perform as well as the whole. Yet, a subset of these non-random models, when compared against a random alternative, do appear to have some explanatory power, so it may be appropriate to attempt to put these tests into perspective.

Table 1.6 Basic Economic Rules

	Pass only if necessary for physical development	Pass only if necessary for physical development with no public facilities problems
Predicted Correctly	71	87
Predicted Incorrectly	54	38
Percent Correct	56.8	69.6

The first point is that the simulation does perform better than any of the alternatives considered here. Given this fact and the absolute level of performance, the authors judge the exercise to have been a success.

The second point is that, although the simple alternatives do appear to have some explanatory power, the basic role of the phenomena which they might represent need not be obvious when placed within the context of the entire decision-making structure which the simulation is supposed to model. An example may make this point more clear. Consider public opinion. Some of the above alternatives that are intended to reflect this phenomena do appear superior as a model to random probabilistic decision making of the type discussed earlier in this section. Further, it is doubtful that any of the human participants in the process would dismiss completely the power of protest by the concerned public. Yet, the simulation model demonstrated strong insensitivity to alterations in the public opinion parameters. One interpretation of this paradox is that the "other factors" bearing on a decision would tend to have produced the kind of decision which the public demanded even in the absence of relevant expressions of public opinion.

The above observations point to one of the uses to which this type of research could also be adapted. The decision makers might find it tolerable, and perhaps useful, to employ a model such as this one as a check on their own decisions and as a device to help clarify vague concepts.

Almost needless to say, the authors are of the opinion that further work along the lines of this study would be helpful. Not only is it desirable that this particular effort be duplicated for other cities which might not have quite the same decision-making structure and procedure as is found in Pittsburgh, but it appears that other areas of political decision making may be suitable for this kind of analysis. Regulatory authorities, certain of the legislative committees, and large parts of the executive establishment seem particularly amenable.

Finally, it seems appropriate to conclude that this study itself is a tribute to the fact that what might appear to some to be an essentially political problem and process in actuality incorporates a large technical component.

Indeed, in the flowcharts and elsewhere, one tends to get the impression that the technical considerations may outweigh the political. Such an impression may or may not be accurate, but one can speculate that it may be more or less true for an ever increasing part of our political life.

NOTES–CASE 1

1. See, for example, Martin J. Bailey, "Notes on the Economics of Residential Zoning and Urban Renewal," *Land Economics,* August 1959, pp. 288-292; Otto A. Davis, "Economic Elements in Municipal Zoning Decisions," *Land Economics,* Vol. XXXIX, No. 4, November 1963, pp. 375-386; Otto A. Davis and Andrew S. Whinston, "The Economics of Complex Systems: The Case of Municipal Zoning," *Kyklos,* Vol. XVII, 1964, pp. 416-446; Allison Dunham, "City Planning: An Analysis of the Content of The Master Plan," *Journal of Law and Economics,* Vol. I, October 1958, pp. 170-186; Allison Dunham, "Promises Respecting the Use of Land," *Journal of Law and Economics,* Vol. VII, October 1965, pp. 133-165; William I. Goodman and Eric Freund (Eds.), *Principles and Practice of Urban Planning,* Washington, D.C. International City Managers' Association, 1968; R.M. Haig, "Toward an Understanding of the Metropolis," *Quarterly Journal of Economics,* Vol. XL, February/May 1926, pp. 179-208, 402-434; S.J. Makielski, *The Politics of Zoning,* The York Experience, New York, Columbia University Press, 1961; Donald H. Webster, *Urban Planning and Municipal Public Policy,* New York, Harper and Brothers, 1958; E.C. Yonkley, *Zoning Law and Practice,* Vol. 2, Charlottesville, Michie Company, 1953.

2. Externalities are probably best described here as the possibility that what is constructed on one site may affect the uses to which another might be suited. For further references, see J.M. Buchanan and W.C. Stubblebine, "Externality," *Economica,* N.S. 29, 1962, pp. 371-384, and David and Whinston, "The Economics of Complex Systems."

3. See, especially, A. Newell and H.A. Simon, "GPS, A Program that Simulates Human Thought," in E. Feigenbaum and J. Feldman (Eds.), *Computers and Thought,* New York, McGraw-Hill, 1963.

4. Richard M. Cyert and James G. March, *A Behavioral Theory of The Firm,* New Jersey, Prentice-Hall, 1963.

5. John P. Crecine, *Governmental Problem Solving: A Computer Simulation of Municipal Budgeting,* Chicago, Rand McNally, 1969.

6. Donald Gerwin, *Budgeting Public Funds: The Decision Process in an Urban School District,* Madison, University of Wisconsin Press, 1969.

7. Unfortunately, the City Clerk is unable to locate the minutes of 32 of the 76 relevant hearings. This is the primary motivation for consulting the local newspapers for reports of the remaining hearings. No information is available for 23 of the hearings.

Case 2
Goal Definition and Influence: A Delphi Case Study

EUGENE CUTULY*

INTRODUCTION

The objective of this study was to use a Delphi procedure to isolate and define the influential goals of an organization. This would facilitate the comparison of stated goals of the organization with those goals of the decision makers within the organization.

The Delphi procedures are based on the discovery by the RAND Corporation that the average of individual opinions without discussion tends to be more accurate than group opinion resulting from discussion. Each Delphi procedure, therefore, is designed to make systematic use of the knowledge of group members in resolving an issue, yet to avoid discussion between or among members. The question of just how effective the Delphi procedures are in reaching valid conclusions has considerable practical importance. If they have merit in terms of validity, ease of use, and user acceptance, they become powerful tools to elicit and process both factual and value judgments. This capability can make available to the organization valuable information previously unattainable.

The function of the Delphi procedure in this effort was to identify and determine the motivational influence of "true" organizational goals. It is well known that stated goals of the organization are often modified in the course of doing business. The modification is the result of decisions committing the organization's resources to ventures which may or may not facilitate the attainment of the stated goals of the organization. The decisions are often made by individuals whose motivation is a complex function of perceived organizational goals, perceived group goals, and personal goals. The purpose here is not to determine the nature or components of this function but to

*University of Pittsburgh

determine its overall influence on the decision-making process. Knowing this, it is possible to determine the goals the organization will seek to attain regardless of the "officially" stated goals. A significant deviation or polarization of influences makes it unlikely that the professed goals will ever be efficiently attained—if attained at all. If this is an undesirable condition, appropriate and timely remedial action of various forms can be taken.

THE ORGANIZATION

The focus of this effort is an organization consisting of nine product-capability groups. Each group is headed by a manager who effectively determines what type of activities will constitute his business. The organization— the Information Systems Division (ISD)—has the charter to engage in the analysis and solution of management, engineering, and scientific problems and in the preparation of the computer support systems necessary to implement them. ISD functions both as an operating profit center and as an internal consulting and applications group. Figure 2.1 illustrates the relevant organizational relationships. The bold lines denote the organizational units to be involved in this effort.

METHODOLOGY

Panel Selection

A Delphi technique calls for the use of an "expert" panel. In this case, each member of the panel was an expert in the sense that he knew best what he would do under various circumstances. Operating managers were chosen as opposed to administration-type managers. An operating manager within ISD makes the decision to commit resources to a project or at least presents possible projects to the administration manager for evaluation.

Under the latter circumstance, he acts as a screen, using his personal, perceived group, and perceived organizational values to allow or not allow evaluation. For these reasons, the operating managers essentially determine organizational direction and, therefore, they seemed appropriate as participants.

Letter of Intent

The first correspondence received by the potential respondents was a letter inviting them to participate in the study.

The letter was written to be cosigned by the ISD division manager, who gave his approval, in order to lend credibility to the effort.

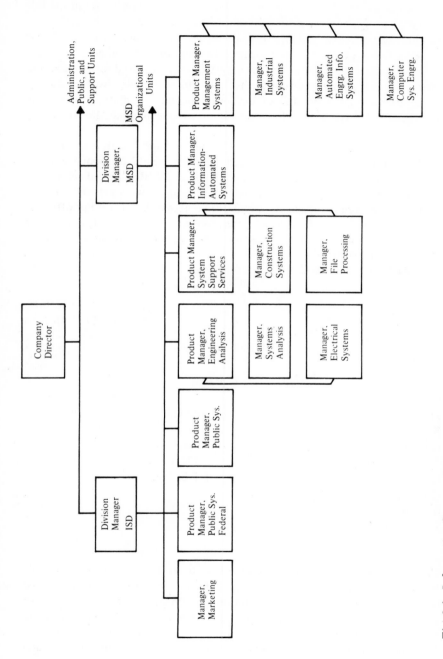

Fig. 2.1. Information Systems Division

Eight individuals were initially selected to receive invitations, but the ISD division manager suggested the addition of the manager of Public Systems as another respondent. Initially, I resisted the suggestion since the Public Systems business environment was much different than the others.

After consideration, however, the suggestion was accepted for two reasons. First, there was the possibility that the study would reveal a distinct polarization of goals because of the heterogeneous orientations of respondents. Second, I felt that Delphi techniques, in general, would be potentially most valuable to this individual.

The letter was as candid as possible, but not so candid as to jeopardize the validity of the study results. For instance, the Delphi technique was not explained in detail, since this may have artificially forced consensus convergence or changes in the respondents' answers. It was explained that the study satisfied a requirement for a Ph.D. seminar and that it was not officially being carried out for ISD. The objective of the study as well as its importance and potential value to ISD were summarized to insure proper cooperation from all participants.

The letter of intent follows.

Date: November 5, 1969
Subject: Goal Analysis

ISD Site

C.R. Arcail
M.A. Axlerad   cc: ISD Site
R.A. Ciorra
G.T. Deaner   P.J. Elk
A.J. Humphries   J.K. Lazor
R.M. Mitchell   T.E. Stein
C.W. Muller
S.R. Rudick
T.L. Sandquist

You, as operating managers representing a relatively homogeneous ISD functional area, are invited to participate in a research study to be conducted by Gene Cutuly. In addition to fulfilling a Ph.D. course requirement for Gene, this unique effort can be of significant value to all ISD managers. It will require approximately two hours of your time, in four half-hour intervals, over the next four weeks. If you are unable to participate or have any questions at any time during the study, please contact Gene at extension 7648.

Study Objective and Importance

There are two major objectives of this study: (1) the measurement and refinement of the <u>perceived</u> operating goals of the combined area you represent, and (2) the evaluation of the measuring technique used in the investigation.

Decisions which commit resources are based, at least in part, on the decision makers' perception of organizational goals—their nature and their importance. Any measurement of goal perception is important and potentially valuable in that it indicates the goals the organization will seek to attain regardless of the "officially" expressed goals. A significant deviation makes it unlikely that the professed goals will ever be efficiently attained—if attained at all. If this is an undesirable condition, remedial action in the form of increased communication of goals between top and operating management can immediately be taken.

The technique to be used in the measurement process was developed by the RAND Corporation for long-range technological forecasting. It is designed to systematically "tap" the intuitive and unarticulated knowledge of a group of experts as efficiently and accurately as possible. The use of the technique in this study gives us an opportunity to gain "hands on" experience as well as an opportunity to evaluate its merits in goal setting and measurement. This technique, if it shows merit, can be of practical value to ISD in that it provides us a tool to elicit and process human judgment. This capability will allow us to efficiently determine the nebulous objectives of many ISD studies related to education, public health, public transportation, etc.

General Instructions

The interrogative measuring technique utilizes four questionnaires over three or four weeks. Comments and instructions are given on each. The general instructions are:

1. Do not discuss this effort in general or in detail with anyone since complete independence of thought is necessary to insure valid results.

2. Express yourself freely. There will be complete anonymity.

3. Apply yourself seriously to the questionnaires and respond fully (within reason) to each question.

4. Observe the due date on each questionnaire. A messenger will collect it at noon on that day.

At the completion of the study, you may request a complete report of the findings.

N. Kefal, Division Manager   E.D. Cutuly, Consultant
Information System Division   Special Projects

Questionnaires

The following comments relating to the questionnaires appear partly in the present tense, because they were written concurrently with the procedural step they describe. This approach eliminates biasing remarks made from hindsight and "bares" my thoughts and findings at that time.

Questionnaire I

This is the most critical of all the questionnaires since it determines the course of the entire study. For this reason, it is deliberately phrased in as vague and unstructured a way as possible. It will personally be delivered to allow me an opportunity to clear up any procedural questions the participants may have. There were no procedural questions, but two of the participants made it a point to question the degree of anonymity that was to be maintained. They were assured that all the answers to the questionnaires would be destroyed previous to the release of the findings. It is clear that the anonymity feature should be emphasized in any effort of this type if any reasonable degree of validity is to be obtained. Most of the participants expressed either a strong academic or practical interest in the study, which indicated at the onset a key advantage of the Delphi approach—acceptability.

The comments on this questionnaire instruct the respondents to assume their current situation except that now they had projects available that facilitated the attainment of every conceivable goal. Since many of the operating managers are faced with a very real profit crisis, it is expected that profit will be emphasized. Because of this possibility, they will be instructed to specify short-, long-, or intermediate-term profit. Short is defined as a year or less, long as greater than three years, and intermediate as one to three years. The mention of profit, on the part of the respondents, is a presumption on my part. Considering the actual situation, though, this assumption seems to be more than reasonably justified.

The first question calls for a listing of the ISD goals *they* would consider in deciding among projects. The second question asks for the allocation of 100 points of each listed goal. It was made clear that one point represented a commitment of one percent of their resources for a full year. The full-year commitment is introduced to provide a tenure equality among projects and to eliminate any academically uninterpretable in-out strategy on the part of the respondent.

Questionnaire I–Findings

Eleven goals were identified by participants as being influential—short-term profit, intermediate profit, long-term profit, staff development, expertise consolidation, market growth, good reputation, full utilization of resources, product development, sales capability development, and employee satisfaction. It was obvious from the definition and interpretation given these goals that the respondents were uncomfortable allocating points to a "single-purpose" goal. A good example of the uneasiness is the comment of one of the respondents, "In most cases, goals are not independent. If market penetration does not imply ultimate profit, then market penetration is completely uninteresting as a goal."

Date: November 7, 1969
Subject: Questionnaire I
Goal Analysis

ISD SITE

C.R. Arcail
M.A. Axlerad
R.A. Ciorra
G.T. Deaner
A.J. Humphries
R.M. Mitchell
C.W. Muller
S.R. Rudick
T.L. Sandquist

Date Due:Tuesday, November 11. A messenger will be around to pick the answers up if I do not receive them by noon on Tuesday.

Our first task is to identify those ISD goals which influence your decisions to commit resources to a project. In addition to your current situation, you are to assume the following conditions:

1. Each future project you commit resources to will aid in attaining only a single goal.

2. There are and forever will be projects and activities available that facilitate the attainment of every conceivable goal.

Question I-1.

Would you please list all the ISD goals (objectives) you would really consider in deciding among the available projects and/or activities. (The goal of profit, if selected, should specify whether short, intermediate, or long term—where short is a year or less, intermediate is one to three years, and long is over three years.)

Question I-2.

Allocate 100 points to the goals listed in I-1 assuming that each point represents a commitment of one percent of your resources for a full year.

Any written comments relating to any of your reasoning are expected and welcome. If you need assistance at interpretation please contact me.

Please allow at least one-half hour to answer as completely as possible.

> Gene Cutuly, Consultant
> Special Projects

Questionnaire II

Using the weights supplied by the respondents on Questionnaire I, the eleven goals were combined into seven goal "categories." Each category was an originally mentioned goal or an implicitly or explicitly suggested "goal string." An example of a goal string would be:

> customer satisfaction—reputation—intermediate profit

This was done to eliminate the goal relatedness mentioned by the participants. Each category was given a definition, which was a combination of several respondent remarks. In addition, all the pertinent comments were also listed under the associated goal or "goal string." The points were reallocated by me to conform to the seven categories. They are to serve as a reference point for the Questionnaire II responses.

In brief, Questionnaire II instructs the participants to consider the feedback information and revise their point allocations. If any of their revised allocations fell above or below the interquartile limits of the revised allocations, they are asked to give their reasoning. It should be pointed out that no great pains were taken to arrive at an accurate reallocation of points. At this point, my interest centers on the rationale for extreme weightings and not the weightings themselves. From the second questionnaire on, it is anticipated that the structuring of goals should provide a basis for accurate weighting. If this is not the case, the respondents have an opportunity to add more goal categories if the seven provided are insufficient. Questionnaire II follows.

Date: November 12, 1969
Subject: Questionnaire II
Goal Analysis

ISD SITE

C.R. Arcail
M.A. Axlerad
R.A. Ciorra
G.T. Deaner
A.J. Humphries
R.M. Mitchell
C.W. Muller
S.R. Rudick
T.L. Sandquist

Date Due: Monday, November 17, 1969. A messenger will pick up the answers if I do not receive them by 2:00 p.m. on Monday. Please use the same identifying marks.

Remember, our purpose is to identify those goals actually influencing your decisions. For the remainder of this study, you will be provided with information generated by your fellow respondents which may aid in pointing out some areas of influence you might have overlooked. Please answer this questionnaire without referring to your previous answers and comments. The time—now. Your current status is applicable.

The first questionnaire was, admittedly, difficult to answer because of its vagueness and the difficulty in neglecting the interrelatedness of some goals. Your comments on these points have enabled me to define and combine these goals so as to minimize further difficulty.

Definition and Comments

Goal or "Goal String"

1. Profit (short-term)—efforts to accrue profit immediately or within one year. This requires the efficient allocation of personnel to projects which precludes any staff, service, or market development.

Comments:

a. "Failure to attain satisfactory short-term profit endangers all further activities."

b. "Section productivity must be maintained, even though unsuitable projects are selected, to insure the survival of the organization."

c. "Because we are new, we need sustaining revenues in the initial months."

d. "I feel I can devote very little effort to achieving objectives other than the short-term profit objective. This requires foregoing a multiplicity of other desirable goals."

2. Employee Satisfaction—efforts will provide employee satisfaction and tend to reduce the desire to leave the organization. These projects are interesting, challenging and enjoyable, but do not develop any further capabilities. This allows utilization of manpower without profit or loss.

   Comment:

   a. "Projects should be as stimulating and challenging as possible if ISD is to attract and hold employees."

3. Sales Capability Development—Intermediate Profit—the development of technical personnel which will substantially contribute to the marketing effort. This will ultimately lead to the goal of intermediate profit.

4. Product Development—Intermediate Profit—the allocation of resources ($10,000-$50,000) to the development of a packaged program which will yield a satisfactory effective return two to three years hence. After this period, it is assumed that competitors will drive the price of the service down so as to make it unmarketable. Staff development is sacrificed in such a task.

5. Staff Development—Intermediate Profit—these are the educational and research projects that will be funded by the organization. It is assumed that the benefits of such development will not be noticeable until two or three years have elapsed.

   Comments:

   a. "Large numbers of experienced and competent individuals are not available. We must develop our own staff to grow at the projected rate."

   b. "We should develop state-of-the-art systems."

6. <u>Customer Satisfaction—Reputation—Intermediate Profit</u>—it is assumed that the short-term profit will be sacrificed in order to give the customer a superior product. This will enhance your reputation and after a year's time will lead to new and repeat business you would not have otherwise secured.

<u>Comments:</u>

a. "A satisfied customer is mandatory for repeat business which should serve as a base loading for ISD."

b. "Bid only those jobs which we have the ability to perform with a high probability of successful completion."

c. "We must satisfy the customer's needs."

7. <u>Market Penetration—Intermediate Profit</u>—this is effort expended to capture more than your projected market share in a particular area. You will utilize your resources to develop and "advertise" your products.

<u>Comment:</u>

a. "Specifically—international trade, distribution control, mass storage and retrieval systems, video display."

QUESTIONNAIRE I FEEDBACK

The following statistics have been obtained through my reallocation of your point rankings to be compatible with the goal or "goal string" definitions. They are, at best, rough approximations since not all of you selected the same goals, and I had to do a lot of subjective estimating to combine some rankings. The median M of a set of point allocations is the middle allocation when these allocations are arranged in order of magnitude. The interquartile limits Q_L and Q_H contain the middle 50% of these ordered allocations.

Goal or "Goal String"	Q_L	M	Q_H
1. Short-term Profit	15	21	24
2. Employee Satisfaction	7	8	10
3. Sales Capability Development— Intermediate Profit	7	9	11

Goal or "Goal String" (continued)	Q_L	M	Q_H
4. Product Development—Intermediate Profit	15	22	25
5. Staff Development—Intermediate Profit	24	33	42
6. Customer Satisfaction—Reputation— Intermediate Profit	8	15	15
7. Market Penetration—Intermediate Profit	34	47	60

QUESTIONNAIRE II

Question II-I.

After considering all of the information contained in this questionnaire, revise your estimates for the seven categories of goals. That is, reallocate your 100 points to reflect the degree of influence each has on your decision making. Be sure to allocate to each one—a zero score is acceptable. If you are influenced by a goal category not listed, then you are to list this goal or "goal string" and explain your reasoning. Also, an explanation as to why it was not mentioned in Questionnaire I would be appreciated.

Question II-2.

If any of your revised allocations fall above or below the interquartile limits, please give a brief description of why you attach that degree of influence. This information is important, so be as specific as possible.

Gene Cutuly, Consultant
Special Projects

Questionnaire II—Findings

The "goal string" approach to related goals proved successful. None of the respondents expressed any difficulty in allocating the 100 points or understanding the "goal string" concept. No other goals were mentioned. A comment of one respondent, however, prompted me to expand the Employee Satisfaction goal to include employee relations activities.

Significant deviations in the allocations were noted for goals (5), (6), and (7). However, this indication may have been false, since the original points were reallocated to conform with the seven goal category format. One thing is certain, the goal definitions acted as a base. This is evidenced by rapid movement of the allocations into various point ranges. (This is graphically shown in the Findings and Conclusions section—Fig. 2.3 (1-4).)

From: Ardmore Site
W   236-7648
Date: November 24, 1969
Subject: Questionnaire III
Goal Analysis

ISD Site

C.R. Arcail
M.A. Axlerad
R.A. Ciorra
G.T. Deaner
A.J. Humphries
R.M. Mitchell
C.W. Muller
S.R. Rudick
T.L. Sandquist

Date Due: Tuesday, December 2, 1969—noon. A late response jeopardizes the validity of the study in that large time lapses between questionnaires allow for many forms of bias.

Please answer this questionnaire without any interruptions so that all the information is equally remembered and considered.

The goal definitions given in Questionnaire II are repeated here for your convenience. You are urged to review them before answering this questionnaire. Note the slight modification in the Employee Satisfaction Goal.

Again, please remember that your current status is applicable, and I am only interested in those goals or "goal strings" which actually influence your decisions.

Questionnaire III

The feedback information consists of the following:

Item	Purpose
1. Goal Definitions	To insure uniformity of understanding among respondents
2. Interquartile Limits from Questionnaire I	To serve as a quantitative reference for reasoning expressed by respondents when their allocations fell beyond those limits

3. Rationale of respondents from Questionnaire II (edited for succinctness and clarity)	To promote recognition of influential goals. The rationale of the other respondents serving to eliminate over-emphasis or under-emphasis of goal influence
4. Medians and Interquartile Limits from Questionnaire II	To serve as a quantitative reference

The respondents were asked to consider the feedback information and revise their point allocations. If any respondent found any of the rationales unconvincing or in error, he was instructed to criticize them appropriately.

Questionnaire III appears on the following pages.

GOAL DEFINITIONS

Goal or "Goal Strings"

1. Profit (short-term)—efforts to accrue profit immediately or within one year. This requires the efficient allocation of personnel to projects which precludes any staff, service, or market development.

2. Employee Satisfaction—efforts will provide employee satisfaction and tend to reduce the desire to leave the organization. These projects are interesting, challenging, and enjoyable, but do not develop any further capabilities. This allows utilization of manpower without profit or loss. Employee relations efforts are associated with this goal.

3. Sales Capability Development—Intermediate Profit—the development of technical personnel which will substantially contribute to the marketing effort. This will ultimately lead to the goal of intermediate profit.

4. Product Development—Intermediate Profit—the allocation of resources ($10,000-$50,000) to the development of a packaged program which will yield a satisfactory effective return two to three years hence. After this period, it is assumed that competitors will drive the price of the service down so as to make it unmarketable. Staff development is sacrificed in such a task.

5. Staff Development—Intermediate Profit—these are the educational and research projects that will be funded by the organization. It is assumed that the benefits of such development will not be noticeable until after two or three years have elapsed.

6. Customer Satisfaction—Reputation—Intermediate Profit—it is assumed that the short-term profit will be sacrificed in order to give the customer a superior product. This will enhance your reputation and after a year's time will lead to new and repeat business you would not have otherwise secured.

7. Market Penetration—Intermediate Profit—this is effort expended to capture more than your projected market share in a particular area. You will utilize your resources to develop and "advertise" your products.

QUESTIONNAIRE III

Question III-1.

Revise your 100 point allocation after considering the previous point allocation summaries and the statements of rationale presented on the remaining pages. It is suggested that you consider the comments relating to a goal and then revise your estimate of that particular goal rather than reading all the comments and then revising your allocations.

Question III-2.

If you found any of the summarized reasonings unconvincing or in error, please criticize appropriately. Identify the statement being expanded, modified, or refuted by its letter-number code (e.g., 6L-2, 7H-1). Any other comments are also invited at this time.

Questionnaire I/II—Response Summary

Allocation Summary	Goal or "Goal String"

1. Short-term Profit
2. Employee Satisfaction
3. Sales Capability Development—Intermediate Profit
4. Product Development—Intermediate Profit
5. Staff Development—Intermediate Profit
6. Customer Satisfaction—Reputation—Intermediate Profit
7. Market Penetration—Intermediate Profit

Goal No.	Q-I ALLOCATIONS		Q-II ALLOCATIONS		
	Q_L	Q_H	Q_L	M	Q_H
1.	15	24	10	20	38
2.	7	10	4	5	7
3.	7	11	3	10	11
4.	15	25	10	15	20
5.	24	42	5	10	14
6.	8	15	15	20	30
7.	34	60	10	10	16

Rationale Summary

Those respondents who exceeded the interquartile limits given on Questionnaire I provided the following rationale:

1.   Short-term Profit

The goal of Short-term Profit should <u>not</u> receive as much weight as indicated by the <u>lower</u> quartile limit because:

1L-1.   Efforts directed toward short-term profit will detract from and lessen the effectiveness of any effort directed toward overall, successful long-term success.

1L-2.   Short-term profit is not that important in a start-up operation.

The goal of Short-term Profit should receive <u>more</u> weight than indicated by the <u>upper</u> quartile limit because:

1H-1.   Without sufficient short-term profit, there will be no ISD future as originally conceived.

1H-2.   Since current status is applicable, other goals are somewhat extraneous. Recent indications (e.g., cutback in personnel) are that if the short-term profit picture does not improve, then the organization is in serious trouble. In comparing forecasts with performance, I am apparently not as inclined as some others to view recent events through fuchsia spectacles.

1H-3.   Immediate profit continues as foremost influencing element in my resource allocation. I cannot associate less weight to an effort having so great a bearing on being a participant in the market.

1H-4.   Most resources must go to short-term profit (until the objective is assured) rather than efforts which have an intermediate return.

2.   Employee Satisfaction

The goal of Employee Satisfaction should not receive as much weight as indicated by the lower quartile limit because:

2L-1.   I cannot place weight on a goal aimed at merely keeping the staff happy without an association to the profitability of the endeavor. Interesting, challenging, yet worthwhile and profitable projects should provide staff members with a sense of belonging and contribution. The attrition rate will be small. We are in business, not participating in academic pursuits.

2L-2.   I think that the general business atmosphere is conducive to employee satisfaction since it is professional, and exposure rate to new ideas and businesses is high. Hence, I think employee satisfaction will take care of itself.

2L-3.   Employee satisfaction should be derivable from any job well done, but as an end in itself, it is always going to get short shrift in a new and struggling organization.

2L-4.   As far as jobs are concerned, anyone's problems that come to us are automatically interesting and challenging— otherwise someone else would have probably solved them.

2L-5.   While recruiting the original staff, special consideration was given to selecting qualified employees who would be satisfied doing the required work. Division of work assignments is certainly considered when staffing jobs.

The goal of Employee Satisfaction should receive more weight than indicated by the upper quartile limit because:

2H-1.   I still think that employee satisfaction is an important goal and involves more than labor turnover.

3.   Sales Capability Development—Intermediate Profit

This goal should receive <u>less</u> weight than indicated in Questionnaire I because:

3L-1.   Sales capability development is within the province of the Marketing Department. Professional people should be able to <u>provide technical support</u> to the sales group after initial contacts are made.

3L-2.   I feel that less than 20% of your tasks should be developmental. We still have got to show a Return-on Investment.

3L-3.   I believe for the present that I have a sufficient technical sales capability. In the natural execution of contracts, additional capability will be developed.

The goal of Sales Capability Development should receive <u>more</u> weight than indicated in Questionnaire I because:

3H-1.   I feel greater emphasis must be associated with development of these sales-related abilities in my own staff area.

4.   Product Development—Intermediate Profit

This goal should receive <u>less</u> weight than indicated in Questionnaire I because:

4L-1.   I believe that we have products already developed which are not being sold not because of competition but due to failure to reach the proper customers.

4L-2.   An important goal which cannot be given more weight in my analysis while the ISD forward movement is so confused. I do not assign greater weight to this area which produces a fixed product(s) without greater assurance of the future moves of my superiors.

5.   Staff Development—Intermediate Profit

This goal should receive <u>less</u> weight than indicated in Questionnaire I because:

5L-1.   Standard educational opportunities for the staff are already available, through the tuition refund program, company-sponsored professional and management courses, and occasional seminars. The need for organizationally funded educational and research projects would be diminished if customer projects were available that junior people could be trained on assignment with the competent and experienced senior individuals who are now employed.

5L-2.   I use project assignment variety to enhance staff skills. Although funded educational projects are occasionally advisable, I use the learning-by-doing as a less costly but equally beneficial approach.

5L-3.   While important, research and educational projects may be too expensive in time, money, and manpower in the initial stages of ISD development.

5L-4.   I choose paying contracts which will permit the training and development of a staff. At this time, an unlimited supply of such jobs are not "available." I choose this item, however, to indicate a willingness of my part to bid jobs with lesser returns (profits) which will facilitate staff development and, thereby, permit long-term market participation.

6.   <u>Customer Satisfaction—Reputation—Intermediate Profit</u>

The weight given this goal should be <u>more</u> than indicated on Questionnaire I because:

6H-1.   I rank customer satisfaction <u>high</u> because it helps in many ways. The obvious ways you know. Some of the not-so-obvious ways are: enhances overall company posture; induces company salesmen (other than ISD) to refer customers to you without the fear of losing them for the company.

6H-2.   Customer satisfaction is felt to be the best way of improving market penetration since not only does respect for work result, but successful implementation and satisfaction of one customer is a valuable marketing aid which can be used on other customers.

6H-3.   A good reputation for quality work will spread and bring new customers as well as repeat business.

6H-4.   Successful and significant market participation will be achieved on technical capability and customer satisfaction. In my opinion, a bad reputation will preclude successful participation and hinder future recruiting efforts.

7.   Market Penetration—Intermediate Profit

This goal should be weighted less than originally indicated because:

7L-1.   In view of current loading, emphasis on productivity, and reduced workforce, I cannot assign greater weight to aggressively "developing and advertising" products for the larger haul. There is no further blood in the turnip.

7L-2.   This goal should be that of the Marketing Department.

7L-3.   Market penetration is not directly related to my task-oriented efforts, but rather a marketing function. However, it is important enough that it should deserve some attention.

E.D. Cutuly, Consultant
Special Projects

Questionnaire III—Findings

The point allocations, represented by the statistical response summary, indicate that there is more agreement than evidenced in Questionnaire II concerning the influencing effect of all goals except (7)—Market Penetration—Intermediate Profit.

Questionnaire IV

The goal definitions are repeated for the convenience of participants and the purpose of the study is again emphasized. The respondents are asked to revise their allocations after considering

1) the point allocation summary from Questionnaire III in terms of the medians and interquartile ranges, and

2) the rebuttals of rationales expressed in support of allocations falling outside interquartile limits.

Comments concerning their perception of the validity, usefulness, and effect of this study are also solicited. This questionnaire appears on the following pages.

Date: December 3, 1969
Subject: Questionnaire IV
Goal Analysis

ISD Site

C.R. Arcail
M.A. Axlerad
R.A. Ciorra
G.T. Deaver
A.J. Humphries
R.M. Mitchell
C.W. Muller
S.R. Rudick
T.L. Sandquist

Date Due: Friday, December 5, 1969—noon. If you are not going to be here, please remit previous to that date.

This is the last questionnaire. The results are, to say the least, extremely interesting and should prove to be of benefit to all concerned. Again, answer this questionnaire without any interruptions so that all the information is equally remembered and considered.

The goal definitions are repeated for your convenience. Please review them before answering this questionnaire. Remember, I am not interested in the goals you would like to pursue, but those you actually would pursue through your decision making.

QUESTIONNAIRE IV

Question IV-1.

Revise your 100 point allocation after considering the point allocation summary from Questionnaire III and the rebuttals of statements offered in support of allocations falling outside interquartile limits.

Question IV-2.

May I have your comments on the following items?

a) Benefits of this study to you and ISD
b) Validity of this study
c) The Delphi technique for obtaining an unbiased consensus of opinion
d) Problems you encountered with the Delphi technique
e) Overall opinion

Question IV-3.

Although my purpose was to identify motivating goals, it is possible that your original sources of influence may have changed as a result of this effort. Please comment.

QUESTIONNAIRE III—RESPONSE SUMMARY

Goal or "Goal String"	Q-III ALLOCATIONS		
	Q_L	M	Q_H
1. Short-term Profit	15	20	35
2. Employee Satisfaction	5	5	5
3. Sales Capability Development—Intermediate Profit	5	10	11
4. Product Development—Intermediate Profit	12	15	17
5. Staff Development—Intermediate Profit	5	10	10
6. Customer Satisfaction—Reputation—Intermediate Profit	16	20	30
7. Market Penetration—Intermediate Profit	10	15	20

Rubuttals to Rationale

1. Short-term Profit

Rationale for less weight:

Concentration on short-term profit alone will preclude long-term success. In addition, it is not important in a start-up operation such as ours.

Rebuttals:

The comments reflect the idealistic approach under which ISD began. The early environment reflected that our success would be in the future, that staff quotas were to be met despite business levels, and that an unprofitable operation in 1969 was inevitable. Paradoxically, sales goals repetitively bounded upward, development funds became virtually nonexistent, budget tightenings virtually eliminated occasions for ISD exposure, billing months were artifically extended, finally the staff was reduced. If the "long-term profits" policy is the appropriate course of action, then the wrong signals are being called in the huddle.

As a start-up operation, our "grace" period is apparently up.

Upper management by its actions has shown that it is primarily concerned with short-term as opposed to long-term profit.

Rationale for more weight:

Without sufficient short-term profit, there will be no ISD future as originally conceived.

Rebuttals:

This assumes that products are available for entry in each of our application areas—which, for the most part, is not the case. It also assumes that we are acquainted with the business of that application area—which, for a number of areas, is not the case either.

Short-term profit would be sacrificed if the probability of considerable future business was high.

Short-term profit is important. However, at this point, prices should be held to a level to entice the customer. In other words, increase bookings, but go for the large profit margin in the intermediate term.

2. Employee Satisfaction

Rationale for more weight:

Employee satisfaction is an important goal and involves more than labor turnover.

Rebuttals:

I continue to strongly disagree with this point as a goal of high priority significance. Only the current revision to the definition permits me to rationalize even a minimal degree of influence (i.e., employee relations efforts).

It seems incompatible with any profit-oriented operation. I cannot visualize myself turning down business because an employee might not be happy.

Employee satisfaction can be maintained through good management, while achieving the goals of the product group.

3. Sales Capability Development—Intermediate Profit

Rationale for less weight:

Sales capability development is within the province of the Marketing Department. Professional people should be able to provide technical support to the sales group after initial contacts are made.

In the natural execution of contracts, additional capability will be developed.

Rebuttals:

Sales capability is not inherent in professional people. The skill required must be developed. Regardless of whose province the task falls in, significant weight must be applied to this vital goal. The Marketing Department has not taken the lead. Is it wiser to wait for them to provide for this area, or seize the initiative in your own area?

If one waits for the natural execution of contracts to provide this capability, there may be too few experiences to develop a capability to keep ISD intact.

4. Product Development—Intermediate Profit

Rationale for less weight:

Although product development is important, the confused state of affairs which exists within ISD precludes pursuing this goal.

Rebuttal:

It's true that the road ahead is not clear, but product identification, documentation, and development is necessary and important to ISD.

5. Staff Development—Intermediate Profit

No rebuttals.

6. Customer Satisfaction—Reputation—Intermediate Profit

No rebuttals.

7. Market Penetration—Intermediate Profit

Rationale for less weight:

This goal should be that of the Marketing Department.

Rebuttal:

Market penetration is what it's all about, considering how small our share of the market is. Since the Marketing Department has such a long way to go, in that they are not familiar enough with our products, capabilities, and marketing in general, it behooves a manager to actively pursue this goal at this time.

E.D. Cutuly, Consultant
Special Projects

Questionnaire IV – Findings

The allocation responses received indicated that four questionnaires were adequate for this study. The degree and amount of allocation changes are slight at this point in the study, as evidenced by lack of line crossing and slope changing. (Refer to Fig. 2.2). Although there was more convergence on four of the seven goal categories, it was very slight and probably attributable to noise in the process. The same could be said of the slight divergence noted in the other three goal categories. The final interquartile summary is presented in Table 2.1.

Table 2.1. Questionnaire IV Response Summary

Goal or "Goal String"	Q-IV Interquartile Allocation		
	Q_L	M	Q_H
1. Short-term Profit	15	20	38
2. Employee Satisfaction	5	5	6
3. Sales Capability Development— Intermediate Profit	6	10	10
4. Product Development— Intermediate Profit	14	15	15
5. Staff Development—Intermediate Profit	5	8	10
6. Customer Satisfaction—Reputation— Intermediate Profit	16	17	20
7. Market Penetration—Intermediate Profit	10	15	20

FINDINGS AND CONCLUSIONS

Delphi Feasibility

There can be no doubt that Delphi techniques are administratively workable. In this study, nine participants completed four questionnaires to indicate either an agreement or disagreement on the degree of influence of goals. No objective evaluation can be made of these results since there are no right or wrong answers. However, an intuitive evaluation can be made in terms of control features, validity, user acceptance, and ease of use. The Delphi technique used need not have been perfect in all of these respects to be of value. It is only necessary that it is judged to be "better" than other techniques such as round-table discussion, interviews, questionnaires, and suggestion solicitation for this type of application.

The features of anonymity, feedback, and statistical response are at least an attempt to control for dominant individuals, interviewer biasing, specious persuasion, and extreme variations. Overall, the technique was viewed as being interesting, useful, and reasonably valid by the respondents. A representative sample of salient respondent comments relating to the validity and efficacy of the Delphi technique is presented here.

"The approach taken has generated relatively true feelings, in my opinion. However, by presenting the response summary you may have caused a bandwagon effect."

"The stumbling block has been the problem of goal relatedness."

"If the study had been conducted on consecutive days within a week period, conclusions could have been less affected by extraneous factors. A weighting of responses might have resulted in more meaningful interpretations."

"Validity is dependent upon (1) the amount and type of information filtering and (2) the availability of time to answer the questionnaires in-depth."

"I don't know if the study is quite valid. It is very subjective and even though you have tried to be unbiased in how you defined the goals, I'm sure that another person would have structured a somewhat different variation of the goals. Also, I was somewhat influenced by the total point distribution even though I tried not to have this happen. I began to read into the strength and weakness of goals based upon whether it got a strong point allocation or a weak one. I don't think the point results should have been passed out, but do think that the comments were appropriate."

"The Delphi technique is much better than any single step process."

"I feel it yields unbiased results for goal definition, but has some flaws in being able to measure the degree of influence."

"Since anonymity was observed and discussion among participants was forbidden, an excellent opportunity for statement of free and unbiased opinions was provided."

"As the environment changes over time, I take a different outlook on, say, product development."

"The format of some of the questionnaires and references to prior replies provided some difficulty."

"The time delays between responses was a problem."

"I had no particular difficulty in responding to the questionnaire except for finding time to answer as completely as I would have liked in some instances."

In retrospect, it would be difficult to state with certainty that a Delphi technique is a valid sociological measuring device. However, quite a convincing argument could be made to present it as yielding "more" valid results than other techniques currently being employed.

Table 2.2. Final Goal Definitions

Goal or "Goal String"

1. Profit (short-term)—efforts to accrue profit immediately or within one year. This requires the efficient allocation of personnel to projects which precludes any staff, service, or market development.

2. Employee Satisfaction—efforts will provide employee satisfaction and tend to reduce the desire to leave the organization. These projects are interesting, challenging, and enjoyable, but do not develop any further capabilities. This allows utilization of manpower without profit or loss. Employee relations efforts are associated with this goal.

3. Sales Capability Development—Intermediate Profit—the development of technical personnel which will substantially contribute to the marketing effort. This will ultimately lead to the goal of intermediate profit.

4. Product Development—Intermediate Profit—the allocation of resources ($10,000-$50,000) to the development of a packaged program which will yield a satisfactory effective return two to three years hence. After this period, it is assumed that competitors will drive the price of the service down so as to make it unmarketable. Staff development is sacrificed in such a task.

5. Staff Development—Intermediate Profit—these are the educational and research projects that will be funded by the organization. It is assumed that the benefits of such development will not be noticeable until after two or three years have elapsed.

6. Customer Satisfaction—Reputation—Intermediate Profit—it is assumed that the short-term profit will be sacrificed in order to give the customer a superior product. This will enhance your reputation and after a year's time will lead to new and repeat business you would not have otherwise secured.

7. Market Penetration—Intermediate Profit—this is effort expended to capture more than your projected market share in a particular area. You will utilize your resources to develop and "advertise" your products.

Findings

Although the point allocations reflecting the motivational influence of goals were important, the development of the workable goal definitions was a major achievement. The purpose of explicit definition of goals or goal categories was to eliminate the confusion resulting from natural goal hierarchy and mutual goal dependence. This task was accomplished with relative ease by combining the respondents' definitions into succinct form and utilizing a means-end chain concept. Its success is substantiated by the fact that no participant offered any major criticisms, and after definition (Questionnaire II—Questionnaire IV) the allocations fell within a different "response band." It is interesting to note that all of the goal definitions except one end with a profit objective.

The final definitions appear in Table 2.2.

The capability of defining workable objectives has broad applicability and, therefore, is of significant value. This type of expertise can be applied to structuring many nebulous objectives of public works programs, for instance, to the satisfaction of the administration as well as the persons affected.

If range is considered a measure of opinion, with a high value representing a large difference in agreement and small value representing a small difference in agreement, then the following is a list of the goal categories ranked from *least* agreement to most agreement.

Rank	Goal Number	Goal	Range
1	1	Short-term Profit	23
2	7	Market Penetration—Intermediate Profit	10
3	5	Staff Development—Intermediate Profit	5
4	3	Sales Capability Development— Intermediate Profit	4
5	6	Customer Satisfaction—Reputation— Intermediate Profit	4
6	2	Employee Satisfaction	1
7	4	Product Development—Intermediate Profit	1

The explanation of the disagreement in the Short-term Profit goal was attempted earlier and will not be repeated here. The variance of agreement in Market Penetration—Intermediate Profit is most likely due to the "survival" stance assumed by some of the managers. That is, it is recognized that the attainment of this goal should be a Marketing function, but, because of Marketing's seeming ineffectiveness, some managers feel that they should assume some of this responsibility if they are to retain their status. The other goal variances are small enough to be attributable to the stochastic nature of the process so no explanations will be offered. It suffices to say that there is general agreement for these goals.

If the median is used as a measure of goal influence, then the following is a list of the goals ranked from greatest influence to least influence.

Rank	Goal Number	Goal	Median
1	1	Short-term Profit	20
2	6	Customer Satisfaction—Reputation— Intermediate Profit	17
3	7	Market Penetration—Intermediate Profit	15
4	4	Product Development—Intermediate Profit	15
5	3	Sales Capability Development— Intermediate Profit	10
6	5	Staff Development—Intermediate Profit	8
7	2	Employee Satisfaction	5

An "attention" index may be developed by multiplying the medians of the goal categories by the ranges of those categories. This index can be thought of as representing a combination of importance and uncertainty. The higher the index, the more likely it is that the organization will proceed toward these goals in an inefficient manner. The computation and presentation of this index should allow the policy setting management of the department to take timely remedial action in the form of further clarification and redefinition. The following list of goals is ranked in order of attention needed.

Rank	Goal Number	Goal	Attention Index
1	1	Short-term Profit	460
2	7	Market Penetration—Intermediate Profit	150
3	6	Customer Satisfaction—Reputation—Intermediate Profit	68
4	3	Sales Capability Development—Intermediate Profit	40
5	5	Staff Development—Intermediate Profit	40
6	4	Product Development—Intermediate Profit	15
7	2	Employee Satisfaction	5

While the earlier Delphi applications dealt almost exclusively with factual judgments (i.e., technological forecasting), this effort was concerned with eliciting "true" responses which were based on both factual and value judgments. The assumption lending hope for success was that value judgments are factual statements of an especially complex and vague sort.

The study was conducted in such a way that the allocation of 100 points among seven goal categories was to reflect the degree of influence of each category. Table 2.3 is a summary of all the responses of all the participants for all questionnaires. Figure 2.2 plots the information contained in Table 2.3. Referring to these plots, we can note the effect of goal definition. This is indicated by the marked shift in responses for Questionnaire II. The succeeding questionnaire responses for all goals remain within the range bounded by the Questionnaire II responses. The Short-term Profit goal influence maintains the greatest variance throughout the study. This result seems to bear out the current state-of-affairs within the department. Some managers have salable programs and expertise and are expected to capitalize on them immediately. Some who have ill-defined responsibilities suspect that short-term profit should be sacrificed for other goals lending to intermediate-term profits. As for the other—they are confused for reasons presented in the verbal response summaries. All of the other goals, except Customer Satisfaction—Reputation—Intermediate Profit (# 5) appear to have a generally agreed-to influence. However, upon closer examination, it will be noted that the wide variance of response for this goal is the result of only two participants. The elimination of extreme values from all responses such as this is accomplished by using a statistical group response. This consists of the interquartile range for variance measurement and the median as a measure of central tendency. The statistical responses for all goals can be seen in Fig. 2.3.

Table 2.3. Individual Responses

Questionnaire	Goal 1				Goal 2				Goal 3				Goal 4			
	1	2	3	4	1	2	3	4	1	2	3	4	1	2	3	4
Respondent																
A	90	85	90	90	0	5	5	5	0	10	5	5	2	0	0	0
B	24	28	28	25	7	0	2	2	12	18	12	12	25	12	12	15
C	10	38	35	38	4	4	5	6	0	2	5	6	22	10	15	15
D	21	0	5	15	0	7	5	5	0	11	12	8	0	15	17	15
E	10	20	10	15	10	5	5	5	0	10	10	10	0	20	20	20
F	50	40	40	40	14	15	11	10	6	3	4	5	15	7	8	10
G	15	15	20	20	0	0	0	0	0	0	10	10	0	25	30	30
H	20	7	16	16	0	5	8	8	0	13	11	11	65	25	14	14
I		10	15	15	—	10	5	5	—	10	10	10	—	20	15	15

Questionnaire	Goal 5				Goal 6				Goal 7			
	1	2	3	4	1	2	3	4	1	2	3	4
Respondent												
A	0	0	0	0	7	0	0	0	1	0	0	0
B	16	14	14	14	9	10	15	15	0	18	17	17
C	0	5	5	5	30	25	20	17	22	16	15	13
D	0	12	10	7	6	20	22	20	73	35	29	30
E	0	5	10	10	8	30	25	20	72	10	20	20
F	0	10	10	8	15	15	17	17	0	10	10	10
G	50	25	0	0	35	35	40	40	0	0	0	0
H	0	20	14	14	15	20	16	16	0	10	21	21
I	—	10	10	10	—	30	30	30		10	15	15

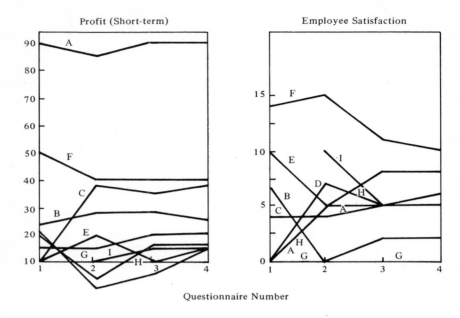

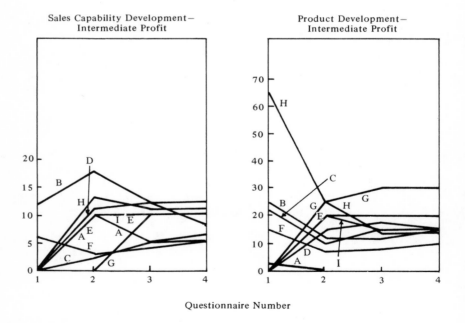

Fig. 2.2. Individual Responses

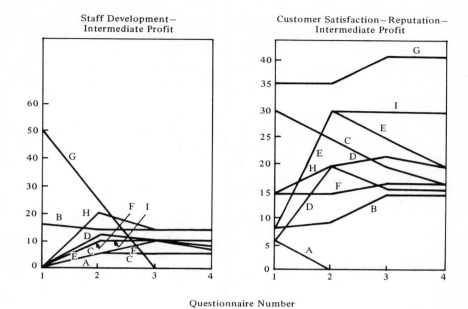

Staff Development—
Intermediate Profit

Customer Satisfaction—Reputation—
Intermediate Profit

Questionnaire Number

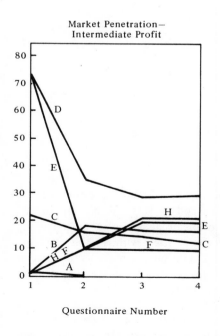

Market Penetration—
Intermediate Profit

Questionnaire Number

Fig. 2.2. Individual Responses (cont.)

These figures dramatically show the convergence process made possible with the Delphi technique. It should be pointed out that the scale employed in each case was selected to illustrate the convergence process and not the relative influence. A convergence can be interpreted to mean that there is general agreement as to the amount of influence attributed to that goal by the respondents.

The interpretation of these results is extremely interesting and enlightening. Table 2.4 is an extended summary table, showing the final questionnaire results along with the value of the interquartile range.

Table 2.4. Final Response Summary

#	Goal	Q_L	M	Q_H	Range
1	Short-term Profit	15	20	38	23
2	Employee Satisfaction	5	5	6	1
3	Sales Capability Development— Intermediate Profit	6	10	10	4
4	Product Development—Intermediate Profit	14	15	15	1
5	Staff Development—Intermediate Profit	5	8	10	5
6	Customer Satisfaction—Reputation— Intermediate Profit	16	17	20	4
7	Market Penetration—Intermediate Profit	10	15	20	10

METHODOLOGICAL COMMENTS

Validity

This study would be academically incomplete without some discussion of the sources of invalidity that were possible and the steps taken in an attempt to control these sources. Fundamental to this discussion is an understanding of internal validity. Internal validity concerns itself with, in this case, the Delphi procedure itself. Did, in fact, the Delphi process make a difference in the responses? Did the process cause a convergence of responses or was it, as desired, the result of true increased understanding?

The events that occurred between Delphi rounds may have produced other than "rational" responses from the respondents. Where a rational respondent is one whose: (1) preferences are mutually consistent or at least when inconsistencies are brought to his attention, he is willing to correct them, and

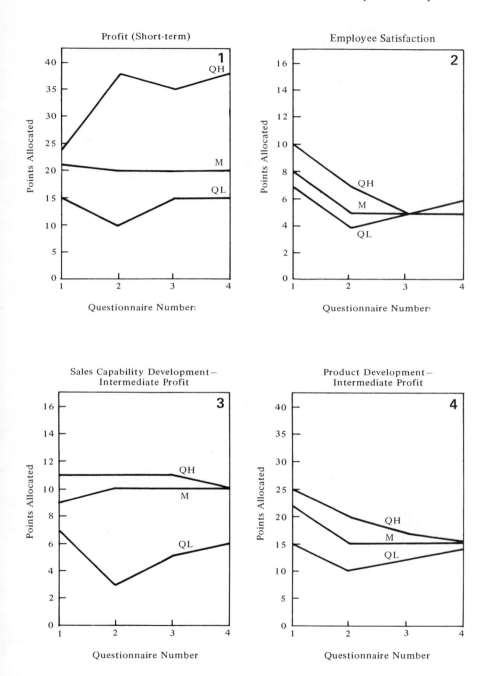

Fig. 2.3. Interquartile Responses

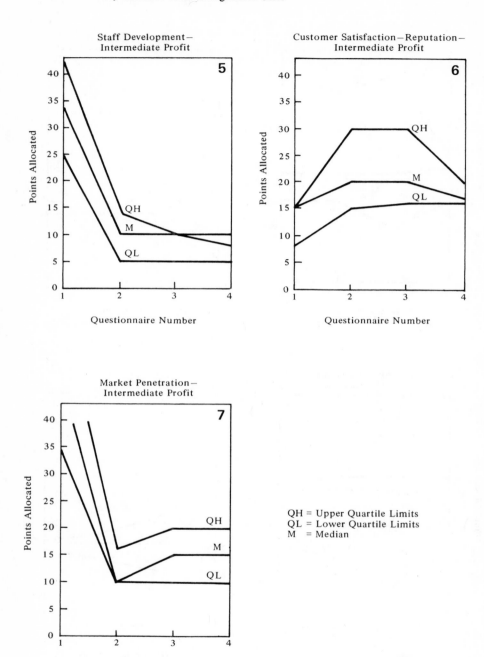

Fig. 2.3. Interquartile Responses (cont.)

(2) personal probabilities are reasonably stable over time, provided he receives no new relevant evidence. The major cause of this type of invalidity is the time lapse between rounds. As the time span between questionnaires increases, prior reasoning becomes difficult to recall and the probability of interference approaches certainty. To control for this possible source of invalidity, the lapse between questionnaires was made as brief as practically possible through immediate processing of the questionnaries. It is interesting to note that midway through the study, a "manpower leveling" took place. In effect, it was a layoff. This must have caused some changes in the degree of influence of some of the defined goals. The wording of the questions and feedback information may have adversely affected the responses. It may have been possible for two respondents to have different interpretations of the same question or comment. To minimize this possiblity, each bit of correspondence was carefully examined to eliminate any ambiguity or emotionally "charged" words. Being the steering component of the process, I may have biased the results by providing too much, too little, or incorrect feedback. In an effort to control this, I was as objective as possible and provided most of the feedback verbatim.

Another factor (for which control is difficult) may have influenced the validity of the study—the subject matter. This could have been perceived as being potentially dangerous. Here were a collectively known group of participants asked not only to define influential goals but, in addition, to state the reasons of influence.

There was a good chance that top management would not be in full accord with all of the reasonings. Therefore, true feelings may have been repressed to some unknown extent. In retrospect, then, I should not have made the participants known either to one another or to the division's top management.

My explanations of some of the rankings may not have been perfectly correct, but they do serve as brief summaries of the verbal responses received during the course of the effort. After carefully studying these results and applying the criterion of "reasonableness," I feel that this was indeed a valid and useful effort. Its value to the department's upper management depends on the use made of the results, if they are considered valid.

The value of this study perceived by the respondents can be summarized by presenting their comments.

"It should give some indication of the current problems in the division as identified by the participants in the study. Whether these problems are real or imaginary could perhaps be commented on by higher management."

"The main value of this study to me has been the opportunity to get some indications of the opinions of other managers on both ISD goals and their relative importance. This is the first definition of ISD goals formally stated that I have seen, and I am curious as to whether these goals are related in any respect to the actual goals of higher management. The benefits of the study to ISD will depend upon the dissemination of results. There seems to be somewhat general agreement that a disproportionate weight must be assigned to the short-term profit goal even though most managers would prefer to concentrate more activity on the intermediate and long-term goals. If the results of the study were made known to professional personnel, I feel certain that many would express dissatisfaction and disappointment with the apparent lack of importance attached to the satisfaction and accomplishment which a professional person should feel toward his job. I do not suggest that jobs should be refused because an employee's dignity may be offended or his professional status degraded. However, one of the most common complaints experienced recently in my employee appraisal interviews is that some current assignments do not require personnel with the high degree of technical competency."

"I think you have more people thinking about what we should be trying to do and why. If you can feed back to top management that there is not a common view of objectives among this group, you will be doing a big service."

"It serves to focus systematic attention as to what goals are and ought to be."

"I have benefited from this study in that it has helped me clarify some of my thinking on the subject of the study. It certainly was a worthwhile experience. ISD can benefit if the comments, results, and thoughts of the study can pinpoint where the goal allocations are markedly different from the goal allocations as seen by upper management."

"Hopefully, some of the comments made during the study will bring more realism into the judgment of ISD managers."

"Gives me a better understanding of the ideas of other managers. May help ISD management by giving them some feeling for the thoughts of their operating managers."

"It gives me an insight into how my peers view their goals in relation to each other. Also, found the comments interesting. I don't think it has any long-lasting benefit to ISD since I believe the staff will continue to do as they have. The key influence on an organization is what the top management views as its policy to get the job done, I don't think the ISD staff knows precisely what this policy is, assuming that it had been formulated. Perhaps top management themselves should have participated in a Delphi analysis. I would like to know what their thinking is."

"It brings into the open the variety of interpretations and emphasis being expressed in the pursuit of a goal. It can facilitate communication and understanding between different levels of management. By examining the results of the study top management can (1) be aware of the grass roots attitudes, (2) determine if adequate communication has been provided, and (3) direct their future efforts accordingly."

Validity Testing

Considering all the possible sources of invalidity, it is difficult in an absolute sense to assess the validity of using the Delphi technique for the purposes of this study. Its true worth, in the sense of yielding more reliable results than conventional methods, can be established in an intuitive sense by the respondents who seem satisfied that it is fair and efficient. In this case, the participants seemed pleased with the opportunity to see how others felt. They interpreted the comments as reflecting accurately the reasons for the general mood within the department.

A possible extension of this study would be an effort to establish its validity in a more tangible manner. Supposedly, the increased understanding of influential goals made possible through the Delphi technique represents a direction in which the organization is proceeding.

If this is truly the direction in which the organization *does* proceed, we will have substantively proved the validity of this technique in a particular application. This could be accomplished through an analysis, at some future time, of the division of labor of the organization, its flow of work, and its allocation of resources as reflected in its budget to determine if the direction has been as predicted.

The Fourth Jetport for Metropolitan New York:
A Case Study *

A.Y. LEWIN[†], M.F. SHAKUN[†], D.R. HORTBERG[†], J.F. HYFANTIS[†],
F.J. IAROSSI[†], and J.C. MILES, II[†]

INTRODUCTION

On a typical day, one out of every five air passengers flying within the United States either takes off or lands at one of the major airports now serving the greater New York area. Three out of every four air passengers traveling between the United States and transatlantic destinations depart from New York. In the last few years, air traffic has increased to the point where the existing facilities at Kennedy International, La Guardia, and Newark Airports cannot meet peak period demands.

This disparity between air traffic demands and present airport capabilities is apparent to most travelers. A late afternoon visit to any of the New York-New Jersey jetports would resolve any doubt. Furthermore, there is little disagreement as to future trends in air passenger traffic. In 1958, the three regional jetports handled nearly 13,500,000 passengers. Ten years later, in 1968, these airports handled almost three times that number—37,000,000 passengers. Current estimates indicate that ten years hence New York area jetports will be faced with a demand to serve over 60,000,000 passengers.

This projected figure, coupled with the growth in air cargo and general aviation traffic, has alarmed aviation-oriented groups in the New York area and throughout the nation. The major fear is that air traffic will be stifled with resulting repercussions on the economic growth of aviation in particular and the New York area in general. There is some indication that air traffic congestion is already taking its toll. Statistics issued by the Port of New York

*Undertaken in 1970
[†] New York University

Authority show that overall revenue passenger traffic for 1968 increased 7.5 percent over 1967. However, the growth rate for 1969 had dropped to an overall 3.9 percent.

The immediate need for action is well established; however, the major participants remain deadlocked over the most appropriate course to follow. Although there are a number of organizations and special interest groups involved in the conflict, the parties generally fall into two categories: those concerned with the economic and industrial decline resulting from lost air traffic, and those concerned with the decline in an ecological sense associated with the proposed solutions. This issue has been smoldering, and sometimes burning, for the past ten years with no agreement in sight.

The present stalemate finds the Port of New York Authority, the Federal Aviation Agency, and various aviation industry groups proposing two sites in northern New Jersey, while representatives of the State of New Jersey (i.e., governor, legislature, and citizen groups) favor sites in central New Jersey. Each side is steadfastly opposed to the position of the other. The main issue is whether a site should be selected on the basis of existing air traffic patterns and the disposition of traffic-generating populations or on the basis of the social, economic, and ecological impact on the State of New Jersey.

It appears that the participants will remain deadlocked until sufficient pressure is developed to force a compromise solution. The aim of this study is to investigate alternate strategies which might lead to the resolution of this interorganizational conflict.

SUMMARY AND RECOMMENDATIONS

In reviewing the fourth jetport controversy with its multiple outcomes, two approaches were taken: an individual citizen's utility model was derived and preference and power functions of each participant were formulated. From the preference-power analysis, coalitions were constructed to determine the likelihood of occurrence of the various outcomes. While the results of these studies are amplified in the Appendices of this report, the basic conclusion arising from this work is that there is no site for the fourth jetport which is agreeable to all the major participants in the controversy.

The primary findings indicate that a fourth metropolitan jetport will not be required until the next decade if certain actions aimed at increasing the capacity of the three existing jetports are implemented rapidly. The following are the specific recommendations necessary to avoid building a fourth jetport.

1. *Improved Air Traffic Control Hardware.* Nearly all of the equipment and the technology to achieve a significant increase in air traffic control capacity is now available. Through use of these new techniques, aviation experts predict that a 50 percent increase in peak-hour,

poor-weather runway capacity could be achieved. Additionally, this development would have international significance since many foreign jetports are experiencing air congestion similar to the New York metropolitan jetports. A recommendation of this nature must be developed on a national level where the direction, funding, and coordination could be accomplished under one roof.

2. *Restriction of General Aviation from the Metropolitan Jetports During Peak Periods.* It is the burgeoning growth in general aviation (i.e., private, corporate, and taxi aircraft) that is the cause of congestion at the metropolitan jetports. While their restriction will solve capacity problems at the jetports, new and attractive facilities (both from an equipment and convenience standpoint) must be provided for them. Toward this end, existing facilities should be upgraded and new facilities created. The technology employed should include STOL ports and IFR navigational equipment. Federal funds for these purposes have been established and are available through the respective state aviation authorities.

3. *Upgrading of Ground Transportation Systems.* Highway access and egress routes to and from the metropolitan jetports must be upgraded to meet the increased passenger demands which will develop in the coming years. The formulation and implementation of specific plans should be the responsibility of the respective state highway departments. Rail service must be provided to the jetports to ease highway congestion. Final negotiations are in progress for rapid transit service to Kennedy International while initial talks are commencing for PATH service to Newark. The Port Authority must assume responsibility for implementating these proposals.

4. *Expanded Terminal and Baggage Facilities.* These facilities must also be expanded to meet increasing passenger demand. Little effort has been directed toward the optimal solution for allocation of terminal floor-space or baggage-handling techniques. It is felt that the investment of minimal time and resources could yield large dividends in this area. The Port Authority should assume the leadership role for the resolution of this problem.

5. *Expansion of Kennedy International into Jamaica Bay.* The additional capacity generated from this expansion would allow additional general aviation traffic at the metropolitan jetports. Opposition to this expansion is already mounting (primarily from the conservationists, since Jamaica Bay is a wild-life sanctuary) hence, its implementation may be impossible.

6. *Need for Strong Coordination at the Federal Level.* There is no obvious need for a coordinated national approach to airport planning. While a National Airport Plan as such exists, it has been ineffectual in meeting the needs of the respective states and the aviation industry. The Department of Transportation (probably through the FAA) must establish a national policy, setting priorities coupled with appropriate long-term funding.

While the immediate need is not seen for a fourth jetport, there can be no doubt that one will be required sometime in the 1980s. It is felt that this jetport will be built in the McGuire/Lakehurst area of central New Jersey. This site represents not only a feasible political solution (one that New Jersey could implement unilaterally) but with projected population growths and the advent of high-speed ground transportation, it could serve not only New Jersey but also New York and Philadelphia. The basic question surrounding this site is not one of feasibility but one of timing. If the previously outlined recommendations fail to be implemented and massive congestion at the existing jetports result, one could expect construction at this site to start in the near future.

PARTICIPANTS

A detailed history of participant involvement is developed in Appendix I. Here we merely list the participants for ease of referral:

I. *State Government*
   New Jersey Governor
   New York Governor
   New Jersey Legislature
   New York Legislature
   Port of New York Authority—created in 1921 as a bi-state agency charged with joint control and development of the New York Port District. In 1947, it inherited the operation of Newark, La Guardia, and Kennedy International.

II. *Federal Agencies*
   Federal Aviation Agency (FAA)—charged with maintenance of the National Air Traffic Control System, encouragement of commerce growth, and promotion of air safety.
   Department of Transportation—charged with formulation and coordination of a National Airport Plan.
   Department of Defense—involved to the extent that several suggested sites are presently military bases.

III. *Others*

Various members of Congress
Airlines (Aviation Development Council)
Aircraft Owners and Pilots Association (AOPA)
Conservationists
Local communities
Airline Pilots Association (ALPA)
Professional Air Traffic Controllers Organization (PATCO)
Airport Operators Council
Civil Aeronautics Board
County governments and planning boards
Governor's Economic Evaluation Committee
Long Island Association
Metropolitan Commuter Transportation Association
National Business Aircraft Association
New York City Council
New York Planning Commission
Regional Plan Association
U.S. Customs Bureau
U.S. Department of Interior

SITES

A list of airport sites under consideration and a map showing their locations appear in Appendix II.

BACKGROUND

Beginning in 1957, the Port of New York Authority made periodic forecasts based on air travel market surveys which indicated a constant and rapid increase in the air passenger traffic utilizing the three New York area jetports. Nearly 25 million passengers were forecast at that time for 1965 and 45 million for 1975. (Actually, traffic reached 25.8 million in 1965 while the 1975 prediction increased to 55 million.) These forecasts led to an evaluation of the existing regional system relative to the projected demand. In December 1959, the Port Authority's preliminary report on airport requirements was published. It stated that the air traffic demand would soon exceed the capacity of the regional system and that an additional major airport was urgently needed to serve the metropolitan area. The Port Authority had examined 15 possible sites throughout the New York-New Jersey region and concluded: "The proposed site in Morris County (Great Swamp) therefore meets all of the requirements for a new major airport to serve the New

Jersey-New York area, and it is the only potential site in the area which does so. . . ."

The report was greeted with immediate opposition. The Great Swamp site was situated adjacent to prime suburban areas. The 10,000-acre tract proposed by the Port Authority included 3,000 homes as well as a vast natural preserve. Concerned community groups and local governments, joined by conservationists, voiced their overwhelming disapproval. The New Jersey Legislature passed a bill (later vetoed by Governor Meyner) prohibiting the construction of a jetport in the seven heavily populated counties of the state.

In 1961, following a thorough study of the situation, the Port Authority submitted a report to the governors and legislatures which analyzed 17 potential sites and confirmed the findings of the preliminary 1959 study. Also in 1961 the Federal Aviation Agency conducted a study of the airport problem in the New Jersey-New York area and confirmed the need for an additional major airport in the metropolitan region. Furthermore, the FAA concluded that the new airport would be compatible with existing air space and air traffic environment only if it were located in the "northwest quadrant," that is, the northwest sector of New Jersey.

Opposition continued to develop within New Jersey following the PA and FAA reports. Regional planning groups challenged the need for a fourth jetport. Local community groups and conservationists increased the pressure on both state and federal authorities. Governor Hughes (N.J.) asked the FAA to study three additional sites in the central and northern portions of the state, while Governor Rockefeller suggested two new sites in New York.

In 1963, the FAA rejected these sites and reaffirmed its position—i.e., a fourth major airport was urgently needed, and it must be located in the northwest quadrant to minimize interference with existing air traffic patterns. To this the Port Authority added that the new facility must be financially sefl-sufficient, therefore, located adjacent to traffic-generating areas. Resistance within the State of New Jersey continued to mount. The criteria used by the Port Authority and the FAA in their site selection studies included air traffic patterns, current disposition of traffic-generating areas, weather, construction costs, and current surface transportation patterns. To the citizens of New Jersey, these studies favored the interests of New York City and ignored the impact of a new airport upon the surrounding area and the necessity of combining airport planning with comprehensive land-use planning.

Late in 1965, the Aviation Development Council, representing ten major airlines, offered a program to meet the metropolitan air terminal needs for the next 15 years without a fourth jetport. By expanding the existing facilities and relegating general aviation aircraft to peripheral airports, the airlines hoped to avoid the cost of staffing and equipping another major terminal. The Port Authority immediately scored the proposal, maintaining that a new jetport would be needed by 1970. The AOPA, representing general aviation interests, strongly resisted the proposal, while the community groups and conservationists continued their opposition to the Great Swamp site.

In 1966, the Port Authority issued a second comprehensive report, which updated previous information but reaffirmed its position that the Morris County site was the only suitable location for the urgently needed fourth jetport. Before the print was dry on this report, a coalition of local community groups and conservationists had arranged to deed a section of the Great Swamp to the federal government for use as a national sanctuary. The Department of the Interior promptly decreed the entire Great Swamp a national landmark and voiced its opposition to any jetport in that area. By the end of that year, the airline association had reversed itself and called for prompt agreement on a site for a new jetport.

Early in 1967, Governor Rockefeller, backed by the Metropolitan Commuter Transportation Authority and Mayor Lindsay, announced plans to build a fourth jetport at Calverton, Long Island, a site 70 miles from New York City. He also proposed that a fifth jetport be built in northern New Jersey. Instead, Senator Case (N.J.) proposed that the Port Authority reevaluate a site in central New Jersey bordered by McGuire Air Force Base and Lakehurst Naval Air Station. This site in Burlington County was long favored by New Jersey, since it was largely undeveloped and would profit by the establishment of a major air terminal. Although both sites enjoyed local support, they also aroused stubborn opposition. The Calverton site centered on an existing facility operated by Grumman Aircraft in conjunction with the Navy. Grumman, a major employer on Long Island, threatened to move its entire operation. In New Jersey, the Port Authority restated its opposition to the Burlington County site, holding that the location was far removed from the prime traffic-generating areas.

Throughout the summer of 1968, air traffic in the metropolitan area was hampered by major delays of up to three hours. The particular problem resulted from action on the part of the air traffic controllers as they sought to publicize the congested facilities and antiquated air controller system. The FAA acted to alleviate the immediate congestion by limiting the number of flights at each of the major airports, while banning general aviation traffic during peak periods. The FAA also reemphasized the need for a fourth jetport and for additional facilities for private aircraft. A delegation of New York Congressmen blasted the FAA for not acting forcefully enough in regard to the fourth jetport. They proposed legislation enabling the federal government to select a site and construct and operate a new jetport in the metropolitan area under the direction of a new federal agency.

In August of 1968, the Port Authority announced that the existing Solberg Airport in Hunderdon County, N.J., would be an acceptable site for a fourth major jetport. By early 1969, the Solberg proposal had received the backing of the FAA as well as major airlines and aviation industry groups. However, political organizations within New Jersey remained opposed to the site on the grounds that air and noise pollution would disrupt major sections of the state.

In November of 1969, William Cahill was elected Governor of New Jersey. Although he made no direct statements on the matter, it was generally understood that he was opposed to the Solberg site. Within three days of his election, a delegation of Congressmen led by the New York representatives inserted a rider to the federal airport funding bill which would have empowered the Secretary of Transportation to select a site for the fourth jetport if the local participants failed to reach agreement within three years. The provision was defeated with the help of all 14 members of the New Jersey delegation.

One week later, the Port Authority, in an unusual public board meeting, acknowledged the opposition of Governor-elect Cahill to the Solberg site. The PA then stated that it would attempt to meet increasing traffic demand by further expansion of the three existing jetports. However, few observers believed that the conflict had ended. Some recalled a similar announcement made by the Port Authority when that agency dropped its plans for a Morris County jetport because of the opposition of the New Jersey Legislature. That announcement was made in September of 1960.

ANALYSIS OF THE
FOURTH JETPORT DECISION-MAKING PROCESS

The initiative in the fourth jetport decision-making process has been held throughout by the New York Port Authority. They originally perceived a need for another jetport in the New York area and they have made the major proposals for jetport sites and have been the primary evaluator of alternatives suggested by others. The pattern of the decision-making process has been: (1) the Port Authority makes a jetport site proposal supported by detailed analyses of alternatives; (2) residents in the area suggested as a site express strong opposition, which their Congressional and legislative representatives echo; (3) comments for and against based on special interest are expressed by peripheral groups; (4) politicians and agencies seeing themselves as mediators or as having responsibility for the "public good" suggest consideration of alternative sites; and (5) after a period of give and take, and when deadlock is clearly seen by all, the Port Authority reevaluates the situation and makes a new major proposal. This sequence has been repeated twice—first for the Great Swamp proposal and then for the Solberg proposal. Currently, the process is in recognized deadlock with no new proposal in sight.

There is substantial disagreement among the participants, both over the need for a new jetport and over the desirability of the alternative outcomes. Air passenger traffic to and from the New York City area has been growing rapidly, and this is forecast to continue. However, the difficulty in the present three jetports handling this traffic, which was originally forecast by the Port Authority in 1959, has not materialized, providing an indication to some participants (that is supported by other analyses) that there are ways to handle increased passenger traffic other than by construction of another jetport. Thus, participants do not agree on the need for a fourth jetport.

The disagreement that also exists over the desirability of the alternative outcomes is in part evaluated by the utility analysis presented in Appendix IV. This analysis hypothesizes three components in an individual citizen's utility for a jetport site: (1) Availability utility consists of the utility provided by access to jet transportation; it is inversely proportional to the distance from the jetport site. (2) Environmental utility—which is negative—derives from environmental degradation caused by a jetport, such as additional noise, pollution, ground traffic, and "undesirable" land development. Environmental utility is a very strong negative factor in the vicinity of a jetport site and negligible factor elsewhere. (3) Economic utility derives from increased spending due to jetport development and to increases in land value (decreases in land values related to environmental degradation are considered part of environmental utility). Economic utility is small except in the vicinity of the jetport, and it is also inversely related to population density.

This utility model explains the strong opposition by area residents to jetport sites in heavily populated areas where the environmental factor dominates. It also explains the mild favoring of jetport sites by local residents in sparsely populated areas where the economic utility outweighs the environmental utility. (The favors are spread over fewer people; hence, each individual's share is much larger.)

Evaluation of the availability utility factor by itself shows that the total utility to all New York area residents is substantially greater for sites in the densely populated area (which includes the three existing jetports) than for sites on the periphery. It shows that New York residents are essentially neutral with respect to all sites in New Jersey, while New Jersey residents are essentially neutral with respect to all sites in New York. Further, Solberg and the central New Jersey sites have approximately the same utility for all groups.

No clear-cut coalitions among the participants have emerged, although some loose alignments are evident. The elected representatives (governors, legislators, and Congressmen) and the local communities all are more or less opposed to a new jetport. The governors favor some areas, primarily outside of populated areas and where there is no strong local opposition to a jetport, but generally reflect the "will of the people" which is the primary motivation of all in this group.

The "technically" oriented organizations—such as the Port Authority, FAA, DOT, airlines and airline pilots—in general favor a new jetport. However, all have their own special requirements that tend to create issues among them. For example, the Port Authority strongly favors a "profit-making" venture (discussed in Appendix III-B), the FAA opposes changes in the air lanes (discussed in Appendix III-C), and so forth.

The other participants represent various special interests, which have only marginal impact. Only the conservationists have a growing influence with elected representatives that tends to strengthen the opposition to any new jetport site. The preference "functions" for all participants are discussed in detail in Appendix V.

In order to evaluate the likelihood of occurrence of the various possible outcomes, it is necessary to consider both the preferences of the participants and their relative power to impose their views. An analysis is presented in Appendix V that uses subjective estimates of the relative power of the participants in order to compute estimates of the combined preferences of all participants for each of the outcomes. This "preference index" for an outcome provides a measure of the likelihood that the current decision-making prcess will choose that outcome.

The preference-power analysis indicates that expansion of present jetports and exclusion of general aviation from present jetports (to provide more capacity for scheduled airlines) are strongly favored outcomes. Neutral and weakly favored are sites on the periphery of the populated area. Strongly opposed outcomes are sites in the densely populated area, northern New Jersey and Westchester County, and also proposals for "ocean" sites.

The preference-power analysis recognizes the present disposition to use power as well as the ultimate power that a participant might possibly use. Thus, the power coefficient for the Congressional participants was relatively modest compared to their great potential power through the enactment of legislation, since their recent actions do not indicate a strong inclination to legislate in this field. Additional discussion is presented in Appendix III-D.

One last observation is that economic pressure to reach a decision seems to be negligible. It would be difficult to demonstrate that any perceived slowdown in economic growth was related to a shortage of jetport facilities (and such a shortage itself has not yet been shown). This is discussed in Appendix III-E.

In summary, Messrs. J.D. Thompson and A. Tuden[1] propose that organizational decision-making processes can be divided into four categories determined by the participants' beliefs about the "causes" of the decision-making problem and by their preferences for the possible outcome. In the case that there is disagreement about both causes and preferences (as in the jetport case) the decision must come by "inspiration" rather than by "compromise," "judgment," or "computation," which are the decision-making mechanisms in the other three categories. In this situation, Thompson and Tuden say the most likely outcome is the decision not to face the issue. This in a sense seems to fit the fourth jetport decision-making process.

RESOLUTION WITHOUT A FOURTH MAJOR JETPORT

The initial Port Authority evaluation, completed in 1959, concluded that the air traffic demand would soon exceed the capacity of the regional system and that an additional major airport was *urgently* needed to serve the metropolitan area. A comprehensive study of the region's airport requirements, completed late in 1961 by the Port Authority, predicted that peak period movements would exceed total capacity by 10 percent in 1965 and 30 percent by 1970. This report, backed by a companion FAA study, again stressed the immediate need for a fourth major airport to serve the New York-New Jersey region. A follow-up report published in December 1966 "confirmed the need beyond all doubt." Furthermore, the Port Authority report concluded "The consequences to the New York-New Jersey metropolitan region of continued inability to provide for its future air transport needs will be an economic catastrophe for its people and its commerce."

The Port Authority's forecasts for total passenger traffic and peak-hour IFR movements have proven to be exceptionally accurate. However the "economic catastrophe" which it predicted in 1959, 1961, and 1966 has not materialized. Whereas its traffic forecasts have been accurate, the Port Authority's conclusion that a fourth major jetport was the only alternative for salvation has not been substantiated during the past decade. While the debate raged over the site for the proposed fourth jetport, two alternative measures were taken which enabled the three existing jetports to meet the increased traffic demands. First, the Port Authority expanded the facilities at both Kennedy and La Guardia (expansion of Newark Airport is nearing completion). Secondly, the FAA took action to restrict the use of these jetports by general aviation during the peak hours. It is appropriate to review the evidence which led to the original Port Authority conclusion to determine if other publicly acceptable alternatives are available which would enable the traffic demand of the next decade to be met without a fourth jetport.

A SOLUTION TO FIT THE PROBLEM

The measurements used by the Port Authority to determine the traffic that can be accommodated at an airport are the number of aircraft landings and take-offs that can be handled in an average peak hour under poor weather conditions when Instrument Flight Rules (IFR) are in effect. The 1961 report predicted the following peak-hour IFR demand and available capacity:

	Passenger Aircraft	General Aviation	All-Cargo Aircraft	Total IFR Demand	Total IFR Capacity	Unsatisfied Demand
1965	112	22	2	136	123	13
1970	130	41	7	178	137	41
1975	143	78	16	237	151	86

The Port Authority's conclusion was that the unsatisfied demand could only be met by construction of a fourth jetport.

In 1966 these predications were updated to include the following modifications:

> The subsonic "jumbo jets" will reduce the number of required movements by doubling seating capacity.
>
> The supersonic "SST" will reduce the number of peak-hour movements since European arrivals and departures will be out of phase. Presently, European arrivals and departures coincide during the peak period. With a supersonic aircraft, non-peak hour departures will be necessary in order to arrive in Europe at acceptable times.
>
> The IFR capacity of the existing jetports was increased.
>
> The prediction for all-cargo aircraft movements was significantly reduced.
>
> The general aviation movements were significantly increased.

With these conditions and estimated future load factors, the Port Authority made the following predictions:

	Passenger Aircraft	General Aviation	All-Cargo Aircraft	Total IFR Demand	Total IFR Capacity	Unsatisfied Demand
1970	141	69	3	213	173	40
1975	137	106	4	247	173	74
1980	152	145	5	302	173	129

Again the conclusion was that the unsatisfied demand could only be met by construction of a fourth major jetport. But these figures reveal the cause of the congestion to be *the overwhelming increase in general aviation* (i.e., private, corporate, and taxi aircraft) rather than commercial aircraft. Between 1965 and 1980, general aviation movements would undergo a seven-fold increase until in 1980 they would constitute nearly 50 percent of the peak-hour movements. It is this segment of aviation that will create the unfulfilled demand. Therefore, one could rationally question whether a giant new jetport is a solution befitting the problem.

Passenger and cargo aircraft movements could easily be accommodated by the existing facilities through 1980 with a modest margin for priority general aviation movements. The remainder of the general aviation segment could best be served by new facilities tailored to its particular needs. Certainly, a one billion dollar, 10,000-acre site with 12,000-foot runways and giant terminal facilities is not required to satisfy this unfulfilled demand. Perhaps a number of new sites or expansion of existing fields to equal those at Teterboro and Westchester County Airports would be more effective, less costly, publicly acceptable alternatives to the Port Authority proposal.

This is not a novel idea. In 1965 the Tri-State Transportation Committee recommended construction of a ring of 29 general aviation fields throughout the metropolitan area. That same year the FAA, as part of its five-year program, recommended construction of six general aviation fields in the New York-New Jersey area in conjunction with a total ban on private aircraft at Kennedy, La Guardia, and Newark. But the Port Authority, resting on the charter mandate not to engage in money-losing operations, has refrained from considering general aviation airports, since they traditionally fall into this category.

Following the major traffic delays during the summer of 1968, the FAA restricted the movement of general aviation aircraft during congested peak periods. By raising the landing fees from $5 to $25 and threatening a further increase to match the $64 paid by commercial aircraft, the FAA has begun the virtual exclusion of these aircraft from the major airports. However, no comprehensive program has been presented to provide the peripheral facilities needed in the metropolitan area. If these sites were situated so as not to interfere with operations at the three major airports, a fourth jetport would be unnecessary through the next decade. Further examination of the 1966 Port Authority forecasts reveals that, in addition to satisfying the total demand, each specific jetport could adequately meet its particular demand.

1966 Forecast for Specific IFR Peak Hour Demand*
(Figures in parentheses represent 1970 capacity)

	Kennedy (74)	La Guardia (50)	Newark (49)	Total (173)
1970	75	33	36	144
1975	62	36	43	141
1980	66	39	52	157

*Less general aviation movements.

INCREASE EXISTING CAPACITY

In the previous evaluation, the demand was analyzed and then appropriately altered to suit a fixed limitation (IFR capacity). A second approach is to examine the specific causes for this limitation and propose alternatives which would increase the IFR capabilities to meet the projected peak period demand including the general aviation segment.

One such alternative was discussed in the 1966 Port Authority report. This proposal involved the addition of two major runways in Jamaica Bay and the extension of Runway 4L-22R, resulting in a triple parallel runway system. This expansion could theoretically add 35 peak-hour IFR movements to Kennedy's capacity in two to three years time at an estimated cost of $100 million. (The proposed fourth jetport could add approximately 75 movements at a cost in excess of $1 billion. One could reasonably question the cost effectiveness of the Port Authority choice.) A traffic simulation study is presently underway by the FAA to determine the feasibility of this plan. If completed, it would add sufficient capacity to provide 67 general aviation movements during peak-hour IFR condition, 39 short of the projected total demand in 1975, and 78 short of the total demand in 1980. However, concerned community groups and conservationists are already forming coalitions to block any further expansion into Jamaica Bay.

These same groups are really upset by a more ambitious plan for expanding Kennedy which calls for location of a new terminal complex on land fill in Jamaica Bay. The new runways and terminals would connect the existing airport with the Navy's Floyd Bennett Field on the west side of the Bay. This would add at least 75 peak-hour IFR movements to the region's capacity and, planners believe, could be completed in five to six years at a cost of about $1.5 billion. However, it would still fall 38 short of the projected demand in 1980 if general aviation movements are included.

To the original thesis, that a fourth major jetport is a poor solution to the phenomenal projected growth of general aviation, one could now add the futility of major expansions to satisfy this demand. The three existing jetports have sufficient capacity to satisfy the passenger and cargo traffic beyond 1980. If general aviation movements are to be included at these sites, a fundamental change in the method of handling poor weather, peak-hour traffic is required.

ADVANCED AIR TRAFFIC CONTROL

The real need is to develop a traffic control system that can handle the capacity of the existing jetports, a peripheral chain of general aviation facilities, and a future STOL network—and do it all on a non-interference basis. The present ATC system stems from an international decision made in

1957 to continue with development of navigation aids or oriented toward ground control rather than cockpit control. One result of this approach is that the controller has to navigate the aircraft from the ground by interpreting his radar presentation and then jamming the airways with a multitude of radio communications to the pilot. The controller must give intensive individual attention to each aircraft, thus limiting the number of aircraft which can be monitored during poor weather, peak-hour conditions. This specific limitation is frequently a direct cause of airport delays.

Mr. John R. Wiley, Director of Aviation for the Port Authority, before a Congressional hearing in August 1968, stated that "while the airports are congested, the fact is that the capacity of the air lanes is being strained also, and this has a very direct effect upon the extent of delayed arrivals and departures on the ground."

While quotes out of context can sometimes be misleading, the following excerpts from Mr. Wiley's presentation leave little room for misinterpretation.

> The visual radar presentation is not sufficiently refined to provide navigational guidance precise enough for current traffic. Obviously it will become even less so as our traffic volumes continue to mount. The controller's radar display miniaturizes miles of airspace into a 22-inch circle, so that aircraft sometimes appear to touch on the screen when actually the aircraft are a mile apart. Because of this imprecision, excessive "blocks" of airspace must be allocated to each aircraft as a margin of safety. Under the present system, aircraft must be separated by three miles within 40 miles of the airport, and five miles beyond that. If these blocks could be safely reduced, a larger number of aircraft could occupy the airspace, more aircraft could approach their destinations and land on our runways.
>
> A computer technology that is so much more rapid and accurate than the gound-based radar system is now available. With this equipment the same terminal airspace could accommodate a significantly larger number of aircraft.
>
> Nearly all of the equipment and the technology to achieve a significant increase in air traffic control capacity is now available. But Federal action is mandatory if this is to be accomplished.

This same thesis was emphasized by Mr. J.E. Steiner, Vice President-Engineering and Sales, The Boeing Company, in a presentation to the New Jersey Legislative Committee on transportation in March 1969.

Quoting from Mr. Steiner:

> Technically, the problem is that of close aircraft control in the immediate vicinity of the runway. This control would be exercised to ensure precise timing of aircraft touchdown and takeoff. The air

traffic control function located on the ground would plan the flow of aircraft in the terminal area to make fullest use of runway capacity. It would do this in an adaptive manner by reacting to ever-changing traffic demands. Substantial use would be made of computer technology to sequence and control the flow of aircraft. Surveillance and navigation equipment required would not tax the state-of-the-art. The pilot, assisted by data link, displays, and computers, would exercise greater authority and control over his aircraft than is the case today. Aircraft would carry modest additional equipment that would permit them to fly time-distance-azimuth profiles generally prescribed by local air traffic control. The air traffic controller would supervise and monitor the operation of the system in an executive capacity, exercising override powers whenever required. Clearly, a great length of time and expenditure of money will be necessary before such a system could be implemented.

In his presentation Mr. Steiner emphasized the significance of improved air traffic control by analyzing the effect of aircraft spacing. By developing an ATC system which would enable a decrease in the air spacing from three miles to two miles, the poor weather, peak-hour capacity of existing facilities would be increased by 50 percent. This represents an aggregate increase of about 85 movements for the metropolitan region without a fourth jetport or further expansion of Kennedy.

The last budget submitted by the FAA requested $27 million for its entire research and development program. Advancements in ATC constituted a small fraction of this sum. That same budget provided over $140 million for development of an "SST." One could logically question this allocation against a hierarchy of needs.

The New York dilemma was also analyzed in an article appearing in *Aviation Week and Space Technology*. Quoting from this article in the October 20, 1969 edition: "Development of area navigation is being counted on to solve some of the present problems, but there is no real definition of what future air traffic control demand or need will be, much less any proposed solution." This coincides with another statement by Mr. Wiley of the Port Authority: "The airlines cannot install the precise and costly equipment that will go far to improve traffic conditions aloft unless and until procedures are developed that will enable the air traffic controller to utilize such airborne equipment and increased capability."

A solution of this nature must be developed on a national level where the direction, funding, and coordination could be accomplished under one roof. In fact it must be programed on an international scale since foreign aircraft operating in the U.S. would have to fit into the advance ATC system. This is hardly a major stumbling block since London and Tokyo are presently experiencing air congestion, as bad as if not worse than New York's. Aviation authorities in Europe and Asia are meeting the same public resistance to further jetport construction as experienced here. This past summer the city of Munich finally reached agreement on the site of a new airport after years of bitter debate. London and Tokyo have been as successful as New York in resolving their problems. As traffic volume increases, other cities throughout the world will be faced with the same debate and there is little hope that public opposition will subside. On the contrary, the public is just beginning to fight for the sanctity of its environment. An advanced air traffic control system which would provide a 50 percent increase in the peak-hour, poor-weather capacity of our metropolitan airports would perform the same miracle all over the world.

SUMMARY

This analysis has developed three alternatives to construction of a fourth major jetport in the New York-New Jersey area—construction of a system of general aviation airports to draw that traffic away from the commercial jetports, further expansion of Kennedy International Airport, and development of an advanced air traffic control system to increase the capacity of the existing facilities. Certainly each alternative requires further study and evaluation before its full merit can be verified. However one point is clear—filling the countryside with additional jetports is not the only, and perhaps not even the best, solution to air traffic congestion.

Comparison of Various Alternatives

Alternative	IFR Capacity	Cost	Time (yrs.)	Remarks
1. Fourth Jetport	50-75	$1-1.5 billion	5-6	Community opposition
2. General Aviation Ports	69-145	?	?	Reduces Peak traffic demands
3. Kennedy Plan #1	35	$100 million	2-3	Community opposition
4. Kennedy Plan #2	75	$1.5-2 million	5-6	Community opposition
5. Advanced ATC	85	?	5-6	Increases worldwide capacity

RESOLUTION—A CENTRAL JERSEY JETPORT

Participants in the site selection controversy for a fourth metropolitan jetport continue to flounder with no solution in sight. The major reason for this is the unwillingness of the New Jersey Governor and Legislature to allow construction of the jetport in heavily populated northern New Jersey—a site which nearly all other participants claim is the only possible and realistic one.

Both the New Jersey Governor and Legislature feel that construction of such a major facility mainly for the sort-range objective of relieving current and conceivably temporary air traffic control problems (which is what they view PONYA's *et al.* solution to be) is not in the best long-term interests of the State of New Jersey. These statements are supported by Table 3-V-5 (Likelihood of Various Outcomes of the Fourth Jetport Controversy) of this report. The preference index developed in this table indicates strong opposition (3.46) to a populated northern New Jersey site and a weakly favorable (2.88) position toward a central New Jersey site. By 1985 New Jersey will be an urbanized state of over ten million people. Current planning indicates six million people in northern New Jersey with similar increases in central and southern Jersey. Current industrial development is concentrating in the center of the state between New Brunswick and Camden. Land availability, transportation potential, water supply, and political climate indicate that this area will continue to grow as an industrial complex. New Jersey already depends heavily upon international trade for its high standard of living and its industrial growth. Additionally, it is a sound assumption that New Jersey will be in a strong position to take advantage of the great growth in international trade forecast for the next 30 years.

"For too long have we been the victims of provincialism. For too long have we thought ahead in terms of years rather than of decades and generations. The tremendous changes in our society demand that we work now toward solutions which serve the best interests not of a particular city or group, but of the greatest number of citizens in the broadest region possible." Under this banner of foresightedness, the Governor's Economic Evaluation Committee for an Intercontinental Jetport for New Jersey (established by Governor Hughes on October 31, 1967) began the task of restudying the crisis of inadequate jetport facilities in the New York-New Jersey metropolitan areas. The major conclusions of this study were:

1. New Jersey's future economic health rests upon a revitalization and expansion of its transportation facilities.

2. New Jersey will need a major *intercontinental* jetport. This major airport should be located in the McGuire/Lakehurst area to meet the needs of the state as a whole and to have ample land reserves for unforeseeable expansion. Additionally, the noise and air pollution generated by this site will disturb the fewest number of people.

3. The estimated cost of the jetports is $663 million. Financial feasibility studies strongly indicate that the construction and operation of the proposed intercontinental jetport can be self-liquidating.

A strong case can be made for New Jersey "going its own way" by building at the McGuire/Lakehurst site. Traffic forecasts at Philadelphia and the three New York metropolitan airports made by the above committee show that *unsatisfied passenger demand* would reach over 134 million enplaned and deplaned per year by 1985, and *unsatisfied inbound* and *outbound cargo demand* would reach over 28 million tons per year.[2] As improved surface transportation puts this airport within acceptable time/distance of Manhattan, Philadelphia, and Wilmington, it will not only serve the state, but will also function as the fourth airport for New York as well as supply the second airport which is being sought by Philadelphia. Additionally, the action of building a jetport at McGuire/Lakehurst could be taken unilaterally by New Jersey and would not require the agreement of other participants in order to implement it. While this site might not result in an optimal solution to the *metropolitan* problem, it is a desirable *political* outcome and could prove very beneficial to New Jersey especially in the long run.

The basic question surrounding the site is not one of feasibility but one of timing. If any of the following events occur, coupled with federal funds which have recently become available, one could expect construction at the McGuire/Lakehurst site to start in the relatively near future.

1. The Economic Evaluation Committee is able to galvanize the New Jersey Governor and Legislature to action by convincing them of the immediate need for a New Jersey jetport.

2. Expansion at the metropolitan jetports (especially Kennedy) is blocked by either conservationists or local citizens.

3. General aviation through the AOPA exerts sufficient political muscle to preclude its being banned from the major jetports.

4. Technological advances in air traffic control are not realized.

5. Severe congestion and traffic delays at the existing jetports clearly demonstrate a lack of capacity.

6. Several airline crashes occur which can be directly traced to overcrowded air space surrounding the existing jetports.

7. New federal legislation is enacted allowing the government to select a site which New Jersey feels would not be in its best interests.

If the above events do not occur, the most probable course of action is for New Jersey to delay its decision to build a jetport until such time as the evidence supporting it becomes overwhelming and hence no longer avoidable.

APPENDIX I—HISTORY OF PARTICIPANTS

United States Congress Position

Background

The members of Congress who represent areas in the metropolitan New York City area are involved in the jetport decision making by taking public positions and by making statements for or against various proposals. The Congress as a whole is involved through the legislation that it enacts to allocate funds for airport development and the various projects of the executive agencies (the Departments of Defense, Interior, and Transportation in particular). It can also enact legislation to provide for air safety, research and development, and other factors that could influence the New York area jetport decision.

The representatives generally express views reflecting their constituents' opinions.

History

1959

Dec. 18	Rep. Frelinghuysen against building jetport in Great Swamp.
Dec. 21	Rep. Celler hints Congress probe of Port Authority.
Dec. 29	Sen. Williams suggests questions for FAA.
	Rep. Frelinghuysen backs Congress probe.

1960

Jan. 26	Rep. Frelinghuysen opposes any site in Morris County.
Nov. 8	Sen. Case opposes any new airport in northern New Jersey.

1961

Aug. 3	Rep. Frelinghuysen urges final resolution of Morris site.
June 2	Rep. Frelinghuysen scores Meyner inaction.
July 16	Sen. Case says FAA confused.
July 28	Rep. Frelinghuysen charges FAA-Port Authority agreement.

1962

Aug. 26	Case reports Port Authority looking at Orange-Suffolk County (New York) sites.

1963

June 15	Case urges McGuire and Lakehurst as sites.
July 18	Case again urges McGuire.

1965

Aug. 23	Sen. Dodd urges site in Connecticut.

1966

Nov. 10	Javits chides FAA on report.
Dec. 22	Javits urges immediate study of need.
Dec. 29	Case and Williams against northern Jersey site.

1967

Jan. 22	Javits urges Senate hearings.
Jan. 28	Case urges McGuire.
Mar. 12	Rep. Pike against Culverton.
Sep. 28	Case again proposes McGuire.

1968

Aug. 3	Seven representatives from New York City area endorse proposal to open Floyd Bennett Field to general aviation.
Sep. 25	Reps. Addaffo and Rosenthal propose Federal New York Aviation Authority to replace New York Port Authority in aviation activities.
Dec. 11	Sens. Monroney says New York City faces traffic losses if fourth jetport is not built.

1969

Jan. 3	Rep. Rosenthal says federal government should select fourth jetport site.
Feb. 7	Sen. Case and Williams discuss use of McGuire with Sen. Land.

Goals

1. Office holders want to stay in office.
2. Promote the economic, environmental, and cultural interests of their constituents.

Influence

The Congress can enact legislation, but it may be difficult to tailor this specifically to the New York situation.

State Government Position

Background

State government is involved in the development of airports, since airports frequently serve several municipalities and countries simultaneously. In the case of airports to serve the New York metropolitan area, the state governments of both New York and New Jersey are involved. The various agents of the state governments influence events in several ways: influence of public opinion through use of the persuasive powers of the state offices, enactment of state laws, execution and enforcement of laws, and control over activities of the Port of New York Authority (the PNYA is somewhat independent but its activities can be vetoed by the states of New York and New Jersey). Involvement in the fourth jetport controversy has been largely of the first type through public comments for or against various proposals. However, the New Jersey Legislature did pass a bill in 1961 banning another jetport in northern New Jersey, which was vetoed by Governor Meyner, and the New York legislature gave a vote of approval to a Governor Rockefeller plan in 1967.

The primary goal of most elected officials is to stay in office so the statements of individual legislators generally relect the expressed feelings of their constituents. The governors tend to take a broader, "general public good" attitude, but they also generally follow rather than lead public opinion on the jetport issue.

History
1959
Dec. 4	Gov. Meyner opposes Great Swamp—noise, ill effects on area.
Dec. 25	New Jersey Legislature urges study for alternate site.

1960
Jan. 13	Gov. Meyner asks legislation study.
Jan. 19	New Jersey Legislature opposes Morris County site.
Jan. 31	New Jersey Sen. Jones, five county's freeholders plan further opposition.
Feb. 5	New Jersey Legislature asks study of Port Authority authorization to choose site.
Mar. 29	New Jersey Senate votes study sites for both New York City and Philadelphia.
July 19	New Jersey Freeholders Association backs New Jersey Senate opposing Morris and favoring southern New Jersey.
July 21	New Jersey Conservation Department starts long-range study of airports needs.

1961
June 1	New Jersey Senate bars site in Morris, six other counties unless required by federal.
June 3	New Jersey Legislature passes bill opposing jetport.
June 29	Meyner favors northern New Jersey and Morris County site.
July 1	Trenton hearings on jetport.
July 15	Hodges and Mitchell urge southern Jersey site.
July 17	Meyner reports mail favoring northern New Jersey site up from 20% to 50%.
Aug. 29	Bill to ban New Jersey site vetoed by Meyner.

1962

Jan. 10	Meyner says jetport vital to New Jersey economy.
Feb. 11	New Jersey Senate group urges barring new jetport by Port Authority.
Apr. 17	New Jersey Senate votes bill barring northern New Jersey site.
Sep. 5	Hughes regrets Port Authority opposition to Burlington site.
Dec. 7	Hughes urges Burlington-Ocean site.

1963

July 4	Rockefeller disputes Halaby that Pine Island, Orange County, is unsuitable.
July 17	Hughes and Rockefeller order New York Port Authority to resurvey Pine Barrens and Pine Island.
Nov. 22	Comm. Roe pledges all-out fight for New Jersey jetport.

1964

Oct. 29	Rockefeller again suggests Pine Island.
Oct. 30	Hughes says Bearfort and Bowling Green would require federal subsidy, wants jetport in New Jersey.

1965

July 30	Rockefeller asks Port Authority definite recommendation by January.

1966

Dec. 23	New Jersey Transportation Commissioner says restudy northern New Jersey. Hughes regrets pledge against Great Swamp site.
Dec. 24	New Jersey Aviation Bureau surveys Hunterdon, Warren, and Sussex Counties.

1967

Jan. 1	Rockefeller asks Met. Com. Trans. Authority for jetport recommendation, urges Culverton.
Mar. 8	Rockefeller asks sum for site acquisition.
Mar. 17	Rockefeller announces plans to build at Culverton and transit unification system.
Apr. 1	New York State Assembly approves Rockefeller plan.
June 7	Hughes reports U.S. review of Pine Barrens.

1969

Jan. 13	Sen. Speno offers bill to order New York State Transportation Department to select jetport site.
Mar. 5	New Jersey legislative hearings open on jetport—any site in

	northern New Jersey termed politically unacceptable by Democratic and Republican leaders.
Mar. 15	Gov. Rockefeller opposes Somers, New York, site.
Apr. 9	Sen. Dumont leads thousands in demonstration against Solberg at Statehouse.
May 6	New Jersey Senate approves bill to form state airport authority to help select jetport site.
May 22	Democratic Governor-Candidate Tonti opposes New Jersey jetport.
Sep. 6	Cahill against jetport, Meyner says "keep options open."

Goals
1. Office holders want to stay in office.
2. Promote economic environmental, and cultural good of constituents.

Preferences
New Jersey: 1. For southern New Jersey site.
             2. Against metropolitan New Jersey site.

New York: 1. For Long Island or Orange County site.

Influence
The state governments could exclude areas in their own states from development as a jetport by passing appropriate legislation. They can also veto proposed actions of the Port of New York Authority.

Federal Executive Branch Position

Background
The major executive agencies involved in the jetport decision are the Departments of Defense, Interior, and Transportation. The DOD is involved primarily through its control of military installations and aircraft operations in the New York City area. However, the Army Corps of Engineers are also involved in flood control development and natural resource projects. The DOI is responsible for control of the environment and for provision of national parks. National parks are a land use that sometimes competes with airport facilities. The DOT is responsible for providing for an adequate national transportation system.

History
1961

| Jan. 12 | Army flood control conflicts with Great Swamp plan. |

1963

| July 4 | U.S.N. denies plans to abandon Lakehurst. |

1966

Oct. 3   U.S. Customs Bureau staff at Kennedy urges fourth jetport to ease congestion.

Dec. 4   U.S. Interior Department says Great Swamp National Landmark, opposes jetport there.

1967

Aug. 12   Transportation Department opposes central New Jersey, Burlington.

1968

Jan. 26   U.S.A.F. opposes McGuire.

Sep. 9   DOD says McGuire still needed for military.

Sep. 12   Sen. Boyd of DOT supports central Jersey site.

Sep. 26   U.S.N. agrees to open Floyd Bennett Field to general aviation.

1969

Sep. 12   CAB Chairman Brown favors fourth jetport, but says local community should select location.

Oct. 13   CAB reports say three New York City area jetports saturated.

Goals

1. National defense.
2. Environmental control.
3. Adequate transportation system.

Influence

The departments control spending of funds allocated by Congress for programs that they administer. They can also influence public opinion by making proposals and offering opinions for or against jetport sites.

The Port of New York Authority Position

Background

The Port Authority, as an interstate agency, is the creature of the legislatures of New Jersey and New York. The authority was originally established in 1921 as a self-supporting agency to plan and develop terminal and transportation facilities in the port area—specifically within a 25-mile radius of the Statue of Liberty. It is governed by a 12-man board, made up of six members appointed by the Governor of New York and six by the Governor of New Jersey, for six-year staggered terms.

Over the years, the Port Authority has concentrated its attention upon bus, truck, and automobile access and airline terminals. Recently it became active in marine container facilities in New Jersey and real estate in New York

City. The Board of Commissioners, predominantly from the financial community, has adhered closely to its charter mandate not to engage in money-losing operations. However, there is a growing feeling that this theme has become a shield, allowing the Authority to remain unresponsive to the wishes of the community.

History
1959
Dec.   PA weighs building fourth major commercial airport in area on 10,000-acre tract in Morris County, N.J., 25 miles west of New York City.

1960
Sep.   PA reports it drops plan for Morris County jetport because of N.J. Legislature's opposition.

1961
June   PA finds Morris County only suitable jetport site of 17 surveyed. Final report submitted to Governors Meyner and Rockefeller.

1962
Aug.   PA announces opposition to southern N.J. sites.

1963
Dec.   PA rejects both the Burlington County (N.J.) and Pine Island (N.Y.) sites proposed by Governors Hughes and Rockefeller.

1964
Oct.   PA rejects as too costly proposed N.J. jetport at either Bearfort or Bowling Green; both sites in northwest corner of N.J. were recommended by Governor Hughes.

1965
Oct.   PA scores proposal to meet N.Y. airport needs through 1980 without building fourth jetport; offered by consortium of ten major airlines serving N.Y.C. PA holds new jetport will be needed in 1970-75.

1966
Dec.   PA reports it is unable to find suitable alternative to Morris County (Great Swamp) as site for fourth jetport; issues final report to Governors Hughes and Rockefeller.

1968

Aug.   PA says Solberg Airport in Hunterdon County, N.J., 44 miles from Manhattan, would be acceptable site for fourth jetport. PA and TWA issue joint statement noting their agreement on need for fourth jetport; deny disagreement between PA and some airlines on need.

Oct.   PA rejects proposal to build fourth jetport in central N.J. near McGuire A.F. Base; holds site not feasible; says costs would be prohibitive.

1969

Nov.   PA, in unusual public board meeting, acknowledges position of Governor-elect Cahill—i.e., Solberg will not be the site of a fourth jetport. PA states it will attempt to meet increasing traffic by further expansion of three existing jetports.

Goals

1. Continue as sole authority in planning and operating major airline terminals in metropolitan area.
2. Refrain from engaging in enterprises which might not be financially self-sufficient.

Preferences

1. Morris County, N.J. (Great Swamp), site.
2. Solberg, N.J., site.
3. Further expansion of existing sites as interim solution.

Influence

The Port of New York Authority must abide by the wishes of the States of New Jersey and New York. It cannot act on a project without their concurrence. Presently it cannot be forced to engage in an enterprise which it deems unacceptable. The PA is essentially powerless to force a solution; however, little can be done in the face of its inaction.

The Federal Aviation Administration

Background

The FAA (Federal Aviation Administration), which draws its authority from legislation dating back to the 1930s, is "empowered and directed to encourage and foster the development of civil aeronautics and air commerce in the United States and abroad." The FAA serves three primary functions: traffic system designer, economic developer, and promoter of safety. The FAA Administrator is authorized and directed "to develop plans for and formulate policy with respect to the use of the navigable airspace under such terms, conditions, and limitations as he may deem necessary in order to ensure the safety and the efficient utilization of such airspace. He may modify or revoke such assignment when required in the public interest." Additionally, in developing the National Airport Plan and in administering the Federal Aid to Airport Program, the FAA was charged by Congress with overall planning for airports developed with federal assistance.

History
1961

FAA stated a fourth metropolitan jetport was required and incorporated this into its National Airport Plan. It set out the desirable site location as an area lying in the "northwest quadrant" of the metropolitan New Jersey-New York region.

1962
Dec. 7

FAA undertakes site selection studies for Pine Island, Suffolk Air Force Base, and the pine-barrens of Burlington County. While initial studies were based solely on air traffic control needs, these studies will also be based on aeronautical needs, population distribution, ground transportation, topography, land cost and use, obstructions, and wind data.

1963
June

FAA restates jetport site must lie in northwest quadrant— rejects Pine Island, Suffolk Air Force Base, and pine-barrens of Burlington County.

1965
Dec. 26

It its five-year plan, the FAA urges:
1. acquisition of land for a new jetport,
2. construction of a network of 17 heliports in outlying sections of New York City to feed passengers to the airports,
3. construction of six airports in greater NYC for private aviation, and
4. banning of private aviation from Kennedy, La Guardia, and Newark.

1968
Feb. 14

FAA warns of one to two-hour delays at peak times by early 70s unless new jetport is built. Also urges major expansion at existing airports, lower fares for off-hour flying, and lower fares for flying into underutilized airports.

Apr. 1

FAA proposes High-Density Terminal Plan. Under this plan,

the FAA would establish large circular zones around the three major airports. The goal: eliminate the mixing in such zones of air traffic operating under guidance from the ground and aircraft flying VFR (visual flight rules).

Aug. 15   FAA threatens to impose limitations on air traffic to ease congestion. Additionally, Agency hopes airlines themselves will voluntarily reduce schedules at the three major airports during peak traffic time.

Sep. 5   FAA acts to reduce congestion, limits flights at each major airport, and bans general aviation traffic during peak hours. Also, it reemphasizes the need for a fourth jetport and for additional facilities for private aircraft.

Sep. 25   Reps. Addabbo and Rosenthal blast FAA. Urge federal legislation enabling the federal government to select a site, construct, and operate a fourth jetport in the metropolitan area. A new federal agency would be created for this purpose.

1969

Mar. 19   FAA testifies before New Jersey Legislature that Solberg is the best site since it is situated in the northwest quadrant of the Metroplex. The Agency rejects a major airport in central New Jersey due to airspace limitations. States that perhaps a smaller airport—for New Jersey's needs only—could be developed.

Goals
1. Promotion and encouragement of aviation.
2. Air safety—especially air traffic control.
3. Site in the northwest quadrant—Solberg.
4. Remain friendly with various interest groups in aviation—that is, airlines and general aviation.

Deficiencies
1. "Bureaucratic" organization—must often by prodded to action.
2. Incredibly poor forecasting and national planning.
3. Subject to strong political pressures.
4. Continually failed to present a strong image and total needs at budget hearings.

Summary
While the FAA could potentially be a leader in solidifying agreement on the fourth jetport site, the Agency has consistently held back—often until conditions reached the point where decisions could no longer be postponed—in pressing its ideas for solving the air traffic congestion problem of the three metropolitan airports. I think this primarily reflects the bureaucratic and political underpinnings of the FAA.

General Aviation Position

Background

General aviation is defined as any non-scheduled operation. It would include air taxi, corporate, and private aircraft. The AOPA (Aircraft Owners and Pilots Association) is the voice of general aviation. With over 200,000 members and a rapidly growing number of small-plane pilots, AOPA is a potent political force already represented in and recognized by both the FAA and Congress.

Critics have charged that general aviation is a major cause of tie-ups, a largely uncontrolled element in the air traffic system, and a hazardous factor in the presently inadequate air safety system. In 1968, 37 percent of the aircraft operations at La Guardia Airport, 25 percent at Newark, and 15 percent at Kennedy International involved general aviation planes.

History

1958   Section 104—Federal Aviation Act of 1958—"Any citizen of the United States has a public *right* of freedom of transit through the navigable airspace of the United States." This section has become the backbone of the general aviation arguments for the past decade.

1967

Jan. 16   AOPA strongly resists proposed banning of general aviation planes from major metropolitan airports. Association points out:

1. Airports were built with public money—and are for public use.

2. General aviation provides a valuable service by serving 100 percent of the country's 2,400 airports.

1968

Jan.   Max Karant, Senior Vice President of AOPA, contends that the current air traffic congestion problem is "a matter of convenience and delay—not safety. On a scale proportionate to our overall operations at the major New York Airports, general aviation is suffering from this inconvenience and delay, just as are the airlines."

Feb.   The AOPA claims "the taxpayer's dollar does the best work for the national interest by having one well-equipped airport to serve all flying activities of communities." Roughly translated, this means: don't exclude our planes from any airport.

Mar. 17   AOPA fights Pan American take-over bid for Teterboro and

Republic Airports. AOPA states Pan Am wants to phase out light craft in favor of business jets.

Oct. 4   General aviation opposes the FAA proposal to limit peak-hour movements at major New York Airports.

Goals

1. Protection and advancement of general aviation.
2. Creation of sufficient airport capacity to meet the future needs of general aviation.
3. Protection of the principal that general aviation craft are equal partners in the aviation industry and can fly anywhere they want to.

Summary

General aviation (and the AOPA) is a very vocal and politically strong interest group. While it has always vigorously opposed any move by anyone that would restrict the the general aviation industry, it hasn't taken a side in the site selection controversy surrounding the proposed fourth jetport. The final solution to the jetport problem, however, will have to take account of the general aviation industry and provide attractive (both from an equipment and convenience standpoint) facilities for it.

Airlines Position

Background

The major airlines are joined together by a loose association called the Aviation Development Council. Mr. George E. Kech, President of United Airlines, presently serves as spokesman for the group. The airlines have seen tremendous growth in the number of passenger trips taken—from 7,000,000 in 1950 to 30,000,000 in 1965 to a projected figure of 67,000,000 in 1975. The industry is on the verge of introducing a new generation of planes (B 747, SST) to meet present and future passenger requirements.

History
1965

Nov. 1   Airline Council offers a program to meet metropolitan needs for the next 15 years without a fourth jetport. Airlines urge expansion of existing jetports and suggest general aviation craft use peripheral airports. Airlines are also worried about the cost of staffing and equipping a fourth jetport.

1966

Dec. 26   Airline Association reverses itself and calls for prompt agreement on a fourth jetport. Airlines urge:
1. early selection of site for fourth jetport,

2. the phase-out of general aviation from the three major airports,

3. improved ground transportation to and from airports.

1967

Sep. 20   Airlines move to induce private and corporate planes to use peripheral airports. Plan hopes to make peripheral airports attractive enough to draw private and corporate plans voluntarily.

1968

Mar. 17   Pan American Airlines files intentions to take over Teterboro and Republic general aviation fields.

May 17   CAB rules in favor of Teterboro for Pan American but rejects Republic bid. CAB states Teterboro takeover is consistent with public interest because Pan Am will improve the facility.

Aug. 1   Airlines agree voluntarily to cut back flights at peak hours but oppose the adoption of a fixed number of allowable operations per hour in major airports.

Aug 15   Airline Association restates the need for a fourth metropolitan jetport. The airlines also urge expansion of the three existing airports.

Oct. 4   Airlines favor FAA proposed ban on general aviation at the three major airports during peak hours.

1969

Mar. 19   The airline industry testifying before the New Jersey Legislature recommends Solberg as the best site for the fourth jetport because of:

1. the expanding needs for transportation in that area,
2. the airspace situation,
3. adequacy of land area.

Goals

1. Profit—dependent upon:
   a. population--passenger requirements,
   b. feeder systems to airport—highway, rail, and air taxi,
   c. cargo volume,
   d. international operation.
2. Air safety—air space.
3. Recommend Solberg site.
4. Urge expansion of major existing airports.
5. Favor banning of general aviation planes from major airports.

Deficiencies

1. Airline Association is loose and subject to internal disagreement.
2. Airlines worried about financing of a fourth jetport—especially user's fees.
3. Airlines faced large bills for transition to new generation of jet aircraft.

Summary

The airline industry is convinced of the need for a fourth jetport. Its primary concern in the site selected for the jetport is that the site allow profitable operation for the airlines—more generally, that the site be located to serve the maximum number of passengers and freight in the metropolitan area. Toward this end, the industry supports Solberg as the site for the fourth jetport.

Airline Pilots' Association Position

This is a union—nothing more, nothing less. It is vocal, well financed, and extremely conscious of how well heeled it is. Its members have little cohesiveness except that necessary to maintain high standards of pay. Overall air safety is left to the plane manufacturer, the FAA, and the airports, although the ALPA makes its contribution by forcing crew changes to minimize fatigue due to a pilot's flying when his biological clock says "sleep." The contradiction lies in the fact that, at least in this area, some influential pilots live in areas where they object to the presence of a jetport. Moreover, some pilots have publicly denounced the FAA for being so rigid in its insistence that some proposed sites are unacceptable due to their interference with present patterns. Patterns are often changed in this area, so that procedure is normal to most airline pilots. Some anti-FAA feeling persists from the Quesada days, when the "casual era" in the cockpit came to a screeching halt.

Pilots are much more critical of the lack of adequate radar, since it contributes to the unnecessary continuation of "flight by sight" in ever filling skies. Although as a unit they object to spending time holding patterns and competing with nearly invisible small craft for landing space, they are in favor of an additional facility only as it pertains to those items.

Goals

1. Maximum pay and benefits..
2. Optimum flight time.
3. Improved safety in the air (includes better hardware).

Outcomes

1. Participate in hearings.
2. Form loose coalition against FAA.

Preference
1. Minimum holding pattern time.
2. Maximum plane spacing.

Conservationists' Position

Background
   Conservationists are involved only where irreplaceable land assets can create an imbalance in the state of nature vis-à-vis the animal kingdom or natural resources. In and of themselves, they constitute a vocal but diverse group. Their record as coalitionists, however, is enviable. Relative to a jetport decision, their best showing to date on the East Coast is the Morris County campaign. In the midst of the sociopolitical debate, the entire Great Swamp was declared a national sanctuary by Department of Interior Secretary Udall. Since no other government body had the power to intervene or overthrow the decision, and since no one had the presence of mind to point out that Jamaica Bay is also a bird sanctuary, the effect of the decision was to close the doors of the Great Swamp in PONYA's face. There were enough factors prior to the conservationists' efforts to eventually close that door, but it is interesting to note how final they made it seem.
   Equally diligent efforts are probably not forthcoming with respect to the preservation of the northern New Jersey forest, central New Jersey Pine Barrens, or Lower New York Bay, but conservationists could be aroused over eastern Long Island, Long Island Sound, or the Jersey meadows.

Goals
1. Maintenance of the "balance of nature" as perceived by the conservationists.
2. Protection of defenseless living things from the encroachment of man.

Outcomes
1. Prevention from occurrence of (1) or (2) above.
2. Coalitions with whatever group presently aligned with efforts to achieve (1) or (2).
3. Independent action to achieve the goals legislatively.

Preference Function
1. Build where disturbance to the natural balance is minimized.

Professional Air Traffic Controllers' Position

Background
   In terms of its basic involvement with the problem of air traffic congestion, the PATC occupies a pivotal position. Relatively speaking, all

other parties are observers and the controllers are the observed. There is little need to expound on the job pressures that have resulted in the New York area paying the highest wage and extracting the greatest toll in controller mental fatigue. In fact, the controllers are not pushing as hard for a new jetport as they must for public and FAA recognition of the potential hazard to life brought by outmoded hardware and methods. Since the entire area is under central control, it is not axiomatic that another facility would alleviate the problems vis-à-vis the controllers. A new facility would provide relief only if it resulted in significant traffic diversion away from the present area.

This group, since it resides in an atmosphere created by the problem, is the link most likely to break first. Considering the increasing difficulty in obtaining qualified controllers, air traffic supply will be limited by the group simply by adhering to established government procedures. It seems reasonable to assume that, left to their own devices and without the relief they seek, the immediate consequences of the jetport non-decision will be generated by the PATC, with unwitting assistance from the FAA.

Goals
1. Reduce the ratio of operations/man/time period to tolerable levels.
2. Press for improved hardware to reduce the job fatigue and mental strain on member personnel.

Outcomes
1. Participate in hearings.
2. Form loose coalition against FAA.

Preference
1. Minimum operations in control area.

Local Communities' Position

Background
From a technological standpoint, the location of any technically oriented facility is subject to criteria and restrictions commensurate with its functional operation. Communities generally comply with the decisions of their zoning boards with respect to the locations of transportation facilities (e.g., trucking terminals, commuter parking) and commercial properties so long as the expected economic benefits in the form of ratables and employment exceed the costs.

Generally, such costs are reasonably clear, categorized as loss of unreplaced recreational land, cost of improvements (e.g., new access roads, traffic control, etc.), or displacement of citizens.

Since the exchange is accomplished between factions who have a need to co-opt to achieve their ends, the items or payments made mutually and to third parties are generally real in the sense that they exist as recognizable entities. One could state that the local community has an ideal preference function whose statement is couched in terms of maintaining a balance between general satisfaction of the citizenry and economic solvency. Exceptions certainly exist, and the demise of communities that allow an extreme unbalance to persist is evident. For example, a religious sect or community of retirees is interested in the general welfare at the expense of economic solvency, but these cases are anomalies. Examples of communities that suffer from the unbalanced state are numerous. Consider beach towns, company towns, and towns that allow industrialization at the expense of both recreational and residential requirements. Northern New Jersey's refinery area is a glaring example. Long Island's southern Nassau County, immediately surrounding JFK airport, is becoming another. In the latter case, the effect lags the cause by the number of years it takes for the indigenous to be gradually replaced by members of a lower echelon economic class, one which is perhaps more tolerant or less able to institute change.

In comparison to other land-consuming commercial facilities, the airport is unique, for reasons of its long-range effects not only on the economic structure but on people. Shopping centers, industries, and highways consume land, true enough. However, they do not render the fabric of local life unrepairable over the long run. Neighborhoods split by superhighways have connecting roads; shopping centers attract traffic, but those problems can be either tolerated or solved; industries provide jobs. All are active for known periods and can be counted upon for periods of "silence." Airports consume their immediate premises and render large adjacent areas of land unlivable—all day, every day. For example, in the Morristown plan, professional estimates placed airport land at 16 square miles, but total uninhabitable land at 23 square miles and semi-inhabitable land at 25 square miles. Even those estimates excluded the imponderable effect of noise on those who remained, human or animal. Aside from actual displacement from the premises, airports create an exodus from its fringes of those best able to leave. Economically, it is axiomatic that whether real or imagined, the market value of property drops. Perhaps no proof of this exists, but no proof is necessary—the evidence is as empirical as it is in integrated neighborhoods. It is equally axiomatic that their replacements are of a lower economic class. Those who do not tend to use their homes as places of concentration are more tolerant of transient noise.

No law says that all the citizens must be pleased. Often enough, the "greatest displeasure of the least" is an acceptable criterion. Such a criterion was used to locate Dulles International Airport. It was also located in a "technically chosen" area, provided with adequate ground transportation and it had the backing of all the technical bodies that are supposedly responsible for airport location. It is a ghost airport now, and unless passenger traffic is forced to it, it will be a ghost airport forever. Detroit's Willow Run Airport, 45 miles out, was expanded based on technical criteria. It is so unsuccessful that Detroit Municipal, once considered unusable, is Detroit's national terminal. It appears that, with the possible exception of L.A. International, the technical criteria are insufficient and perhaps partially irrelevant.

Goals

1. Maintenance of balance between economic benefits and loss of irreplaceable assets (taxpayers, ratables, land).
2. Minimum disruption of the existing social fabric.
3. Minimum change in the prevailing power structure (e.g., no outsiders or changes in relative power).

Outcomes

1. Acceptance, if goal (1) is satisfied.
2. Rejection, if failure on goal (2) or (3) is perceived as being the result of acceptance.
3. Coalition, however loose or distasteful, to achieve rejection if its own power is insufficient.

Preference Function

1. Don't build it here (Morris, Hunterdon).
2. Build it here, we need it (Burlington, Ocean).

It must be built where it is not an anomaly to the local population.

Miscellaneous

A large number of peripheral groups have submitted their respective inputs at stages of the jetport non-decision. In rough chronological order, they are:

1957

| Jan. | Burlington County Planning Board | Feasibility study of international airport in southern Jersey. Request for concurrence from CAA (now CAB, FAA) not answered. Preferred placement in Burlington County. |

1965

| Oct. then **1966** Sept. | Metropolitan Airline | R. Dixon Speas report recommended general aviation expansion and increases in existing facilities. Preferred this action coupled with search to result in a new facility by 1980. |

1967

| Mar. | Metropolitan Commuter Trans. Authority | Report recommended fourth (N.J.) and fifth (N.Y., L.I.) facility. |

Dec. and 1968 July	New Hanover Township McGuire Jetport Corp.	Apply to USAF for joint use of AFB by scheduled carriers. Turned down by DOD in 1/68; FAA refused to intervene. Re-requests ATA, DOT, and USAF for joint use of McGuire.
July	Governor's Economic Comm. for an Int'l Jetport in N.J.	Albert E. Blonquist & Assoc. issues report concluding that south central Jersey is best location; Lakehurst or McGuire.
Sept.	Long Island Assoc.	Proposes L.I. Sound location with appropriate bridge and tunnels. Lockwood, Kessler, and Bartlett are consultants.
1969		
Mar.	Dun & Bradstreet Munic. Service Div.	Economic consideration relative to airport financing, subsidizing, and development.
	Aerospace Safety Research & Data Inst. Cornell University	Relative strength of aircraft pollutants in total pollutant problem. Study recommended central Jersey site, Middlesex, Monmouth County. Details not yet available.
	Flight Safety Found.	Goals and preference similar to those of PATC and ALPA.
	National Audubon Society	Conservationist, hence covered in other section.

APPENDIX II—AIRPORT SITE: LOCATIONS AND EVALUATIONS

The airport sites under consideration are shown on the Location Map, Fig. 3. II-1. Seventeen sites were evaulated in the Port Authority 1961 "Report on Airport Requirements and Sites in the Metropolitan New Jersey/New York Region"; six additional sites were subsequently studied. All site evaluations were periodically updated. We do not reproduce these detailed site evaluations here.

A basic requirement was that any potential site for another airport should complement the operations at the existing airports. Accessibility of the site to air passengers and airspace criteria were the main considerations in this site evaluation work.

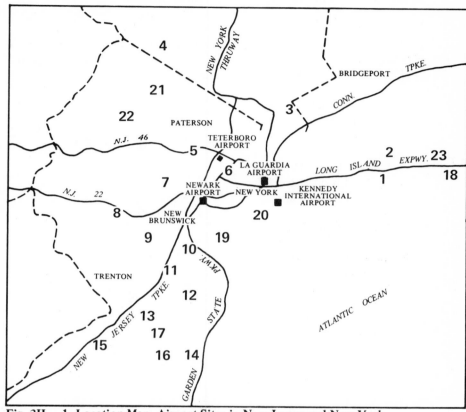

Fig. 3II − 1. Location Map. Airport Sites in New Jersey and New York

Site	1	MacArthur Airport	Site	13	Mount Holly-Burlington A
Site	2	St. James	Site	14	Toms River
Site	3	Westchester County	Site	15	Mount Holly-Burlington B
Site	4	Pine Island	Site	16	Lebanon Forest
Site	5	Caldwell	Site	17	McGuire Air Force Base
Site	6	Jersey Meadows	Site	18	Suffolk County Air Force Base
Site	7	Morris County	Site	19	Lower Bay
Site	8	Solberg-Hunterdon	Site	20	Floyd Bennett NAS
Site	9	New Brunswick	Site	21	Bearfort
Site	10	Matawan	Site	22	Bowling Green
Site	11	Hightstown-Jamesburg	Site	23	Colverton
Site	12	Lakewood			

APPENDIX III—REANALYSIS OF PARTICIPANTS' POSITION

Appendix III-A—Sites and Previous Air Traffic Proposals

1. *Agreement on a New Site*

Of the 23 sites proposed in 1961 and allegedly reevaluated in 1966 by PONYA, there are a number of sites that, by any one of the several criteria, need not be covered again, under the categories below.

   a. *Shortage of available land*
      1. Caldwell
      2. New Brunswick
      3. Matawan
      4. Hightstown-Cranbury
      5. Floyd Bennett Field
      6. Monmouth County
      7. Westchester
      8. MacArthur Field

   b. *Politically Unavailable*
      1. Solberg
      2. Great Swamp
      3. Calverton
      4. Long Island Sound
      5. Republic Aviation Field

   c. *High Construction Costs*
      1. Toms River
      2. Bearfort
      3. Bowling Green
      4. Long Island Sound

   d. *Remote from Projected Growth in Population (N.J.)*
      1. Bearfort
      2. Bowling Green
      3. Pine Island
      4. Stewart A.F.B.

This list is neither exhaustive nor exclusive in that the elimination of sites (b-1) through (b-5) casts a different light on those sites in (c) and (d) as well as the following other possible sites:

McGuire-Lakehurst
Pine Barrens (Burlington, Ocean County)

Allentown
Lower New York Harbor

Prior to entering into an evaluation process, one must dwell on the fruits borne of the specific delay regarding the New York jetport.

In 1969, extensive hearings were held by the House Committee on Interstate and Foreign Commerce regarding Bills HR 12374, HR 12780, and other related bills, providing for the expansion and improvement of the nation's airport and airway system. In large part, these hearings exemplified the New York monologues on a national scale. Groups that had provided input to the local process also presented their cases to the Congressmen. Some local groups, like PONYA, were not seen, but their presence was felt through statements made by regional Congressmen (Messrs. Addabbo, Ottinger, and Hastings of New York, to name a select few).

With regard to the local problem, testimony is minimal. With regard to the national problem (many facets of which are common to the local problem), the testimony is quite illuminating. By covering the following items, 2 through 4, first, considerable clarity can be gained, so that full coverage of the question of agreement on a new site will be delayed until item 5, "Resolution".

2. *Further Expansion of Existing Physical Plant*

It is patently evident that expansions of Newark, La Guardia, and J.F.K. are stop-gap measures. The real limitations of these facilities are built into their environments.

a. *Noise abatement procedures.*

In the case of J.F.K., two major runways are limited to "half capacity" (i.e., no landing on one, no take-offs on the other).

b. *Surrounding real estate.*

Except for J.F.K., which could probably expand into Jamaica Bay, land for expansion does not exist.

c. *Terminal facilities, especially parking.*

One study established that about two-thirds of the terminal population at these major hub airports (O'Hare, Love Field, J.F.K.) is non-air passengers, consisting of sightseers (42%), employees (16%), and suppliers (7%). The same study also established that, to service the expected passenger car arrivals at J.F.K. in 1972, a 12-lane highway from the L.I.E. to the J.F.K. causeway would be needed. This acute problem of access has prompted the manager of L.A. International Airport to claim that his facility will never face saturation—the access roads cannot supply enough passengers.

d. *Financing.*

Under the existing (1958) FAAP, appropriations for airport assistance have lagged behind requests. For instance, in 1969 the difference was $455.2 million (requests) minus $30 million (FAAP appropriations) or $425.2 million. Even under new legislation, with new taxes, the expected federal deficit is $460.4 million in 1970, and $5,692.8 million for the period 1970-1979. In terms of the local problem, the burden falls on PONYA, and its willingness to invest in these facilities is limited. As an interesting aside, it is perhaps ironic that, in the testimony of several federal and state officials, a multi-state authority was recommended as a means of making the airport location decision less provincial and more regional. Terms such as "self-sufficient," "port district," and "nonpartisan" were mentioned frequently. One would suppose that, despite the frequent view that PONYA wears blinders, the absence of any such legislative creature is worse.

e. *FAA traffic limitation.*

Perhaps the most significant and irrefutable limitation concerns the peak air carrier movements imposed by the FAA. These are variable, depending on time of day, and are specifically 40 for Newark (each hour), 48 for La Guardia (each hour), and 80 (5 to 8 p.m.) and 70 (remaining hours) for J.F.K. Given the inability of the FAA to either assign more controllers or install better hardware, these limitations will not change.

All of these categories are, of course, predicated on the absence of any major change in the "way things are done" now. Items a and b and e are self-evident. Item c is the least inflexible, but involves concepts and restructuring not presently being considered. Some of these deserve mention:

1) Aircraft
   a) Reduce vehicle flow (e.g., large aircraft, higher load factor, discrimination).
   b) Improve vehicle throughput on the ground through group service and maintenance techniques.

2) Automobile
   a) Segregation by purpose of trip to airport.
   b) Premiums on unnecessary parking (e.g., penalty for private auto use if adequate public transportation is available).
   c) Underground parking.
   d) Improved access roads.

3) People
   a) Stagger shifts for airport employees and peripherally located industries.
   b) Discriminate against sightseers and visitors in congested passenger areas.

4) Baggage
   a) Greater automation.
   b) Limitation of size and number of pieces.

5) Ticketing and Movement to the Aircraft
   a) Remote terminals in potential passenger origination points (downtown offices, airline terminals such as W.S.A.T.).
   b) Moving sidewalks.
   c) Jitney buses.

6) Others
   a) The all-cargo airport, using standard containerization.
   b) Reliever airports, using V/STOL.
   c) Satellite collection and distribution of passengers, using V/STOL, HSGT, or public transportation.

3. *Reschedule and Reroute*

In 1968, all airlines held a continuous one-month session during which every operation at the five major hub airports was evaluated under the FAA operation limitation criteria.

The resulting operation schedule appears to be final. If one considers the factors of (a) time zone differentials, (b) aircraft utilization, (c) aircraft maintenance, and (d) economic justification (MC=MR, load factor, passenger demand), it becomes clear that the benefits to traffic flow, if any, are severely limited.

International carriers have expressed desire to overfly J.F.K. for other parts, but not at the expense of reducing the J.F.K. operations. Our international agreements limit the alternatives in this area. Evidently, the reduced growth rate at J.F.K. (10% vs. 13% national average) reflects some voluntary rescheduling now by domestic carriers.

Rate reductions have allegedly proven that the demand for passenger service is inelastic. Reductions of up to 30 percent have been offered to entice passengers to travel during the "off-peak" hours. Supposedly, the inconvenience of arrival at an "odd hour" exceeds the utility of the cost saving. It is interesting to note that the trials were made (1) on the N.Y. to Washington shuttle, where (a) passengers are reimbursed for their fares and (b) the exclusive purpose of the trip is to maximize usable working hours at the destination; and (2) on the Miami runs, where the traffic is generally pleasure-bound and the passenger is very likely a member of the upper middle class. In neither case is the traveler especially price sensitive, and it is true that the latter case presents special problems, since there is generally no time-zone change.

4. Accept Growth Limitation

Conservative estimates are that a dollar spent on airports is respent about 20 times in the affected area. In addition, the industrial attractiveness of an area with adequate air passenger and cargo facilities is attested to by the growth of New York City as a port. An equally valid statement can be made for the migration of industry out of an area experiencing or facing stultifying congestion.

Several institutions have made estimates of the business costs of air traffic delays, and one can pick one's own number.[3] There is no question that the traffic will go elsewhere if congestion on the air or ground continues. Air cargo users have already begun to desert J.F.K. because of excessive delays in warehouse throughput. On the other hand, one could speculate that the decline of New York as a viable port is inevitable, and that the resulting diversion can be healthy on a national scale, especially if it forces the governing bodies to abandon the provincialism that is choking New York.

5. Resolution

Several characteristics of the conflicting participants are evident, but one is common and that one is "frozen positions." The FAA is frozen in its position regarding flight patterns. PONYA is frozen in its position regarding financing. New Jersey is frozen in its position regarding the northwest quadrant. The local communities are frozen in their aggregate positions regarding the adverse effects of the jetport on them. Evidently, the choice of a site cannot occur within the constraints of these fixed positions. One then can suggest the need for a superordinate goal or the need for reevaluation under the aegis of a national airport plan. In any case, the sites most likely to be reevaluated are listed below:

a. *Bearfort.*
   In 1964, PONYA estimated costs at $870 million. By now these costs could be $1,320 million, using an inflater of 10 percent per annum. J.F.K. cost $420 million when new. In addition, PONYA figured that it would require 598,000 operations per year, based on the 1964 structure. With the assistance of HR 12374, the number of operations would not drop to the PONYA-recommended level of 350,000 per year.
   Traffic flow to the area is not aided by the existing road network or proposed rail links. Moreover, residents of counties south of Morris

would be attracted to it only by alternate facilities being relatively unavailable.

b. *Bowling Green.*

Since 1964, costs would have escalated from $764 million to $1,118 million. Traffic flow and passenger appeal are similar to Bearfort, although Bowling Green, being south of Bearfort, is relatively more readily serviced by existing rail (E-L, D-L&W) and road (I-80, I-287). Both locations suffer from the faults generally associated with airports on mountains. This is, slope of the runway relative to the surrounding land, or vice versa, are considered to be hazards, due in large part to the apparent distortion of the $3°$ glide path to the pilot flying with IFR. Both locations also suffer from the disenchantment of the local communities with the airport as a potential neighbor.

c. *Lakehurst-McGuire.*

Cost estimates made in 1967 put this site at $663 million, or about $799 million now. Ground traffic is not adequate now, and it is estimated that it would appeal to only 17 percent of the metropolitan flying population whereas Solberg would have appealed to 56 percent (Speas' figures).

Two objections raised to this site are (1) interference with existing air patterns and (2) reluctance of DOD to allow joint use. Item (1), of course, requires a thaw by the FAA. Item (2) is effectively minimized by section 12(e) of the Senate Bill HR 14465, the companion of the House's Hr 12374 and 12780. Proponents of this site point to (1) community willingness to tolerate the jetport due to its inherent economic benefits, and (2) the projected growth of New Jersey population and industry into the belt along U.S. 1 (I-95) between Elizabeth and Camden. In a system where a jetport becomes a point of aircraft movement and satellite airports account for passenger collection and distribution, a remote site offers the distinct advantage of ease of expansion and freedom to innovate in terminal design.

d. *Allentown.*

Costs for this site are currently estimated at $882 million. It is northeast of McGuire-Lakehurst, and poses more problems relative to (1) displacement, (2) noise abatement, and (3) interference with existing patterns, especially the Colt's Neck holding area for J.F.K. In terms of passenger appeal, it would probably exceed the 17 percent figure given for McGuire-Lakehurst, since it is located nearer to the fast growing Middlesex and Monmouth County areas. Access by road is by I-95 (5 miles) and rail CNJ (5 miles) or PC (12 miles). Local cooperation has not been active, either pro or con.

e. *Lower New York Bay.*

By and large, this proposal is opposed by the airlines, FAA, and ALPA as being too dangerous a site. Objections pointed to are (1) V. Bridge towers, (2) Staten Island Hills, (3) J.F.K. approaches. It is feasible from the engineering standpoint, since the proposed site is relatively shallow. About 20 square miles of fill are required, at a current estimated cost of $300 million (no land acquisition costs). It would automatically reduce the capacity of J.F.K., viewed in its present role of the major overseas embarkation point. Major realignment of the area's navigation facilities is required, and this cost is not available. As in the case of the McGuire-Lakehurst, the final FAA report did not reflect even a rough estimate of relocation costs. However, also as in the case of McGuire-Lakehurst, the attractiveness of this site is high, in the light of SST sonic boom problem.

Agreement is predicated on the unfreezing of positions and the role of the federal government viz. HR 14465.

With respect to local communities, the preponderance of the anti-jetport sentiment voiced by Rep. Morris and the Hunterdon County groups centered about the noise factor. In any of their present configurations, and by any reasonable noise standard, airports are bad neighbors. Whether perceived or real, the devaluation of property values offsets the economic advantage of the facility.

Techniques used by local communities to limit airport growth or presence fall into the general category of zoning restrictions. In essence, these restrictions are the real limitations to expansion of all the existing major hub airports. Nearly half the 30 metropolitan airports are 100 percent impacted. Communities have failed to either (1) provide expansion land in the original plan, or (2) prevent subdivision encroachment on the airport.

Typically, the sponsoring body, FAA, state agency, or local enthusiasts have left the development of terminal facilities to "the others." The FAAP provided no funds for terminals; local governments provided no bonds to construct access roads and vehicle accommodations. Even in the exceptional case of PONYA, access to facilities like Newark or J.F.K. is on the horizon due to the highway planners, not the local body.

In general, successful long-term obligations undertaken by municipalities for airport facilities are rare. Detroit, Chicago, Atlanta, and San Francisco are large enough to afford the issuance of bonds, since they can impose specific taxes (e.g., head tax) and build in sufficient concessions to aid in amortization. Most localities are legally shackled by debt ceilings related to local revenue, and most simply do not see airport construction as a high priority item. There is, on the aggregate, little economic motivation to view any airport construction as a viable alternative to subdivisions or industrial parks, both of which generate as many new problems as revenue.

The unfreezing process must take several forms.

a. *Noise*

There is a sound argument for planning a jetport such that the feeder facilities (such as access roads, utilities, and rail links) are located along the route of highest PNDB (perceived noise decibels). Correct local zoning can contribute to further isolation of the general dwelling area by locating peripheral industries and service facilities along the edges of the maximum noise area. As in any site, the community would be required to accept the noise as a cost, and the economic influx as a benefit offsetting this cost. To the best of our knowledge, the proponents of Great Swamp and Solberg never made an effort to bring the affected communities into the dialogue by exposing a representative group to the anticipated noise levels.

b. *Access*

HR 14465 has included in it some broad statements regarding the placement of airports in local communities, with their approval obtained only after hearings. Also contained in the Bill are provisions for full coordination of the various federal and state agencies involved, especially the administrators of the highway funds. Since the funding structure of the Bill allows latitude in appropriations to terminal facilities, it appears that part of the financing burden has been lifted from local shoulders. Highways and rail links pertinent to the airport in a metropolitan transportation system are eligible for aid.

c. *General Financing*

State aeronautic authorities are empowered to disburse federal funds, but local authorities must submit proposals to the state agency, not directly to the federal level, as in the case of OEO. Limitations on the federal amount of financing (50% max.,) require that localities be prepared to issue general obligation bonds to support the facility. Some amortization can come from head taxes and user's fees, but new methods of revenue generation (such as a "proximity tax" for peripheral firms that demand to be located nearest the airport for ease of access) can be created.

d. *Economic Benefits*

The spectrum of choice with regard to local airports ranges from the "one town—one airport" to the "system first—locality last" philosophies. Each is valid in its own right, from the standpoint of local revenue generation in case 1 to avoiding overlapping facilities in case 2. There is no question that the communities must rethink their economic positions. The ongoing growth of the airport area, not the immediate construction payroll, is the prime consideration. Most locales have not been sold on the airport as a revenue generator, but on its disruptive effect. The advent of a national airport plan will, of course, force the

New Jersey communities to rethink their objections through to logical rather than emotional conclusions.

The forces that bind a community together are based on the power of each group to maintain its bargaining position in the structure. The influx of new potential members of that structure constitutes a disruptive force of unknown proportions. Since the airport brings an unknown into the picture, it is bound to disrupt existing coalitions. Many communities in the Morris County dispute felt that this problem area was the most dangerous, because coalitions were old and stable. Younger, less populous communities can withstand additional coalition members without breaking, although they also harbor fears of disruption. On this behavior premise, one can predict that the location of the jetport in less inflexible communities is the only viable solution, because these will be more willing to approach the problems with true negotiation in mind.

Appendix III-B—Port Authority Financial Criteria

The Port Authority was originally established in 1921 as a self-supporting agency to plan and develop terminal and transportation facilities in the port area. Over the years, this requirement for self-sufficiency has become the foundation of all its activities. The Port Authority has steadfastly refused to engage in operations which could not support themselves—an enviable position in the eyes of the business community, an increasingly unpopular position in the eyes of the general public.

This position has had a direct bearing on choosing suitable locations for the proposed new jetport. The Port Authority has maintained that any new facility must lie adjacent to the region's traffic-generating centers so as to realize its full potential. This thesis has received overwhelming opposition— the region's traffic-generating centers don't want a major jetport for a neighbor. So far the Port Authority has refused to bend; so far there has not been agreement on the location of a fourth jetport. If this position is maintained, there may never be a fourth jetport.

A number of sites have been proposed which lie outside of the immediate metropolitan area. These areas are sparsely populated and have generally received favorable local response. Most of these sites are in potential population growth areas, although they would not be convenient to a major segment of the population at this time.

The Port Authority has maintained that a new jetport in these areas would not attract sufficient travelers to financially support the facilities. They could not exist without a subsidy. This evaluation merits further consideration. If air traffic congestion at the three existing jetports gets as bad as the P.A. predicts it will, the prudent air traveler might be willing to trade 20 minutes longer on the road for a two-hour delay at the terminal.

Furthermore, the Port Authority's mandate requires it to be self-supporting. It does not necessarily hold that each specific operation must be self-supporting in order for the aggregate to be so. The air terminal complex of the Port Authority could conceivably be financially sound even if one of the four component facilities did require a modest subsidy from the operations of the other three. If inaction will create the "economic catastrophe" the Port Authority predicts it will, a fourth jetport in one of these locations might enhance overall operations sufficiently to compensate for its subsidy.

Appendix III-C—FAA Flight Patterns

The primary directive of the FAA is to "develop plans for and formulate policy with respect to the use of the navigable airspace under such terms, conditions, and limitations as may be deemed necessary in order to ensure the safety and the efficient utilization of such airspace."

The FAA has stated from the outset that a fourth *metropolitan* jetport must be located in an area that will not hinder the airport's operations by airspace conflicts (either departure or arrival flights or holding patterns) with the three major existing jetports. The FAA develops its airspace requirements at a large airspace simulator complex in southern New Jersey.

It has outlined the airspace considerations to be as follows:

1. Runway alignment—a northeast-southwest alignment for the primary instrument runway is required to ensure that instrument approaches into the regional complex of airports do not conflict.
2. Major traffic directions—departure and arrival routes must be provided in all directions in order to accommodate domestic requirements.
3. Holding airspace—holding areas must be 16 statute miles long and eight miles wide. These areas must also be clear of air routes which would be in use at the same time that the holding stack is in use.

The most recent position statement of the FAA was delivered to the New Jersey Legislature on March 18, 1969. The key recommendations were the following:

1. If a major airport is to best serve the needs of northern New Jersey and Metropolitan New York areas, it should be situated in the northwest quadrant of the Metroplex.
2. Recent FAA air traffic analyses have indicated that a major airport should preferably not be located in central New Jersey, due to air space limitations. If, however, an airport were contemplated in this area to serve a *smaller volume of traffic for the needs of New Jersey* alone, the FAA could probably develop traffic patterns to accommodate such an installation.

All of the above analysis is based on current technology for airspace control. The FAA doesn't see any major technological breakthroughs on the horizon. Additionally, the FAA allocates a very small portion of its budget to research activities on this problem.

Appendix III-D—Federal Intervention

The presence of the federal government in the jetport problem environment has been confined to the activities of the FAA. This body is, as previously noted, dedicated to the growth of aviation and concentrates on the maintenance of the airways. Broadly interpreted, the Federal Airport Act of 1958 charged the FAA with incorporating sufficient funds into its annual appropriations request to allow for airport expansion commensurate with public safety.

To prove how well the FAA has responded to its responsibilities, consider a typical year, 1968. FAA budget figures were:

General Operations	$ 617.4 M
Facilities and Equipment	54.0
Aid to Airports (excl. terminals)	70.0*
R & D	27.0
SST	142.4
Residual (incl. construction)	8.9
TOTAL	$ 919.7 M

*Requested 66.

Note that only 5.8 percent was allocated to improve airways hardware and staffing (F & E), and only 2.8 percent was allocatd to the potential improvement of technology (R & D). In the following year, the R & D percentage declined. On the other hand, the FAA saw fit to indulge in the SST to the tune of 15.5 percent of its budget.

In the same year, total requests for airport aid were $392.4 million, generating an annual deficit of $322.4 million, just for aiport aid alone.

When testifying before Congress in July of 1969, FAA administrator Shaffer grandiosely projected FAA R & D requirements of $60 million/yr., average, and F & E requirements of $215 million/yr., average over 1970 to 1979. Evidently, under the onus of shouldering the blame for the current airway crisis, the FAA has become sensitive to the obsolescence, and perhaps the danger, of their existing hardware.

Historically, the federal government in general and the FAA in particular, have done little to aid in the financing of hub facilities. By their own estimates, federal funding of the 23 major hubs has averaged 21 percent. Local revenue bonds (70%) and state assistance (9%) have borne the burden of capital expenditures for new and improved facilities. So much 'for historical trends.

Department of Transportation (DOT) Secretary Volpe, during the same hearings, submitted a ten-year projection of revenues from new users taxes and expected expenditures. Over the 1970 to 1979 period, the average expected revenue is $913 million/yr., or over twice the annual appropriation asked for by the FAA (this includes F & E, Aid, Capital Improvements, and construction of about $150 million requested in 1969). Expenditures are expected to average $1,477 million/yr., creating an average deficit of about $569 million/yr., nearly the size of the present FAA budget. In 1967, the only year for which the CAB has figures, the airlines generated only $183 million in revenues (i.e., landing fees, terminal rentals, etc.).

Locally, the figures boil down to a precious few. The final enactment of HR 14465 includes the following provision.

1. Approval of a plan by DOT is based on (a) consistency with the current National Airport Plan, the first DOT version of which is due in January 1971. (b) Availability of the balance of the costs not borne by DOT (i.e., the tax capacity of the sponsor). (c) Ability of the sponsor to:
   1. hold title,
   2. exercise authority (e.g., condemnation to acquire land),
   3. meet general DOT requirements.
   (d)Completion without undue delay.

It becomes the sponsor's responsibility to take action to restrict land usage in and around the site to activities commensurate with FAA flight and landing rules. In addition, there is the sponsor's responsibility to maximize "self-sustenance" by appropriate rental fees, etc., and to insure that adequate public hearings have been held so that the site does not conflict with local urban plans (e.g., HUD Master Plan).

In the case of a non-decision, Secretary of DOT has the power to "exercise such of his authority under (the law) as he may deem appropriate to carry out the provisions of this (law)."

Specific dollar appropriations have been set for the next three years:

	1970	1971	1972
1. CAB certificated airports	$150M	$180M	$240M
2. Non-CAB certified airports	25M	25M	25M
3. States (½ proportional to area, ½ proportional to population)	48.5M	58.2M	77.6M
4. Sponsors (proportional to enplanements in U.S. at similar hubs)	50M	60M	70M
5. Secretary's discretion	50M	60M	80M

In the case where the facility overlaps state lines, the split is according to the percentage of area in each state.

In the case of New Jersey, one of the 27 states with an existing state agency eligible for funds, a case could be made for obtaining jetport funds based on its population and enplanements at Newark and Teterboro, as well as the urgency of obtaining some of the discretionary funds.

Appendix III-E—Economic Costs of Delaying Decision

No economy just stands still. It it doesn't move forward, it declines. Each day the economy of a whole region faces a greater threat of strangulation.

The New Jersey-New York Metropolitan Area owes its economic pre-eminence to a vast and intricate network of communications and transportation services. Its leadership and prosperity will continue to depend on maintaining not only adequate but superior transportation links between the region and distant markets, both domestic and overseas.

During the 20 years since World War II, there has been a 33 percent increase in employment and 31 percent increase in population in the area. The business responsibilities arising from this growth involve extensive commerce with and travel to and from distant divisional headquarters and markets, and they generate tremendous employment and business opportunities which are essential to the economic well-being of the region.

There is much evidence of the close relationship between manufacturing and air service. The New York Metropolitan Region Study findings with respect to the vast industrial complex in this metropolitan area pointed out that their products are swiftly changing and that demand for them is geographically widespread and highly variable. Additionally, air cargo has undergone tremendous growth. As an example, foreign air cargo volumes moving through the region's airports have increased from virtually zero at the end of World War II to 142,469 tons valued at $2.3 billion in 1965. The new jetport itself would have a significant effect upon the economic well-being of the region. Estimates predict 30,000 employees earning $250 million (in 1965 dollars) within the new airport's boundaries. In addition, it is estimated that the airport could generate thousands of additional direct jobs at off-airport offices and other locations.

The old adage that the marketplace must cater to the convenience of the customer still holds true. If the level of air service in this metropolitan area should be stultified and allowed to deteriorate, the short-run and long-run economic growth in the New Jersey-New York Metropolitan Area would be severely handicapped.

Yet with stakes such as these—nothing less than the continued prosperity and economic well-being of the whole metropolitan region—we are faced with demand for air service which the existing airports are hard pressed to meet today and which by 1975 will have peak-hour deficiencies of 62 plane movements. A lack of airport capacity of these magnitudes would result in severe delays and dislocation of travel schedules and would certainly constitute a severe barrier to the free flow of travel which is so important to the health of the region's economy.

Appendix III-F—General Aviation

There is sufficient evidence to disqualify each of the 25 sites as a jetport. Under the existing rules of the game, and without the presence of a superordinate goal, negotiations that could unfreeze the participants' attitudes will not take place. However, using the concept of peripheral or feeder airports, some of these sites could serve the useful purpose of "reliever" airports.

This concept is predicated on the following premises:

1. Removal of general aviation from major air facilities substantially reduces:
   a. peak IFR demand,
   b. auto flow and related parking shortages,
   c. passenger flow and related terminal congestion,
   d. air traffic control workload.

2. Installation of IFR equipment at these reliever airports.

3. Substantial rescheduling of feeder flights and air taxi flights to the reliever airports.

4. Construction of ground transportation networks dedicated to handling the inter-airport passenger traffic.

Using the sites enumerated, and assuming the present jetport stalemate will continue, a listing of potential activities that allows concentration of commercial traffic at Newark, J.F.K., and La Guardia, and diversion of general aviation to reliever sites is as follows:

AIRPORT	REQUIRED IMPROVEMENTS			FUNCTION	
	IFR	HWY	RR	C/D	SR
Caldwell	X	X	/	X	X
Morris	X	X	X	X	X
Solberg	X	X	/	/	X
Linden	X	X	X	X	/
Millstone	X	X	X	X	X

AIRPORT	REQUIRED	IMPROVEMENTS		FUNCTION	
	IFR	HWY	RR	C/D	SR
Red Bank	X	/	X	X	/
Manhattan					
STOL	/	/	/	X	X
Teterboro	/	X	/	X	X

Note: C/D is passenger collection and distribution.
        SR is short range (500 mi) to other metropolitan airports.

According to figures submitted under HR 14465, DOT can provide expansion funds of up to $150 million to CAB airports in 1970 alone. If New York and New Jersey qualified for as little as five percent of that, at least $7.5 million could be made immediately available to provide hardware improvements at existing airfields.

APPENDIX IV—UTILITY ANALYSIS

The jetport would be built to serve the public's interest; hence, the utilities of interest in comparing alternative sites and other outcomes are the utilities of the public, divided into appropriate groups. The utilities of the various organizational participants are of interest in evaluating the likelihood of various outcomes but are not relevant in comparing the relative worth of the outcomes. That is, these organizations exist to serve the public interest so their utilities should reflect the utilities of the public.

The utility of the public is a function of three general factors: (1) the availability of air transportation provided by the jetport; (2) effects on the environment such as noise, pollution, degradation of natural resources, and so forth; and (3) economic effects such as changes in property values and additional spending in local economies during and after jetport construction.

Observation of the reaction of various groups of the public during the jetport "negotiation" during the past ten years provides insights about these factors. First, it is apparent that the major consideration in availability is the travel time from an individual's residence or business to the jetport. The greater the travel time the less the "availability utility."

The environmental effects have two components—effects on the living environment of people residing in the vicinity of the airport and effects on natural resources such as virgin countryside and watersheds. The former effects are very localized, apply only close to the airport, and are very intense. The latter apply to the public at large and have minor importance to most individuals, but the cumulative effect may be significant. Ignoring these general effects, the "environmental utility" of a jetport is strongly negative for people close to the airport and negligible for others. The validity of this is indicated by the observation that it is only local groups in the vicinity of a suggested site that comment or take action relevant to the suggestion, and they are frequently strongly opposed because of (as stated) adverse environmental effects.

Economic effects may be negative to the extent that adverse environmental effects lower property values. This predominates in high population density, built-up areas where property values are already high. However, in low density areas positive economic effects that have nothing to do with environmental changes predominate. These effects are increased property values due to purchase of property for the jetport and for commercial development around the jetport and due to increased spending in the local economy as a result of the development. In low population density areas this factor is most important and leads to active promotion of the area as a jetport site. Southern New Jersey and eastern Long Island are examples of this. Thus, "economic utility," which is independent of environment changes, is inversely related to population density. The reason this factor is so important in low density areas may be that there is more investment required, particularly for surrounding area commercial development, than in high density areas, and this investment is spread among fewer people. Thus, each individual's economic utility is much greater in low density areas.

A mathematical model of an individual citizen's utility function based on these observations might have the form:

$$U = \frac{A_1}{\ell} + X\left(\frac{A_2}{d} - A_3\right),$$

where A_1, A_2, and A_3 = constants,

ℓ = travel time to airport,

d = population density in region of airport,

$X = \begin{cases} 0 \text{ for individual outside airport region} \\ 1 \text{ for individual within airport region} \end{cases}$.

With $A_1 = 200$, the availability utility for an individual is $200/\ell$, where ℓ is the distance from the individual's residence or business to the jetport, expressed in minutes of travel time. In this analysis the counties in the metropolitan New York City and Philadelphia areas are considered as units. The distances in minutes from each county to each of the sites that are considered are given in Table 3-IV-1. The availability utility for each individual in each county is also given, as well as the county's population (in 1968). The total utility in each county for each site is found by multiplying the individual utility by the population (in millions of people). Thus,

$$
\left.
\begin{array}{l}
\text{Total Availability} \\[4pt]
\text{Utility for } i^{th} \\[4pt]
\text{Jetport Site}
\end{array}
\right\}
= \sum_{j=1}^{n} P_j \, \frac{200}{\ell_{ij}} \, ,
$$

where p_j = population of jth county (millions), and

ℓ_{ij} = travel distance in minutes from j^{th} county to i^{th} jetport site.

APPENDIX V–PREFERENCE FUNCTIONS, PARTICIPANT POWER, AND LIKELY OUTCOMES

A condensed list of possible outcomes of the "fourth jetport" controversy is given in Table 3-V-1. In many cases these lump together several different sites, which from the point of view of the overall problem are essentially indistinguishable.

A summary of the expressed preferences of the participants is given in Table 3. V-2. Five categories of preference are used: statements for or against; implied, but not stated, preferences for or against (some judgment is involved in placing outcomes in these categories); and no opinion stated or implied. Of the 176 preferences expressed by the 16 participants for the 11 outcomes, approximately 50 percent were "no opinion," and the rest were approximately equally divided for and against.

The Governors of New Jersey have been for a northern New Jersey site (Meyner in 1961, and Hughes in the late 1960s) and opposed (Hughes in the early 1960s, and Cahill at present). The New Jersey State Legislature has been consistently opposed to a northern New Jersey site and passed a bill banning a jetport there in 1961 that was vetoed by Governor Meyner. Governor Hughes also favored a north-rural New Jersey site, if a federal subsidy could be obtained. The Legislature, by its negative attitude, has taken an implied position in favor of taking no action. It has also tended to the position that New Jersey should look after its own needs, independent of New York.

The Governor of New York (Rockefeller throughout) has actively promoted several New York sites and tends to be against a "do nothing" approach. The New York Legislature has not been much involved, although they did second a Rockefeller proposal for a Long Island site in 1967.

A number of New Jersey Congressman have been strongly opposed to a northern New Jersey site; for example, Representative Frelinghuysen and Senators Case and Williams, and Representative Pike opposed a Long Island site. Senator Case has urged adoption of a south-central New Jersey site. The Congress as a whole responded to leadership from New Jersey Congressmen in removing a provision from the 1969 Airport Funding Bill that would have

Table 3.IV.I Distance Estimates and Individual Resident Utilities for All Jetport Sites

	1968 Population (millions)	McGuire		Solberg		Morris County		Pine Island		Culverton		Kennedy	
		Distance Minutes	Individual Utility	Distance Minutes	Individual Utility	Distance Minutes	Individual Utility	Distance Minutes	Individual Utility	Distance Minutes	Individual Utility	Distance Minutes	Individual Utility
New York													
Kings	2.7	90	2.2	70	2.9	60	3.3	100	2.0	40	5.0	20	10.0
Queens	2.0	100	2.0	80	2.5	60	3.3	80	2.5	40	5.0	30	6.7
Nassau	1.5	120	1.7	100	2.0	90	2.2	120	1.7	30	6.7	30	6.7
New York	1.6	90	2.2	70	2.9	50	4.0	75	2.7	50	4.0	40	5.0
Bronx	1.5	95	2.1	75	2.7	55	3.6	50	4.0	50	4.0	40	5.0
Richmond	.3	80	2.5	60	3.3	50	4.0	100	2.0	60	3.3	30	6.7
Westchester	.9	105	1.9	85	2.3	65	3.1	40	5.0	70	2.9	50	4.0
Rockland	.2	100	2.0	80	2.5	60	3.3	30	6.7	80	2.5	60	3.3
New Jersey													
Middlesex	.6	30	6.7	30	6.7	30	6.7	120	1.7	100	2.0	70	2.9
Union	.6	40	5.0	30	6.7	25	8.0	110	1.8	90	2.2	60	3.3
Essex	1.0	60	3.3	30	6.7	20	10.0	100	2.0	100	2.0	70	2.9
Bergen	.9	90	2.2	60	3.3	30	6.7	40	5.0	70	2.9	50	4.0
Passaic	.5	90	2.2	60	3.3	30	6.7	30	6.7	80	2.5	60	3.3
Hudson	.6	80	2.5	60	3.3	40	5.0	70	2.9	60	3.3	50	4.0
Camden	.5	30	6.7	50	4.0	60	3.3	170	1.2	170	1.2	140	1.4
Burlington	.3	10	20.0	40	5.0	50	4.0	150	1.3	150	1.3	120	1.7
Ocean	.2	20	10.0	40	5.0	60	3.3	170	1.2	140	1.4	110	1.8
Monmouth	.4	30	6.7	40	5.0	60	3.3	130	1.5	120	1.7	180	2.5
Mercer	.3	20	10.0	30	6.7	50	5.0	140	1.4	130	1.5	90	2.2
Somerset	.2	40	5.0	20	10.0	20	10.0	120	1.7	110	1.8	80	2.5
Morris	.4	70	2.9	25	8.0	10	20.0	50	4.0	110	1.8	80	2.5
Pennsylvania													
Bucks	.4	50	4.0	30	6.7	50	4.0	90	2.2	180	1.1	150	1.3
Philadelphia	2.0	30	6.7	50	4.0	70	2.9	170	1.2	180	1.1	150	1.3

required the Transportation Secretary to pick a site if a local area could not pick a site within three years after notification of the need for a new jetport by the federal agency. This action implies a position of "no action" with respect to new airports in the New York City area.

The Department of Defense (DOD) has opposed suggestions that it vacate military bases on Long Island and in south-central New Jersey to make way for a fourth jetport.

The Department of Transportation (DOT) has opposed a south-central New Jersey site on the grounds that it would be incompatible with the air lanes, and it has stated opposition to "no action," but promoted the idea that the local area should pick a jetport site.

The Department of the Interior (DOI) has opposed the Great Swamp site on conservation grounds. It is probably opposed to expansion of Kennedy because this would involve disruption of the natural state of Jamaica Bay.

The FAA has favored a jetport in the "northwest quadrant" which would not disrupt existing air lanes. It has also favored separate general aviation facilities.

The airlines are generally for a new jetport that does not disrupt established air lanes, and that is not so far from the centers of population that it would not get substantial use.

General aviation strongly favors continuing present mixing of general and scheduled air traffic at all airports. They also favor expansion of existing, airports.

The airline pilots both favor a new jetport and favor policies governing traffic that would promote air safety. Thus, they oppose additional traffic at existing airports.

The traffic controllers are primarily in favor of an improved air traffic control system and jetport facilities and locations that promote this.

The conservationists oppose enlargement of land areas required for jetports and strongly oppose new jetports in "virgin," wild areas and areas where jet pollution would be particularly objectionable.

The local communities strongly oppose jetports in populated areas and there is great sympathy for areas other than "one's own" for which a jetport may be proposed. In unpopulated areas the economic rewards to the few people in the area may cause the local community to favor a jetport.

The Port Authority has favored Morris County and Solberg, and opposed most other sites that have been mentioned.

No clear-cut coalitions among the participants have emerged, although some loose alignments are evident. The elected representatives (governors, legislators, and Congressmen) and the local communities all are more-or-less opposed to a new jetport. The governors favor some areas, primarily outside of populated areas, and where there is not strong local opposition to a jetport, but generally reflect the "will of the people," which is the primary motivation of all in this group.

The "technically" oriented organizations—such as the Port Authority, FAA, DOT, airlines and airline pilots—in general favor a new jetport. However, all have their own special requirements that tend to create issues among them. For example, the Port Authority strongly favors a "profit-making" venture, the FAA opposes changes in the air lanes, and so forth.

The other participants represent various special interests, which have only marginal impact, except for the conservationists, who have growing influence with the elected representatives that tends to strengthen the opposition to a new jetport.

The state and federal government participants all are in good positions to influence public opinion and to propose courses of action that will get wide consideration. The legislative groups can also enact legislation, which gives them, perhaps, the greatest power of any of the participants. The United States Congress, in particular, has a broad range for possible legislative action and potentially could dictate an outcome to the other participants. In the near passage of a clause in the 1969 Airport Funding Bill (which would have given the DOT the responsibility to dictate a site if the local area did not within three years of notification) they almost made a major change in the structure of the negotiation process. However, the power of New York area Congressmen is much less than the total power.

The state governors have the power to veto legislation of their respective legislatures and also the power to initiate and carry out studies and investigations which can have great influence. The governors (either or both together) can also veto any action proposed by the Port Authority.

The federal executive agencies, DOD, DOT, and DOI, have considerable influence in proposing legislation to the U.S. Congress. They also have influence locally through the control of federal expenditures of certain types within the local areas. The DOD has control of military reservations and military air traffic, giving them a special mandate for leadership in the area of air transportation and also the technical expertise to be very influential. The DOI controls federal parks and lands, some of which are involved in the jetport issue, and also exercises leadership in the field of conservation, which also is involved.

The FAA controls the air traffic lanes and administers allocation of funds under the new federal aid program for airport funding. It also has considerable prestige and technical expertise, which makes its opinions very influential.

The airlines have some influence when they speak as a group, since they certainly are very knowledgeable about the economics and operations of air transportation. They also have economic power in the latitude they possess concerning flight scheduling, route selection, advertising, and pricing.

The general aviation group is influential primarily through governmental lobbying. This is also essentially the position of the Airline Pilots' Association and the air traffic controllers.

The conservationists' power consists primarily in their ability to influence elected representatives. This power is growing rapidly as conservation and pollution become major political issues. They also have some power to stimulate enforcement of federal conservation legislation.

The local communities have very strong powers to block jetport construction in their own areas through zoning, political pressure, and so forth. There is also great sympathy in other areas for the area that is specifically threatened with jetport construction, which reinforces and broadens this power.

In order to evaluate the likelihood of occurrence of the various possible outcomes, it is necessary to consider both the preferences of the participants and their relative power to impose their view. To do this in a systematic way, relative power coefficients for each of the 16 participants were estimated using subjective judgment. The estimates are listed in Table 3. V-3. These represent an averaging of the independent judgments of four members of the study team, which were fairly similar. This allocates 56 percent of the power to the elected representatives and the local communities—the groups most closely aligned with and sensitive to the political "will of the people." It allocates 28 percent of the power to the technical organizations with specific responsibilities to propose and administer programs relevant to air transportation, but with somewhat limited decision-making power. Finally, 16 percent of the power is given to special interest groups, of which the conservationists get 6 percent.

The preference functions of the participants, shown in Table 3.V-2, are quantified by scaling from 1 to 5 the five categories from "expressed for" to "expressed against." A "preference coefficient" was computed for each outcome by multiplying the preference number (1, 2, 3, 4, or 5) for each participant by the power coefficient for the participant (listed in Table 3. V-3) and summing over all participants. The preference coefficient is a measure of the likelihood of occurrence of the various possible outcomes of the fourth jetport decision-making process. Mathematically, we have:

$$\begin{pmatrix} \text{Preference coefficient} \\ \text{for } j^{th} \text{ outcome} \end{pmatrix} = \sum_{i=1}^{n} x_{ij}\, p_i \,,$$

where
$$\begin{cases} 1 \text{ if } i^{th} \text{ participant has expressed preference for } j^{th} \text{ outcome} \\ 2 \text{ if } i^{th} \text{ participant has implied preference for } j^{th} \text{ outcome} \\ 3 \text{ if } i^{th} \text{ participant has no opinion about } j^{th} \text{ outcome} \\ 4 \text{ if } i^{th} \text{ participant has implied preference against } j^{th} \text{ outcome} \\ 5 \text{ if } i^{th} \text{ participant has expressed preference against } j^{th} \text{ outcome} \end{cases}$$

p_i = power coefficient of ith participant

The computation of the preference coefficient values for the 11 outcomes that were considered is shown in Table 3. V-4.

The resulting "preference coefficients" (the totals in Table 3. V-4) are listed in Table 3. V-5. These are grouped somewhat about the neutral point, 3.00, since strong preferences are, in most cases, counterbalanced by strong opposition. The outcomes appear to separate into four groups.

The most likely outcomes are continued expansion of present jetports and exclusion of general aviation from these jetports to provide for expansion of scheduled airline traffic. In the "weakly favored" and "neutral" groups are sites in the low population density areas. The "strongly opposed," least likely outcomes are those sites in densely populated areas.

Table 3.V-1 Condensed List of Possible Outcomes

1. No action—This includes limiting traffic, rescheduling flights to spread traffic more evenly throughout the day, and minor expansion and modernization of present facilities

2. Separate general aviation airports—this includes proposals for STOL ports and so forth

3. Expansion—this includes major expansion of Newark or Kennedy, such as is indicated in the *Aviation Week* article

4. Ocean Sites—build in ocean off Long Island, in Sandy Hook Bay, etc.

5. Consider New Jersey needs separately from New York and Pennsylvania needs

6. Metropolitan New Jersey—this includes Morris County and other high population density areas

7. Rural northern New Jersey

8. Rural south-central New Jersey

9. Long Island

10. Westchester County

11. Pine Island

Table 3. V-2. Preference of Participants

Preference	State of New Jersey		State of New York		Congress	Federal			Port Authority
	Governor	Legislature	Governor	Legislature		DOD	DOT	DOI	
Expresses in Favor of	8		9, 11	9	8				
Implicit in Favor of	3	1, 3, 5		1	1	1		1	
No Opinion	1, 2, 4, 5, 9, 10, 11	2, 4, 8, 9, 10, 11	2, 3, 4, 5, 6, 7, 8, 10	2, 3, 4, 5, 6, 7, 8, 10, 11	2, 3, 4, 5, 10, 11	2, 3, 4, 5, 7, 10, 11	2, 3, 4, 5, 6, 7, 9, 10, 11	2, 5, 7, 8, 9, 10, 11	
Implicit Opposed to			1					2, 4	
Expressed Opposed to	6, 7	6, 7			6, 7, 9	6, 8, 9	1, 8	6	

Preference	FAA	Airlines	AOPA	APA	Controllers	Conservationists	Local Community	Port Authority
Expresses in Favor of	2, 3, 6, 7	2, 3, 6		1, 6, 7, 11	1, 6, 7, 11		8, 9, 11	6, 7
Implicit in Favor of	5	1	1, 3			1	1, 3	2, 3
No Opinion	4	4, 5	1, 4, 5, 6, 7, 8, 9, 10, 11	2, 4, 8, 9, 10	2, 4, 9, 10	2, 5, 7, 9, 10, 11	2, 4, 5	5
Implicit Opposed to	1, 10			3, 5	8			
Expressed	8, 9, 11		2			3, 4, 6	6, 7, 10	1, 4, 8, 9, 10, 11

Table 3.V-3—Relative Power Coefficients for
Participants in New Jetport Decision-Making Process

Participant	Power Coefficients
New Jersey Governor	.09
New Jersey Legislature	.07
New York Governor	.09
New York Legislature	.07
Congress	.09
DOD	.02
DOT	.05
DOI	.02
FAA	.09
Airlines	.04
AOPA	.02
APA	.02
Controllers	.02
Conservationists	.06
Local Communities	.15
Port Authority	.10
	1.00

Table 3. V-4 Computation of Preference Coefficients for Possible Outcomes of Decision-Making Process

Participant	No Action	Exclude General	Expand	Ocean Sites	Separate N.J.	Metrop. N.J.	Rural No. N.J.	Rural So. N.J.	Long Island	West-chester	Pine Island
N.J. Gov (.09)	.27	.27	.18	.27	.27	.45	.45	.09	.27	.27	.27
N.J. Leg (.07)	.14	.21	.14	.21	.14	.35	.35	.21	.21	.21	.21
N.Y. Gov (.09)	.36	.27	.27	.27	.27	.27	.27	.27	.09	.27	.09
N.Y. Leg (.07)	.14	.21	.21	.21	.21	.21	.21	.21	.07	.21	.21
Congress (.09)	.18	.27	.27	.27	.27	.45	.45	.09	.45	.27	.27
DOD (.02)	.04	.06	.06	.06	.06	.10	.06	.10	.10	.06	.06
DOT (.05)	.25	.15	.15	.15	.15	.15	.15	.25	.15	.15	.15
DOI (.02)	.04	.06	.08	.08	.06	.10	.06	.06	.06	.06	.06
FAA (.09)	.36	.09	.09	.27	.18	.09	.09	.45	.45	.36	.45
Airlines (.04)	.08	.04	.04	.12	.12	.04	.16	.16	.16	.16	.16
AOPA (.02)	.04	.10	.04	.06	.06	.06	.06	.06	.06	.06	.06
APA (.02)	.02	.06	.08	.06	.08	.02	.02	.06	.06	.06	.02
Controllers (.02)	.02	.06	.08	.06	.08	.02	.02	.10	.06	.06	.02
Conserv. (.06)	.12	.18	.30	.30	.18	.30	.18	.24	.18	.18	.18
Local (.15)	.30	.45	.30	.45	.45	.75	.75	.15	.15	.75	.15
PA (.10)	.50	.20	.30	.50	.30	.10	.10	.50	.50	.50	.50
Total	2.86	2.68	2.59	3.34	2.88	3.46	3.38	3.00	3.02	3.63	2.86

Table 3. V-5. Likelihood of Various Outcomes of the Fourth Jetport Controversy

Outcome	Preference Coefficient*	
Expansion	2.59	) Strongly favored
Exclude general aviation	2.68	)
Pine Island	2.86	)
No action	2.86	) Weakly favored
Separate N.J. Airport	2.88	)
Rural southern N.J.	3.00	) Neutral
Long Island	3.02	
Ocean Site	3.34	)
Rural northern N.J.	3.38	) Strongly opposed
Metropolitan N.J.	3.46	)
Westchester	3.63	

*The preference coefficient can take values from 1 to 5 with 1 indicating all participants favor an outcome, 3 indicating participants are neutral or there is equal weight for and against, and 5 indicating all participants oppose an outcome.

NOTES–CASE 3

1. James D. Thompson and Arthur Tuden, "Strategies. Structures and Processes of Organizational Decisions," in H.J. Leavitt and L.R. Pondy (Eds.), *Readings in Managerial Psychology*, Chicago, University of Chicago Press, 1964, pp. 496-515.

2. While these figures appear at odds with passenger and cargo demand tables presented earlier, they are based on the following different assumptions: (a) the technological events forecast earlier will not come to fruition; (b) a broader region is being considered (the megalopolis from Philadelphia to New York City, as opposed to metropolitan New York).

3. FAA estimates that at J.F.K. in the 7/26/66 to 8/26/66 period. cost was $6.81 million, or 18,953 hours, just as a sample of the numbers.

Case 4
National Policies Toward Foreign Private Investment

ANGELOS A. TSAKLANGANOS* and AMBAR G. RAO[†]

INTRODUCTION

Planned economic development is increasingly being recognized as a necessity for many countries suffering from a low level of material well-being. Economic development requires large inputs of capital and organizational and technical skills; planners in many countries have sought to obtain these inputs from foreign sources—both private and public. The predominant form of foreign assistance in the past was foreign aid and foreign loans. This pattern is, changing, however, and it is expected that foreign private investment will play a larger and more vital role in the economies of the developing countries.

Many incentives are offered to make a country attractive to the foreign private investor. The most common is the grant of some kind of income tax reduction or exemption. Permission to repatriate profits and/or capital, after a certain number of years is another incentive—one that attempts to protect the investor from the vagaries of changing political and social climates. Others are accelerated depreciation, deferred tax payments, and the permission to employ foreign consultants and experts with minimal restrictions. Of course, many other variables enter the picture—the reader is referred to the work by Tsaklanganos[1] for a discussion. Planners hope that the granting of incentives will maximize profit opportunities for foreign businessmen and thereby compensate them for the inherent risks of investing in a less developed and potentially unstable environment.

While incentives are likely to stimulate the rate of flow of foreign investment into a country, they simultaneously reduce the impact of this

*Temple University
† New York University

flow on the domestic economy. Thus, the planner is confronted with the typical operations research problem—the balancing of opposing forces to optimize some desired goal—where the controllable variables are the level of incentives offered to foreign investors. Many of the factors affecting investment and its impact on an economy have been studied in the literature but their simultaneous and interacting effect within a framework of optimization has not been investigated. The reason for this is probably the difficulty of formulating a set of consistent and comparable goals for the development of an economy. Nevertheless, any set of incentives offered to foreign investors *implies* a set of goals; although the trade-offs between goals may not be obvious, planners should be able to compare sets of implied goals and select those that are best.

The approach in this paper to the problem of determining the optimal incentive policy, although not solving the issue of goals, circumvents these difficulties. In the next section we show how the various, perhaps conflicting, goals of a developing economy can be formulated in terms of a set of constraints. Then we show how this set, together with the consequences of incentive policy can be incorporated into the framework of optimization, to demonstrate the effects of various types of incentive policy. Finally, a numerical example illustrating the proposed methodology is presented.

DETERMINING GOALS

The development goals of most developing countries usually relate to desired rates of growth for various sectors together with social requirements— for example, the reduction of unemployment and underemployment, increases in per capita consumption, and so forth. A common management science approach to multigoal problems has been to try to develop trade-offs between each goal and a common measure and express each goal as a function of this measure. The sum of the individual functions then can serve as an objective function in the appropriate optimization problem.

This approach, although conceptually attractive, is both difficult and dangerous. The difficulties arise because most often neither the data, nor the ability to experiment in order to determine the individual trade-offs is available. Thus, the analyst must make assumptions about the trade-offs. The consequences of these assumptions are usually not fully clear to the decision maker; thus, "optimal" policies can in fact be quite unoptimal. Hatry[2] discusses this problem in the context of planning for health systems.

We shall avoid this traditional approach and deal directly with the various goals. As stated before, we assume that the host government seeks through various means, including foreign investment, to drive several goal or criterion variables to desired ("better") values. For example, the government may wish to reduce unemployment by at least a percent, or increase consumption by not more than b percent. It is quite possible that several of these targets are inconsistent or not achievable simultaneously; if so, the government would like to come as close to its various targets as possible. Also, some targets may be more heavily weighted than others—thus, achieving target 1, say, may be considered more important than achieving target 2.

We therefore seek a set of incentives that moves the criterion variables as close as possible to the target values. The philosophy of this approach is thus akin to that of "satisficing." Instead of maximizing one criterion while constraining the others to attain given values, however, we seek solutions that bring all criterion variables as close as possible to desired levels. Let $n = (x_1, \ldots, x_n)$ be the vector of incentives that the planner can control; the x_i represent tax rates, depreciation rates, percentage of profit allowed to be repatriated, and so on. Let $f_j(x)$ represent the functional relationship between x_i's and the jth criterion variable $j=1,\ldots,m$, and let bj be the target level for this variable. Let y_j^+ and y_j^- represent positive and negative deviations, respectively, from these target values. Finally let $g_k(x) = 0$ $k=1,\ldots,p$ represent a set of internal consistency constraints that must exist among the x_i's. We now formulate the problem of determining the optimal incentives as one where we

$$\text{minimize} \quad \sum_j y_j^+ + \sum_j y_j^- \qquad\qquad 1(a)$$

$$\text{subject to} \quad f_j(x) - y_j^+ + y_j^- = bj \quad j=1,\ldots,m \qquad 1(b)$$

$$g_k(x) \qquad\qquad\quad = 0 \quad k=1,\ldots,p$$

$$y_j^+ \qquad\qquad\qquad \geqq 0$$

$$y_j^- \qquad\qquad\qquad \geq 0$$

$$x_i \qquad\qquad\qquad\quad \geq 0$$

where

$$y_j^+ \cdot y_j^- = 0 \qquad\qquad\qquad\qquad 1(c)$$

is the necessary condition for minimization, giving us the following three possibilities in our optimal solution:

a. exact attainment of goals—i.e.,

$$y_j^+ = y_j^- = 0; \qquad\qquad\qquad\qquad 1(d)$$

b. positive discrepancy or overattainment of goals—i.e.,

$$y_j^+ > 0, y_j^- = 0; \qquad\qquad 1(e)$$

c. negative deviation or underattainment of goals—i.e.,

$$y_j^+ = 0, \; y_j^- > 0. \qquad\qquad 1(f)$$

If some targets are weighted more heavily than others, or if negative deviations are to be avoided more than positive ones, then this can be reflected in the objective function 1(a) through the selection of appropriate weights w_j^+ and w_j^- and modification to the form

$$\text{minimize } \Sigma w_j^+ y_j^+ + \Sigma w_j^- y_j^-. \qquad\qquad 1(g)$$

Thus we have formulated the problem as one of goal programming. A detailed discussion of this approach when the constraints are linear can be found in the books by Charnes and Cooper and by Ijiri.[3]

Of course, in general, the effects of incentives will be manifested over a planning period that may embrace several years, and the incentives may be changed within the planning period. In this case, let $x_t = (x_{1t},...,x_{nt})$ be the values of the incentives in year t; let X_t represent the vector $(x_1, x_2,...,x_t)$ t = 1,...,N, where N is the length of the planning period in years. Introduce the functions $f_{jt}(X_t)$ to represent the relationships between the historical incentive policies and the value of the jth criterion variable in period t, and the functions $g_{kt}(X_t)$ to represent the internal consistency requirements as before. Finally, let b_{jt} be the desired value of the jth criterion variable in period t; y_{jt}^+ and y_{jt}^- the deviations from these values; and w_{jt}^+ and w_{jt}^- the weights associated with these deviations. Then we can write the general problem of determining the best set of incentives as one where we

$$\text{minimize } \quad \Sigma w_{jt}^+ y_{jt}^+ + \Sigma w_{jt}^- y_{jt}^- \qquad\qquad 1(h)$$

$$\text{subject to } \quad f_{jt}(X_t) - y_{jt}^+ + y_{jt}^- = b_{jt} \quad j=1,...,m$$

$$t=1,...,N$$

$$g_{kt}(X_t) \qquad\qquad\qquad = 0 \quad k=1,...,p$$

$$y_{jt}^+ \geq 0, \; y_{jt}^- \geq 0 \quad x_t \geq 0$$

MODEL DEVELOPMENT

Now we present an illustration of the approach outlined previously. In this section we develop the functions $f_{jt}(X_t)$ and the consistency requirements $g_{kt}(X_t)$. In the next section a numerical example of the solution of this kind of problem will be presented. Suppose the government wants to maximize economic growth and/or minimize unemployment. If we let r_t stand for growth and U_t for unemployment, then we have

and

$$r_t = Y_t - Y_{t-1} \tag{2}$$

$$U_t = LS_t - LD_t, \tag{3}$$

where LS_t is the labor supply in year t, LD_t is the labor demand in year t, and Y_t and Y_{t-1} are income (say GNP) for year t and t-1. The actual increase in income and the actual decrease in unemployment, rather than the percentage rate, have been chosen in order to avoid nonlinear relationships.

Now suppose that the labor supply increases at a constant rate α—i.e.,

$$LS_t = (1 + \alpha) LS_{t-1} \qquad 0 < \alpha < 1 \tag{4}$$

and that the demand for labor is a function of income—i.e.,

$$LD_t = \Psi Y_t \qquad\qquad 0 < \Psi < 1 \tag{5}$$

where Ψ is the coefficient of labor demand/income relationship.

Let us assume that income is a function of labor and capital (production function) or, assuming a constant labor/capital ratio and a constant relation between flow of capital and level of capital, we can have a simpler form where income is a function of domestic and foreign capital—i.e.,

$$Y_t = K_t (I_{dt} + TCBFI_t), \tag{6}$$

where K_t is the investment multiplier which is assumed the same for local and foreign investment, I_{dt} is the local investment, and $TCBFI_t$ is the total capital invested, which is generated because of foreign private investment.

We can further assume a constant (h) increase in the domestic investment:

$$I_{dt} = (1 + h) I_{dt-1}, \quad 0 \le h < 1. \tag{7}$$

Now $TCBFI_t$ consists of
   a) foreign private investment (FPI_t),
   b) investment made by the local government, or local investors (LGI_t), to match certain ownership percentage if there is a restriction on ownership by the foreign investor,

c) capital borrowed by the foreign investor from the local government or other domestic sources (B_t),

d) cost of the feasibility study paid by the foreign investor or the local government (CFS_t),

e) capital expatriated (CE_t), and

f) retained and reinvested earnings (RE_{t-1}) from year t-1.

That is,

$$TCBFI_t = FPI_t + LGI_t + B_t + CFS_t - CE_t + RE_{t-1}. \tag{8}$$

These forms of capital generated because of foreign private investment will be discussed in detail later in this paper.

The realized FPI_t produces a certain income every year over the planning horizon of the life of the investment. This income stream depends on the sector of the economy in which the investment is made, the technological structure and the marginal efficiency of the investment, the overall absorbing capacity of the host country, and the conditions of demand for the goods produced in the local market as well as in the world market. It is affected also by tax policies, wage and employment regulation, and transfer of income to the parent country. We assume that foreign private investment (FPI_t) is equal to the present value of the expected income stream over the planning horizon, discounted at an interest rate equal to the expected rate of return of the foreign investor. That is,

$$FPI_t = \sum_{j=t}^{N+t} YF_j (1+i)^{t-j}, \tag{9}$$

Where YF_t is the net expected revenue by the foreign investor in year t, and i is the expected rate of return by the foreign investor for his investment, and N is large.

We further assume that YF_t is the portion of income exported or retained and reinvested by the foreign investor—i.e.,

$$YF_t = (\lambda_{1t} + \lambda_{2t}) YFP_t, \tag{10}$$

where YFP_t is the total net income after deducting wages and salaries (W_t), depreciation (R_{tt}), and interest (INT_t) generated by the foreign investment in year t. λ_{1t} and λ_{2t} stand for the proportion of total net income (YFP_t) reinvested and exported respectively in year t.

In other words, we have

$$YFG_t = YFP_t + W_t + R_{tt} + INT_t, \qquad (11)$$

where YFG_t is the gross income generated by the foreign investment before wages and salaries (W_t), depreciation (R_{tt}), and interest (INT_t).

Now YFP_t—the total net income after wages and salaries, depreciation, and interest—is the income taxed by the local government. The remainder is retained by the corporation for reinvestment and further expansion of business, or is transferred abroad (exported) to the parent company or the individual investor as has already been described in equation (10). Letting RE_t stand for retained and reinvested earnings, EP_t for exported profits, and TX_t for income taxes, then

$$YFP_t = RE_t + EP_t + TX_t \qquad (12)$$

and

$$RE_t = \lambda_{1t} YFP_t \qquad 0 \leq \lambda_{1t} \leq 1 \qquad (13)$$

$$EP_t = \lambda_{2t} YFP_t \qquad 0 \leq \lambda_{2t} < 1 \qquad (14)$$

$$TX_t = \lambda_{3t} YFP_t \qquad 0 \leq \lambda_{3t} \leq 1 \qquad (15)$$

where λ_{3t} is the proportion of total net income (YFP_t) taxed, λ_{1t} and λ_{2t} are as defined earlier in equation (10) the proportion of total income reinvested and exported respectively, and where

$$\sum_{i=1}^{3} \lambda_{it} = 1. \qquad (16)$$

If we accept λ_{1t} as greater than 1, this means that we have new investment or capital inflow, from income exported in previous periods. Allowing λ_{1t} to be negative means that we have expatriation of capital invested in previous periods of time.

We should note here that λ_{2t} and λ_{3t} are some of the controllable variables which can be used by the local government to attain its goals. λ_{1t} is not only controlled by the local government, where $\lambda_{1t} = 1 - \lambda_{2t} - \lambda_{3t}$, but also is subject to control by the foreign investor where he can retain RE_t from net income but not reinvest it. However, we exclude such a possibility in the present study, assuming that income retained (RE_t) in period t is reinvested in period t+1.

Because of the instability of local economic and political conditions, we may assume that the foreign investors will prefer to export their profits rather than reinvest them, thus giving greater weight to expatriated profits. To reflect this preference for the repatriation of profits, we discount reinvested income by some constant factor, which will be explained in more detail in the numerical example.

It should be noted that many developing countries do not tax YFP_t at all, but only EP_t or YFP_t-RE_t, leaving RE_t free of tax as an extra incentive for reinvestment of profits. Many of the developing countries treat local corporations in the same way, leaving all reinvested earnings free of tax. The same phenomenon can also be observed in some of the developed countries, where further expansion and growth is a highly weighted economic goal.

Now the total income realized by the foreign private investor in year t (YF_t) is

$$YF_t = RE_t + EP_t = \lambda_{1t}YFP_t + \lambda_{2t}YFP_t = (\lambda_{1t} + \lambda_{2t})\,YFP_t \qquad (17a)$$

or

$$YF_t = (1 - \lambda_{3t})\,YFP_t, \qquad (17b)$$

which is the total of retained earnings plus exported income as discussed in equation (10).

The income (YF_t) realized by the foreign investor is a very important measure in determining the rate of return of FPI and for ranking alternative investment opportunities.

The total net benefit (YFF_t) for year t for the recipient country affected by the foreign private investment is the total income spent in all various forms in that country—that is, the total of local wages plus taxes on wages of foreign personnel plus taxes on corporate income plus the portion of foreign personnel wages spent in the recipient country plus retained earnings invested in the country. Thus, YFF_t can be used to determine the marginal productivity of the foreign private investment and also the social rate of return of the recipient country.

It should be noted that YFF_t is the increase in aggregate demand at the end of the first year which will generate further investment through the acceleration principle, provided the economy doesn't operate below full capacity. However, the total effect of the first year is equal to $FPI_t + YFF_t$, where the multiplier effect will produce an income multiple to FPI (the multiplier works only on FPI).

Concerning taxation of the income produced by the foreign investment, it should be noted that the donor country may also tax income received by investors who have invested overseas as well as income earned from wages realized abroad. There are, however, many agreements and treaties among the various countries for avoiding double taxation.

The restriction on equity share imposed by the recipient country has a major effect on foreign investment. This ownership split differs to a large extent in the various countries, up to the complete absence of any restriction at all in many of them.

Let δ be the maximum share by the foreign investor where $0 \leq \delta \leq 1$ and $1-\delta$ the share by a local investor or government, then the local investment (LGI_t) and the total generated capital investment (TGI_t) resulting from foreign private investment in the developing country is

$$TGI_t = FPI_t + LGI_t = FPI_t + \frac{1-\delta}{\delta} FPI_t \qquad (18)$$

where $\dfrac{1-\delta}{\delta} FPI_t$ is the local investment (LGI_t) at year t. We should note that δ is not a constant percentage applied to all investment projects. It is rather an average percentage of all investment projects, each of which may have a different δ depending on the importance of the industry and the project as well as the area or region where the investment is made. It should also be noted that the lower δ is, the better it is for the developing countries and the process of development (if it has or can find the funds for investment) because of the extra capital investment generated as a result of the foreign private investment. However, higher δ attracts more foreign investors because of the privilege of control. In most cases, the critical question that affects the final decision of investors is whether δ is greater or less than 0.50. It is often the most controversial subject in negotiations between the foreign investor and the government of the developing country.

The extra capital generated because of FPI (i.e., $\dfrac{1-\delta}{\delta} FPI_t$) is financed either by increasing domestic savings, by local private or public loans, by foreign loans from private or public organizations or individual investors, or by foreign aid.

Many countries, as part of their incentive program to foreign investors, grant some kind of financial assistance. This financial assistance can be in many forms, such as

a) providing loans with very low interest rates,
b) subsidizing for interest expenses (interest rebates),
c) providing cash grants,
d) providing land, factories, and services free of charge, etc.

Some of these means of financial assistance and the extent of their importance, depend upon

a) the contribution to the economy of the foreign investment,
b) the location of the plant to be established,
c) the contribution to employment and labor training,
d) the use of domestic raw materials,
e) the technological content of the investment,
f) the contribution to exports or the substitution of imports, etc.

In our model, we assume that the foreign investor has credit and can borrow an amount B_t from local sources, with reduced interest rate i'_t where $0 \leq i'_t \leq$ market i_t. Assume also that

$$B_t \leq b_t FPI_t \qquad 0 \leq b_t \leq 1 \qquad (19)$$

where b_t is the proportion of capital provided by the government or governmental agencies to the total amount imported and invested by the foreign private investor. The total investment (TI_t) taking place in the developing country because of the foreign investment is now

$$TI_t = (1 + b_t)\ FPI_t .\qquad(20)$$

It is obvious that the higher b_t is, the more investment is generated if there is money available. The interest expense (INT_t) paid by the foreign investor annually is

$$INT_t = i'_t B_t = i'_t b_t\ FPI_t \qquad 0 \leq i'_t \leq \text{market interest rate}\qquad(21)$$

which may be zero if the local government subsidizes interest expenses (i.e., if $i'_t = 0$).

An important variable controlled by the government is the maximum capital expatriation rate. Constraints dealing with maximum depreciation rates, amount of wages paid to local personnel, payroll taxes on foreign wages, expatriation rates of foreign wages, etc., also have an important effect on the foreign investment decision-making process. In the interests of simplicity, however, we shall not deal with these variables and constraints here. They are discussed in detail by Tsaklanganos.[4]

A NUMERICAL EXAMPLE

In this section we present a two-goal-three-period numerical example as an illustration of the model and its solution. The goals used are a desired rate of growth of GNP and a desired rate of reduction in unemployment for each of the three time periods.

The following target values for GNP growth and unemployment reduction have been chosen for this example:

$$r_1 = \$3.2 \text{ billion } (11.6\%),$$
$$r_2 = \$4.0 \text{ billion } (13.0\%),$$
$$r_3 = \$4.7 \text{ billion } (13.3\%),$$
$$u_1 = 5.5 \text{ million people } (18.0\%),$$
$$u_2 = 3.3 \text{ million people } (14.0\%),$$
$$u_3 = 1.0 \text{ million people } (5.0\%).$$

These can be considered as very ambitious goals for a developing economy.

No effort was made in this example to estimate the values of the parameters. The values have been chosen arbitrarily but within a realistic range. The purpose here is merely to present a numerical example and the type of results that may be expected in a real situation.

Before formulating the objective function of the optimization problem, we note that the scales on which the deviations from the respective targets are measured have a major influence in the relative importance of each goal. In our case, the deviations from the GNP target are measured on a scale of dollars, while the deviations from the unemployment target are measured in a scale of numbers of people. Utilizing the deviations without transforming scales obviously imposes a utility function of a specific kind on the problem. We shall, however, weight the two goals equally. In order to do so, we define a constant β_t t = 1, 2, 3 such that

$$GNP_{Gt} = \beta_t U_{Gt},$$

where the subscript G denotes target values. The deviations from the unemployment target are then weighted by β_t in the objective function. Thus, reducing the deviation from the unemployment target by a unit amount is accorded the same importance as reducing the deviation from the GNP target by a unit amount. The values of β_t used are $\beta_1 = 1466.67$, $\beta_2 = 2076.92$, and $\beta_3 = 3100.00$. The economic implication of this treatment is to say that there is a definite quantity by which GNP must be increased in period t to provide employment for one extra person in that period.

EQUATIONS FOR THE NUMERICAL EXAMPLE

$$\text{Min. } \sum_{t=1}^{3} [Y_{1t}^+ + Y_{1t}^- + \beta_t Y_{2t}^+ + \beta_t Y_{2t}^-] \tag{1}$$

s.t.

$$r_t + y_{1t}^+ - y_{1t}^- = \bar{r}_t \qquad t = 1, 2, 3 \tag{2}$$

$$U_t - y_{2t}^+ + y_{2t}^- = \bar{U}_t \tag{3}$$

$$r_t = Y_t - Y_{t-1} \tag{4}$$

$$U_t = LS_t - LD_t \tag{5}$$

$$LD_t = \Psi Y_t \qquad 0 < \Psi < 1 \tag{6}$$

$$LS_t = (1 + \alpha) LS_{t-1} \qquad 0 < \alpha < 1 \tag{7}$$

$$Y_t = K_t (I_{dt} + TCBFI_t) \tag{8}$$

$$I_{dt} = (1+h)I_{dt-1} \qquad 0 < h < 1 \tag{9}$$

$$TCBFI_t = FPI_t + LGI_t + B_t - CE_t + CFS_t + RE_{t-1} \tag{10}$$

$$FPI_t = \sum_{j=t}^{N+t} YF_j (1+i)^{-j+t} \tag{11}$$

$$YF_t = (\lambda_{1t} + \lambda_{2t}) YFP_t \qquad 0 \le \lambda_{1t} \le 1 \tag{12}$$
$$0 \le \lambda_{2t} \le 1$$

$$YFP_t = YFG_t - W_t - R_{tt} - INT_t \tag{13}$$

$$YFP_t = RE_t + EP_t + TX_t \tag{14}$$

$$RE_t = \lambda_{1t} YFP_t \qquad 0 \le \lambda_{1t} \le 1 \tag{15}$$

$$EP_t = \lambda_{2t} YFP_t \qquad 0 \le \lambda_{2t} \le 1 \tag{16}$$

$$TX_t = \lambda_{3y} YFP_t \qquad 0 \le \lambda_{3t} \le 1 \tag{17}$$

$$LGI_t \le (1 - \delta) FPI_t \qquad 0 \le \delta \le 1 \tag{18}$$

$$LGI_t \le \overline{LGI_t} \tag{19}$$

$$B_t \le b_t FPI_t \qquad 0 \le b_t \le 1 \tag{20}$$

Note that the signs of the deviations, y_{1t}^+, y_{2t}^-, y_{2t}^+, and y_{2t}^- are in reverse order. This is because we wish to *reduce* unemployment and *increase* income.

SUMMARY OF RESULTS

We have conducted three sets of sensitivity studies, varying the values of the parameters λ_1, λ_2, and λ_3 which are, respectively, the retained and reinvested earnings, the exported profits, and the tax rates. In order to reflect the preference of foreign investors for repatriating their earnings rather than reinvesting them, money reinvested has been discounted by a constant 20 percent.

We should also note that convertibility of currency is an important factor to be considered by foreign investors. It has been assumed that there is free convertibility of currency and no exchange controls are imposed by any country according to Article VIII of the International Monetary Fund Agreement.

Study I

In the first study we hold λ_1 (retained and reinvested earnings) constant at the level of 40 percent and vary λ_3 (tax rates) and hence λ_2 (expatriated profits). The results are summarized in Table 4.1 and Fig. 4.1. We observe that as the tax rate is increased and the expatriation rate of profits is decreased, the amount of foreign private investment is decreased. This means that foreign investors are very sensitive and responsive to changes in the tax rate and the expatriation of profit rates. We also observe that the total capital generated because of foreign private investment is decreased as the tax rate is increased and the expatriation rate of profits is decreased. As a consequence, the value of the objective function is increased—that is, the deviations from target goals are increased, worsening the achievement of our national objectives.

Table 4.1 Summary of Sensitivity of λ_3, λ_2

λ_3 TX	λ_2 EP	$\overline{\lambda_1}$ RE	MOF Obj. Function	TCBFI	FPI	B
.10	.50	.40	8,437	3,529	3,043	409
.20	.40	.40	8,833	3,509	2,842	352
.30	.30	.40	9,398	3,479	2,592	736
.40	.20	.40	10,233	3,435	2,331	782
.50	.10	.40	11,334	3,377	2,032	736

Key: λ_1 = proportion of income retained and reinvested in year t.

λ_2 = proportion of income exported in year t.

λ_3 = proportion of income available for taxes in year t.

TCBFI = total capital invested in period t which is generated because of foreign private investment.

FPI = amount of money invested by the foreign private investor in period t.

B = amount of money the foreign investor can borrow from local sources.

MOF = value of objective function.

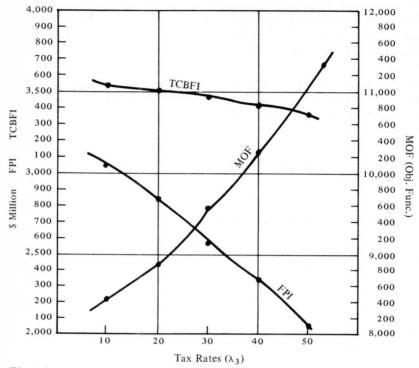

Fig. 4.1

Key: λ_3 = proportion of income available for taxes in year t.

TCBFI = total capital invested in period t which is generated because of foreign private investment.

FPI = amount of money invested by the foreign private investor in period t.

MOF = value of objective function.

Study II

In the second study we hold λ_2 (expatriated profits) constant at the level of 40 percent and vary λ_3 (tax rates) and hence λ_1 (retained and reinvested earnings). The results are summarized in Table 4.2 and Fig. 4.2, and are similar to those obtained in Study I. As tax rate is decreased and retained and reinvested profit rate is increased, foreign private investment is increased, as is the total capital generated because of foreign private investment. This results in a closer approach to our target goals—that is, the value of the objective function is decreased.

Table 4.2 Summary of Sensitivity of λ_3, λ_1

λ_3 TX	λ_1 RE	λ_2 EP	MOF Obj. Function	TCBFI	FPI	B
.10	.50	.40	7,757	3,565	3,183	233.4
.20	.40	.40	8,560	3,523	2,994	317.0
.30	.30	.40	9,618	3,468	2,760	794.4
.40	.20	.40	11,077	3,391	2,519	913.0
.50	.10	.40	12,918	3,294	2,256	817.0

Key: λ_1 = proportion of income retained and reinvested in year t.

λ_2 = proportion of income exported in year t.

λ_3 = proportion of income available for taxes in year t.

TCBFI = total capital invested in period t which is generated because of foreign private investment.

FPI = amount of money invested by the foreign private investor in period t.

B = amount of money the foreign investor can borrow from local sources.

MOF = value of objective function.

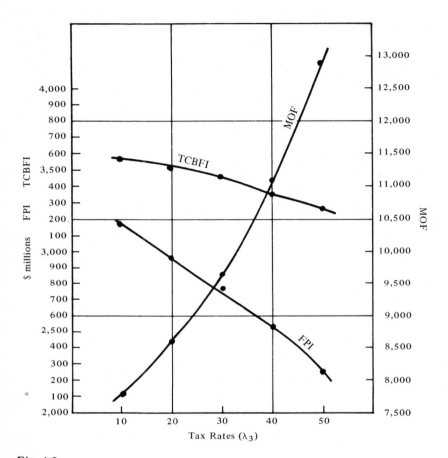

Fig. 4.2

Key: λ_3 = proportion of income available for taxes in year t.

TCBFI = total capital invested in period t which is generated because of foreign private investment.

FPI = amount of money invested by the foreign private investor in period t.

MOF = value of objective function.

Study III

The results of the third study are summarized in Table 4.3 and Fig. 4.3. In this study we hold λ_3 (tax rates) constant at the level of 20 percent and vary λ_1 (retained and reinvested profits) versus λ_2 (expatriated profits). The results of this study are extremely interesting as we observe that as retained and reinvested earnings are decreased and expatriated profits are increased, foreign private investment flow is increased because of the incentive of repatriation of profits. However, expatriation of profits does not benefit the local economy and it is demonstrated by the increase in the value of the objective function.

Table 4.3 Summary of Sensitivity of λ_1, λ_2

λ_1 RE	λ_2 EP	$\overline{\lambda_3}$ TX	MOF Obj. Function	TCBFI	FPI	B
.10	.70	.20	7,223	3,594	2,713	229
.20	.60	.20	7,776	3,565	2,758	271
.30	.50	.20	8,314	3,536	2,800	311
.40	.40	.20	8,833	3,509	2,843	351
.50	.30	.20	9,339	3,482	2,885	390
.60	.20	.20	9,830	3,457	2,898	429
.70	.10	.20	10,317	3,432	2,964	455

Key: λ_1 = proportion of income retained and reinvested in year t.

λ_2 = proportion of income exported in year t.

λ_3 = proportion of income available for taxes in year t.

TCBFI = total capital invested in period t which is generated because of foreign private investment.

FPI = amount of money invested by the foreign private investor in period t.

B = amount of money the foreign investor can borrow from local sources.

MOF = value of objective function.

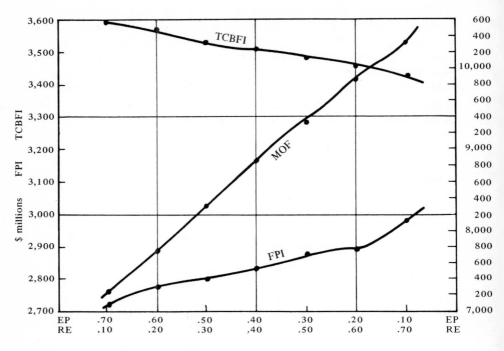

Fig. 4.3

Key: TCBFI = total capital invested in period t which is generated
        because of foreign private investment.

        FPI = amount of money invested by the foreign private
        investor in period t.

        MOF = value of objective function.

        RE = retained earnings.

        EP = exported profits

NOTES–CASE 4

1. Angelos A. Tsaklanganos, "National Strategies Concerning Foreign Private Investment: An O.R. Approach," unpublished Ph.D. Dissertation, New York University, 1971.

2. Harry P. Hatry, "Measuring the Effectiveness of Non Defense Public Programs," *Operations Research,* Vol. 18, No. 5, 1970, pp. 772-784.

3. A. Charnes and W.W. Cooper, *Management Models and Industrial Applications of Linear Programming,* New York, Wiley, 1961, 219ff; and V. Ijiri, *Management Goals and Accounting for Control,* Amsterdam, North Holland Publishing Company, 1965.

4. Tsaklanganos, "National Strategies."

Case 5
Effecting Change in Public Policy:
Financing Urban Transportation in the
New York, New Jersey, and Connecticut Region*

ERNEST KURNOW,[†] RICHARD P. BRIEF,[†] and IRWIN H. SILBERMAN[‡]

INTRODUCTION

This study[1] was undertaken to provide basic financial data and to make recommendations to the Tri-State Transportation Commission[2] for its development of immediate action and long-range programs for financing transportation services in the New York Metropolitan Region.[3] The financing of intraurban facilities in the region includes expenditures on streets, roads and highways, bridges, tunnels, commuter railroads, buses and public transit, as well as street cleaning, parking, lighting, sidewalks, storm sewers, and traffic and highway police. The study does not include facilities devoted solely to interregional travel or to the shipment of goods.

We have adopted an "enterprise" approach that would be applicable to the study of financing urban transportation systems in any metropolitan area. This approach to accounting for regional transportation systems reflects the view that an overall, coordinated effort is required to obtain a balanced transit network in metropolitan regions. Thus, both the methodology and the statistical findings themselves should be of interest to transportation specialists and to those involved in public administration.[4] In addition, the study sheds some light on the more general process of influencing public policy. It provides an eight-year history of both successful and unsuccessful efforts to achieve change in transportation financing in the New York Metropolitan Region.

*Appeared originally in the *Highway Research Record,* Vol. 476, 1973, pp. 49-56, without the appendices. Reprinted by permission.
† New York University
‡ Irwin H. Silberman & Associates, Inc.

We shall first present an analysis of the sources of transportation funds and then analyze the expenditures on transportation. The difference between the sources of funds and expenditures on transportation—the "transportation surplus"—is discussed next. In the following section we elaborate on our general approach to the study of financing transportation and the implications of the specific findings for public policy. We then summarize the study recommendations, mention some of the institutional constraints which influenced their implementation, and summarize subsequent events.

SOURCES OF TRANSPORTATION FUNDS

The tri-state region generated $2.6 billion in 1962 to finance transportation disbursements (see Table 5.1). The three major sources of funds are classified as direct users, indirect users, and borrowing.[5]

Direct users are those who contribute to the transportation system in direct relation to the use they make of transportation facilities. Their payments for transportation services are direct and their benefits are also direct. All funds provided by direct users are recorded at the level of government that initially receives the funds.

Funds provided by direct users include user taxes, user charges, and miscellaneous related income directly associated with the use of transportation facilities.

1. *User taxes* include federal and state motor fuel taxes, motor vehicle license fees, and other motor vehicle related excise taxes. These taxes are viewed as direct payments for the use of transportation services and, insofar as possible, the allocation procedures attempted to estimate the user charges actually earned in the region. For example, motor vehicle taxes were allocated to the region on the basis of gasoline sales, an index that would be expected to reflect the amount of mileage driven and, therefore, the user taxes paid by motorists for traveling on the region's roads and highways.

2. *User charges* consist of fares, tolls, and parking fees paid to local governments for the use of transportation facilities.

3. *Related income* consists predominantly of income from concessions directly associated with the operation of some transport facilities. Interest on investments is also included in this category of funds.

Indirect Users include persons, firms, and entire communities—all deriving an indirect benefit from the transport facilities. The contributions of indirect users usually do not bear a direct relationship to the use they make of

Table 5.1. Sources of Funds to Finance Transportation, by Facility* 1962 (millions of dollars)

Source of Funds	Government Roads and Highways	Authority Toll Roads, Bridges, and Tunnels	Mass Transit	Commuter Railroads	Private Bus Companies	Total	Percent of Total
Direct Users							
Federal User Taxes Earned	375.9					375.9	
State User Taxes Earned	430.2					430.2	
User Taxes Earned	806.1					806.1	31.1
User Charges Earned	22.1	202.2	331.0	122.7	153.3	831.3	32.4
Related Income	7.8	23.3	9.2	10.3	2.9	53.5	2.1
Total – Direct Users	836.0	225.5	340.2	133.0	156.2	1690.9	65.6
Indirect Users							
General Fund Appropriations, Special Assessments, and Other (Local)	268.9	–	161.1	5.7	–	435.7	16.9
Borrowings	106.0	209.6	129.7	5.5	–	450.8	17.5
Total Sources	1210.9	435.1	631.0	144.2	156.2	2577.4	100.0
Percent	46.9	17.0	24.5	5.6	6.0	100.0	

*Interfacility transfers and tax relief eliminated.

219

transportation facilities. These contributions are considered to reflect the payments for the social benefits received by localities from the transportation system. The present level of economic and social activity in the region would, of course, be impossible without the vast transportation system entwined throughout the region. Those who may not actually use the facilities, or those who make less than average use of them, nevertheless benefit from the system.

In the absence of a more precise measure, the statistical analysis assumes that the following sources of funds represent the contributions of indirect users:

1. *General fund appropriations for transportation services in excess of legal government user charges and related income.* Local user charges, transportation-related income of local governments are considered as payments by direct users. However, most local governments in the region channel such payments by direct users into their general funds. Therefore, these amounts are excluded from general fund appropriations in order to avoid double counting.[6]

2. *Special assessments.* Theoretically, special assessments are generally imposed in rough proportion to benefits directly received by the property owner. However, actual methods of assessment vary widely among local governments in the region and many governments report only one total for special assessments and real property tax yields. Therefore, special assessments are included in measuring the contributions by indirect users. However, this practice tends to understate the contributions of direct users.

A resident of the region, then, contributes to the transportation system in a dual capacity. For example, each time he registers his automobile or purchases gasoline, he contributes as a "direct user." Each time he pays his real property tax or a sales tax, he contributes as an "indirect user" to the extent that these payments may be allocated to transportation.

This system of classifying funds and the methods for allocating them to the region have the advantage of giving a clear picture of the flow of funds generated by the transportation system. It offers a more meaningful basis for evaluating financial policy than a system which restricts sources of funds to those which are actually made available for transportation purposes. Even though certain user payments flow directly into general funds and are then appropriated "back" to transportation, either wholly or in part, it is essential to provide a measure of the total contribution of the users to the region's transportation system.

This approach is at variance with the view that all user taxes returned to a region by the federal and state governments constitute subsidies to its transportation system. It is reasoned that if user taxes and charges are earned in a region, calling them a subsidy when they are returned is inappropriate. Transportation in a region is considered subsidized only to the extent that federal and state expenditures exceed user taxes earned there. Any particular region may, therefore, have a surplus or deficit of user taxes over federal and state expenditures on transportation.

Although transfer payments among individuals and governments are used to promote equity for all regions, it is important to identify the sources of all such transfer payments. If it is found that the donor is ailing, the transfer payment may not be justified on equity grounds; in fact, it may make no economic sense at all.

Out of the total of $2,579.4 million raised to finance transportation, direct users provided 65.6 percent ($1,690.9 million), indirect users—16.9 percent ($435.7 million), and the balance of 17.5 percent ($450.8 million) was obtained through borrowing.

Government roads and highways were the major source of funds, accounting for $1,210.9 million or 46.9 percent of the total. Mass transit followed with $631.0 million (24.5%). Authority toll roads, bridges, and tunnels accounted for $435.1 million (17.0%) and private bus companies contributed $156.2 million (6.0%) while commuter railroads provided the remaining $144.2 million (5.6%).

EXPENDITURES FOR TRANSPORTATION

Over two billion dollars were expended in 1962 to operate, maintain, and expand transportation facilities in the region. Operation and maintenance of facilities cost $1,082.9 million (51.3%), debt service accounted for an additional $309.3 million (14.7%), while the remaining $718.2 million (34.0%) represented capital outlay (see Table 2).

In addition to expenditures made by local governments in the region, maintenance includes monies spent by the state in the region on state highways, including the maintenance of condition, snow removal, traffic services, general administration expense on highway-related expenditures of appropriate state departments, and budget appropriations made to the region for highway purposes. Similarly, capital outlay expenditures include monies from the state and federal governments as well as local governments in the region for right-of-way, engineering, and construction expenses.[7] Thus, the accounting system used herein considers all capital outlays in the region financed by the states and federal governments as user taxes that are returned to the region. Since such capital outlays vary substantially from year to year, an attempt was made to ascertain whether the 1962 figures are representative. It was found that capital outlays financed with federal and state user taxes in 1962 overstated average annual expenditures for such purposes. To this extent, the estimate of a typical "transportation surplus" is understated.

In New York State, the average amount ($166.4 million) of contracts "let" in the region for the three-year period 1961-1963 was used as the estimate of construction expenditures, the major component of capital outlay. The balance of expenditures for capital outlay in New York includes $33.8 million for right of way and $8.1 million for engineering. This figure is apparently high because it reflects the atypical $230 million of contracts let in 1961, primarily for highways relating to the World's Fair. For example, the six-year average, 1958-1963, for contracts let was only $130.9 million. As a further test, both the Commission and the New York State Department of Public Works made estimates of capital expenditures on the basis of work completed during the year. The Commission estimate on this basis was approximately $170 million, compared with the $140 million-figure arrived at by the Department of Public Works. Thus, the estimate of $166.4 million for construction costs is toward the upper end of the range.

In New Jersey, the State Highway Department's estimate of $88.2 million was included as the capital outlay in the region. This figure compares favorably with the average of $90 million of capital outlay for the three fiscal years ending in 1962. In Connecticut, the State Highway Department's estimate of $39.8 million was included as the capital outlay in the region. This figure is approximately $8 million above the average outlay in Connecticut for the three years ending in 1962.

In terms of transportation facilities, expenditures on roads and highways and allied services amounted to $1,176.9 million and accounted for 55.7 percent of all disbursements for transportation in the region. Of this total, $843.2 million went for highway facilities operated by governments in the region and the remainder of $333.7 for authority operated roads, tunnels, and bridges. Expenditures on mass transportation amounted to $626.1 million (29.7%), while commuter railroads and private bus companies spent only $154.5 million (7.4%) and $152.9 million (7.2%).

THE TRANSPORTATION SURPLUS

The data presented above indicate that although $2,577 million were provided to finance the region's transportation "enterprise," only $2,110.4 million were applied to secure facilities and finance operations. Therefore, when viewed from a regional point of view, a transportation surplus of $467.0 million existed in 1962. The composition of this surplus is shown in Table 3.

The major components of the "regional surplus" are $203.1 million of state and $154.9 million of federal user taxes earned on government roads and highways but not expended on transportation in the region. This basic finding concerning the disposition of user taxes is in agreement with research conducted in other metropolitan areas in the United States. User taxes earned

Table 5.2. Expenditures by Type of Transportation Facility: 1962 (millions of dollars)

Expenditure	Government Roads and Highways*	Authority Toll Roads, Bridges, and Tunnels	Mass Transit	Commuter Railroads	Private Bus Companies	Total	Percent of Total
Operating Expenses	332.1**	67.2	392.8	149.0	141.8	1082.9	51.3
Debt Service	72.3	114.4	122.6	n.a.	‡	309.3	14.7
Capital Outlay	438.8	152.1	110.7	5.5	11.1	718.2	34.0
Financed by:							
Federal Government	220.8	3.0	—	—	—	223.8	10.6
State Governments	115.5	—	—	—	—	115.5	5.5
Borrowed Funds and Cash Reserves	102.5	149.1	110.7	5.5	11.1	378.9	17.9
Total	843.2	333.7	626.1	154.5	152.9	2110.4	100.0
Percent	39.9	15.8	29.7	7.4	7.2	100.0	

n.a. — not available.

* Includes expenditures on streets, toll and non-toll highways, ferries, parking, street cleaning, lighting, sidewalks, storm sewers, and police. State expenditures for these purposes as well as costs of tax collection have been allocated to the region.

**Financed by state funds, $111.6 million; federal funds, $0.2 million; and local funds, $220.3 million.

‡ Interest on debt included in operating expenses.

in high density areas are often used to finance transportation and other government services outside of the area.[8] In addition local governments realized a surplus of $6.2 million on current operations.

Toll roads, bridges, and tunnels in the region that were operated by public authorities earned a surplus of $40.9 million on current operations.

Current operations of private bus companies showed a surplus of $14.4 million. While the private bus industry is in a seemingly profitable position in the region, it is in part due to numerous tax concessions granted by various government agencies.[9] Losses of $10.3 million and $14.1 million were incurred by commuter railroads and mass transit facilities, respectively. The deficit for mass transit would have been substantially larger if it were adjusted for $161.1 million provided by New York City to finance the operating deficit.

Table 5.3 Analysis of the Transportation Surplus: 1962
(millions of dollars)

Government Roads and Highways	
Excess of Federal User Taxes over Federal Expenditures	154.9
Excess of State User Taxes over State Expenditures	203.1
Increase in Current Reserves of Local Governments	6.2
	364.2
Public Authority Toll Roads, Bridges, and Tunnels	40.9
Net Operating Surplus	
Mass Transit	
Net Operating Deficit	(14.1)
Commuter Railroads	
Net Operating Deficit	(10.3)
Private Bus Companies	
Net Operating Surplus	14.4
Total Current Operating Surplus	395.1
ADD: Change in Working Capital due to Capital Transactions of Public Authorities, Local Governments, and Private Bus Companies	71.9*
Total Surplus	467.0

*Includes $3.5 million surplus of borrowings over capital expenditures of local governments.

Source: Table 5.1, Table 5.2, and Table 5.4.

The remaining $71.9 million reflect changes in fund balances due to capital transactions of public authorities, local governments, and private bus companies. This last item is a residual, resulting mainly from temporary differences between sources and uses of funds provided from bond issues and applied to capital construction. An illustration is the temporary increase in funds of the New York City Transit Authority (NYCTA), resulting from bond sales that were $19.0 million in excess of the capital projects undertaken during the year under study.[10] This residual is, therefore, not meaningful for this analysis and is not considered in the study.

An analysis of the $395.1 million current transportation operating surplus by type of facility is presented in Table 5.4. The current operating surplus is computed on a cash-flow basis indicating the excess of current sources of funds over current expenditures. Since bond issues are viewed as non-current transactions, neither the funds provided by borrowings nor the capital outlay financed with borrowings are considered as current transactions. However, debt service on borrowings is viewed as a current expenditure. Where capital outlay is financed out of user taxes, it is regarded as part of current expenditures.

POLICY IMPLICATIONS

This overall approach to the financial analysis of a region's transportation system differs from those that seek to measure the economic profit or loss earned on particular transportation facilities. Such calculations involve a great deal of conjecture with respect to the magnitude of implicit costs and benefits such as depreciation, the value of time, etc. Furthermore, the calculation of economic profits is not of primary importance when studying the problem of financing transportation. As a practical matter, what is required is an estimate of the system's surplus funds that might be made available to finance the region's transportation needs. This estimate is provided by the procedures outlined in this study.

If only the $1,690.9 million of direct user taxes and charges earned in the region had been available to finance all of the $1,731.5 million of current disbursements—i.e., current operating expenses, debt service, and capital outlay financed with federal and state user taxes—the region's transportation system would have operated at a deficit of $40.6 million. This deficit is not distributed evenly among the various facilities. Government roads and highways, authority toll roads, bridges and tunnels, and private bus companies earn surpluses. The deficits of mass transit and commuter railroads more than offset these surpluses. Thus, transportation facilities may be classified as "winners" and "losers" and, because of the nature of the present underlying demand and the cost structure of each of these facilities, the same pattern will probably continue. However, if all the facilities are viewed as parts of a single enterprise, users alone would appear to contribute virtually enough funds to finance all disbursements.

Table 5.4. Analysis of the Transportation Current Operating Surplus by Type of Facility: 1962 (millions of dollars)

	Government Roads and Highways	Authority Toll Roads, Bridges, and Tunnels	Mass Transit	Commuter Railroads	Private Bus Companies	Total
Funds Provided by Direct Users	836.0	225.5	340.2	133.0	156.2*	1690.9
LESS: Operating Expenses, Debt Service, and Capital Outlay Financed with Federal and State User Taxes	740.7	184.6	515.4	149.0*	141.8	1731.5
Surplus (Deficit) Funds Provided by Direct Users over Expenditures	95.3	40.9	(175.2)	(16.0)	14.4	(40.6)
ADD: Funds Provided by Indirect Users	268.9	—	161.1	5.7*	—*	435.7
Surplus (Deficit) Funds Provided by Direct and Indirect Users over Expenditures	364.2	40.9	(14.1)	(10.3)	14.4	395.1

*The following adjustments were made in consolidating the statements of the region's facilities:

a. Tax relief of $12.7 million granted to commuter railroads in New York State and $1 million in Connecticut was not included in operating expenses nor in funds provided by indirect users.

b. Tax relief of $3.0 million granted to bus companies in New York State was not included in operating expenses nor in funds provided by indirect users.

c. User taxes and charges of $7.8 million paid by private bus companies for the use of toll roads, bridges, and tunnels were eliminated from funds provided by direct users and from the operating expenses of these companies.

Source: Basic data from Tables 5.1 and 5.2

226

In addition, indirect users contributed $435.7 million to maintain and improve the transportation system. Of this amount, $268.9 million were provided for the maintenance of local streets and roads and the operation of allied services. The balance, $166.8 million, was provided primarily for mass transit.

It is, of course, difficult to determine whether the funds provided by indirect users would have been provided to the transportation system if all direct user taxes earned in the region were returned to it. Nevertheless, it is also clear that communities should help to finance the transportation system in return for the social and economic benefits provided to the community at large.

Based on direct user charges and taxes and assuming continued financial support for those "externalities" or benefits accruing to the community at large, it can be stated that the transportation system more than pays for itself. In fact it appears to have "earnings" that justify expansion and/or improvement.

The major policy implications of the statistical findings are these—adequate funds for financing all mass transportation services in the region would be assured if

a) all funds earned in transportation at each level of government were pooled,
b) transportation services would have priority in the use of funds earned in transportation,
c) the allocation of funds earned in transportation to a region were in rough proportion to the monies earned in it, and
d) all transportation planning and administration were coordinated in one agency for the region or in a group of cooperating agencies.

IMPLEMENTATION OF RECOMMENDATIONS

A series of recommendations incorporating these policy implications were made in 1965 and are summarized in the accompanying Exhibit I. It is interesting to note that these recommendations reflect the legal and institutional constraints that impinge upon the decision-making process. Thus, no overall regional agency was proposed because of the legal difficulties in creating an interstate compact among three states, and the resistance that the then existing state and local organizations had to such an arrangment.

To date, all the organizational changes have been implemented:

1. A Federal Department of Transportation has been established.
2. Each of the three states—New York, New Jersey, and Connecticut—has coordinated the administration of all modes of transportation in one department.
3. In each state a commuter transportation agency has been organized with overall responsibility for mass transit facility operations. In fact,

the Connecticut Transportation Authority and New York's Metropolitan Transportation Authority have joint responsibility for the operation of the New Haven Railroad, which services both states. The three commuter agencies eventually could be combined into a single regional organization responsible for all mass transit operations in the region.

The recommendations relating to the flow of funds into the transportation system have as yet not been implemented. However, there has been some recent movement on the federal level in this direction:

1. President Nixon has called for the creation of a transportation fund in connection with his special revenue-sharing proposal for transportation and the requisite legislation has been introduced in Congress.
2. Secretary of Transportation Volpe and many Senators have urged the use of monies from the Highway Trust Fund for mass transit purposes until a Transportation Trust Fund is created.
3. On the regional level, surplus automobile tolls in New York and New Jersey now are being used to finance mass transit.

The slowness in implementation of the financial recommendations can be attributed to the greater impact of institutional constraints on such changes rather than those that are purely organizational. Thus, the automobile lobby on the federal and state level is still effective in its opposition to the creation of a single transportation fund, but it has yielded in its blanket opposition to the use of any automobile funds for other transportation purposes. In addition, on the federal level, the majority of the Senate and the House represent other than metropolitan areas; hence, these legislators have resisted the creation of a single transportation fund and oppose any shift in the present balance in the use of funds as between highways and mass transit facilities.

On balance, the major organizational changes that we proposed have been adopted. Although there has been some progress in the direction of the recommended methods of financing, concerted action is still required in this area. Crisis methods of financing, including the use of questionable bookkeeping procedures, are the dominant practice. A unified approach to financing does not yet exist. Thus, the financial data remain essentially the same and a study conducted in 1971 reveals the same basic needs.[11]

The deficit of the region's mass transit system increased to $420 million in 1969-70 and can be expected to increase substantially in the future. While no data are available on the "transportation surplus" for this period, we would conjecture that an overall surplus existed. Furthermore, even in the absence of a surplus, our financial recommendations would have made it possible to take a more balanced approach to financing transportation and to simplify the problem of allocating funds among individual forms of transportation in order to maximize the effectiveness of the system as a whole. Recommendations for financing mass transportation in the 1972 report[11] also reflected this philosophy. Thus, the organizational changes recommended and adopted were only a first step for attaining a balanced and financially sound system.

Studies, however, are only the first step in the slow process of implementing change. One is reminded of the old saying that "you can lead a horse to water but you can't make him drink." Hopefully, if you lead him there often enough he is sure to drink if he wants to survive. The process in government decision making is similar. Studies of the type presented here may help to show the way. Sooner or later, governments must act if metropolitan transportation systems are to remain viable.

Exhibit I

Summary of the Proposed Organizational
Framework and Flow of Funds for Financing
of Transportation

Governmental Level	Agency	Function	Source of Funds	Use of Funds
Federal	Department of Transportation	1. Coordinate transportation system for nation 2. Administer Federal Transportation Trust Fund to be set up by federal government	The Federal Transportation Trust Fund would be credited with all revenue from transportation related taxes	1. Payments to states for transportation projects; approval of regional planning agency required 2. Surpluses to General Fund of federal government
State	Department of Transportation	1. Coordinate transportation system in state 2. Administer state-operated transportation facilities 3. Construct state highways 4. Administer State Transportation Trust Fund to be set up in each state	The State Transportation Trust Fund would obtain funds from the following sources: 1. All revenue from transportation-related taxes 2. User charges from state-operated transportation facilities 3. Federal Transportation Trust Fund in proportion to funds raised in the region	1. Defray costs of state-operated transportation activities and construction of state highways 2. Transfer to a region of funds from Federal Transportation Fund 3. Payments to region from state transportation funds for transportation projects in proportion to funds raised by state in the region 4. Payments to local governments 5. Surpluses to General Fund of state

230

	Portion of each State in Region		
Mass Transit Commuter Authority	1. Operate or contract for the operation of mass transit and commuter service 2. Plan for improvement and expansion of mass transit and commuter facilities	1. User charges from operated facilities 2. State Transportation Trust Fund (including federal funds) 3. Receipts from local governments (station maintenance, etc.)	1. Carry out planning, operating, and investment functions relating to mass transit-commuter operations
Local Government	1. Operate and maintain local streets and roads and provide for allied services (including capital outlay)	1. User charges from operated facilities 2. State Transportation Trust Fund 3. General funds	1. Carry out indicated functions

231

APPENDIX I

The following methods of allocations and sources of data were used for Table 5-1.

I. Government Roads and Highways
   A. Federal User Taxes Earned
      Motor Fuel Tax. In all states, allocated on basis of ratio of gasoline station sales in counties in region to total gasoline sales in the state.
      Motor Vehicle Use Tax. In all states, on basis of ratio of truck registrations in region-portion of state to total for state.
      Automobile Tax. In all states, on basis of ratio of passenger cars and taxis registered in region-portion of state to total registrations in state.
      Truck, Buses, and Trailer Tax. In New York on ratio of trucks, buses, and trailers registered in region-portion of state to total registrations in state. In New Jersey and Connecticut, on basis of ratio of buses and commercial vehicles registered in region-portion to total in state.
      Parts and Accessories Tax. In all states, on ratio of region-portion of state total motor vehicle registrations to total registrations in state.
      Tires and Tube Tax and Tread Rubber Tax. In all states, on ratio of total motor vehicle registrations in region-portion of state to total registrations in state with trucks weighted one and one-half times.
      Source. U.S. Department of Commerce, Bureau of Public Roads, *Highway Statistics 1963,* Tables E-7 and E-8, and *Highway Statistics 1964,* Tables E-7 and E-8; *1963 Census of Business, Retail Trade,* Table 3 in respective state volumes.

   Data have been aggregated in this paper. Detailed breakdowns of the data by state and by facility may be obtained by writing to the authors.

   B. State User Taxes Earned
      Motor Fuel Tax. Allocation same as for federal taxes.
      Sources. 1963 Annual Report of Comptroller, State of New York, p. 36; *Fiscal Report, 1963,* New Jersey, Department of Treasury, p. IV; *Annual Report, 1962,* Comptroller, State of Connecticut, Schedule G-3.
      Motor Vehicle Tax.
         New York. Directly from *Annual Report, 1963* of New York State Department of Motor Vehicles.
         New Jersey. Allocated in proportion to motor vehicle registrations in region-portion to total for state. *Fiscal Report, 1963,* p. IV.

Connecticut. Total receipts from *Facts: 1962*, Connecticut State Motor Vehicle Department, p.38. All Parkway Toll Plate receipts allocated to region. Remainder distributed in proportion to motor vehicles in region to total for state.

Highway Use Tax.

New York. Total state receipts reported in the *1963 Annual Report of Comptroller*, p.36, were allocated in proportion to the sum of the estimates of motor fuel tax, motor vehicle tax, and fines and penalties in region to the total revenue from these sources in the state.

New Jersey. None.

Connecticut. Total state receipts reported in the *Annual Report, 1962*, Comptroller p.54, were allocated on the same basis as in New York.

Fines and Penalties.

New York. Total fines from *1963 Annual Report,* p.37, were allocated in proportion to mileage of state highway, arterial highway and interstate system in region to total in state as reported in *1963 Annual Report* of N.Y.S. Dept. of Public Works, p. 130.

New Jersey. One-half of collections reported in *Highway Statistics, 1962*, p. 42.

Connecticut. The total collected in the state as reported in *Highway Statistics, 1962*, p. 42, was only $2,000 and was not included.

C. User Charges Earned

Bus Excise Tax. New Jersey only. Receipts reported in *Fiscal Report 1963*, p. IV, were allocated in proportion to bus registrations in region to total in state.

Motor Vehicle Truck Increase. New Jersey only. Receipts reported in *Fiscal Report 1963*, p. IV, allocated in proportion to bus and truck registrations in region to total in state.

Parkway Tolls. In New York and New Jersey all tolls are collected by public authorities. In Connecticut all tolls on Wilber Cross-Merritt Parkway were allocated to the region. *Financial Report 1962* of Highway Dept., p. 7.

D. Related Income

Connecticut Only. Mainly gas station rents and royalties, rents of residences, land, and buses, and sales of commodity and services on Wilber Cross-Merritt Parkway as estimated by State Dept. of Highways.

E. General Fund Appropriations, etc.

New York City. Annual Report of the Comptroller of the City of New York 1962-63, p. 82, to which was added cost of traffic police and school crossing guards.

Rest of New York State. Compiled from IBM runs of Local Highway Finance Report received from N.Y. State Dept of Public Works.
New Jersey and Connecticut. Compiled directly from Local Highway Finance Reports submitted by local governments in region to Highway Departments of their respective states.

F. Borrowings
Same sources as I(E).

II. Authority Toll Roads and Bridges

The following authorities operated wholly in the region: Triborough Bridge and Tunnel Authority, Nassau County Bridge Authority, Jones Beach State Parkway Authority (Causeways and Southern State Parkway), East Hudson Parkway Authority (excluding non-region portion of Taconic Parkway). Data for these authorities are from their annual reports and consultations with authority officials. Only the moneys retained by the Triborough Bridge and Tunnel Authority on its Coliseum operations are included and make up part of the related income total.

The following authorities operate facilities that extend beyond the boundaries of the region: New Jersey Turnpike Authority, New Jersey Highway Authority, Connecticut Turnpike, New York State Thruway Authority, and New York State Bridge Authority. Data were derived from annual reports of these authorities and allocations were made from detailed breakdowns of revenues provided by authority officials.

Some of the operations of the Port of New York Authority are not included in the definition of transportation as used in this study (e.g., airports, marine terminals). Data, therefore, refer only to the bridge and tunnel, inland terminal, and heliport operation of the Authority. Data sources include published reports of the Authority and discussions with officials.

III. Mass Transit

The operation of PATH (Port Authority Trans-Hudson), New York City Transit Authority, Manhattan and Bronx Surface Transit Operating Authority, and Staten Island Rapid Transit are included in this category. Data were derived from authority reports and discussions with authority officials and staff of the New York City Comptroller's office.

IV. Commuter Railroads

The following commuter railroads are included: Long Island Railroad, New York Central, New York, Hartford and New Haven, Pennsylvania Railroad, Erie Lackawanna, Central Railroad of New Jersey and New York, and Long Branch Railroad. For methods of revenue and cost allocations, see Richard P. Brief, *An Aanlysis of Costs and Revenues of Suburban Service and Their Relationship to Government Service*, Tri-State Transportation Commission, 1965, mimeographed.

V. Private Bus Companies

Reports filed by 127 private bus companies with the Public Service Commission of the three states were reviewed with the assistance of officials of these agencies. Not included are small Class II or Class C lines generally owning only one or two buses, the Carey airport service, and the Fifth Avenue and Surface Transit lines in New York City, which terminated as privately owned carriers early in 1962.

APPENDIX II

The following methods of allocation and sources of data were used for Table 5.2

I. Government Roads and Highways
  A. Operating Expenses
    1. From State Funds

        a. *Maintenance of State Roads:* Includes maintenance of condition, snow and ice removal, and traffic services. In New York data were provided by Department of Public Works to which was added entire maintenance cost of maintenance of Palisades Parkway and portion of costs (allocated on basis of mileage in and out of the region) of Taconic State Parkway, as reported in *The Executive Budget 1962-63,* pp. 214-15, 217.

        In New Jersey and Connecticut, data were furnished by the respective Highway Departments.

        b. *Administrative Expense:* Total costs of various functions are from the budgets of all states and Highway Departments reports in New Jersey and Connecticut and discussions with officials of Dept. of Public Works and other departments in New York. The method of allocation is generally in proportion to a measure of the service offered in the region-portion to the total of that measure for the state. The agencies whose expenses were allocated and measure used follow:

        In New York, Motor Vehicle Department (registrations); Department of Public Service (buses registered, commercial vehicles registered, and railroads on opinion of office of Local Government); Department of Public Works (budget in region, local highway assistance, state road maintenance, and state capital outlay for highways); Department of Taxation and Finance (tax receipts); Office of Transportation (all); Office of Local Government (provided by office); Department of Audit and Control (state capital outlay for highways).

In New Jersey, State Highway Department (all railroads, state aid grants, highway construction expenditure); Department of Treasury (gasoline service state sales); Department of Public Utilities (all railroads, and motor carriers on basis of bus and truck registrations).

In Connecticut, State Highway Department (allocated by Highway Department's reporting system); Department of Motor Vehicles (registrations); Safety Commission (registrations); Public Utilities Commission (10% for railroads, bus, and trucks by registration); State Tax Department (motor fuel taxes collected).

c. *State Police:* In New York, in proportion to maintenance and general administration of state highways in region to total for state. State police costs on New York Thruway are reported as cost of the authority. In New Jersey and Connecticut, cost data were obtainable from the Division of State Police and the Department of State Police, respectively.

d. *Other:* In all states, the state's share of the Tri-State Transportation Commission studies. In Connecticut, also a portion of Highway Department's research and development costs.

e. *Assistance:* New York shares revenue from Motor Fuel Tax and Motor Vehicle Tax, and makes reimbursement for snow removal. In addition, all states make appropriations for road purposes from state General Funds. The aggregate amount of this contributed is considered part of the state-financed cost of operational. Data are from the Local Road Finance Work Sheets for all local governments but New York City. For New York City, data are from *1963 Annual Report of the Comptroller, State of New York,* p. 81.

2. From Federal Funds

The $0.2 million represent emergency relief storm damage received by New Jersey.

3. From Local Funds
Same source as Appendix I, I(E).

B. Debt Service
Same source as Appendix I, I(E).

C. Capital Outlay

1. Financed by Federal and State Funds
In New Jersey and Connecticut, the State Highway Departments provide data on federal and state expenditure on highways in the region for right-of-way, construction, and engineering.

In New York, data on right-of-way and engineering expenses were provided by the Department of Public Works. Data on construction were derived by applying the appropriate federal and state percentages to contracts let for each individual contract-interstate, ABC, and non-federal aid. An average for the three fiscal years 1961-1963 was taken.

2. Financed by Local Government (borrowed funds and cash reserves).
Same source as Appendix I, I(E).

II. All Other Modes of Transportation
Expenditures for other types of facilities were allocated and taken from sources as described in Appendix I.

NOTES–CASE 5

1. This study is a revised version of our report, "Transportation Finances in the Tri-State Region, A New Method of Reporting," Tri-State Transportation Commission, March 1968. The recommendations contained in this study were part of another report, "The Financing of Transportation in the Tri-State Region," undated. Our work began in September 1964. We are grateful to the Tri-State Transportation Commission, state and local governments, public authorities and private transportation agencies for making possible the collection of detailed data on which this study is based. However, the findings, conclusions, and opinions expressed in this paper are our responsibility, and the various governmental agencies involved in this study do not necessarily agree with them.

2. The name of the Tri-State Transportation Commission was changed to the Tri-State Regional Planning Commission in 1971.

3. The tri-state region covers an area of 8,000 square miles including New York City and seven additional New York State Counties (Dutchess, Nassau, Orange, Putnam, Rockland, Suffolk, and Westchester), ten New Jersey counties (Bergen, Essex, Hudson, Mercer, Middlesex, Monmouth, Morris, Passaic, Somerset, and Union), and six planning regions in Connecticut (Ansonia-Derby, Greater Bridgeport, Southwestern, Central Naugatuck, and South Central), including the hundreds of local government jurisdictions in these areas.

4. There is, in fact, a paucity of comprehensive data relating to the sources and uses of funds arising in transportation in metropolitan areas. The Bureau of Public Roads has provided such data for sample Metropolitan areas (excluding New York) but has limited its study to highway finance (Stanley F. Bielak and James F. McCarthy, *Highway Incomes, Expenditure, and User Tax Earnings in Standard Metropolitan Statistical Areas*, Bureau of Public Roads, 1965, mimeographed). The CED compiled aggregate data for large cities in the U.S., but also limited itself to highway finances (Committee for Economic Development, *Developing Metropolitan Transportation Policies*, April 1965). And Netzer prepared rough estimates for the New York Metropolitan Area but he was handicapped by lack of basic data (Dick Netzer, *The Financial Problem of New York Region's Suburban Rail Service*. Consultant's report to Regional Plan Association, Inc., Jan. 31, 1961, mimeographed). Although the data in this study relate to the year 1962, we know of no later data available.

5. All allocation procedures and data sources used for Table 5.1 are described in detail in Appendix I.

6. Therefore, the amount recorded as general fund appropriations of local governments under indirect users is net of these direct revenue sources.

7. All allocation procedures and data sources used for Table 5.2 are found in Appendix II.

8. Cf. G.P. St. Clair, "Congestion Tolls—An Engineer's Viewpoint," *Highway Research Record,* No. 47, 1964, pp. 93 and 95; Philip H. Burch, Jr., *Highway Revenue and Expenditure Policy in the U.S.,* New Brunswick, N.J., Rutgers University Press, 1962, p. 123; Robert W. Harbeson, "Some Allocation Problems in Highway Finance," *Transportation Economics,* New York, National Bureau of Economic Research, 1965, pp. 138-165; and J.R. Meyer, J.F. Kain, and M. Wohl, *The Urban Transportation Problem,* Cambridge, Mass., Harvard University Press, 1965.

9. These tax concessions are enumerated in detail in the *Special Report of the Law Committee,* American Transit Association, February 1964.

10. A similar increase of $60.5 million is reflected in the operations of Authority roads, tunnels, and bridges, and $3.5 million in operations of local governments. The balance reflects a decrease in accumulated surplus of private bus companies to finance capital outlays during the year.

11. Ernest Kurnow, Richard P. Brief, and Regina Reibstein, *Financing Mass Transportation, A Positive Approach,* Final Report of the Governor's Special Commission on the Financing of Mass Transportation, April 1972.

Case 6
Statement by Texaco, Inc., to the Air and Water Pollution Subcommittee of the Senate Public Works Committee, June 26, 1973*

MR. JOHN K. McKINLEY, President, and DR. W.J. COPPOC, Vice President

STATEMENT BY JOHN K. McKINLEY, PRESIDENT OF TEXACO INC.

Mr. Chairman, members of the Subcommittee. My name is John K. McKinley. I am President of Texaco Inc.

With me is Dr. W.J. Coppoc, Vice President in charge of our environmental protection activities.

Texaco welcomes the opportunity to offer its views concerning the recent decision of the Administrator of the Environmental Protection Agency to suspend for one year the 1975 Automobile Exhaust Emission Standards.

A longer and more technical paper covering Texaco's comments and suggestions will be submitted for the record.

As is generally recognized, the 1970 Amendments to The Clean Air Act constituted landmark legislation. They put our nation on the road to cleaner air and boldly challenged every citizen to help meet the high standards they set. Texaco fully supports these objectives. Back in 1970 it was impossible for anyone to foresee with any degree of accuracy many of the developments

*On June 26, 1973, Mr. John K. McKinley, President of Texaco, Inc., accompanied by Dr. W.J. Coppoc, Vice President of Texaco's Environmental Protection Department, presented a statement to the Air and Water Pollution Subcommittee of the Senate Public Works Committee covering Texaco's views concerning the recent decision of the Administrator of the Environmental Protection Agency to suspend for one year the 1975 automobile emission standards. Reprinted by permission of Texaco, Inc.

The additional material comprises supporting information to the statement offered on June 16, in compliance with Mr. McKinley's advice that such submission would be made for the record.

that have occurred in these two and a half years. Much new information on the atmosphere has become available; data have been obtained on the effects of exhaust emission control on automobile performance and fuel economy; shortages in the supply of petroleum fuels have become more evident; and the movement of crude petroleum and its products in world trade has assumed increasing international significance, while the balance of payments problem for America has worsened.

Texaco considers the deliberations of this committee on this subject to be of extreme importance to our nation and, indirectly, to the entire world.

Statement of Shortage

While the basic reasons for the 1973 shortages of petroleum products are both complex and controversial, there is little argument among those who have followed the matter closely that a very major factor is a lack of adequate refining capacity within the United States coupled with an inadequate supply of the correct kind of crude oil while demand for these products continues to soar. Whatever reasons each of us may feel are responsible for this refinery shortage, the fact remains that it cannot be corrected in a short period of time. The refinery shortage will exist in the United States for at least four years and perhaps longer. In the meantime, it behooves all of us to study every method through which the available refining capacity can most efficiently be used.

Looking to the years ahead, it is important to emphasize the growing nature of the United States' domestic crude oil shortage. The present total U.S. crude oil production of about 9.3 million barrels a day cannot fill the present domestic refining capacity of over 13 million barrels a day. Thus, major imports are already required.

As new U.S. refining capacity begins to come on-stream in significant quantities, the shortfall in domestic crude will be even more serious. It will take very large expenditures of capital and effort even to maintain U.S. crude oil production at the present 9.3 million barrel-a-day level for the remainder of this decade.

In the 1980s, the shortfalls will increase even further. What this means, of course, is that the nation will be increasingly dependent on imported crude to fill its energy gap because no other sources of energy—atomic, coal, shale, or tar sand—can make a major contribution in this time-frame. I need not repeat for this group what these growing imports mean to our trade balance.

It is against this background that we welcome an opportunity to review with you possibilities for amending automobile emission control standards in a way which will most intelligently conserve the natonal energy resources.

Emission Standards and Fuel Consumption

Of all the energy used in the United States, 25 percent is used in transportation—and half of that amount is used in motor vehicles. Petroleum is the energy source for cars because of the many advantages of liquid fuels. Because we are literally a nation on wheels, the United States today consumes about 60 percent of all the gasoline used in the world. Therefore, the miles per gallon obtained by U.S. automobiles has a major effect on the energy demand picture. In this context, it is important to examine the impact of exhaust emission controls on fuel consumption by U.S. automobiles.

Chart 1 presents a Texaco projection of additional petroleum demand which would result from meeting federal emission standards as currently mandated. The baseline for this projection is the National Petroleum Council forecast of December 1972. This study, as you know, assumes a given mix of car sizes over the period projected. Texaco has used the same assumption in its projection on this chart. If the actual mix were to reflect a larger proportion of smaller cars, it is evident that overall consumption would be lower. The proportionate petroleum losses, however, could be essentially the same.

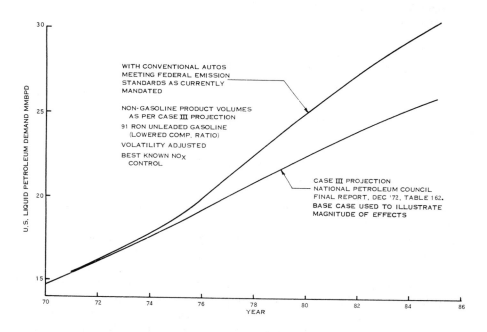

Chart 1. Impact of 1976 Emission Controls on U.S. Petroleum Demand to 1985

As you can see, the differential goes to over four million barrels a day by 1985. This represents more than 30 percent of the industry's present refining capacity.

A number of factors have combined in recent years to lower the gasoline mileage being obtained by the American automobile. From an average of slightly less than 14 miles per gallon in the early 1970s, there has been a significant drop, particularly in the 1973 model cars. Every day, all across the nation, our service station operators hear complaints from American motorists about the low mileage of their 1973 cars. There can be no questioning the fact that the consumers are becoming aware of this problem.

The factors to blame are several. Certainly larger cars with more power-driven accessories are among them. However, it is also clear that the emission control measures taken by the automotive industry to date have played a significant part and can, unless changes in presently planned requirements are made, play an even larger part in the future.

Energy Resource Losses

The specific automotive exhaust emission control measures which result in significant impact on the nation's energy resources fall primarily into two categories:

First, those associated with controlling the emissions of hydrocarbons and carbon monoxide with catalysts. These include

a) increased fuel consumption caused by lower compression ratios beginning with 1971 model cars (this was done in anticipation of the need for unleaded gasolines which present catalyst technology would require),

b) losses in refinery yields due to the manufacture of high-octane components required to replace tetraethyl lead used in fuels, and

c) inventory requirements for a lead-free, third grade of gasoline.

Second, the exhaust recycle devices being installed to control the level of nitrogen oxides are serious mileage reducers.

The combined impact of all of these measures is shown in the next chart (Chart 2). The baseline, once again, is the National Petroleum Council's forecast. The catalyst-related and the nitrogen oxide-related energy losses have been broken out separately. As you can see, by 1985 the loss associated with the catalytic devices alone would be accumulating at a rate of 1.2 million barrels of crude oil a day.

The nitrogen oxide penalties are shown for three different NO_X emission levels. One of these is the 1976 federal standard of 0.4 grams per mile which

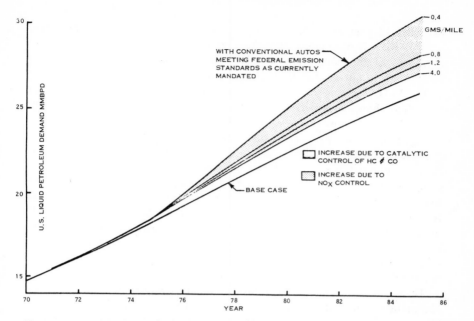

Chart 2. Impact of 1976 Emission Controls on U.S. Petroleum Demand to 1985

is the mandated 90 percent reduction from the 1971 models. The other two, 0.8 and 1.2 grams per mile represent 80 percent and 70 percent reductions.

The combined fuel penalties for exhaust emission control to the indicated levels would amount to more than 4 million barrels per day in 1985. The total penalty for the 1975-85 period is 10 billion barrels of oil, nearly one-fourth of the nation's total proven crude reserves, including Alaska.

Alternative Emission Control Strategies

Now let's examine the question "is there a better way to control automobile emissions?"

In view of many recent developments, we believe there is:

The stringency and time tables of present emission standards are forcing the automotive industry to adopt catalytic and exhaust recycle devices which, as has been seen, result in serious problems for the nation. Aside from the losses in fuel economy and the need for a special type of fuel, the manufacture of which itself is wasteful of crude, these devices will result in significant expense and maintenance difficulty for the American motorist. In light of these circumstances, this committee may wish to consider an alternative approach.

First, let us consider what could be done to remove the necessity for the use of catalytic control of hydrocarbons and carbon monoxide. If the nation were to accept the presently-stated 1975 interim standards for HC and CO

(1.5 and 15 grams per mile, respectively) as average—not maximum—values until 1980, it is our opinion that these levels could be met without the use of catalysts. As the committee is aware, the automotive industry has several options open to it for reaching such standards on an average basis.

By 1981 there is reasonable expectation that new engine technology (stratified charge or other) will be available and new, lower standards could reasonably be set now—to be accomplished by 1981.

Acceptance of these standards for the 1975-80 period would have important benefits for the American consumer. Since these standards could be met without the use of catalysts, it would be possible to resume pre-1971 compression ratios and the use of leaded gasoline. The secondary gains from these changes would be significant. The American motorist would be freed from dependence on an expensive and unproven temporary device; he would once again have automobiles with the economy and performance to which he is accustomed; and the oil industry would be freed from expensive conversion to a special fuel at a time when capital is badly needed for refinery expansion and the discovery of new oil and gas reserves.

Texaco recognizes that the return to higher compression ratios and the acceptance of leaded gasoline represent a sharp change in plans which have been underway for several years. Texaco itself has participated in these plans in good faith; many months ago it appropriated and has largely spent about $200 million in the installation of equipment to produce high-octane low-lead gasoline. This equipment is scheduled for completion in time to meet the EPA schedule for unleaded gasoline in 1974. It is also preparing to set aside the inventories and create the marketing facilities to handle this special fuel on a widespread basis.

Texaco is increasingly convinced, however, that in the face of the refining capacity and crude oil shortages we see in the years ahead, it is just not in the national interest to go ahead with the present catalytic technology which is wasteful of crude, wasteful of refinery capacity, and wasteful of capital sorely needed to increase our national energy resources.

Now let us look at the nitrogen oxide problem. The EPA has recently announced its conviction that nitrogen oxides are not presently of significance as an air pollutant in most parts of the nation. If, in addition to the steps outlined above for hydrocarbon and carbon monoxide standards, nitrogen oxide levels could be returned to those of the 1971 model cars (about four grams per mile) as an average requirement—once again, I stress the word "average"—exhaust recycle could be removed on all cars except those built to operate in California. We believe it feasible to establish California nitrogen oxide levels at 3.1 grams per mile for 1975 models and at 1.5 grams per mile for models from 1976 through 1980.

What is suggested involves a two-car strategy—one type car meeting more rigid NO_x standards for California and perhaps other critical areas, another type for marketing in the rest of the nation. This is a simple and a practical approach since neither type of car would require catalysts or special fuels.

Chart 3 illustrates the effect of this two-car strategy on energy demand. The actual HC,CO, and NO_x emission levels assumed for our calculations are included in the box on the chart for reference.

You will recall that my first chart showed a four million barrel-a-day crude loss from automotive emission control measures by 1985. These alternatives would save three million of these four million barrels a day—a tremendous incentive when added to the other advantages already cited. We believe it is worthy of your consideration.

However, it is predicated on the acceptance of leaded gasoline as the primary automotive fuel for the 1975-80 period and, inevitably, on acceptance of somewhat higher levels of automotive emissions over the period. Such levels would be higher than those that would result if original 1976 standards were achieved, but lower than actual emissions at present.

Stratified Charge Engine Technology

The strategy which we have asked you to examine is, of course, dependent upon the development of new engine technology by 1981 which will provide a continued lowering of those pollutants which come from automotive sources. Our basic point is that the nation will be better off by avoiding temporary catalyst technology and permitting the automotive industry to

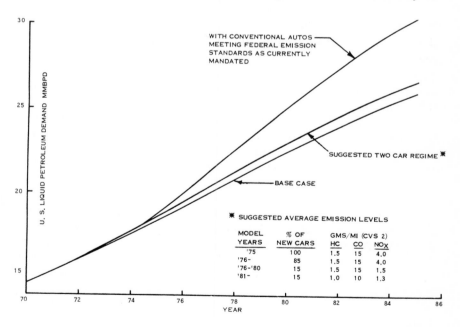

Chart 3. Effect of Suggested Emission Schedule on U.S. Petroleum Demand

focus directly on the development of internal combustion engines which will provide more energy-efficient means of controlling emissions.

Texaco has been interested in the development of such an engine for many years and, along with other organizations, has done research work on a stratified charge engine. Texaco does not represent itself as an engine builder and we do not offer our version of the stratified charge engine as any panacea for the present problem. Work with the engine, however, has given our research people at Beacon, New York, detailed background on combustion behavior and some of the possibilities offered by the stratified charge engine.

Even at its present stage of development, the stratified charge engine would have a significant effect on fuel demand. Our research indicates that multi-fuel stratified charge engines, if introduced around the end of this decade, could by 1985 be saving an additional two million barrels a day of crude beyond the two-car strategy which we have discussed. It is recognized, of course, that there are other approaches to new engine technology which are equally promising.

Ambient Air Standards

A very important factor in the whole energy picture is the ambient air quality standards. These were established by EPA in accordance with the Act, which required that a very rigid criterion for health effects be applied and, in addition, called for an adequate margin of safety. Primary, or health-related, standards are to be achieved by 1975, with provisions for up to a two-year delay.

Automobile exhaust emission controls have been an important part of the implementation plans presented by several states for meeting hydrocarbon, carbon monoxide, nitrogen dioxide, and oxidant standards.

Even if the 1975-76 automotive emission standards were implemented on schedule, it has become evident in recent weeks that many parts of the nation expect to experience great difficulties in meeting the standards on the required time table. This is further substantiated by a review of the letters from state governors who have submitted transportation control plans outlining their programs designed to meet ambient standards by 1975.

The plans proposed by EPA for some of the states whose plans were considered unsatisfactory would cause severe hardships. Certainly, these standards and the plans devised to meet them should be reviewed to determine whether such hardships are necessary to protect human health and whether the margin of safety in the plans is greater than the anticipated benefits justify.

Sulfur Limitations

Now, let's examine some of the problems which relate to supplying adequate quantities of low-sulfur fuels.

Sulfur restrictions are, of course, an important part of the nation's clean air program—and real progress is being made. For example, the sulfur dioxide content of New York City's winter air has dropped to 35 percent of its value three years ago.

On the other hand, there are serious problems connected with the supply of low-sulfur fuel oil. A continuing construction program involving expensive desulfurizers, which in no way add to overall capacity, must be undertaken at the very time that refinery capacity increase is a pressing national need.

Nor can imports be looked to for a solution. In Texaco's view, it is not realistic for the United States to count on major volumes of gasoline and low-sulfur fuel imports over the next few years because of the close energy balance that exists throughout the world. These products are coming into increasingly short supply as the other developed nations of the world want them in ever-growing quantities.

For these reasons, it would appear prudent to review the legislation and regulations relating to sulfur restrictions to ensure that they are no more stringent than actually necessary for the regions involved.

Non-Degradation and the National Environmental Policy Act

Two other related subjects require brief comment:

The first of these is the recent Supreme Court decision upholding "non-degradation" as a principle of The Clean Air Act. At this time, it is not possible to evaluate completely the far-reaching implications of this decision. Nonetheless, we have a deep-rooted concern that new refinery construction could be brought to a halt or significantly delayed by this interpretation of the law. We fail to see why projects designed to fulfill the basic needs of the people should be at issue provided that these projects meet ambient standards that are realistically set for the protection of health and welfare. We urge the Congress to reconsider the non-degradation principle by adopting an appropriate amendment to the law.

Similarly, we are concerned about the time requirements for the preparation and approval of impact statements required by The National Environmental Policy Act. Whereas we are in complete agreement with the overall objectives of this program, we attach the utmost importance to close cooperation of all concerned so that vital new construction projects are not unduly delayed.

Major new product volumes for the U.S. markets cannot be expected until new refining capacity is actually in operation.

Summary

In summary, Texaco suggests that you may wish to consider the following four changes in the law:

First, to consider amending The Clean Air Act to empower the appropriate governmental agency to establish new standards for hydrocarbon and carbon monoxide emissions over the 1975-80 time period which would eliminate the need for catalytic exhaust devices.

Second, to review the nitrogen oxide situation. If it is determined that the EPA evaluation is correct, consideration should be given to relaxing the nitrogen oxide standards for non-critical areas so that exhaust recycle will not be required. We also suggest that you consider a two-car strategy so that exhaust recycle-equipped cars, not requiring catalysts or special fuels, would be sold in California and other critical areas.

Third, to consider a reevaluation of the national standards for ambient air quality and the criteria used for setting those standards. It might be well to review the health and welfare bases of the standards and the time tables for their implementation. We also suggest consideration of the varying geographical and meteorological conditions that exist across the nation. A single standard for clean air quality on a nationwide basis may not be defensible.

Fourth, to review the time requirements for implementation of sulfur standards. The growing energy supply problems of the nation will need to be balanced against its health and welfare needs.

Conclusion

I want to close by reaffirming Texaco's support of the objectives of The Clean Air Act. The suggestions which have been made here today have stemmed from our belief that national circumstances have changed significantly since the Act of 1970 was passed.

The health, welfare, and social aspects of these proposals are matters for your judgment. If these proposals are acceptable in that regard, it is our judgment that they would result in a major improvement in the national energy situation.

Thank you very much. Dr. Coppoc and I are ready for any questions you may have.

SUPPORTING INFORMATION

Statement of Shortage

Introduction

The United States is heavily dependent upon petroleum for its energy needs and at the present time consumes daily some 17 million barrels of oil, or slightly more than 700 million gallons. This, plus 60 billion cubic feet per day of natural gas, constitutes 78 percent of the nation's total energy requirements.

The present shortage of petroleum products has been caused by factors rooted in the total energy supply dilemma we are experiencing today. The obvious cause of this scarcity is unprecedented demand and restricted supply. Restrictions on free market action, both in the past and at present, have increased supply problems at a time when U.S. crude oil production has leveled off and is now declining.

For many years, the industry has pointed out the need for additional incentives and for the relaxation of government restrictions. In the past two years, industry groups and individual companies have repeatedly warned the country of the impending shortage through statements before Congress and state and federal agencies and in advertisements and other publications.

The specific causes of the shortage, which are discussed below, include the long-standing federal controls on natural gas prices, the environmental restrictions on the use of coal and high sulfur fuel oils, the declining domestic crude production, the lack of adequate refining facilities, the accelerated increase in gasoline demand and the lack of development of alternate energy sources.

Shortage of Natural Gas

The imposition of controls on prices of natural gas by the Federal Power Commission has been a major reason for the developing energy shortage in the United States. These controls have kept prices at unrealistically low levels for some 15 years while costs of exploring for, developing, and marketing this resource have increased sharply. These low prices have made natural gas very attractive to consumers but unattractive to producers, who had little economic incentive to assume the heavy financial risks of exploring for new reserves of natural gas. Thus, these artificially low prices contributed to a serious imbalance between the demand for and supply of natural gas.

Moreover, the recent decline in the production of natural gas resulted in an increased demand for middle distillates (home furnace oil, diesel fuel, and jet fuel are all middle distillates) by industrial users due to the environmental restrictions on the use of high sulfur coal and residual fuel oil which could otherwise have been substituted for natural gas. As gas became scarce, public utilities and other large users of natural gas were forced to use middle distillates despite the fact that this was clearly an undesirable use of these fuels. Electric utility demand alone has risen to 186,000 barrels per day in 1973 from an insignificant 8000 barrels per day in 1967.

Decline in Domestic Crude Oil Production

Domestic production has not kept up with increased demand and has, in fact, decreased in recent years despite the fact that the major oil fields in the U.S. have been producing at their maximum efficient rate. Proved crude oil reserves decreased 1.7 billion barrels in 1972.

The potentially large reserves of crude oil in the Outer Continental Shelf have not been tapped due largely to strong expressions of environmental concern. An estimated 10 billion barrels of crude oil in Alaska has not been used to meet the energy needs of the U.S. because of opposition to the construction of a pipeline.

The high cost of exploration activity has also been a cause of the increased shortage. Whereas incentives are needed to encourage industry to explore new areas, Congress in passing the Tax Reform Act of 1969 increased the tax burden on the oil industry by $500 million annually, thereby depriving the industry of funds which might otherwise have been used for drilling of exploratory wells.

Restrictions on Coal and High Sulfur Fuels

The U.S. has vast coal reserves which, it is estimated, could supply our energy needs for the next 300 years. Nevertheless, as a result of the artificially low price of natural gas, environmental opposition to the mining of coal, and restrictions on the use of high-sulfur content coal, this mineral today supplies only 18 percent of the nation's energy. Moreover, the development of technology for the removal of sulfur from coal has not yet reached commercial reality. Certainly the necessary provisions must be made to make this huge energy reserve available for use.

As explained above, environmental restrictions have also limited the use of residual fuel oil with high sulfur content as a source of industrial energy. Manufacturing and commercial businesses turned first to natural gas and, as this supply dwindled, to middle distillates. This unprecedented demand for middle distillates contributed to the recent fuel oil and gasoline shortages.

Lack of Adequate Refining Facilities

As a result of the increasing demand for petroleum products in the United States, refineries have been operating at their highest levels and production of gasoline and middle distillate fuels is today at an all-time high. Nevertheless, there is not sufficient refinery capacity in the United States to meet demand. Moreover, due to the worldwide product shortage, it has been difficult to find foreign products for importation into the U.S. Also, the controlled product prices in the United States are generally below those on the world market.

The lack of refinery construction has been at least partially caused by difficulties in finding sites due to environmental considerations. For example, although 40 percent of U.S. petroleum demand is in states along the eastern seaboard which have only 12 percent of domestic refinery capacity, plans for two major new refineries for the northern Atlantic Coast area were shelved as a result of environmental restrictions.

The uncertain availability of crude oil in the future has also been a factor in delaying the construction of refining capacity, as has been the uncertainty which has prevailed over whether to plan for leaded or unleaded gasoline, for example.

Increase in Gasoline Demand

The U.S. energy shortage has been substantially aggravated by the very large increases in gasoline consumption which have occurred over the past ten years and particularly in 1972 and 1973. This is borne out by the fact that the gasoline consumption increase of 6.7 percent between 1971 and 1972 has grown to 7.7 percent between comparable periods of 1972 and 1973.

Contributing to the increased consumption are the record auto sales (a 19 percent increase in the first quarter of 1973 over the like period of 1972) and drastic reductions in mileage per gallon. This reduction has arisen as a result of increases in optional equipment on autos such as air conditioners and power equipment and because of automotive emission control devices.

Lack of Development of Alternate Energy Sources

The energy shortage today is due also to failure to develop alternate sources of energy such as nuclear energy, which had been counted on to supply much of the increase in stationary power-generating capacity.

Although some nuclear power plants are being constructed, they have not been built and completed at the rate which was anticipated in the late 1950s and early 1960s. In 1968 the Department of Interior estimated that reactor capacity by 1973 would be three times what it is today.

The U.S. has substantial reserves of heavy oil, tar sands, and oil shale, but the expense of developing such reserves has been so great as to make development unattractive to investors under prevailing product price levels.

Emission Standards and Fuel Consumption

Of all the energy used in the United States, about 25 percent is used in transportation—and half of that amount is used in motor vehicles. These figures were calculated from the data in Table 22, page 37, of *U.S. Energy Outlook*, National Petroleum Council, December 1972. These data indicate that in 1970 the total U.S. energy demand was 67.8 quadrillion BTUs (British Thermal Units), of which 16.3 quadrillion BTUs (24.1%) was required for transportation. Since estimates of growth in the transportation sector for the decade 1970-1980 were projected in that table as about the same as the average for all sectors, the percentage is felt to be valid in 1973 as well. The statement that about half of the energy demand for transportation was used in motor vehicles was derived by comparing the BTUs represented by the 65,649 million gallons of gasoline used in U.S. passenger cars in 1970, 8.0 quadrillion, with the 16.3 required for transportation. This gives 49 percent.

The United States today consumes about 60 percent of all the gasoline used in the world. Data compiled by our Economics and Finance Department indicate a total free world demand in 1972 of 10,829,000 barrels per day (BPD), of which the U.S. demand was 6,422,000 or 59.2 percent. Therefore, the miles per gallon obtained by U.S. automobiles has a major effect on the energy demand picture. In this context it is important to examine the impact of exhaust emission controls on fuel consumption by U.S. automobiles.

In order to show the total impact of imposing the automotive emission standards of 1975 and of 1976 and beyond on passenger vehicles in the U.S., Chart 1 was presented on June 26. The National Petroleum Council Study for the Department of the Interior, Summary Report "U.S. Energy Outlook" dated December 1972, Case III, was used as the reference base for this chart. Case III assumed a 4.2 percent average annual energy consumption growth rate for the period 1971-1985. This growth rate was an intermediate value chosen for a range of growth rate values 3.4-4.4 considered probable by the National Petroleum Council (NPC). The NPC study also assumes a given mix of car sizes over the period projected. Texaco has made these same assumptions in its projection on Chart 1. If the actual mix were to reflect a larger proportion of smaller cars, it is evident that overall consumption would be lower. The penalty for emissions control, however, would still be a substantial factor.

The detail of the accumulation of fuel economy penalties associated with the control of the hydrocarbon, carbon monoxide, and oxides of nitrogen is covered in the discussion of the specifics of Charts 1 and 2 under the caption "Energy Resource Losses."

In the calculation of the cumulative effect of the emission controls of the amount of fuel required for the period through 1985 the rate of replacement of old cars by new models was taken into account. Historical data on new car sales from industry figures and vehicle scrappage estimates were used in the projection of the car population by model year. The fuel economy factors associated with the engine modifications necessary to meet the applicable emission standards and the fuel processing demands in the refineries to meet the necessary special fuels were also taken into account.

Since all the factors have been estimated as percentage deviation from the base case, the magnitude of the total penalty would be applicable to any other base case used. This is true provided due cognizance is given to the degree to which the pertinent factors are considered in the overall study.

By comparing the two curves in Chart 1, it can be seen that the differential is over four million BPD in 1985. Since the U.S. petroleum industry refinery capacity[1] as of January 1, 1973, is 13.38 million BPD, the differential in Chart 1 represents more than 30 percent of that capacity.

A number of factors have combined in recent years to lower the gasoline mileage being obtained by the American automobile. Without making an attempt to analyze the reasons for the decrease, Fig. 6.1 shows[2] a plot of the miles per gallon of the average car in this country for the period 1954-1970. One can see the decrease from a value of about 14.6 in 1954 to a value of 13.6 in 1970. Similar data on the miles per gallon of an average car in the car population for years subsequent to 1970 is not currently available from the same source. However, to indicate the trend from 1970 to the present, we have attached Table 6.1 which contains uncorrected data from the EPA report "Fuel Economy and Emission Control," published in November 1972. The data on which that report was based have been statistically analyzed by Texaco and the results obtained are shown in Table 6.2. Both sets of data indicate a decrease in miles per gallon for 1971-1973 cars relative to 1957-1967 cars. The amount of economy loss is generally higher with the heavier cars.

The data in Tables 6.3 and 6.4 were obtained during comparable periods from 1972 and 1973 on Texaco employee cars used in normal suburban service. On the basis of these data the 11.3 average mile per gallon figure for 1972 cars dropped 7 percent to the 10.5 miles per gallon figure in 1973. The 1973 cars differed from the 1972 models by only 1.9 percent in average weight.

Additional data covering both independent work and analysis of the EPA data mentioned above were covered in the paper by E.N. Cantwell *et al.* of

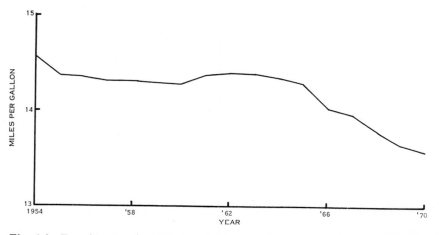

Fig. 6.1. Trend in Average Miles Per Gallon Obtained. Basis Total Car Population

Source: *Automotive Facts and Figures,* 1956-1972.

Table 6.1. Average (Uncorrected) Fuel Consumption for 1957-67, 1968-70, and 1971-73 Cars

Inertia Weight	1957-67 Base Gal/Mi x 100	1968-70 Gal/Mi x 100	1968-70 % Change From 1957-67	1971-73 Gal/Mi x 100	1971-73 % Change From 1957-67
		Automatic Transmission Cars			
2000		4.58*	—	4.37*	—
2250		5.37	—	4.82*	—
2500	4.94*	6.05	22.5	5.29	7.1*
2750	6.20	5.66	8.7	5.74	-7.4
3000	6.93	6.86	-1.0	6.40	-7.7
3500	7.72	7.82	1.3	7.40	-4.2
4000	8.30	8.69	4.3	9.08	9.4
4500	8.83	9.28	5.1	9.99	13.1
5000	9.28	10.36	11.6	10.97	18.2
5500	9.72*	10.19	4.8*	11.51	18.4*
		Manual Transmission Cars			
2000	4.34	4.64	6.9	4.31	-0.7
2250	4.78*	5.15	7.7*	4.91	2.7*
2500	5.04*	5.44	7.9*	5.14	2.0*
2750	5.88	5.11*	-13.1*	5.67	-3.6
3000	6.14	5.86	-4.5	7.03	14.5
3500	6.98	7.82	12.0	7.72	10.6
4000	7.51	8.94	19.0	9.75	29.8
4500	7.89*	8.07*	2.3*	10.38	3.2*
5000	—	—	—	10.05	—
5500	—	—	—	12.84*	—

*Based on less than five (5) cars.

Source: EPA, "Fuel Economy and Emission Control," November 1972.

Table 6.2. Fuel Consumption for 1957-67, 1968-70, and 1971-73 Cars From Statistical Analysis by Texaco

Inertia Weight	CID*	1957-67 Gal/Mi x 100	1968-70		1971-73	
			Gal/Mi x 100	% Change From 1957-67	Gal/Mi x 100	% Change From 1957-67
Automatic Transmission Cars						
2000	100	4.42	4.84	10.0	4.23	−4.0
2500	150	5.51	5.65	3.0	5.40	−2.0
3000	200	6.47	6.46	0	6.53	1.0
3500	250	7.30	7.27	0	7.64	5.0
3500	300	7.79	7.75	0	8.07	4.0
4000	300	8.00	8.09	1.0	8.72	9.0
4000	350	8.43	8.57	2.0	9.14	8.0
4500	350	8.57	8.90	4.0	9.77	14.0
4500	400	8.94	9.38	5.0	10.17	14.0
5000	400	9.02	9.72	8.0	10.79	20.0
Manual Transmission Cars						
2000	75	4.42	4.79	8.0	4.36	−1.0
2000	100	4.67	4.83	3.0	4.61	−1.0
2500	150	5.30	5.30	0	5.64	6.0
3000	200	5.99	6.04	1.0	6.76	13.0
3500	300	7.31	7.54	3.0	8.61	18.0
4000	300	7.53	8.34	11.0	9.28	23.0
4000	350	8.14	8.96	10.0	9.96	22.0

*CID − cubic inch displacement (a measure of engine size)

Source: Texaco analysis of EPA, "Fuel Economy and Emission Control," November 1972.

DuPont before the May API Meeting in Philadelphia.[3] Their data for a six-car matched fleet showed an average increase in fuel consumption of 9.4 percent for the 1973 cars compared with 1970 of equal weight. These data indicate that, although there is some variation in the magnitude of the differences depending on the method of measurement, car selection, driving mode, etc., there is basic agreement that 1973 cars consume more fuel than comparable cars of the past years. There can be no questioning the fact that the consumers are becoming aware of this problem.

Table 6.3. Fuel Economies of Vehicles on a Texaco Employee Car Test

1972 Vehicles

Make	CID*	Vehicle Wt., Lbs.	MPG**
Buick	350	3571	9.8
Chevrolet	250	3198	11.9
Chevrolet	307	3250	11.4
Chevrolet	350	4115	10.3
Chevrolet	350	4685	8.8
Chevrolet	350	4350	10.9
Chevrolet	400	5201	8.0
Chevrolet	400	4829	10.2
Oldsmobile	350	3425	12.2
Pontiac	400	4006	10.8
Pontiac	400	4855	10.3
Ford	351	4051	11.6
Mercury	351C	3351	14.0
Chrysler	400	4330	11.8
Plymouth	318	2900	16.3
Plymouth	318	3357	13.8
Plymouth	360	3830	10.4
AVG		3959	11.3

*CID — cubic inch displacement
**MPG — miles per gallon

The factors to blame are several. Certainly larger cars with more power-driven accessories are among them. However, it is also clear that the exhaust emission control measures taken by the automotive industry to date have played a significant part and can, unless changes in presently planned requirements are made, play an even larger role in the future.

Energy Resource Losses

Measures necessary to meet automotive emission standards have a significant impact on the nation's energy resources. These may be grouped in

Table 6.4. Fuel Economies of Vehicles on a Texaco Employee Car Test

1973 Vehicles

Make	CID*	Vehicle Wt., Lbs.	MPG**
Chevrolet	350	5795	9.1
Chevrolet	350	4226	9.4
Chevrolet	307	3859	11.1
Oldsmobile	455	4684	7.4
Oldsmobile	350	4387	8.3
Pontiac	400	4477	9.0
Pontiac	350	3442	11.2
Ford	302	3642	8.4
Ford	351C	3642	10.3
Ford	351	4100	11.6
Ford	351	4545	9.1
Ford	400	4098	12.3
Plymouth	225	3045	14.5
Plymouth	318	3163	10.5
Plymouth	318	3211	14.6
Plymouth	360	3860	12.4
Plymouth	360	4420	9.3
	AVG	4035	10.5

*CID — cubic inch displacement
**MPG — miles per gallon

terms of their effects into factors related to control of (1) hydrocarbons (HC) and carbon monoxide (CO) and (2) oxides of nitrogen (NOx). These are discussed in the following sections.

Control of HC and CO

In 1966, control of automobile exhaust emissions was initiated in California and followed nationwide in 1968. Since that time, the degree and extent of the controls have increased in severity at specified intervals. The automotive manufacturers have, in general, been able to comply with the established standards up to the present time by various engine and vehicle modifications as well as by supplementary devices such as air injector reactors. However, in viewing the future standards originally set for 1975 and 1976 by The Clean Air Act Amendement of 1970, it appeared that the engine modification route would no longer be adequate. It was generally concluded that catalytic converters would be required in the exhaust systems of cars to meet the future low limits.

These devices, however, would require an unleaded gasoline in order to achieve an acceptable service life. Further, it was recognized that the petroleum industry would be unable to supply an unleaded gasoline with octane numbers of the leaded fuels currently marketed and cars would have to be made capable of operating knockfree with a lower octane quality fuel. Therefore, beginning with 1971 model cars, engine compression ratios were lowered in anticipation that future catalyst technology for exhaust emissions control would require unleaded gasolines of nominal 91 Research Octane Number.

Reduced compression ratio decreases engine efficiency which, in turn, increases fuel consumption. Considerable information has been published on the magnitude of the fuel consumption increases between 1970 and 1971 model cars due to compression ratio and associated changes in vehicles, ranging up to about 7 percent. Texaco, for the purposes of this calculation, has used 5.4 percent for this penalty. This loss was determined from an analysis of the data contained in the Environmental Protection Agency Report, "Fuel Economy and Emission Control," November 1972. The analysis provided for correction of the data for car weight and car population factors. Such a loss creates an increase in refinery crude run of 2.7 percent.

In addition, the requirement for unleaded gasolines generates a refinery yield loss due to the need to manufacture high octane components to displace the tetraethyl lead normally used in fuels to produce satisfactory octane levels. Commercial gasolines are composed of a number of blending components. The overall octane quality of these fuels can be upgraded by changing the octane quality of the individual blending components, a major one of which is reformed gasoline. However, as octane upgrading occurs, a reduction in gasoline yield is obtained. This is illustrated in Fig. 6.2 which shows the octane-yield relationship of a typical Texaco reforming unit with a typical charge stock. The overall effect of producing unleaded gasoline on the gasoline base pool avails is shown in Fig. 6.3. Here, a typical gasoline base pool quality unleaded of 88 Research Octane Number is noted. If it is necessary to increase this to 91, a loss of 1.7 volume percent in total gasoline avails is experienced. This is equivalent to an additional requirement of crude run in a refinery of about 0.8 percent and is the penalty Texaco has assigned in its calculations for increased crude demand for the manufacture of unleaded gasoline.

It has been proposed by some members of the automotive industry that more restrictive distillation specifications should be adopted for the control of gasoline volatility.[4] Such restriction would serve to eliminate some of the fractions currently used in making motor fuels and would serve to reduce the volume available. Texaco conservatively estimates that its operations would require another 2.6 percent of crude to compensate this loss.

The foregoing has dealt with penalties from engine changes and unleaded fuel manufacture. Additionally, there would be an initial requirement to fill the distribution facilities of a third-grade sytem with unleaded gasoline. This represents a large volume of fuel that would not be available to the motorist. However, since it is a one-time occurrence, no allowance has been assessed against it in the calculation of increased energy demand due to automotive exhaust emission controls.

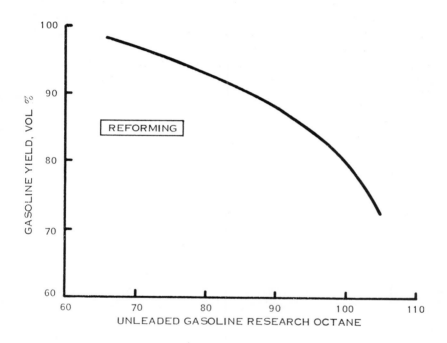

Fig. 6.2 Reformed Gasoline Yields vs. Quality

Control of NOx

Essentially, the control of NOx can be attained either by inhibiting its formation during the engine combustion phase of the cycle or through the use of reducing catalysts in the exhaust system. The rate of oxidation of nitrogen is a function of the ratio of fuel and air and is also temperature dependent. This latter effect can be controlled in an engine by reducing peak combustion temperatures through such means as exhaust gas recirculation or by retarding the timing of the combustion event in the engine cycle—by late spark timing, for example. It may also be alleviated by retarding combustion to reduce the rate of temperature rise during the combustion process. However, any means used to reduce combustion temperatures degrades engine efficiency. This fundamental fact cannot be circumvented.

Reducing catalysts are under development for NOx control. These also impart a fuel economy loss to engine operation since the engine must be operated with an air-fuel mixture rich enough to produce a suitable level of carbon monoxide (CO) to permit the catalytic reduction of nitrogen oxides (NOx). In dual catalyst control practice, the reducing catalyst is generally placed next to the engine and is followed by an oxidizing catalyst. The latter operates with supplementary air, converting unburned hydrocarbons and any remaining CO to water and carbon dioxide.

In 1973, the imposition of a maximum limit of 3.1 grams per mile for automotive exhaust NOx control fostered the use of exhaust gas recirculation

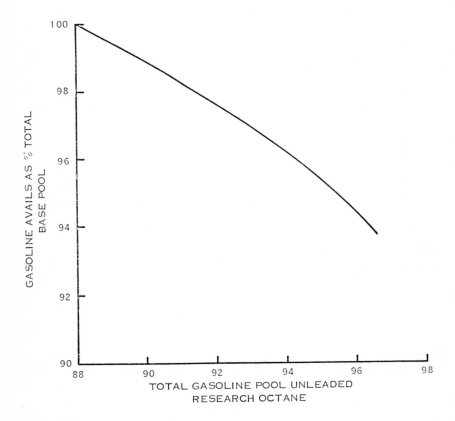

Fig. 6.3. Gasoline Avails vs. Quality

and retarded ignition timing on most engines for its compliance. Current 1976 standards severely increase this control standard requirement to 0.4 grams per mile. This standard will have a significant deleterious effect on automobile engine fuel economy as noted in Fig. 6.4. This figure presents a compilation of data obtained from a study of the effect of NO_x control on fuel economy made by the Aerospace Corporation in 1971 for the Environmental Protection Agency. Their report covers consideration of automotive industry prototype systems. Also included are information from Toyota, a summary report by the Inter Industry Emission Control (IIEC) program and tests by Texaco on its stratified charge TCCS engine. Some of the Texaco data were obtained in a conventional "Jeep" engine (L-141) converted to operate as a stratified charge engine. The engine was modified to meet 1976 emission standards, operated for 50,000 miles at 40 mph level road load in an M-151 ¼ ton 4 x 4 truck and continued to meet 1976 standards at the end of the test. Figure 6.4 indicates that at an NOx level of 4 grams per mile, there is essentially no fuel economy penalty. This is the average level of NOx emissions taken for uncontrolled 1971 model passenger cars. However, as permissible levels of exhaust NOx are reduced, fuel consumption increases exponentially until at the 1976 level of 0.4 grams per mile it amounts to a penalty of 30-40 percent.

In calculating the effect of 1976 emission control standards on energy demand, Texaco has used a vehicle fuel consumption penalty of 30 percent from Fig. 6.4 corresponding to a NOx limit of 0.4 grams per mile. This represents an increase in crude run of 15.0 percent. To evaluate the effect of less severe NOx restrictions, incremental energy demand increases were also calculated for 0.8, 1.2, and 4.0 grams per mile. The applicable fuel economy penalties taken for these were 10, 5, and 0 percent with equivalent increases in crude run requirements of 5, 2.5, and 0 percent, respectively.

The incremental factors discussed above were used to calculate the increase in energy requirements due to exhaust emission controls as plotted in Charts 1 and 2 of the presentation made to the Air and Water Pollution Subcommittee of the Senate Public Works Committee on June 26, 1973. A summary of these factors is shown in Table 6.5. A review of these reveals that in some instances, the tabulated figures are higher than those shown in the text for a given factor. This occurs in those instances where an added increment must be included to account for additional refinery fuel required for the processing of increased volumes of motor gasolines. Specifically, this applies to the compression ratio and NOx penalty factors. The fuel volatility estimate contained a processing allowance and required no further adjustment.

In developing the curves of Charts 1 and 2 presented to the Subcommittee on June 26 showing the effect of exhaust emission controls on energy demand, the National Petroleum Council (NPC) base curve was used as a datum. To this was added an incremental amount each year from 1970 to

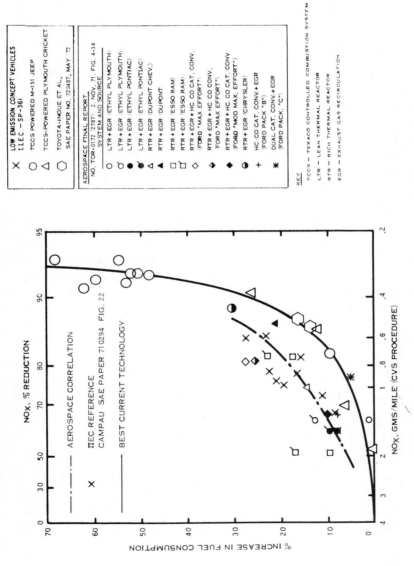

Fig. 6.4. Effect of NO$_X$ Concentration in Engine Exhaust on Fuel Consumption

Table 6.5. Engine Efficiency and Fuel Processing Penalties Associated with Control of Exhaust Emissions Basis for Charts 1 and 2 of the Texaco Presentation

Model Year	Emission Component Controlled (Gms/mi)	Modification Applied	Engine Penalty, % Fuel Consumption over 1970	Demand Penalty, % Crude Requirement — Increment	Total	Comments
1971 1972	Plan for low lead fuel. HC 3.4 CO 39	Reduce compression ratio 1970 9.3 to 1971 8.7 to 1972 8.4	5.4	3.0	3.0	Demand penalty is 1/2 fuel consumption increase (50% yield gasoline from crude assumed) plus refinery fuel increment for processing the additional fuel for equal car miles traveled
1973		Compression ratio	5.4	3.0	3.0	As for '71
1974	NOx 3.1	EGR (Exh. gas recycle) & spark retard	0	0	3.0	No penalty since EGR rate varied with car model, although penalty real
1975	HC 1.5 CO 15 NOx 3.1	Same as 1974 plus unleaded 91 RON volatility change. Catalytic muffler	5.4	3.0 0.8 2.6		As for '71; Refinery fuel for processing
			0	0	6.4	Refinery fuel for processing
1976 and later	HC 0.41 CO 3.4 NOx 0.4	Items in '75 plus more EGR & retarded combustion	5.4 3.0	6.4 17.3	23.7	As for '75; Includes refinery fuel increment as for '71
	NOx 0.8 NOx 1.2 NOx 4.0	Less EGR and retarded combustion No EGR or retard combustion	10 5 0	5.6 2.9 0	12.0 9.3 6.4	

1985 based on increased energy demand as calculated using the factors of Table 6.5. The increment for a particular year contributed by a group of cars, say the 1973-1974 model year cars, is the demand penalty for that group (3.0%) multiplied by the refinery crude runs for that year and further multiplied by the fraction of total car miles accounted for by that group. The fraction of total miles was obtained by first projecting a car population breakdown by model years to 1985 from historical annual new car sales and car retirement rates varying with age as correlated from car registration data. To this was applied the relative distance driven per car, which also varies with car age logarithmically. The sum of the individual increments for each group of cars then determined the total increase in energy demand for each year and, when added to the NPC base curve, provided the basis for the upper plots of Charts 1 and 2.

The development of these plots indicated that the effect of planned and proposed automotive emission controls on petroleum energy demand would be severe, amounting to over 4 million barrels per day by 1985. It is also obvious from the estimate that *control of exhaust NOx levels to 0.4 grams per mile is a major contributor to this penalty. Any relaxation of this requirement would significantly alleviate future energy demand and, should it be established at 4.0 grams per mile, the 1985 energy penalty could be reduced from about 4.45 to approximately 1.24 million barrels per day.* Lesser relaxations of 0.8 to 1.2 grams per mile for NOx would provide intermediate relief of the 1985 projected energy shortage of 2.28 and 1.78 million barrels per day.

During the testimony to the Subcommittee on June 26, three questions were raised under this category. One related to a request for an explanation of how gasoline is made in a refinery, another questioned what impact the introduction of the diesel engine into passenger car service might have on the fuel situation, and the last inquired as to the range of swing available in a refinery between gasoline and fuel oil production.

Attached hereto for the record is a copy of a brief explanation of refinery processing. It is an excerpt from a manual which Texaco has prepared for instruction of its employees in various facets of its operations.

Before discussing diesel fuel, a few comments on the diesel engine itself would be in order. Whereas this type engine has a distinct advantage over its gasoline counterpart in a number of aspects, it also has several disadvantages when its use for passenger car applications is considered. These are summarized below from the prepared "Statement of Daimler-Benz AG" before the EPA on June 27, 1973, and a similarly titled document supplied to the Senate Subcommittee on Air and Water Pollution dated May 18, 1973. Because of the thoroughness of the latter presentation, only major captions and page references to this statement will be given here.

Advantages and Disadvantages
of Diesel When Compared to Gasoline
Engines In Passenger Car Service

"Statement of Daimler-Benz AG"

Advantages	Page	Disadvantages	Page
Fuel Economy	11	Low Specific Power	16
Maintenance	13	Acceleration	18
Reliability & Durability	14	Fuel Requirements	18
Driveability	14	Lubricant Requirements	19
		Noise	20
		Smoke	21
		Odor	22
		Higher Initial Cost	22
		Starting	23

Emission levels attainable are discussed in the presentation to EPA in considerable detail and are summarized in the presentation to the Senate Subcommittee on pages 24 through 29. These should be reviewed in the light of contemplated emission levels to assure proper conclusions.

The summary provided on pages 38 and 39 places the alternatives between the diesel and gasoline engine in proper perspective.

Should it be decided that the advantages outweighed the disadvantages, and if the automobile industry were to install diesel engines in passenger cars, it is estimated that the changeover in primary fuel from gasoline to diesel fuel would occur over a period of ten or more years. The rate would be determined by how fast and the degree to which diesel engine usage in passenger cars developed.

During the transition period, the industry would face large investments to make the significant modifications required to minimize gasoline yield and maximize the higher boiling diesel fuel yield. This would be done by eliminating cracking of middle distillate to gasoline and installing processing to convert higher boiling oils to the diesel boiling range. During this period, the industry would be challenged to supply the increased winter demands of furnace oil and diesel fuel which compete for the same boiling range fractions.

However, about 25-30 percent of most crudes is gasoline boiling range material and unsuitable for diesel fuel. Conversion of this gasoline to diesel fuel would be very costly with present technology. If sufficient gasoline-powered vehicles continued to be made, to consume this gasoline, additional crude consumption might be avoided. In the foregoing statement of Daimler-Benz A.G. before the Subcommittee they stated "our 220 Diesel showed a 75 percent greater fuel economy than model year 1973 gasoline cars of the same weight class (3,500 pounds)." If this is realized, some savings in crude consumption might accrue. However, it should be borne in mind that for equivalent weights, the diesel has poorer performance than the gasoline engine. If is our opinion that as the disadvantages of the diesel engine are such, it is unlikely that it will become a significant contender as an alternative power plant for U.S. passenger car service in the foreseeable future.

It should be further pointed out that although diesel fuel is now supplied to some service stations, we would require another distribution system for its widespread use. A consideration similar to this has been the background of much of Texaco's planning for the investment in a third-grade system for the presently mandated unleaded fuel.

With respect to refinery swing, it is generally accepted industry practice to shift refining operations from maximum manufacture of gasoline for the summer motoring season to maximum manufacture of middle distillates in autumn. It is a common misconception that refineries have the ability to make large variations in output between gasoline and heating oil. In Texaco's domestic refineries, the swing between so-called summer or gasoline operation and winter or heating oil operation is approximately three percent. On the basis of Texaco's U.S. crude runs of about one million barrels a day, this swing amounts to approximately 30,000 barrels a day.

Refining

Petroleum From Well to Market

In general, the operations in a refinery involve the manufacture of fuels, lubricating oils, and possibly greases, asphalts, and petrochemicals. Texaco manufactures most of the numerous products made from petroleum and natural gas. New products and new uses for existing products are constantly being developed in the ever-expanding petroleum industry.

Distillation Principle

The manufacture of a wide variety of petroleum products is made possible largely through application of the distillation principle. The importance of distillation in refinery processing results from the fact that petroleum is a complex mixture of organic compounds (hydrocarbons) with different boiling points. The boiling points may vary from below freezing to above 1000 F. Distillation allows the separation of these hydrocarbons into fractions or cuts of similar boiling range (e.g., gasoline, kerosine, lubricating oil).

The simplest type of petroleum distillation operation and that first used in petroleum refining was the Pot Still. An illustration of a simple Pot Still is shown in the accompanying diagram. This batch-type operation is no longer used due to the many improvements that have been made both in distillation

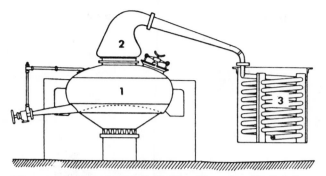

Diagram A. Simple Pot Still, Fire-Heated, with Condenser

(1) Boiling vessel; (2) still-head; (3) condenser worm
(Haslam Foundry Co., Ltd., Derby).

equipment design and operation. The primary improvement has been the development of continuous-type distillation processes. The early continuous units were Shell Stills, but these have been replaced in modern petroleum refining by Fractional Distillation units.

The operation of a Pot Still illustrates the principle of distillation. Crude oil is placed in a Pot Still and heated by internal steam coils. As the crude oil is heated, the gasoline vapors boil off first. As the vapors flow out of the Pot Still and through the condenser coils, the gasoline vapors condense and are pumped to gasoline storage. As more heat is applied to the crude oil, kerosine vapors boil off next, are condensed, and then pumped to kerosine storage. Likewise, the application of additional heat results in gas oil vapors boiling off, followed by lubricating oil vapors. The residue remaining in the pot is called fuel residuum and is used in fuel oil manufacture.

Fractional Distillation or Fractionation, below, is actually a series of distillations conducted in a fractionating tower and offers the following advantages over batch distillation:

1) higher thruput of petroleum possible,
2) better control of product uniformity and quality,
3) higher operating efficiency, and
4) greater flexibility.

Fractional Distillation Operation

In operation, petroleum is first heated to high temperature (usually between 600 and 700 F.), by pumping it through rows of steel tubes heated in a furnace. Next it enters the lower part of the closed vertical tower or fractionating column where part is vaporized. The unvaporized portion or residuum is drawn from the bottom of the tower.

As vapors rise in the tower, they bubble through perforated trays designed to hold a few inches of liquid on each. At the same time, a stream of gasoline,

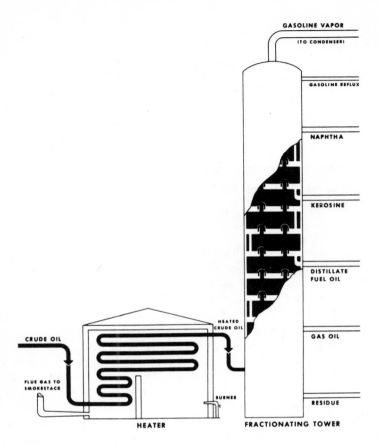

Diagram B. Heater and Fractionating Tower

referred to as reflux, is pumped into the top of the tower and flows down over the trays. Its cooling action condenses the heavier hydrocarbons. In turn, the hot vapors cause part of the reflux to vaporize.

As this operation continues, different "fractions" of petroleum condense on different trays: heavier fractions, with higher boiling points, on the lower (and hotter) trays; lighter fractions, with lower boiling points, on the higher (and cooler) trays.

From the proper trays, primary products of petroleum can be drawn off through pipes in the side of the tower, as indicated in the diagram. The whole operation proceeds continuously.

Vapors of the lightest group of hydrocarbons, suitable for blending into gasoline or for use as reflux, reach the top of the tower. They are taken off through a large pipe and condensed by passing through water-cooled tubes.

Manufacture of Fuels

Introduction

Since the manufacture of fuels is complicated, the Pictorial Flow Diagram has of necessity been simplified and does not represent any one refinery. Likewise, the individual flow diagrams of the various units have been simplified.

The basic processes in a refinery related to the manufacture of fuels that will be discussed are:

1. Natural Gasoline Plant
2. Crude Desalting
3. Vacuum Pipe Stills
4. Isobutane Decarbonizing
5. Catalytic Reforming
6. Cracking
   a. Catalytic
   b. Thermal
   c. Hydrocracking
   d. Delayed Coking
7. Polymerization
8. Alkylation
9. Udex Extraction
10. Hydrotreating
11. Treating and Finishing of Light Products

Natural Gasoline Plant

An oil well produces varying quantities of gas along with the crude oil. This wet gas is sent to the Natural Gasoline Plant which separates the wet gas into natural gas, liquid petroleum gas (LPG), and natural gasoline. The natural gasoline obtained is used primarily as a blending component in motor gasoline.

Crude Desalting

Prior to the initial distillation, the majority of the crude oil is desalted to remove various inorganic salts (sodium, calcium, magnesium, etc.), solids (sand, silt, rust), and formation water. The inorganic salts are deleterious to processing and particularly to heat transfer.

The desalting operation is accomplished by electrostatic precipitation. The unrefined crude oil is heated and mixed with hot water to form an emulsion. The metallic salts are soluble in the water phase. The emulsion is passed through an electrostatic field with a potential in excess of 30,000 volts. This high-voltage potential breaks the emulsion and causes the water droplets to agglomerage. As the water settles to the bottom of the vessel where it is withdrawn, it carries both the water soluble and many of the insoluble contaminants with it. The desalted crude is then ready for further processing.

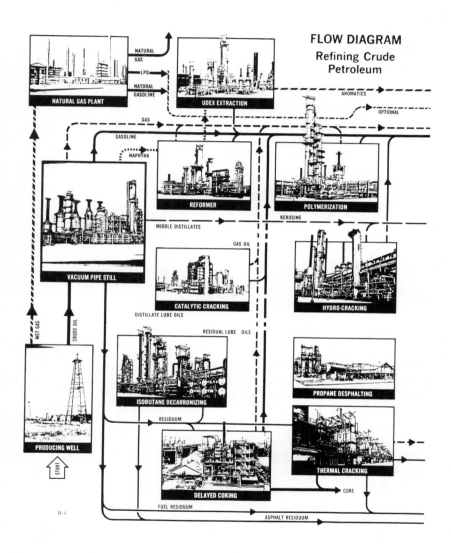

Diagram C.

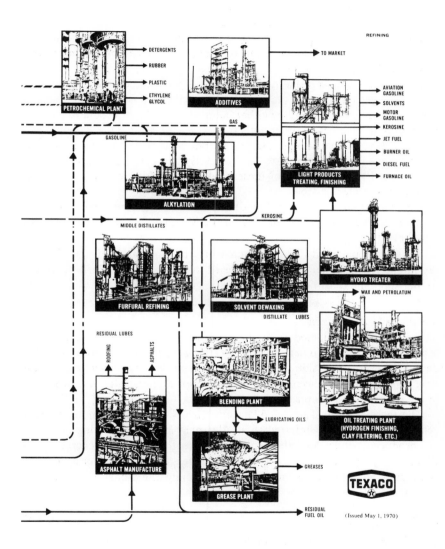

REFINING

PETROCHEMICAL PLANT
→ DETERGENTS
→ RUBBER
→ PLASTIC
→ ETHYLENE GLYCOL

ADDITIVES → TO MARKET

GAS

GASOLINE

ALKYLATION

LIGHT PRODUCTS TREATING, FINISHING
→ AVIATION GASOLINE
→ SOLVENTS
→ MOTOR GASOLINE
→ KEROSINE
→ JET FUEL
→ BURNER OIL
→ DIESEL FUEL
→ FURNACE OIL

KEROSINE

MIDDLE DISTILLATES

HYDRO TREATER

FURFURAL REFINING

SOLVENT DEWAXING

DISTILLATE   LUBES

WAX AND PETROLATUM

RESIDUAL LUBES

ROOFING   ASPHALTS

BLENDING PLANT

OIL TREATING PLANT (HYDROGEN FINISHING, CLAY FILTERING, ETC.)

LUBRICATING OILS

ASPHALT MANUFACTURE

GREASE PLANT
→ GREASES

TEXACO

→ RESIDUAL FUEL OIL

(Issued May 1, 1970)

Vacuum Pipe Stills

In the Pictorial Flow Diagram, only one Vacuum Pipe Still is shown. In a refinery producing a full line of fuels and lubricating oils, several such stills would be used for greater flexibility, see Diagram D.

At the refinery the crudes are evaluated and selected for either fuel or lubricating oil manufacture. However, all crudes contain some fuel. For the purposes of the following discussions, it is assumed that the crude being used contains materials for a full line of products from gas to asphalt. In practice this would be an unusal crude.

The gasoline and kerosine fuel fractions are produced on the Atmospheric Tower; the gas oil fraction, on both the Atmospheric Tower and the Vacuum Tower. These fractions may be either pumped to the Light Products Treating and Finishing Plant or to other units for further processing. For example, the heavy portion of the gasoline fraction (naphtha) is routed to the Reformer. The kerosine and gas oil may go to the Hydrotreater, depending on the nature, quality, and end use of these products. In addition, some of the gas oil is used for cracking stock.

The lubricating oil stocks produced on the Vacuum Tower will be discussed in the subsequent sections on the Manufacture of Lubricating Oils and Asphalts.

The remaining undistilled fraction from the Vacuum Tower is the fuel residuum. This product can either be used in heavy fuel oil blending or sent to the Isobutane Decarbonizing Unit for further treatment.

Isobutane Decarbonizing

The residuum obtained from the fractionation of crudes is a mixture of asphaltenes, resins, aromatics, and paraffinic-type hydrocarbon oils. The deasphalting of a residuum produces a clean oil by concentrating the paraffinic oils in the solvent phase and the asphaltenes, resins, and aromatics in the solvent-insoluble phase (asphalt).

The terms "deasphalting" and "decarbonizing" are almost synonymous. In general, the process is referred to as "deasphalting" if lubricating oil stocks are produced, while "decarbonizing" refers to the process if charge to the Fluid Catalytic Cracking Unit is being produced. Similarly, either propane or isobutane can be used as the solvent to separate the asphaltic constituents from the residuum.

Catalytic Reforming Unit

The naphtha from the Vacuum Pipe Still is charged to the Reforming Unit. Most straight run gasolines are relatively low in octane number. With increasing octane requirements in modern automobiles, it is necessary in many cases to upgrade this material. In this process a straight run gasoline is upgraded catalytically under suitable conditions of temperature and pressure

Vacuum Pipe Still

Reference to the accompanying flow chart will show that the gas and naphtha are separated after passing overhead from the atmospheric fractionating tower. Three sidestreams, naphtha, kerosine and gas oil, are withdrawn from the same tower. The hot reduced crude is pumped to the vacuum still heater and subsequently flashed for the separation of vapors and bottoms. The vapors are then fractionated by passing counter-current to reflux pumped back from exchanger coolers connected to a side stream withdrawn from the tower. The bottoms are sent to storage or other units as are the sidestreams of gas oil, light, medium and heavy lubricating distillates.

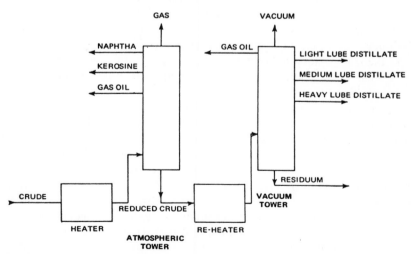

Diagram D. Two Stage Distillation Unit

to improve the octane number. The primary reaction in the process is dehydrogenation of naphthenes to produce aromatic hydrocarbons which have considerably higher octane characteristics than the original naphthenes. Other important secondary reactions are the isomerization of low-octane naphthenes to aromatics, the hydrocracking of long-chain paraffins, and the dehydrocyclization of paraffins to aromatics.

Reforming, therefore, is one way to improve octane rating of fuels. Gasoline from the Reforming Unit is pumped to the Light Products Testing and Finishing section of the refinery.

Cracking

Gas oil from the Vacuum Pipe Still is charged to cracking units. Cracking is the process of breaking up and rearranging the molecular structure of complex high-boiling hydrocarbons. Materials such as olefins and diolefins, which do not exist in crude oils, are produced in cracking. Also aromatics are formed by dehydrogenation of naphthenes and cyclization of olefins. These reactions, plus the production of short-chain and branch-chain paraffins account for increased octane number of cracked gasoline. Cracking is a method of making lighter materials (gasoline) out of heavier materials (gas oil). This cracked gasoline has relatively high octane number. In the upgrading of heavy oils to gasoline, four general types of cracking are used; namely, catalytic cracking, thermal cracking, hydrocracking, and coking.

Catalytic cracking, as its name implies, consists of charging heavy hydrocarbons generally in the gas oil boiling range over a catalyst at elevated temperature. This results in cracking or breaking down of the gas oils into gas, naphtha and a cycle material in the gas oil boiling range which is either recycled back to the unit, charged to a furfural extraction unit or a thermal cracking unit, or disposed of in various middle distillates or in fuel oil. The cracked naphtha produced by this process is of relatively high octane number. The fluid catalytic cracking unit is illustrated in Diagram F.

In thermal cracking the charge stock, consisting of gas oils, topped crude, or, in some cases, whole crude, is cracked by the use of high temperature and pressure without the use of a catalyst.

Hydrocracking is a fixed bed catalytic process in which cracking occurs in a hydrogen atmosphere at high temperature and pressure. Gas oils from the Catalytic Cracking Unit, Coking Unit, or Crude Unit can be charged to the Hydrocracker. The gas oil charge stock is converted to a full range of products, most important of which are high quality light gasoline, heavy naphtha for catalytic reformer feed, and distillate. The distillate is used in manufacture of diesel or jet fuel; however, distillate production can be eliminated by cracking it into lighter products. Hydrocracking also produces good yields of isobutane for alkylation feedstock. Hydrocracked products are typically lower in olefins and aromatics than those produced by other cracking processes. Information on the Hydrocracking Unit is presented in Diagram G.

Catalytic Reforming Unit

This flow diagram is that of a typical Reforming unit for motor gasoline production. The unit may be divided into three sections: a feed preparation section, a reactor section, and a stabilization section. The catalyst is a platinum type divided into two or more beds in series. For manufacture of motor gasoline, straight run and/or cracked naphthas, boiling in the range of 150-400 F., may be used for charge stock. The reactor temperature is in the range of 850-900 F. when operating at pressures from 300-500 pounds per square inch.

The motor gasoline component made by Reforming is stable with a high-octane rating and good response to various lead antiknock compounds.

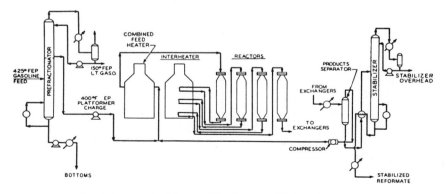

Diagram E. Schematic of Typical Reforming Unit

Fluid Catalytic Cracking Unit

The Fluid Catalytic Cracking Process, as shown in the diagram below, was developed originally for producing motor fuels of improved quality but also can be used for the manufacture of aviation gasoline base stocks and for providing large volumes of the lighter hydrocarbons required as feed stock for alkylate and butadiene plants. The normal charge is gas oil. This process represents a technique for contacting catalyst with oil vapors and for regenerating spent catalyst in a continuous operation as compared with static or moving bed operations. The catalyst is in powder form, and by aeration is maintained continuously in a free flowing condition in the system.

A unique feature of the process is the circulation of the catalyst without moving parts and at pressures not exceeding 15 pounds per square inch at the top of the reaction vessel. This is done by the application of the gas-lift principle for handling liquids. Build-up of sufficient pressure to promote catalyst circulation is done through the use of a standpipe containing catalyst of high density which provides a gravity fluid head against a leg of catalyst of lower density.

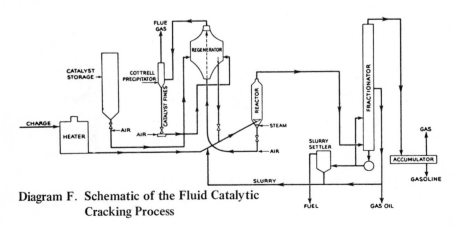

**Diagram F. Schematic of the Fluid Catalytic
Cracking Process**

Hydrocracking Unit

Gas Oil charge is pumped to the first reactor through heat exchange with the first stage effluent. The feed is then combined with heated recycle gas. The combined stream downflows through the first reactor where sulfur and nitrogen compounds are removed. The effluent is combined with more hot recycle gas and enters the second reactor. Hydrocracking occurs here and the gas oil is converted to lighter products. The reactor effluent is cooled by heat exchange with the charge as it flows to the separator. Gas off the separator is recirculated with the recycle gas compressor.

The second stage is a single reactor which hydrocracks gas oil that is not cracked in the first stage. Feed to the second stage is Fractionator bottoms which is combined with heated recycle gas as it enters the reactor. The reactor effluent is cooled as it flows to the separator.

Liquid from the bottom of the separator is fed to the fractionator. The overhead from the fractionator is light gasoline and lighter products which is further processed for butane recovery. Two sidestreams are withdrawn from the fractionator, heavy naphtha, which is upgraded further by catalytic reforming, and distillate which is used as a component in diesel and jet fuels. The bottoms are sent back to the second stage.

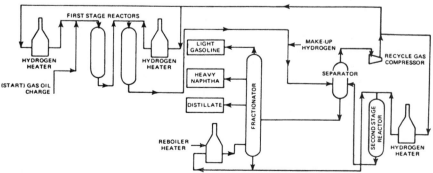

Diagram G. Schematic of Hydrocracking Process

In cases where it becomes necessary to dispose of heavy residual oils, it is sometimes desirable to charge these oils to a delayed coking unit where the primary products are gas, naphtha, and coke. The naphtha is usually of relatively poor quality as compared with that obtained with thermal and catalytic cracking.

Polymerization

The Pictorial Flow Diagram shows that refinery gases that are generated on other processing units are charged to the Polymerization Unit. The polymerization process is used to convert these gases (propylene and/or butylene) to materials boiling in the normal gasoline range by contact with a catalyst under controlled pressure and temperature. The resulting product is a relatively high octane gasoline. However, the currently high octane level of domestic motor gasolines is gradually forcing polymerization into an unfavorable economic position. The polymer gasoline produced is pumped to the Light Products Treating and Finishing section for use in motor gasolines.

Alkylation

Alkylation (Diagram H) is similar to polymerization since both are based on the combination of two molecules to give gasoline. However, in alkylation, a saturated hydrocarbon is combined with an unsaturated hydrocarbon. The product of this reaction is called Alkylate which has a much higher motor octane than polymer gasoline. Iso-butane and one or more of the three butylenes and propylene are reacted in the presence of concentrated sulfuric or anhydrous hydrofluoric acid catalyst.

Udex Extraction

The Udex process is a selective, liquid-liquid solvent extraction method developed for the purpose of separating aromatics from hydrocarbon mixtures. This process is widely used in the refining industry for the separation of catalytic reformed gasoline into very high (aromatic) and low (paraffinic) octane fractions and is used primarily to adjust the octane number of the refiner's premium gasoline. However, some of the low-octane fractions are used in jet fuels.

Referring to the flow diagram (Diagram I) heavy catalytic reformed gasoline from the Catalytic Reforming Units is charged to the Udex Extractor. The light and heavy raffinates and the extract products require no further treating and are segregated for gasoline and/or jet fuel blending. The light raffinate and extract are used in motor gasoline blending and the heavy raffinate in jet fuel blending.

This process is characterized by its high recovery of all aromatics even though the feed may be a complex mixture with a low concentration of aromatics.

Sulfuric Alkylation

Alkylate used in gasoline manufacture is the product of reacting isobutane with butylenes and/or propylene present in refinery gases. Following the reaction, the mixture of hydrocarbons and acid is separated from the acid catalyst in a settler, the hydrocarbon mixture then being caustic washed. Bottoms from the isobutane tower go to a debutanizer where the alkylate is recovered and used in the manufacture of aviation gasoline.

The gasoline produced from this process is of extremely high quality with respect to octane number. It is used primarily in the production of Aviation and Motor Gasolines by blending it with other suitable components.

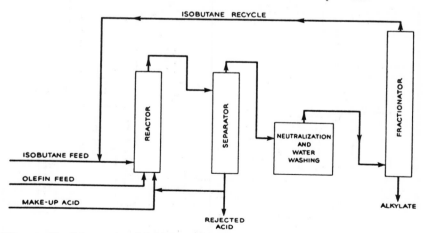

Diagram H. Schematic of Sulfuric Alkylation Process

Udex Unit

Heavy Catalytic Reformed Gasoline is charged to an intermediate point in the liquid-phase extractor tower where it is contacted with a selected aqueous glycol solvent. The raffinate, which is almost completely paraffinic, leaves the top of the extractor, is cooled and water washed, and then sent to the Raffinate Splitter for further reduction to a light and heavy raffinate stream. The aromatic extract withdrawn from the solvent stripper is washed with water and taken directly to storage for subsequent gasoline blending.

The combined wash-water streams and water from the stripper overhead accumulator are collected in a water accumulator for reuse as stripping water. The solvent from the stripper is recovered in a solvent regenerator and reused.

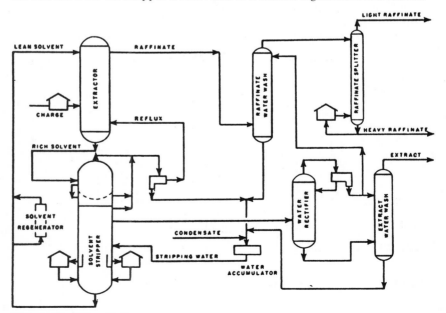

Diagram I. Udex Unit

Hydrotreating Unit

Referring to the Pictorial Flow Diagram, kerosine boiling range distillates from Vacuum Pipe Stills are charged to the Hydrotreating Unit (Diagram J). The use of hydrotreating in the fuel section of a refinery represents an effective method of upgrading sour or marginal kerosine distillates to produce color-stable products. The distillate products from the hydrotreating reaction, after fractionation to the proper front end boiling range and removal of hydrogen sulfide, are routed to tanks for kerosine and jet fuels.

Treating and Finishing of Light Products

The Light Products Treating and Finishing Plant is the last operation shown in the refinery fuel section on the Pictorial Flow Diagram. In an actual refinery this plant is very complicated with many pipe lines leading to and from the units in the fuel section. Coke and heavy fuel oils are by-products. These materials are handled as direct as possible from the refinery to the customer.

Gasolines from the Natural Gasoline Plant, Vacuum Pipe Stills, Reforming, Polymerization, Fluid Catalytic Cracking, Thermal Cracking, and Alkylation Units are pumped to the Treating and Finishing section. The kerosines and gas oils are likewise pumped here.

Treating or Removal of Impurities

Almost universally, both straight run and cracked naphtha distillates, as they come from the stills or from gasoline manufacturing units, contain constituents that are objectionable in motor fuels. The most common of these constituents to be removed or modified to a less objectionable form are sulfur compounds, colored constituents, and some of the most active of the unsaturated products of cracking.

Sulfur compounds are objectionable as they may contribute to corrosion of metal parts of an engine, cause disagreeable odors, decrease the antiknock characteristics of the gasoline, and lower its response to lead antiknock compounds.

Unsaturated compounds produced by cracking are of high antiknock properties, but sometimes have high color or produce gummy reaction products upon storage.

Straight run gasolines generally have good color and gum stability and require no treatment except for the removal or conversion of odorous sulfur compounds (mercaptans) unless the sulfur content is high. Cracked gasolines, on the other hand, almost always require some form of treatment for the reduction of sulfur or improvement of color, gum, or stability. Alkylate and catalytic reformate require no further treatment.

The general treating methods include acid treating with its various modifications, solvent refining, treatment with metal salts, clay treating, and inhibiting.

Hydrotreating Unit

The Hydrotreating process upgrades Kerosine boiling range distillates by fixed bed catalytic treating in the presence of hydrogen. The reaction removes sulfur, nitrogen, reduces organic acids, and produces a doctor negative product with a Saybolt color of +30. Make-up hydrogen requirements in the process is furnished from the Catalytic Reforming Unit. The Hydrotreating Unit produces a color stable distillate product for Kerosine and jet fuel productions and a naphtha stream to the Catalytic Reforming Unit.

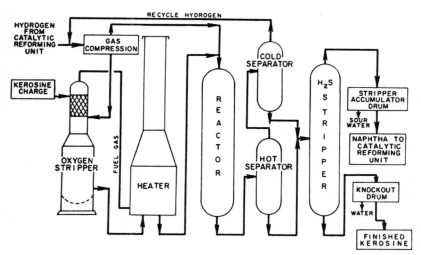

Diagram J. Schematic of HydrotreatingUnit

Sulfur compounds in gasolines are usually more chemically reactive than hydrocarbons and can be removed by selective adsorption or reaction with chemicals or other materials which are, in themselves, insoluble or can otherwise be separated from the gasoline hydrocarbons. For example, some sulfur containing hydrocarbons can be removed due to the fact that they are relatively more soluble in strong sulfuric acid or caustic solutions than hydrocarbons having no sulfur atoms in the molecule. Likewise, solid absorbents such as Bauxite (a natural form of aluminum oxide) may act as a catalyst to cause the rupture of sulfur-containing molecules to yield mainly hydrogen sulfide and unsaturated hydrocarbons.

Cracked gasolines containing the more active olefins or diolefins may be rendered less susceptible to gum formation by adding a chemical inhibitor. Oxidation plays an important role in this deterioration (gum formation), but inhibitors have been found which have a retarding effect on the reaction which causes gum formation. The most active gum inhibitors are derivatives of phenols, cresols, and similar aromatic compounds containing one or more nitrogen-containing groups called amines.

Many gasolines contain foul-smelling compounds called mercaptans, and there are two general types of processes which are used for their removal. One involves the removal of the mercaptans, which automatically reduces the sulfur content, and the other merely converts them to other compounds called disulfides, which remain in the gasoline, but do not have a bad odor. Any process which eliminates mercaptans from a gasoline is known as a sweetening process, whether they are removed or converted.

When mercaptans are contacted with an alkali, the hydrogen is replaced by the alkali metal with the formation of mercaptides. Sodium mercaptide, for example, is highly soluble in caustic but not in gasoline or water. Sometimes a solubility promoter or solutizer is added to improve the solubility of the mercaptan in the caustic. By separating the caustic containing the mercaptide from the gasoline, it is possible to reduce the sulfur content of the gasoline.

When mercaptans are contacted with caustic solution of certain metal salts, usually lead or copper, the metal mercaptides are formed. The addition of free sulfur converts these metal mercaptides to the corresponding metallic sulfides which are gasoline insoluble and a hydrocarbon disulfide which is gasoline soluble. No sulfur reduction takes place since the odorous sulfur is merely converted to a non-odorous variety. Copper sweetening, while it does not remove free sulfur from the gasoline if present, has the advantage that it is not necessary to add additional free sulfur to complete the reaction, as is necessary with lead (Doctor) sweetening.

Finishing

Finishing of fuels consists of blending for desired characteristics and incorporating additives and inhibitors. The operations carried on in this section of the refinery are involved. Samples from the various operations are sent to the control laboratory for quality control testing. Products of uniform quality result. A description of the various products made in the fuel section of the refinery follows.

Natural Gas

Natural gas is a mixture of gaseous hydrocarbons which comes from the ground with or without crude oil. It is classified as wet gas or dry gas depending on whether or not the majority of hydrocarbons present are near their condensing temperature under atmospheric conditions. A portion of wet gas is used in making natural gasoline. The remainder and dry gas is used for many purposes including LPG, commercial natural gas for domestic and industrial uses, and engine fuel.

Propane

Propane is a gaseous hydrocarbon having three carbon and eight hydrogen atoms (C_3H_8). It is found in most natural gas and is usually the first product found naturally in the crude which is commonly used as an engine fuel. Propane is also produced during cracking operations in the refinery. As a rule, it is mixed with butane in varying proportions to make LPG, bottled gas, etc.

$$
\begin{array}{c}
\text{H H H} \\
\text{| | |} \\
\text{Chemical formula: } C_3H_8 \text{ or } H-C-C-C-H \\
\text{| | |} \\
\text{H H H}
\end{array}
$$

Propane is C_3 paraffin or saturated C_3.

Butane

Butane is a gaseous hydrocarbon having four carbon and ten hydrogen atoms (C_4H_{10}). Like propane, it is present in natural gas and is often used as a part of the product which is sold commercially as LPG, bottled gas, or liquefied gas. It is used in motor gasolines for giving front end volatility.

$$
\begin{array}{c}
\text{H H H H} \\
\text{| | | |} \\
\text{Chemical formula: } C_4H_{10} \text{ or } H-C-C-C-C-H \\
\text{| | | |} \\
\text{H H H H}
\end{array}
$$

This is n-butane (normal butane), a straight chain normal C_4 paraffin or saturated C_4.

Liquefied Petroleum Gas

Liquefied petroleum gas is known generally as LP-Gas and LPG. As a rule, it is a mixture of propane and butane and/or refinery gases under sufficient pressure to be in liquid form. It is used as fuel in tractors, buses, trucks, stationary engines, and for power generation where natural gas is not available.

Natural Gasoline

Natural gasoline is a gasoline made from wet gas which vaporizes at a relatively low temperature and has a high antiknock value. For these reasons, natural gasoline is used as a blending stock to provide the starting fraction of the gasoline and to improve antiknock quality.

Gasoline

ASTM defines gasoline as "A refined petroleum naphtha which, by its composition, is suitable for use as a carburant in internal combustion engines."

ASTM defines petroleum naphtha as "A generic term applied to refined, partly refined, or unrefined petroleum products and liquid products of natural gas, not less than 10 percent of which distills below 347 F and not less than 95 percent of which distills below 464 F when subjected to distillation in accordance with ASTM Method D 86, Test for Distillation of Petroleum Products.

Note: The 'naphthas' used for specific purposes such as cleaning, manufacture of rubber, manufacture of paints and varnishes, etc., are made to conform to specifications which may require products of considerably greater volatility than set by the limits of this generic definition."

Although no hard and fast rules can be laid down, gasoline usually is considered as containing a mixture of hydrocarbons having a boiling range of about 90 F to 420 F. Some of the individual hydrocarbons may boil considerably below 90 F, but these materials alter the apparent boiling range as given above. Gasoline will contain hydrocarbon molecules with as low as four carbon atoms and as high as twelve to sixteen carbon atoms.

Two primary requirements for good gasoline are (1) sufficient antiknock quality (octane number) to provide freedom from knock (detonation) in automotive engines, and ʼ(2) properly balanced volatility to provide quick starting, fast warm-up, and freedom from vapor lock. Volatility is controlled by the relative amounts of high and low boiling stocks blended in the gasoline. Octane rating is dependent on the type of hydrocarbons in the gasoline and on the use of antiknock compounds. For example, straight-chain hydrocarbons have low octane ratings, branched-chain and aromatic hydrocarbons usually have higher ratings, and cycloparaffin-type hydrocarbons intermediate ratings. In addition to optimum use of high-octane components it usually is necessary to add small quantities of antiknock fluids to obtain octane levels needed by modern engines. The original and still most widely used antiknock agent is tetraethyl lead, although use of tetramethyl lead is increasing.

Knock in an engine is a relatively high-frequency noise caused by uncontrolled ignition or explosion of the last portion of the fuel-air mixture. Detonation can be prevented by gasoline of sufficiently high antiknock quality. When most current high compression engines are adjusted to develop their maximum power and fuel economy, they require gasoline of 94-100 + octane number. In contrast to knock, another noise phenomenon known as "rumble" can occur in engines even when gasoline octane number is high enough to prevent detonation. Rumble is a low-pitched thudding noise accompanied by engine roughness; it probably is caused by high rates of pressure rise associated with multiple deposit-induced ignition. Hydrocarbon composition is a factor in surface ignition and rumble, and additives are available which alleviate this problem by modifying the chemical nature of combustion chamber deposits.

Antioxidants are used in gasoline to protect against the formation of gum and peroxides in storage, and metal deactivators are used to prevent trace amounts of copper picked up in piping or fuel systems from acting as a catalyst for the formation of undesirable materials. Modern refinery processing produces inherently more stable gasoline components, thereby reducing the amounts of antioxidants and inhibitors needed.

Other widely used gasoline additives include antirust agents, anti-icers to prevent carburetor icing and fuel line freeze-up, detergents to keep carburetor passages clean, and compounds to minimize formation of deposits on intake valves and ports.

The blending operation is complicated and requires careful control testing to assure proper octane number, volatility, and other characteristics desired in the finished gasoline. Antiknock compounds and other additives are precisely metered under carefully controlled conditions.

Solvents

Solvents made from petroleum refers to products having solvent properties and in the general boiling range of gasoline and kerosine.

There are many names applied to such materials, including cleaning naphthas, rubber solvent, paint and varnish solvent, petroleum spirits, and mineral spirits. ASTM defines petroleum spirits as "a refined petroleum distillate with volatility, flash point and other properties making it suitable as a thinner and solvent in paints, varnishes and similar products." The term "turpentine substitute" as applied to petroleum spirits is to be deemed as false and misleading. In Great Britain the term "petroleum spirits" is applied to a very light hydrocarbon mixture having a flash point below 32 F.

Jet Fuels

The new era in jet aviation has found Texaco to be a front runner in supplying jet fuels for both domestic and military requirements.

Current military requirements specify a "wide-cut" gasoline-type turbine fuel such as JP-4 or a high flash point, kerosine-type fuel like JP-5. Domestic requirements, however, demand highly refined, low freezing point, kerosine-type fuels which are made from selected stocks. These fuels have maximum freezing points of minus 40 F for most domestic flights and freezing points of minus 58 F for long-range internatonal flights.

In view of the constantly increasing demand for jet fuels, requiring a constantly increasing percentage of the crude barrel, jet fuel specifications represent the maximum compromise between performance and availability. Critical performance parameters include low temperature handling (controlled by freezing point and low temperature viscosity), engine starting (governed by distillation, flash point, and viscosity) and combustion characteristics (controlled by smoke point, aromatics content, distillation, and sulfur content). Since most jet fuels are straight-run products these characteristics are obtained by crude selection and distillation limits. Other properties, such as copper corrosion, water separation, mercaptan content and acidity which affect compatibility with handling and aircraft systems, are controlled by subsequent treating processes such as hydrotreating, doctor or Linde treating as well as clay filtration.

Kerosine-Stove Oil-Burner Oil

Kerosene was originally a trade name for illuminating oil distilled from coal. With the advent of the petroleum industry, kerosine (note: product from petroleum spelled with "ine") came to be more extensively used as the world-wide trade name for a refined product distilled from petroleum.

Kerosine is composed of a mixture of hydrocarbons of generally higher boiling points than those contained in gasoline.

Some types of crude posses certain desirable inherent characteristics which enable the manufacture of a higher quality kerosine than do other crudes. This fact, together with careful refining supervision, assures the following properties in the finished products:

a. When used as a fuel, they:
   burn without smoke,
   develop uniform heat,
   give a uniform flame,
   develop no objectionable odors,
   contain no foreign matter which might clog burners or wicks,
   contain no water.

b. When used for illuminating purposes, they:
   burn without smoke,
   give a brilliant and dependable light,
   show no tendency to flicker,
   develop no objectionable odors,
   contain no impurities to clog the wick,
   contain no water,
   show no tendency to carbonize surface of wick.

As an illuminating oil, kerosine is normally burned by means of a wick. Kerosine is extensively used in heating stoves and for cooking. It is used also in operation of certain engines, such as tractors. However, as Texaco tractor fuels are especially manufactured for tractor use, they are recommended for this purpose.

The kerosine fraction is used in the manufacture of such products as stove oil, burner oil, jet fuels, and light grades of diesel fuel.

ASTM defines kerosine as "A refined petroleum distillate suitable for use as an illuminant when burned in a wick lamp.

Note: The flash point may not be below 73 F, as determined by the Abel Tester (which is approximately equivalent to 73 F as determined by the Tag Closed Tester, ASTM Method D 56). In the United States of America, local ordinances or insurance regulations require flash points higher than 73 F."

Gas Oil-Diesel Fuel-Furnace Oil

Gas oil is a petroleum distillate obtained between the kerosine and light lubricating oil cuts. So named because it originally was heated in retorts to generate illuminating gas and is presently used to enrich illuminating gas. Great quantities are used as a charging stock in cracking stills. Furnace oils and diesel fuel are made from the gas oil fraction.

ASTM defines gas oil as "A liquid petroleum distillate having a viscosity intermediate between that of kerosine and lubricating oil.

Note: It should be understood that oils, other than gas oil as defined above, may be and are used in the manufacture of gas."

Furnace Oils

Furnace oils are middle distillates for use primarily in domestic-type burners. In some instances they are used industrially where clean combustion and low sulfur content flue gases are required. Also rebrands of furnace oils are often used a second-grade diesel fuels.

One of the most important characteristics of all distillate fuel oils is their storage stability, particularly with fuels used for home heating. Poor storage stability causes sludge formation resulting in filter plugging. Although the composition of these sludges varies, a typical analysis would show approximately 50 percent water, 40 percent fuel oil, 8 percent rust and dirt, and only 2 percent organic sediment. This small amount of organic sediment is considered responsible for practically all the difficulties since it acts as a stabilizer for the sludge and prevents disintegration of the sludge, therefore causing filter plugging.

The most widespread practices used in solving this sludge problem are (1) to stablize the fuel against the formation of this insoluble organic sediment by further refining of the fuel and (2) to use additives which will disperse any sludge that may form so that it will pass through filters and screens and be burned with the oil.

Other properties such as corrosion and color stability can also be improved through the use of additives. Texaco incorporates blends of various organic additives to impart to fuel oils all of the properties necessary for optimum performance.

Fuel Oil

Heavy fuel oil is the material remaining after all gasoline, kerosine, and gas oil stocks have been distilled from the crude or charge stock. Such material from some units would be too viscous for handling, so very often the commercial product sold under such descriptive names as Bunker Oil C, Fuel Oil C, or Fuel Oil No. 6 is mixed with lighter viscosity fuel for reducing viscosity. This type fuel oil is used in industrial plants for generation of steam for heating and power, in oil burning type steam locomotives and in large ships. Heavy fuels are handled separately and as direct as possible from the refinery units to the customer by tank truck, tank car, barge or tanker and occasionally by private pipe line.

The following ASTM definition of fuel oils includes the heavy fuel oil just discussed along with furnace oils:

> "Fuel Oil.—Any liquid or liquefiable petroleum product burned for the generation of heat in a furnace or firebox, or for the generation of power in an engine, exclusive of oils and a flash point below 100 F (38 C) Tag Closed Tester, and oils burned in cotton or woolwick burners. Fuel oils in common use fall into one of four classes:

Small Modern Refinery

Texaco Canada Limited's Edmonton, Alta., 18,000 bbls. per day refinery. From left to right may be seen the fluid catalytic cracking unit gas recovery section, catalytic unit, crude unit fractionator, vacuum distilling unit, catalytic unit fractionator, delayed coking fractionator and coking drum, and the process heaters.

This refinery produces a full line of fuel products with the emphasis on a maximum yield of high octane Sky Chief and Fire Chief Gasolines.

Desalted, preheated crude is charged to the crude furnaces and then to the atmospheric distillation tower. Kerosene and diesel fuel are taken from the primary fractionator for finished product blending. Gasolines are withdrawn for octane upgrading by catalytic reforming (heavy straight run) and treating (light straight run), while gas oil and reduced crude are further processed.

Reduced crude is reheated and distilled under vacuum to provide gas oils for feed to the catalytic cracking unit, and residuum which is then thermally cracked. The products of thermal cracking are gasoline, diesel fuel, thermal gas oil, and coke.

Atmospheric, vacuum, and thermally cracked gas oils are combined and charged to the fluid catalytic cracking unit. Gasoline from this unit is included in final blended products after treating, while distillates are blended after desulphurization.

Gases from the cracking units are routed to a vapour recovery system and gasoline is obtained by a combination of absorption and polymerization.

1. residual fuel oils, which are topped crude petroleums, or viscous residuums obtained in refinery operations;
2. distillate fuel oils, which are distillates derived directly or indirectly from crude petroleum;
3. crude petroleums and weathered crude petroleums of relatively low commercial value;
4. blended fuels, which are mixtures of two or more of the three preceding classes."

Coke

Petroleum coke is the residue remaining in a coking still after the charge has been distilled-to-dryness, meaning that distillation of all volatile materials including tar have been removed. Coke constitutes on an average about 5 percent of the crude oil. It is used to make products where extremely high heat is encountered, such as electric arc light carbons, etc.

Small Modern Refinery

The refinery operation described in the Pictorial Flow Diagram (Diagram C) represents a complete refinery where fuels, oils, greases, and asphalts are made. A second type of refining operation is the Small Modern Refinery. In this refining operation, the plant is designed to manufacture fuels. The fuels include gas, various grades of gasoline, kerosine, burner oil, jet fuel, diesel fuel, furnace oil, fuel oil, and coke. This represents the Texaco Canada Limited plant at Edmonton, Alberta, Canada.

Alternative Emission Control Strategies

A review of all the undesirable ramifications of the present course of emissions regulation raises the question "Is there a better way to control automobile emissions?" Texaco's consideration of the question indicates that a preferable approach for consideration might be one involving a two-car strategy.

In the preparation of the Texaco-suggested two-car strategy many factors have been considered. In presenting this strategy the material has been grouped into the following four sections:

A. Vehicle Emission Standards
B. Petroleum Demand and Crude Oil Savings, Two-Car Strategy
C. Vehicle Emissions and Air Quality
D. Use of Leaded Fuels

A. Vehicle Emission Standards

The Texaco-suggested two-car strategy is based on the use of Critical Area Emission Standards to control the emissions from vehicles used in the critical smog areas of the U.S., viz. California South Coast Air Basin. Nationwide emission standards would be used to control emissions in the rest of the U.S.

In order to provide the time required for the development of emission-control technology and of improved-efficiency engines, the following emission standards and timetable are offered.

Table 6.6. Two-Car Strategy Emission Standards

Alternate Standard	Model Year	Nominal % of New Cars	Gms/Mi (CVS-2) Average Values		
			HC	CO	NO_x
Nationwide	1975 & beyond	85	1.5	15	4.0
Critical Area	1975	15	1.5	15	3.1
Critical Area	1976-1980 incl.	15	1.5	15	1.5
Critical Area	1981 & beyond	15	1.0	10	1.3

1975 Standards

Our suggestion for 1975 differs from the present interim standards established by EPA in three respects:

1. The standards are based on the *average* instead of *maximum* values for a given model car produced in that year and the timetable is different.
2. The standard for the Nationwide NO_x emissions is increased from the currently mandated 3.1 gms/mile *maximum* to 4.0 gms/mile *average*.
3. The Critical Area Emission Standards are proposed as follows in comparison with the U.S. Interim Stds. for California.

Table 6.7.

Component	U.S. Interim (Calif.) gm/mi max.	Critical Area gm/mi avg.
HC	0.9	1.5
CO	9.0	15.0
NO_x	3.1	3.1

Each of these changes is discussed below.

The use of *average* values rather than *maximum* levels for the exhaust pollutants is felt to be an acceptable basis for control. Average as used here means that of all the cars manufactured in a given year, some would have higher and some would have lower emissions than the standards require.

However, the average for all cars produced would comply with the standards. If standards are written as maxima, the automotive industry would have to target to meet levels approximately one half of those specified in order to allow for production variations and to ensure that each individual car manufactured fell below the specified limits. This would have the net effect of increasing the stringency of control standards and directionally further aggravating the energy shortage.

The levels selected can be met by the automotive industry without use of catalysts. Testimony by car manufacturers in the U.S. and Japan have indicated that maximum levels of 2.0 gm/mi HC, 24 gm/mi CO, and 3.1 gm/mi NO_x could be achieved without catalytic devices.[5] Elimination of these devices will avoid the potential increase in emissions as a result of failure of catalytic units. The lack of durability of these units in testing to date suggests that in public service they will not perform their required function. Conventional engines tuned for low emissions without such devices are more likely to have better emissions level stability. Such engines can be maintained by the trained mechanics currently available without the need for expensive schooling in the diagnosis of catalytic devices on a nationwide basis.

Acceptance of the nationwide standard of 4.0 grams per mile for NO_x would obviate the need for reducing catalysts and/or exhaust gas recirculation with their attendant heavy fuel economy penalties. This is supported by The Clean Air Act Amendment of 1970, having accepted 4.0 grams per mile as the uncontrolled NO_x level for 1971 vehicles from which a 90 percent reduction was regulated for 1976.

1976 and Later Years

It is recommended that the proposed nationwide standards for 1975 (see Table 6.6) be continued.

For California and other known smog-prone areas only, a reduction of NO_x emissions is suggested from the level of 3.1 gms/mile *average* in 1975 to 1.5 gms/mile *average* for the period 1976-80 inclusive. These levels are believed to be achievable without the use of catalysts for either NO_x or HC and CO emissions control.

This five-year period would provide the time needed to extend current technology to the development of new non-catalytic control means including alternate engine types. It is felt that this effort could result in the availability of cars that could meet reduced standards for all three pollutants for the period 1981 and beyond. It is suggested that Congress may wish to consider establishing a mechanism whereby progress in this area is periodically determined.

The suggested average levels for 1981 and beyond are (in gms/mile) 1.0–HC, 10–CO, and 1.3–NO_x. Since such levels would require some sacrifice in fuel economy when compared to engines meeting the higher levels

Table 6.8. Engine Efficiency and Fuel Processing Penalties Associated with Control of Exhaust Emissions Basis for Chart 6.3 of the Texaco Presentation Two-Car Strategy—Conventional Engines

Model Year	Emission Controlled	Modifications Applied	Engine Penalty % Fuel Cons. Increase Over 1970	Demand Penalty & Crude Req. Increase	Comments
1971-74		Reduced Comp. Ratio	5.4	3.0	As for Charts 6.1 & 6.2
For Nationwide Cars (85% of Total) Leaded Fuel & Increased Comp.					
1975-	HC 1.5 CO 15.0 NO$_x$ 4.0	Air Pump & Spark Retard or Lean & EGR + Retard	6.4	3.5	Includes refinery fuel increment for processing the additional gasoline
For Critical Area Cars (15% of Total) Leaded Fuel & Increased Comp. Ratio					
1975	HC 1.5 CO 15.0 NO$_x$ 3.1	Same as above	6.4	3.5	
1976-1980	HC 1.5 CO 15.0 NO$_x$ 1.5	Thermal Reactor EGR & Spark Retard	10.0	5.5	
1981-	HC 1.0 CO 10.0 NO$_x$ 1.3	Same	10.0	5.5	

for non-smog-prone areas, it is suggested that the application of these lower standards to a given area of the U.S. be carefully considered.

B. Petroleum Demand and Crude Oil Savings, Two-Car Strategy

Table 6.8 summarizes the assumptions used in evaluating the effect on U.S. petroleum demand of the suggested two-car strategy.

All cars are to operate on leaded fuel of approximately today's octane number, which would permit an increase in compression ratio with resultant increase in power and fuel economy. For 1975 a penalty of 6.4 percent in fuel consumption has been allowed for all cars for control to the suggested emission levels. No distinction has been made between nationwide and critical area car penalties, for the sake of calculation, even though the latter have a stricter NO_x standard and would be expected to consume somewhat more fuel. The corresponding increase of crude demand in 3.5 percent of crude (being half the fuel consumption penalty basis of 50 percent yield of gasoline from crude plus an increment representing refinery fuel required to process the additional gasoline demand).

The suggested standards for critical areas for 1976 and later entail a larger fuel consumption penalty of 10 percent to allow for the means of controlling further NO_x reductions. The corresponding crude demand penalty is 5.5 percent, which includes an increment for refinery fuel. From 1981 and on, it is assumed improved technology will permit meeting more restrictive standards without further fuel consumption penalty.

The method of calculation of the demand increments and resulting U.S. liquid petroleum demand for this case is the same as that explained in the section, Energy Resource Losses, page 244, covering the development of Charts 1 and 2 presented to the Subcommittee on June 26.

The engine efficiency improvement permitted with the use of leaded fuel and the improved refinery operation such fuels permit, can be converted to equivalent crude oil input to the refinery. When this is done for the two-car strategy, the incremental crude saving by year from 1976 to 1985 is as tabulated below.

The cumulative saving through 1985 of Texaco's suggested two-car strategy in comparison with the application of the currently mandated U.S. standards amounts to 8 billion barrels or 18 percent of the U.S. total liquid petroleum reserves.

C. Vehicle Emissions and Air Quality

Acceptable ambient air quality can be achieved at a reasonable cost by utilizing the two-car strategy and vehicle emission standards proposed under Section A.

In order to illustrate the effect of the alternate emission standards on air quality, the total emissions for various pollutants and air quality for Phoenix, Arizona, based on light-duty vehicle emission standards have been projected.

Table 6.9. U.S. Liquid Petroleum Demand and Crud Oil Savings
(Millions of barrels per day)

Year	NPC Base Case	With Currently Mandated Fed. Stds.	With Texaco 2-Car Strategy	Saving Col 3 − Col 4
1975	18.4	18.7	18.6	0.1
1976	19.2	20.0	19.5	0.5
1977	20.0	21.2	20.3	0.9
1978	20.9	22.6	21.3	1.3
1979	21.7	23.8	22.2	1.6
1980	22.5	25.1	23.0	2.1
1981	23.3	26.2	23.8	2.4
1982	24.0	27.4	24.6	2.8
1983	24.7	28.5	25.4	3.1
1984	25.4	29.5	26.1	3.4
1985	26.0	30.4	26.8	3.6

Phoenix is an area of moderate air pollution problems, but involving fewer complications than the South Coast Air Basin of California. The need for transportation controls has been indicated in the Phoenix Implementation Plan, submitted by the State of Arizona to the EPA.

Air Quality Computations

The calculation of emissions and air quality used in our projection was based on the data contained in "The State of Arizona Air Pollution Implementation Plan—Transportation Control Strategies, April 1973" prepared by the Arizona State Department of Health Division of Air Pollution Control for the Federal Environmental Protection Agency. The method of calculating the relation between total emissions and air quality in the Arizona plan is the "Roll-Back Model." Pierrard[6] and associates have shown that this method considerably overestimates the vehicular emissions reductions necessary to achieve the ambient air quality standards, especially for carbon monoxide. Nevertheless, to be conservative, we have projected the emissions for Phoenix to 1985, using the "Roll-Back" model for hydrocarbons and nitrogen oxides. For projection of the air quality and emission levels for CO, we have used a "Modified Roll-Back Model" based on Pierrard's data.

Details of the emission and air quality calculations are shown in the last part of this section.

Emission Trends

Emission trends for Phoenix have been estimated for hydrocarbons, carbon monoxide, and nitrogen oxides through 1985. These are shown in Figs. 6.5, 6.6, and 6.7, respectively. Each figure shows three trends for each

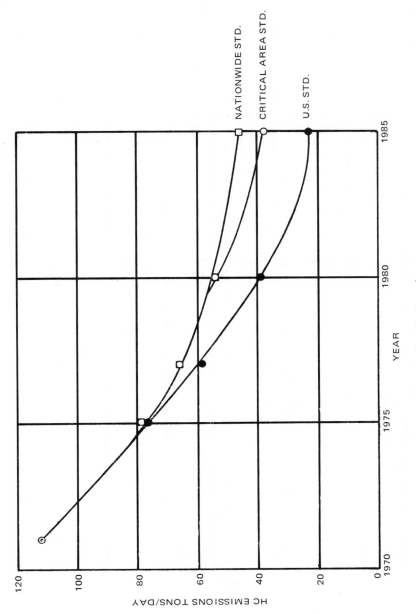

Fig. 6.5. Phoenix Emissions and Air Quality Hydrocarbons

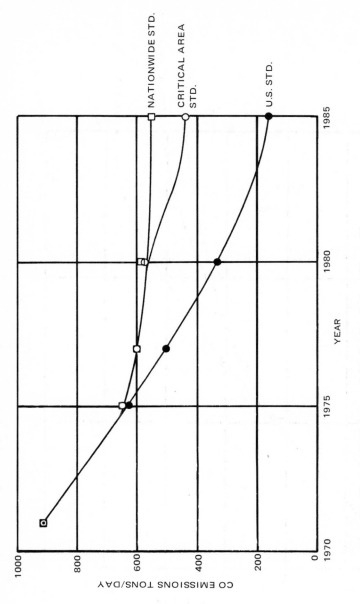

Fig. 6.6   Phoenix Emissions and Air Quality Carbon Monoxide

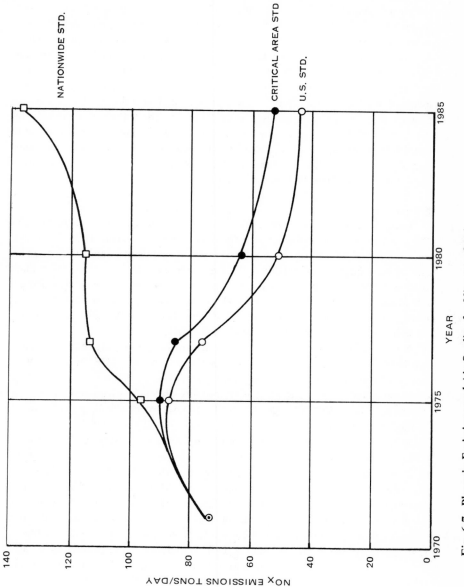

Fig. 6.7. Phoenix Emissions and Air Quality for Nitrogen Oxides

pollutant, one for each of the three emission standards. For the case of the hydrocarbon and CO, air quality improves from 1971 on because emissions of these pollutants continues to decrease. In the case of nitrogen oxides, however, emissions increase for the nationwide standards case while decreasing for the U.S. and critical area standards. It should be pointed out that the increase in nitrogen oxides emissions estimated for the nationwide standards case is a direct function of the 6.8 percent vehicle growth rate assumed by the compilers of the Phoenix Plan. If a more moderate vehicle growth rate of 0-3 percent is assumed for Phoenix, then the increase in nitrogen oxides emissions shown for the nationwide standards in Fig. 7 will not materialize and only a moderate increase in nitrogen oxide emissions would be estimated. This matter is discussed further under the caption Emission and Air Quality Calculations, below.

Compliance with Ambient Air Quality Standards (AAQS)

Table 6.10 indicates when Phoenix is in compliance with the AAQS for the years shown and utilizing the vehicle emissions standards listed. It should be emphasized that Phoenix is not projected to be in compliance with the CO ambient air quality standards by 1975 according to the Implementation Plan filed with the EPA by the State of Arizona. This is based on the projected emissions from the Roll-Back Model and therefore requires imposition of transportation controls. Using a "Modified Roll-Back Model," we predict Phoenix will be in compliance with the CO standard by 1975.

After 1975, both hydrocarbons and carbon monoxide emissions are estimated to be in compliance with the appropriate AAQS through 1985 under all three sets of vehicle emission standards. In the case of NO_x, emissions under the nationwide standards are not estimated to be in compliance in 1985 with NO_2 AAQS if the 6.8 percent vehicle growth factor is used in the calculations. If a more moderate vehicle growth rate of 0-3 percent is assumed for Phoenix, then compliance with NO_2 AAQS through 1985 would be forecast.

It is evident from the emission curves and the AAQS Compliance Table that the imposition of the U.S. standards would be unnecessarily severe for this area since compliance with all AAQS will be achieved by 1977 with the nationwide standards. The emission and air quality forecasts made for Phoenix illustrate the situation believed to exist in most of the U.S.—namely, that the imposition of the severe U.S. vehicle emission standards is not necessary to achieve and maintain satisfactory air quality. Careful, well-documented studies are required in potentially critical smog areas before the critical area standards are extended beyond the California South Coast Air Basin. In the meantime, the benefits of the nationwide standards can be realized by the adoption of the recommended two-car strategy and the associated nationwide and critical area emission standards.

Table 6.10. Compliance with Ambient Air Quality Standards*

Hydrocarbons — Primary Std. — 0.24 PPM (6-9 A.M.)

Standard	Year				
	1971	1975	1977	1980	1985
U.S. Standard	No	No	Yes	Yes	Yes
Texaco Nationwide	No	No	Yes	Yes	Yes
Texaco Critical Area	No	No	Yes	Yes	Yes

Carbon Monoxide — Primary Std. — 9 ppm (8 Hr Max)

Standard	Year				
	1971	1975	1977	1980	1985
U.S. Standard	No	Yes	Yes	Yes	Yes
Texaco Nationwide	No	Yes	Yes	Yes	Yes
Texaco Critical Area	No	Yes	Yes	Yes	Yes

Nitrogen Dioxide — Primary Std. — 0.05 PPM (Annual Arith. Mean)

Standard	Year				
	1971	1975	1977	1980	1985
U.S. Standard	Yes	Yes	Yes	Yes	Yes
Texaco Nationwide	Yes	Yes	Yes	Yes	No*
Texaco Critical Area	Yes	Yes	Yes	Yes	Yes

*Based on 6.8 percent vehicle growth; however, compliance is estimated for all vehicle growth rates up to 3 percent.

Emission and Air Quality Calculations

In our calculations the extension of the data to 1985 was performed by linearly projecting the vehicle population to this date using the 6.8 percent growth rate assumed in the Phoenix report. While this growth rate may apply to the entire Phoenix-Tuscon area, it cannot be expected to apply to the central business district of Phoenix or Maricopa County, which already have the highest population and vehicle density in the state. The vehicle population in such areas is more likely to remain almost constant.

The age deterioration factors for catalytic muffler system effectiveness and for non-catalytic muffler effectiveness (HC and CO) were obtained for 1985 by extrapolation of the values used in the Phoenix report. The age deterioration factor for NO_x emissions reduction obtained by catalytic muffler was the same as that used for hydrocarbons. The age deterioration factor for NO_x reduction obtained by non-catalytic muffler methods was unity.

In the calculations for NO_x emissions, the emission factor was 4.0 g/mi for uncontrolled cars. The speed factor used was inversely proportional to that for CO. It was 1.0 for 1971, 1980, and 1985. It was 1.1 for 1975 and 1977.

The emissions calculated are those of the light-duty vehicle population. These were the only emissions considered in calculating the degree of control necessary for compliance with the ambient air quality standards.

Calculation of compliance with the ambient air quality standard for hydrocarbons and NO_2 is made by assuming the maximum ambient concentration decreases in proportion to the decrease in total emissions—that is, the "Roll-Back Model" assumption. The geometric mean used for the appropriate pollutant was obtained from air quality data[7] for a city whose 1962-1968 maximum was that of Phoenix in 1971. The projected air quality data was plotted on a log-probability chart parallel to the 1971 Phoenix base case, and the percentage of time the air quality exceeded the ambient air quality standard was read from this chart and multiplied by 365 days per year. Complicance was obtained when the calculated number of days exceeded was one or less.

Pierrard[8] has shown that the emissions totaled over an air shed are not directly proportional to peak CO concentrations encountered at specific points in the air shed. He has also shown that the highest levels of carbon monoxide concentration are encountered near central business district traffic rather than near metropolitan area traffic. This traffic is at a saturation level and should have no growth to speak of. Finally, the calculation of allowable emission level should be based on the air quality value which is exceeded once per year rather than the worst value over the sampling period. When these factors are taken into consideration, the CO emission level as calculated by "Roll-Back" is found to be too high by a factor of 2.5. Thus, to obtain a relation between air quality and total emissions in tons/day a "Modified Roll-Back Model" should be used as shown below, where

"Roll-Back Model" $[(EAQ) (GF)-(B)] R = (GF) (EAQ)-(AQS)$

becomes for the case under consideration:

"Modified Roll-Back Model" $(AQS) = (EAQ) \dfrac{(1-R)}{(2.5)}$

Using this model we have computed the projected CO compliance status of Phoenix for 1975, 1977, 1980, and 1985. In the above equation:

$$EAQ = \text{existing air quality}$$
$$GF = \text{emission growth factor}$$
$$B = \text{background air quality}$$
$$AQS = \text{air quality standard}$$
$$R = \text{fractional emission rate reduction required to achieve desired air quality.}$$

D. Use of Leaded Fuels

A description of a typical refinery has been provided under the discussion of Energy Resource Losses. As pointed out in that discussion the octane number of a typical gasoline currently manufactured in a U.S. refinery is lower than required for a modern passenger car engine. The average unleaded gasoline pool Research Octane Number for the U.S. is about 88. This is raised to the currently required pool octane level of about 96.4 through the use of tetraethyl lead additives. It has also been indicated in other sections that the use of lead in gasolines permits the use of more efficient engines and that it avoids the waste involved in manufacturing high-octane unleaded fuels.

It is being argued by some people that lead in gasoline represents a health hazard. Texaco has carefully reviewed all information presently available on this subject and finds no evidence to substantiate that opinion. Our findings on the subject have been communicated to EPA in previous correspondence.[9]

Even though there is no health problem, the emission of lead into the environment by automobiles can be controlled, effectively and economically, by the use of muffler lead traps. Such traps are now available[10] and can be incorporated in new cars as well as retrofitted to in-use cars. Trapping efficiencies of such devices on new cars are of the order of 90 percent; retrofit trap efficiency is about 70 percent.[11] The use of muffler traps has been compared with the EPA proposal for lead-free gasoline and gasoline lead reductions as a means for reducing vehicular lead emissions. Following cases were considered:

Case 1: Unleaded gasoline for new cars, no lead reduction in gasoline for in-use cars;

Case 2: Unleaded gasoline for new cars, reduced lead in gasoline for in-use cars;

Case 3: Leaded gasoline at present levels for all cars, muffler traps on new cars, and retrofitted on in-use cars over a four year period.

The effectiveness of these three approaches to reducing the total lead emissions is shown in Fig. 6.8. The comparison shows that the use of muffler traps provides the most rapid initial decrease in total emissions. Only after 1981 does the EPA proposal (Case 2) show a slight advantage. This comparison, however, assumes the muffler traps to work at the present level of efficiency, and neglects probable improvements over the years. One also notes that all three cases produce reductions in lead emissions below the 65 percent goal set by EPA. It is interesting that the muffler lead trap case reaches this point at the earliest date.

Comparison of these three cases on a cost basis shows the muffler trap to emerge as the most economical solution by far. The figures are summarized in Tables 6.11 and 6.12 below.

Table 6.11. Motorists' Total Incremental Costs, Dollars (85,000 miles)

	Post 1974 New Car			1971-74 Car			Pre 1971 Car		
Case	Fuel[b]	Cost	Total	Fuel[b]	Cost	Total	Fuel[b]	Cost	Total
1	142	66[c]	208	142	29[c]	171	0	14.5[c]	14.5
2	142	66[c]	208	142	39[c]	181	0	19.5[c]	19.5
3	0	28.5[d]	28.5	142	18.7[e]	160.7	0	18.7[e]	18.7

(a) Study assumed Prem. at 2.5 g Pb/gal, Reg. at 2.0 g Pb/gal.
(b) Incremental cost due to increased fuel consumption; study assumed 5% decrease in economy for cars designed to operate on 91 RON lead-free gasoline.
(c) Incremental cost due to lead removal, study assumed 1¢/gal increase in cost for lead removal[12]
(d) Cost long-life muffler trap[13]
(e) Cost retrofit muffler trap[14]

Table 6.12. Annual Savings from Muffler Lead Traps (millions of dollars)*

Car	$/car/yr	1976	1978	1980	1985
Post 1974	21	361.2	863.1	1379.7	2547.3
1971-74	2.4	99.1	94.1	80.9	28.6
	Total, $MM	460.3	957.2	1460.6	2575.9

*Calculated from Table 6.11.

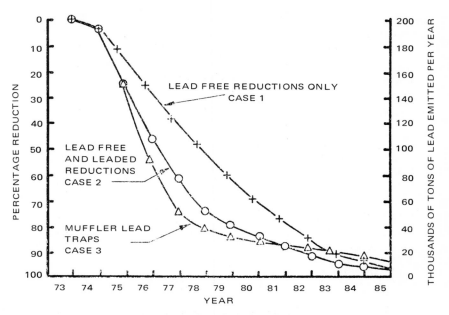

Fig. 6.8. Reductions in Lead Emissions from Muffler Lead Traps and
Gasoline Lead Regulations

LEAD REDUCTIONS ESTIMATED BY:

    CASE 1   EPA, PUBLISHED IN OIL DAILY 1/29/73
    CASE 2   EPA, PUBLISHED IN OIL DAILY 1/29/73
    CASE 3   TEXACO

Clearly, the economic advantages of the use of muffler lead traps over
removing lead from gasoline are substantial: $460 million for 1976 up to over
$2500 million for 1985. Such cost differentials are compelling arguments for
continued use of leaded gasolines in conjunction with lead trapping mufflers,
if lead emission control is eventually decided to be necessary.

THE REDUCTION OF VEHICLE LEAD EMISSIONS
BY SIMPLE CATCHMENT*

INTRODUCTION

Although there is no scientific evidence that lead in the
atmosphere presents a hazard to health, it still may be thought
desirable to reduce that which arises from the use of lead in
gasoline.   It is universally recognised that the reduction of
lead in gasoline would be costly.   A more economically attractive
alternative would be to reduce the quantity of lead emitted by
the vehicle, particularly if the device used was inexpensive,
easy to fit and did not impair vehicle performance.   Such a device
has been developed by The Associated Octel Company and is described
in this report.   The efficiency of this device in drastically
reducing lead emissions is illustrated on a number of vehicles
together with its effect on vehicle performance, fuel consumption,
exhaust gas back pressure and silencing.

DETAILS OF THE DEVICE

The device takes the form of a filter which can be incorporated
into any design of exhaust system.   It is effective over the
lifetime of the exhaust system and will be renewed as part of
the standard system.   For this reason, it is applicable to used
cars and will begin reducing lead emissions immediately after
its introduction.

The filter package consists of a stainless steel wool matrix
as a support for a coating of alumina.   A typical package is
illustrated in Figure 1 and an installed system in Figure 2.

Tests have shown that the filter retains lead due to a
combination of chemical and mechanical actions, for example,
above certain temperatures lead in the exhaust gas reacts with
the alumina to form non-volatile alumina lead compounds.   Since
most vehicle exhaust systems contain two expansion or silencer
boxes, replacing these with the filter units ensures that at
least one of the filters operates in a suitable temperature regime
for chemical catchment at all engine operating conditions.

THE RESULTS OBTAINED WITH THESE FILTERS

1)   The effectiveness of these filters in reducing
      lead emissions

The reduction in lead emissions achieved by these filters
has been examined on a number of vehicles operated over considerable
mileage periods on tape controlled dynamometers.   For mileage
accumulation, a typical journey containing open road, suburban
and city driving was used.   A breakdown of the journey is given
in Table 1.

For these tests, the highest permissible lead content for
the fuel (0.84g Pb/litre) was used, representing the most arduous
testing conditions for these filters.

The lead emissions of three vehicles with standard exhaust
system and when fitted with filter exhaust systems shown in
Figures 3, 4 and 5.   Lead emissions were measured using the
technique described in Appendix 1.

*The Associated Octel Company Limited, Engine Laboratory, Bletchley

In all cases, the filters reduced lead emissions to a fraction of what they were with the standard exhaust.   Correlatory tests are now being conducted with vehicles on the road.

2)   The effect on vehicle performance

This is indicated in Figures 6, 7 and 8 which compare the results for standard and filter exhaust system.   There was no effect on power output and fuel consumption on these vehicles, even in those cases where inclusion of the filter resulted in a slight increase in exhaust gas back pressure.

3)   Filter durability

The results in Figures 3, 4 and 5 show that these filters were durable and still effective up to 25,000 miles (40,000 Km) under the specified running conditions.   The tests were terminated at this point as representing the average life of current exhaust systems.

Excellent control of lead emissions can be achieved in the type of driving operation described.   However, it is accepted that the filter must stand up to sustained high speed and load operation which can be experienced, for example, on the motorway systems of Western Europe.   Tests are being conducted at such conditions and one test has now covered a total of 24,000 miles, 18,000 of these at the 80 mph condition.   There has been no failure of the filter, impairment of lead catchment efficiency or detrimental effect on the engine.   This test is continuing.

Three points of particular interest have arisen during this test.

i)   Although lead emissions increased during the 80 mph operation up to 48%, they were still significantly lower than would be expected from the standard exhaust system (previous experience and published data indicate that virtually all the lead going in and much of that previously deposited will be exhausted with a standard system under these test conditions.)

ii)   There was no evidence that lead previously retained by the filter under the lighter loads and speeds was blown out by the more severe operating conditions.

iii)   The sustained high speed operation did not impair the efficiency of the filter, i.e. when the test was returned to the lower average speed, urban type driving, the catchment efficiency was at least as good as that obtained previously; i.e. less than 10% of the ingoing lead was emitted.

4)   The effect of the filter on the particle size of the emitted lead

This was investigated using a technique suggested by Habibi (Reference 1), detailed in Appendix 2.   Figure 9 shows the

average of several test results obtained with a standard system
and with a filter exhaust system.

With the standard system 36% of the emitted lead is of
a particle size greater than 1.0 micron, i.e. 64% is sub-micron:
with the filter system 74% of the emitted lead is greater than
1.0 micron, i.e. 26% is sub-micron.

This work is continuing.

5)   The efficiency of the filters as silencers

The silencing properties of these filters have been tested
on a variety of vehicles using the British Standard test procedure.
Typical results are shown in Table 2.   The silencing properties
of these filters are at least equal to those of standard silencers.

6)   The effect of the lead content of the fuel

Work has been done on a test bed using a standard design
of filter and varying lead concentrations in the fuel.   The
engine was operated for 60 hours at 50 mph constant speed, road
load.   The percentage of ingoing lead retained by the filter
at different lead levels is shown in the following table.

Lead content of fuel g/l	% ingoing lead retained by filter	
	1st Test	2nd Test
0.8	44.2	47.2
0.6	48.8	45.6
0.4	45.9	44.9
0.2	43.4	54.0

The results show that the filter is equally effective at all
lead levels.

7)   The effect of engine malfunction

In the event of engine malfunction, large quantities of unburnt
fuel can pass through the engine into the exhaust system and cause
failure in exhaust "afterburner" use.   The filters described have

been tested over the complete engine speed and load range up
to 70 mph with one or two cylinders misfiring. In all cases,
the filters satisfactorily withstood these tests.

8)   The effect of the filter on gaseous emissions

Tests have shown that the device does not influence gaseous
emissions. It in no way conflicts with the currently accepted
methods of controlling gaseous exhaust emissions to meet the standards
required in Europe.

CLOSURE

The results given in this report, indicate the potential
of this type of filter device for reducing vehicle lead emissions,
even at this early stage of its development. Work is continuing
to minimise back pressure effects and optimise designs. For
example, Figure 10 compares the performance and back pressure
of a vehicle (1) with its standard exhaust system and (2) our
latest design of filter. Some increase in back pressure has
occurred with mileage on the prototype designs, but this does
not appear to significantly affect vehicle performance or fuel
consumption. The latest designs of filters should minimise any
such increase.

Production costs and means of mass producing these devices
are currently being investigated. It is expected that the cost
will be comparable with that of a standard exhaust system.

These filters reduce overall lead emissions and also change
the particle size so that even in the relatively small quantity
of lead emitted, the proportion which will remain airborne is
also reduced.

The facility with which such devices can be incorporated
into exhaust system design, without penalty to vehicle performance,
offers a more economic alternative to limiting the use of lead
in gasoline and would avoid the consequent upheaval to the petroleum
and automotive industries.

REFERENCE

1.   HABIBI, K., JACOBS, E.S., KUNZ, W.G. and PASTELL, D.L.
        'Characterization and control of gaseous and
        particulate exhaust emissions from vehicles',
        E.I. Du Pont de Nemours & Co. (Inc.), Wilmington,
        Delaware, 1970 (Paper for presentation to the APCA
        West Coast Section 5th Technical Meeting 8th-9th
        October, 1970, San Francisco, California.)

TABLE 1

ANALYSIS OF DRIVING CYCLE USED FOR MILEAGE ACCUMULATION

SPEED RANGE GROUP (mph)	% TIME IN[+] GROUP	DISTANCE IN * GROUP (MILES)	% DISTANCE IN GROUP
0 - 10	12.8	1.28	2.1
10 - 20	11.2	3.35	5.4
20 - 30	24.0	12.00	19.4
30 - 40	23.0	16.10	26.0
40 - 50	14.2	12.80	20.6
50 - 60	10.5	10.60	17.1
60 - 70	3.3	4.8	6.9
70 - 80	1.0	1.50	2.4
TOTALS	100.0	61.91	99.9

AVERAGE SPEED FOR THE TWO HOUR JOURNEY = 31 mph

NOTES:-

[+] From analysis of a two hour speed/time trace.

* Assuming the average speed for each speed range group is the mid point of the speed range.

TABLE 2

SILENCING PROPERTIES

(Noise measurements by the BS 3425 - 1966, procedure)

| VEHICLE | Noise measured dB(A) | | | | SOUND LEVEL * | |
| | Standard silencers | | Octel filters | | STANDARD SILENCER | OCTEL FILTERS |
	RH side	LH side	RH side	LH side		
1600 cc	81.0 82.0 82.0	83.5 83.5 83.5	82.0 82.0 82.0	82.5 82.5 82.5	83.0	82.0
1200 cc	84.0 84.0 84.5	84.5 85.5 85.0	82.0 82.0 82.5	81.5 82.5 82.5	85	82
2000 cc	78.5 79.0 78.5	76.0 76.0 77.0	77.5 77.5 77.5	77.0 76.0 76.5	79.0	78.0

* The average of each set of three readings on either side
  of the vehicle was calculated. The higher average,
  corrected to a whole number (fractions of a decibel being
  ignored), was taken as the sound level of the vehicle.

FIGURE 1. LEAD FILTER – TYPICAL CONSTRUCTION

FIGURE 2.   LEAD FILTERS – TYPICAL INSTALLATION

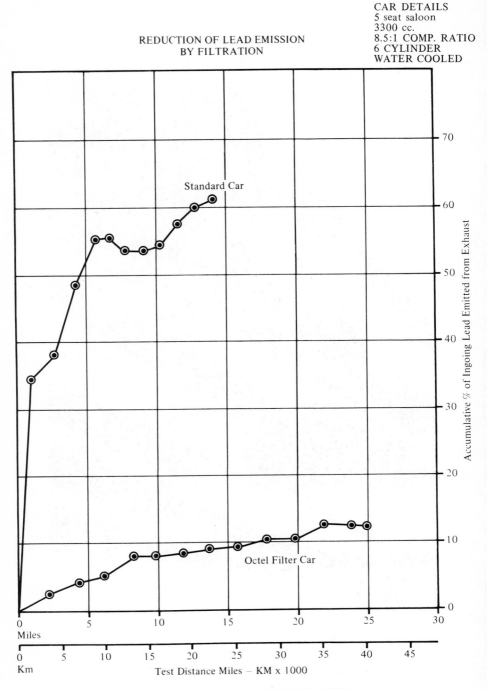

FIGURE 3. REDUCTION OF LEAD EMISSION BY FILTRATION

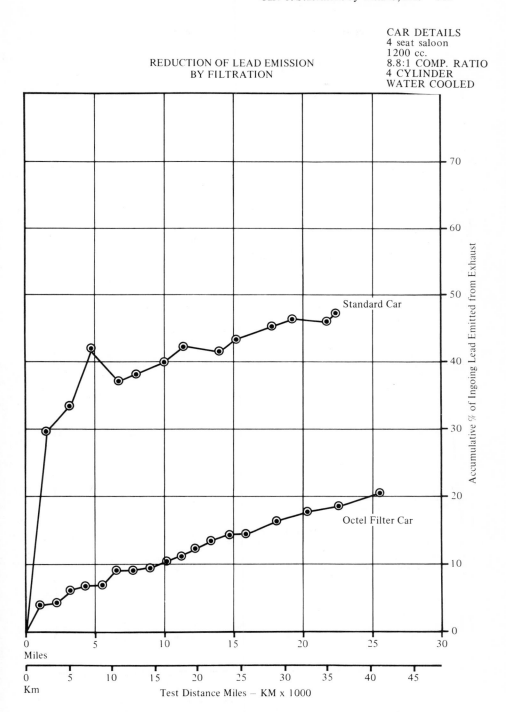

FIGURE 4.   REDUCTION OF LEAD EMISSION BY FILTRATION

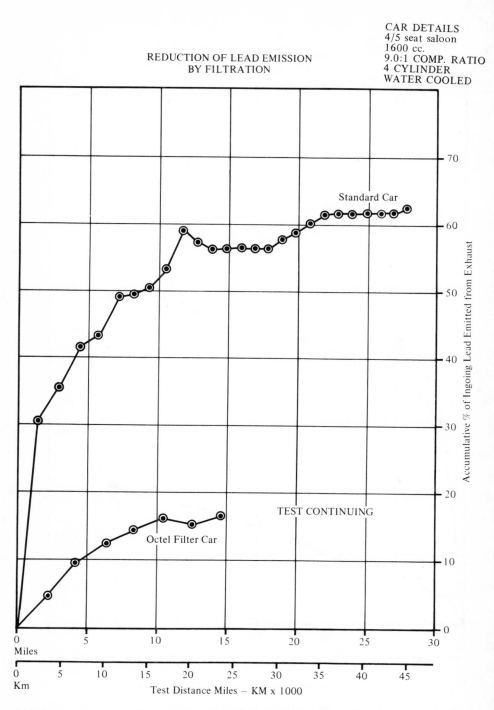

FIGURE 5. REDUCTION OF LEAD EMISSION BY FILTRATION

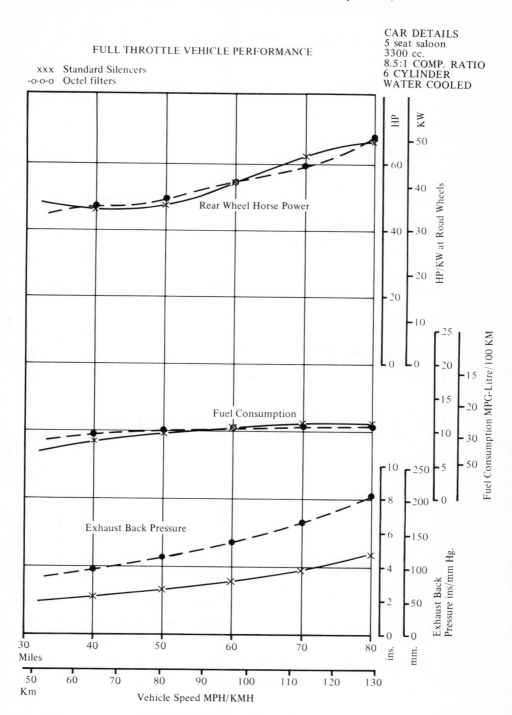

FIGURE 6. FULL THROTTLE VEHICLE PERFORMANCE

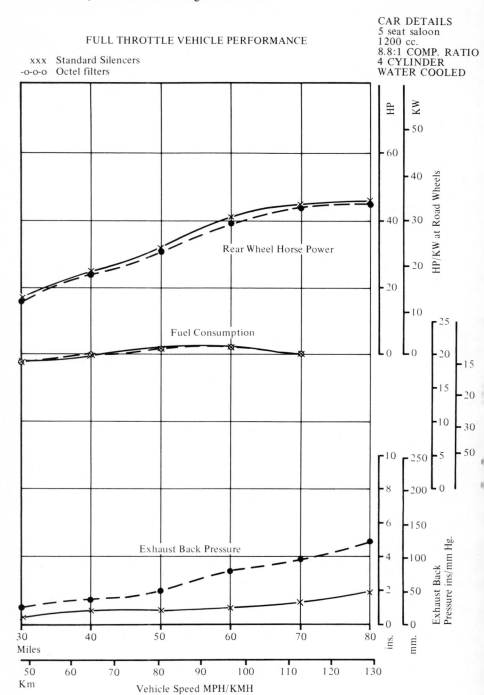

FIGURE 7. FULL THROTTLE VEHICLE PERFORMANCE

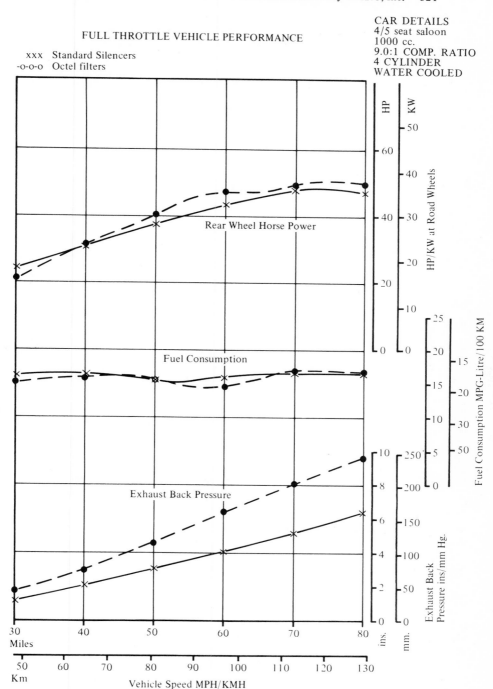

FIGURE 8.   FULL THROTTLE VEHICLE PERFORMANCE

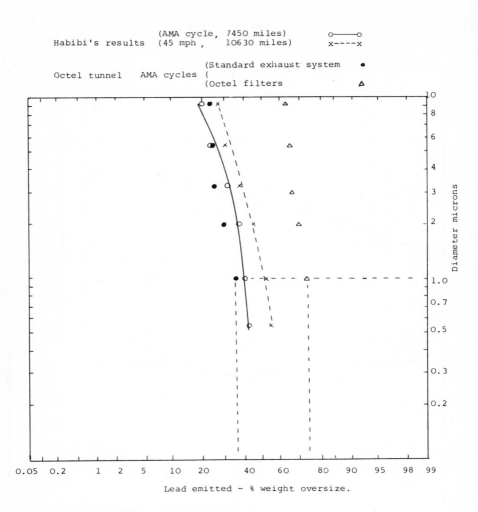

Fig. 9. Effect of Filters on Particle Size

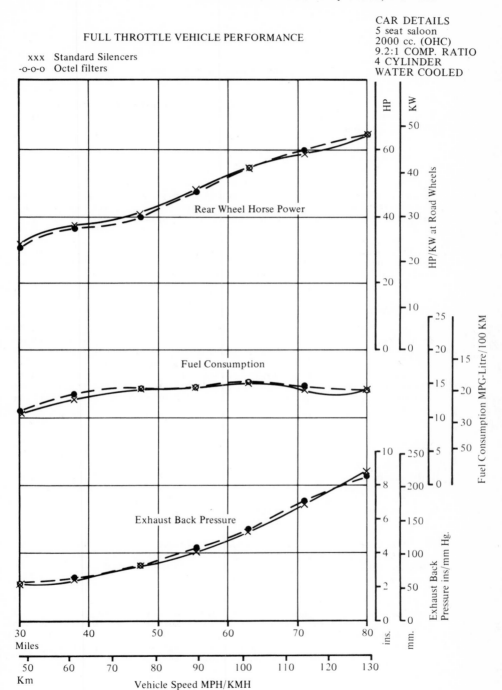

FIGURE 10. FULL THROTTLE VEHICLE PERFORMANCE

APPENDIX 1

LEAD EMISSION MONITORING

A high efficiency, large surface area, low pressure drop glass fibre filter media filter, attached to the vehicle tail pipe, is utilised to monitor lead particulate emissions.

Construction

The filter is constructed on a stainless steel cylindrical framework having dimensions as shown in the accompanying drawing. The fibre glass is held in place on the outside circumference with a square mesh screen and retained internally with a seam strip and spring bands.

Two layers of fibre glass mesh are used; a coarse layer on the inside - grade 25, 24 inches wide and a fine layer on top - grade 50, 36 inches wide with circular sections to complete end cover. The material is available from the American Air Filter (GB) Company Limited.

Application and use

Two of the above-mentioned filters are used in series by enclosing in an outer steel container sealed at the inlet plate end with a quick-release clamp and vent connection tube at the rear. The primary filter media is changed every 1000 - 1200 miles of operation, the secondary filter at less frequent intervals; up to 10,000 miles. The secondary filter is a pre-cautionary measure in the event of occasional split filters due to engine malfunctions. When utilised for vehicles incorporating "Lead Traps" the change period can be extended.

Analysis

Each filter is dismantled and the fibre glass is wetted with an organic solvent ('Fluorisol' - $Cl_2FC - CClF3$) to prevent loss of dust, and is torn to a workable size - about 2-3 inch squares. Fluorisol is used because it is low boiling, non-toxic and non-flammable. The material is then ground and disintegrated until finely divided in a "Shearmix" blender to form a slurry with the wetting agent.

The fibre glass is removed from the blender and the majority of solvent removed by filtration. The material is transferred to a 20-litre reaction vessel, equipped with a water-cooled distillation and reflux condenser and 10 or 15 litres of 20% HCl is added.

The flask is heated under total reflux and agitated for a minimum of two hours, and a filtered sample is removed whilst hot, for analysis. The sample is analysed for lead by polarograph (Method D3). During the first part of the heating to reflux, the tap at the base of the condenser is left open to drain the residual solvent. The large volumes of acid are required to prevent crystallisation of lead chloride at room temperature.

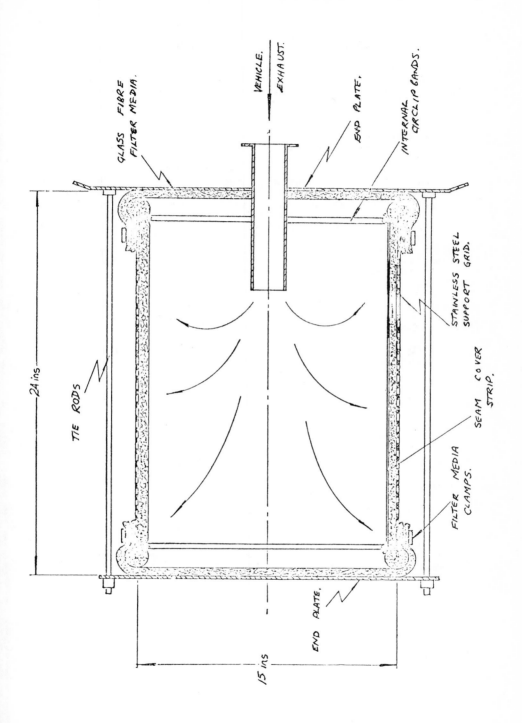

APPENDIX 2

A temporary rig similar in character to that of Habibi but smaller in size, has been set up to investigate the particle size distribution on small European cars.   The rig, in spite of its agglomerate characteristics and deposition from turbulence, is an adequate instrument for comparison work on a car.

For the tests, the vehicle is operated in a chassis dynamometer and the total exhaust stream from the vehicle is led into a tunnel and mixed with a stream of filtered ambient air.   The tunnel, with a flow of 300 cfm of a mixture of exhaust gases and ambient air, is ten feet long and 8" diameter.   Two probes placed at the pump end of the tunnel facing the flow are connected to the sampler with back-up filters and reference filters. The probe for the sampler is 0.5" diameter and sucks 28.3 1/min of gas and the one for reference filters is 0.297" diameter and sucks 125 1/min. The reference filters which are connected in parallel with the sampler and back-up filters are to record any deviations from the isokinetic sampling by the sampler probe.   The flows in the two sampling lines are metered by rotameters and the filters used are Gelman metricel GA9, pore size 0.10µ; maximum pore size 0.26 - 0.30µ.

The tunnel deposits during the test were obtained by cleaning the tunnel with a rag soaked in paraffin and then analysing the soaked rag for deposits.   The fuel consumption during a run was measured by weighing a can of fuel before and after a run.

Only seven out of the possible eight stages of the sampler were used. The stages used were as follows :-

Stage	Particle Size µ
0	> 30
1	> 9.2
2	5.5 - 9.2
3	3.3 - 5.5
4	2.0 - 3.3
5	1.0 - 2.0
6	< 1.0

All the tunnel deposits were classified as above 30µ because of their high settling rate, and all the deposits on the back-up filter were classified as below 1µ and included in stage 6 deposit of the sampler.

APPENDIX 3

VEHICLE PREPARATION AND OPERATING CONDITIONS

1.   Vehicle preparation

Each test is started with a vehicle which has been fully run in on lead-free gasoline.   In the case of cars with previous test mileage, the engine is de-leaded.

The lubrication system of the engine is thoroughly flushed, to remove residual lead deposits (usually part of the end of test procedure from a previous test).   The combustion chambers of the engine are cleaned and the cylinder heads prepared to the maker's recommended standards.   The vehicle is then fitted with a new exhaust system of the appropriate type (i.e., maker's original or Octel manufactured filter system).

All other components of the test vehicle are maintained in standard and serviceable condition.

2.   Operating conditions

Vehicles are driven on automatically controlled dynamometers, according to a pre-recorded road circuit.   This road circuit contains sections of unrestricted (70 mph) cruising and sections of low-speed - high traffic density - city driving.   The total length of the circuit is 60 miles, and the average time for the journey is 2 hours.   (Speed analysis of the journey is given in Table 2 of the report).

Test vehicles are driven according to this cycle for 4 hours.   They are then stopped, and cooled down to ambient temperatures by using external oil and water coolers, supplemented by a large fan to cool transmission components.   The vehicle dynamometers are located in the open air, and this rapid cool-down period takes only 30 minutes.

The mileage accumulation is completed by operating on the above programme for 24 hours per day, 5 days per week.   During this operation critical vehicle temperatures are continuously monitored and correlation between road and dynamometer temperatures is good.

Stratified Charge Engine Technology:
The Texaco Controlled System—TCCS

This combustion system was invented by a Texaco scientist over 30 years ago and has been under development since that time. During that period, considerable knowledge has been gained of stratified engine operation. Further, information has been published on this concept and its advantages as development progress has warranted.[15]

Inherent in the concept is the ability to operate on a wide range of fuels without a requirement for octane or cetane number, the achievement of high levels of fuel economy under normal vehicle driving conditions, and low exhaust pollutant levels compared to conventional engines.

The combustion system operates as follows. During the downward stroke of the piston, air is drawn in through an intake port that directs the air so that it swirls in the cylinder as shown on Fig. 6.9.

When the cylinder is filled with its air charge, the piston then reverses to compress the air. At the time when the air is highly compressed and combustion is to start, fuel is injected into the cylinder in the direction of air rotation. The spark plug fires very soon after the fuel injection is initiated.

In this manner a combustion zone is established into which fuel is fed by the injector with fresh air being supplied by its rotary motion.

Low levels of engine power demand are met by injection of a small amount of fuel impregnating a small portion of the air. For full engine power, the fuel injection continues until all or nearly all the air has been impregnated with fuel. In either case the fuel and air are mixed in the vicinity of the fuel injection and enter the flame front, which is in reality stationary in the area of the spark plug.

At part load conditions, it can be seen that one zone of the combustion chamber can be relatively "rich" in fuel while only air is present in the rest of the chamber. This is the essence of the TCCS stratified charge combustion concept. The presence of excess air in the cylinder permits the products of combustion to mix with the air for more complete oxidation.

Because this mixing of combustion products and excess air cannot, of course, be perfect, there is some hydrocarbon and carbon monoxide remaining in the exhaust products. In a TCCS engine, CO is considerably less and HC's are somewhat lower than in the premixed charge engine.

Now let us consider the manner in which such a combustion system contributes to the inherent advantages mentioned at the start of this discussion.

Operation on a Wide Range of Fuels

Since the fuel is ignited as soon as it mixes with the air in the cylinder, the possibility of engine knock is eliminated. Such knock in other engines is caused by the spontaneous combustion of a relatively large volume of a mixture of fuel and air before the spark-ignited flame front reaches it.

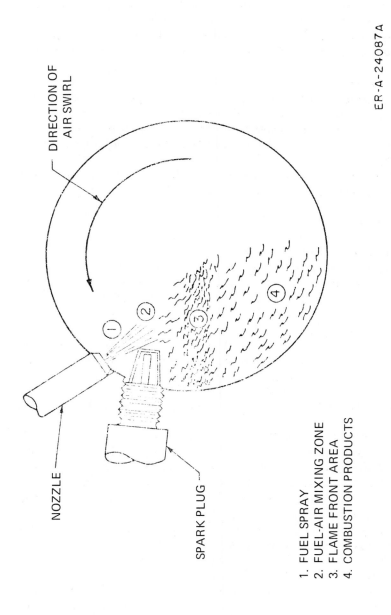

ER-A-24087A

Figure 6.9 Texaco Controlled–Combustion System

Elimination of the possiblity of knock removes a requirement for fuel octane value which is a measure of a fuel's resistance to spontaneous ignition.

Diesel engines operate on a principle of spontaneous ignition of the fuel. These engines have high compression ratios that provide the high temperatures and pressures conducive to the spontaneous ignition so that no spark plug is required. The ease of a fuel's ignition in a diesel engine is measured as cetane number. Again, the TCCS requires no such fuel quality specification.

Good Fuel Economy

The engine draws in a full charge of air. The energy loss associated with the throttling inherent in carburetted engines is not necessary. Small amounts of fuel can be ignited and completely burned, providing high efficiency at the normal part load conditions that represent a major portion of passenger car operation.

Extensive testing programs have demonstrated that TCCS engines have a 30 percent or more fuel economy advantage over carburetted engines.

Low Emissions

Hydrocarbon and Carbon Monoxide

The existence of excess air in the cylinder and its contribution to the complete combustion of the fuel required for part load operation was discussed. This reduces the emission levels of both HC and CO.

Oxides of Nitrogen (NO_x)

It is known that the reaction between nitrogen and oxygen, both components of the air, occurs under high temperature conditions. The most conductive circumstance occurs when the fuel-air mixture contains slightly more air than the theoretical quantity required for complete combustion. Mixtures of fuel and air that are either richer or leaner than this condition yield reduced quantities of NO_x at a given temperature.

Recalling the concept of TCCS one can see that the initial combustion of the fuel occurs in a locally rich mixture which inhibits NO_x formation. The later combustion completion through mixture of the combustion products with the excess air is believed to be a condition in which the NO_x formation is inhibited by the reaction quenching effect of the excess air. This quenching action is a well-known combustion concept and is postulated to explain the demonstrably low oxides of nitrogen levels achievable with stratified charge engines relative to carburetted engines.

Discussion of the TCCS has been provided to the Senate Committee for this presentation to provide a basis for our discussion of the effects of emission controls on engine performance. It must be understood that such a novel engine concept is only viable when it has stood the rigors of extensive study and testing in a potentially marketable vehicle.

Further, the introduction of a new engine type brings with it many problems that must be solved once testing programs have indicated marketing feasibility. Among the areas that must be pursued are the supply of fuel injection equipment in sufficient quantities in the case of TCCS, alteration of engine production lines, and perhaps changes in some vehicle components such as transmission and rear axle ratios. Engine control linkages must be considered as well as auxiliary equipment such as air cleaners, fuel-feed pumps, and fuel filters.

Introduction of such a new concept is normally and sensibly achieved by a pilot production which is expanded in subsequent years until the desired percent of total output is achieved.

Experience has shown that commercialization of such a major component concept in the automotive industry takes at least seven or eight years.

Stratified charge engines are currently being considered by the automotive industry as a means for meeting future requirements. To study the impact of such a move, we have drawn on our experience with the Texaco Controlled Combustion System and have evaluated the fuel demand picture for the foreseeable future for the application of such engines.

The effect on the U.S. petroleum demand of the introduction of stratified charge engines such as the TCCS has been calculated based on the assumptions appearing in Table 6.13. The schedule for phasing in the new engines has been made optimistic in view of the engine's similarity to current power plants as well as development already completed. The 20 percent reduction in fuel consumption as compared with a conventionally powered car of 1970 model year is considered conservative. Credit has been taken for a two percent reduction in crude demand relative to current engine gasoline for the processing of the wide-cut fuel which is suitable for TCCS. Such a fuel could have a boiling range of $100°F$ to $600°F$ and no octane or cetane number requirement. The penalty for emission control is somewhat less than was used for conventional engines in recognition of the inherently lower emissions of the TCCS engine.

The petroleum demand for a two-car strategy calling for the introduction of stratified charged engines to meet the requirements of critical areas and the rest of the U.S. is tabulated in the third column of Table 6.13. For comparison purposes, the demand for the Texaco-suggested two-car strategy based on the use of conventional engines only is shown in the second column.

The saving affected by the stratified charge engine approach is seen to amount to approximately 2 million barrels per day in 1985 as detailed in Table 6.14.

Ambient Air Quality Standards

The present national ambient air quality standards were issued in 1971 in accordance with the requirements of the 1970 Clean Air Act Amendments. The standards were established to protect the public health and welfare with

Table 6.13. Engine Efficiency and Fuel Processing Penalties Associated with Control of Exhaust Emissions Basis for Case Involving TCCS-Powered Autos

Introduction Schedule

TCCS-powered cars phased into production as follows:

1977	10% of new cars
1978	20% of new cars
1979	40% of new cars
1980	80% of new cars
1981 & later	100% of new cars

Model Year	Emission Component Controlled		Modification Applied	Engine Penalty, % Fuel Consumption Increase Over 1970	Demand Penalty, % Crude Requirement Increase		Comments
					Increment	Total	
For Nationwide Cars (85% of TCCS-powered cars)							
1977 & later	HC	1.5	Inherent TCCS economy	-20	-11		
	CO	15.0	Wide-cut fuel		- 2		
	NO_x	4.0	Emission control engine adjustments	3.5	1.8	-11.2	
For Critical Area Cars (15% of TCCS-powered cars)							
1977- 1980	HC	1.5	TCCS economy	-20	-11		
	CO	15.0	Wide-cut fuel		- 2		
	NO_x	1.5	EGR & retarded combustion	7.5	3.8	- 9.2	
1981 & later	NO_x	1.3	Same as above			- 9.2	Refinery fuel saving

Table 6.14. U.S. Liquid Petroleum Demand.
Millions of Barrels Per Day—Two-Car Strategy

	Conventional Engines Only*	Conventional & TCCS Engines	Saving, Col 2 - Col 3
1977	20.3	20.3	0
1978	21.3	21.2	0.1
1979	22.2	21.9	0.3
1980	23.0	22.5	0.5
1981	23.8	23.0	0.8
1982	24.6	23.5	1.1
1983	25.4	23.9	1.5
1984	26.1	24.3	1.8
1985	26.8	24.6	2.2

*From suggested Two-Car Regime Curve of Chart 6.3 presented to the Subcommittee, June 26, 1973, and as described in detail under Automotive Emission Control Strategies

an adequate margin of safety. The air quality mandated by these air quality standards can only be met by implementing emission controls. As we are now learning from the implementation plans submitted by the various states, not only are mobile and stationary source emission controls required, but in some instances, severe transportation and land use controls are required as well.

The more restrictive the air quality standards, the greater degree of emission control required. Because the cost of emission control goes up exponentially with the degree of control, overly restrictive air quality standards will result in a totally unjustified economic penalty to every citizen of the United States because there will be negligible accompanying benefits in public health and welfare. At present, the full costs of meeting the present ambient air quality standards are not known. However, it is evident from the severe transportation controls which have been proposed[16] to supplement the mobile and stationary source emission standards, that the fuel costs of meeting the present air quality standards may be prohibitively large.

A critical review of the information which formed the basis for the national air quality standards for carbon monoxide, nitrogen dioxide, hydrocarbons, and photochemical oxidants indicates that these standards are unduly restrictive. The adverse effects associated with the pollutants at the low levels of the standards are not substantiated by the data. Moreover, in setting the standards, proper attention was not given to studies which showed no adverse effects at these concentrations. This has resulted in standards which are exceeded in many instances by emissions arising from natural sources alone. There follows a summary of the present situation for each ambient air quality standard.

Carbon Monoxide

The present national ambient air quality standards for carbon monoxide are shown in Table 6.15. These standards are "intended to protect against the occurrence of carboxyhemoglobin levels above 2 percent."[17] The standards are based heavily on studies by Beard and Wertheim[18] which were reported in 1967 and which have since been shown to be in error by numerous other researchers.[19]

The newer information cited above would indicate that exposure to carbon monoxide at levels in excess of the present standards does not produce harmful effects and that carboxyhemoglobin levels up to approximately three percent are generally safe. In balance, all of the available reliable information would indicate that the present carbon monoxide air quality standards are unduly restrictive.

Nitrogen Dioxide

The present nitrogen dioxide standards (see Table 6.15) are based on a single study conducted near a TNT plant located just outside of Chattanooga, Tennessee.[20] A comprehensive critique[21] of this study concluded that the results of the Chattanooga study are not sufficient to be the sole basis for setting a nitrogen dioxide standard. EPA has since indicated that the Chattanooga study is to be repeated. Additional epidemiological studies are needed to confirm or disaffirm the present standard.

Hydrocarbons

Hydrocarbons are generally recognized to be harmless at present atmospheric concentrations.[22] However, they can react to produce oxidant and other harmful products under certain meteorological conditions. The present hydrocarbon standard, (see Table 6.15) is based solely on the probability of non-methane hydrocarbons reacting to produce oxidant.[23] Since there is an oxidant air quality standard, the hydrocarbon standard is redundant and, in fact, not desirable. The State of California recognized this and did not set a hydrocarbon air quality standard.

Although an air quality standard for hydrocarbons is redundant, hydrocarbon emissions to the atmosphere must be controlled in order to meet the oxidant standard. The degree of control of hydrocarbon emissions which is necessary to protect the oxidant standard varies between various regions because of differences in meteorology and sunlight. The present hydrocarbon standard is based on a "worst case" oxidant-hydrocarbon relationship and contains an excessive factor of safety for all but the most smog-prone areas of the U.S.[24]

If it is necessary that there be a hydrocarbon standard, then in order to meet the realities of a general hydrocarbon-oxidant relationship, hydrocarbon air quality standards should be developed on a regional basis and set at levels which would protect the oxidant standard in the various regions. Another factor, however, which must be considered in setting regional hydrocarbon standards is the fact that hydrocarbon emissions from natural sources exceed the present standard in some areas.[25]

Photochemical Oxidants

The photochemical oxidant standard (see Table 6.15) is based on epidemiological studies carried out in Los Angeles.[26] The oxidant standard is based primarily on an estimate of increased frequency of asthma attacks in some subjects on days when the estimated hourly average concentrations of oxidant reached 0.16 ppm[27], on a finding of impaired athletic performance on days of high oxidant concentrations,[28] and on a finding of an apparent increase in respiratory complaints in the Los Angeles area as compared to the rest of the state.[29] A detailed analysis[30] of these studies concluded that whereas an oxidant effect might be present at concentrations in the range of 0.15 ppm, questionable extrapolations are necessary to infer effects at the 0.08 ppm level.

Table 6.15. National Ambient Air Quality Standards

Pollutant	Averaging Time	Primary Std. $\mu g/m^3$	Primary Std. p.p.m	Secondary Std. $\mu g/m^3$	Secondary Std. p.p.m.
Sulfur Dioxide	Annual Arithmetic Mean	80	0.03	60[a]	0.02[a]
	24 hour*	365	0.14	260[a]	0.1[a]
	3 hour*	—	—	1300	0.5
Particulate	Annual Geometric Mean	75	—	60	—
	24 hour*	260	—	150	—
Nitrogen Dioxide	Annual Arithmetic Mean	100	0.05	Same as primary	
Hydrocarbon[b]	3 hour* (6 to 9 AM)	160	0.24	Same as primary	
Carbon Monoxide	8 hour*	10,000	9	Same as primary	
	1 hour*	40,000	35		
Photochemical Oxidant	1 hour*	160	0.08	Same as primary	

*Maximum levels not to be exceeded more than once per year.
(a)   EPA has proposed reconsideration of these standards
(b)   Non-methane hydrocarbon

The photochemical oxidant standard must also be considered in relation to background levels. Background oxidant levels range up to 0.06 ppm[31] with average background concentrations in the 0.03-0.05 ppm range.[32] These concentrations have been present in the atmosphere during the entire span of man's existence on earth. In summary, the present photochemical oxidant standard of 0.08 ppm is so close to the natural background levels as to be unreasonable.

Sulfur Limitations

The overall demand for fuel oil is increasing at an unprecedented rate and a major factor contributing to shortages has been the environmental restrictions on sulfur emissions. A most important factor in this situation is the unavailability at U.S. refineries of adequate supplies of both foreign and domestic low sulfur crude oils.

In order to meet the current demands for fuel oil throughout the free world, desulfurization facilities capable of processing one million barrels per day have been built[33] to supply fuel oils meeting the allowable sulfur contents of the major geographical areas. Unfortunately, desulfurization does not increase the supply of fuel oil since this process only removes sulfur with no significant change in the volume of product manufactured. Therefore, from forecasts of heavy fuel oil demands, allowable sulfur contents, and availability of crude oils (both high and low sulfur) during the next five years, it is estimated that an additional 3.6 million barrels per day of desulfurization capacity will be needed for the heavy fuels only. This is illustrated in Fig. 6.10.

One way to alleviate the need for desulfurization of fuel oils would be to remove the sulfur from the stack gases of large consumers such as power plants. This method of handling sulfur is currently being broadly investigated and developed. However, to date none of the known processes under development has demonstrated long-range reliability or the ability to operate without creating other problems. Assuming, however, that stack gas removal processes were available and could compete economically with low sulfur fuel oil, it is doubtful that they could be installed in sufficient quantity to have a significant impact before the 1980s.

Desulfurization for fuel oil production usually involves the heavier portions of the crude and the processing required is quite expensive to build—usually costing in excess of $1,200 per daily barrel of oil feed. The projection of facilities required in Fig. 6.10 assumes that the equipment can be built by the times shown and does not consider the delays in gaining caused by prior commitments on the part of engineering contractors. It is not unreasonable to anticipate a three to five year period between the decision to build and initial operation. Thus it may be optimistic to assume that the indicated capacity can be installed by the times indicated.

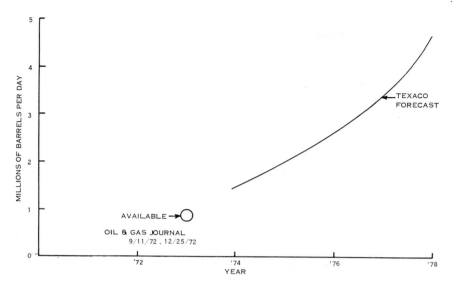

Fig. 6.10. Free world Total Desulfurization Capacity Required

In the presentation to the Subcommittee on June 26, it was noted that progress in controlling sulfur in the air is being made. Particularly cited was New York City, with a reduction of 65 percent during the last three years[34] (1969-1972). This suggests that it might be permissible to relax sulfur restrictions in those areas imposing the most stringent standards for a period of five years. The result of such action would be to ease the supply and cost of fuel oil. During this time, the provisions of The Clean Air Act regarding sulfur emissions could be reexamined by an appropriate governmental agency to consider a more uniform sulfur restriction policy based upon prevailing geographical needs. Also, a realistic timetable could be set to implement sulfur restriction standards which would balance both the nation's health and its economic needs.

Non-Degradation and the National Environmental Policy Act

As mentioned in Texaco's testimony on June 26, it is too early to determine the scope of the non-degradation doctrine upheld as a principle of The Clean Air Act by the recent Supreme Court decision. It is that very uncertainty, however, that could serve to discourage refinery expansion and other plans so vital to the long-term solution of the nation's energy shortage problems. It is, perhaps, ironic that this factor of uncertainty should emerge just as refinery expansion activities were encouraged by the repeal of crude oil quotas.

It also is possible that the non-degradation principle will serve to aggravate near-term energy problems. As President Nixon stated in his recent message on national energy policy, current state and local fuel oil sulfur restrictions should be no more stringent than necessary to implement the primary national ambient air quality standards for sulfur dioxide (SO_2). More stringent fuel sulfur specifications needed to implement the secondary SO_2 standards should be delayed for several years. If this procedure were followed, current sulfur restrictions in many areas could be relaxed somewhat for the next few years, permitting the use of higher sulfur coal and fuel oil that otherwise could not be used to alleviate projected fuel shortages.

With the emergence of the non-degradation principle, however, it is uncertain whether state and local authorities will be able to relax fuel sulfur restrictions currently in effect. Indeed, we are concerned that the principle may even present an obstacle to the adoption by state and local authorities of temporary emergency fuel oil sulfur relaxations such as were granted last winter when the low sulfur fuel shortage began to make its presence felt.

Texaco hopes that Congress will consider amending The Clean Air Act so as to avoid the possibility of such inequities. Section 110 of the Act, and EPA regulations recently adopted thereunder, already ensure that no new construction will be allowed which could prevent the attainment or maintenance of primary or secondary national ambient air quality standards with their built-in safety margins. Texaco fails to see the desirability of more stringent non-degradation land-use safequards which could serve to discourage or prevent activities designed to fulfill the basic energy and other needs of the public. We urge the Congress to reconsider the non-degradation principle and adopt an appropriate amendment to the law.

NOTES–CASE 6

1. *Oil and Gas Journal*, April 2, 1973.

2. *1956-1972 Automotive Facts and Figures,* published annually by Motor Vehicle Manufacturer's Association of the U.S., Inc.

3. E.N. Cantwell, W.E. Bettoney, and J.M. Pierrard, "A Total Vehicle Emission Control System," API, Philadelphia, May 15, 1973.

4. Address by E.N. Cole, President GM Corp., to the API, Pebble Beach, California, September 26, 1972.

5. Typical values (EPA hearings, March 1973): Chrysler–1.7, 24, 2.7; Toyota–2.1, 24, 3.1; American Motors–2.2, 24, 3.1. All in grams/mile maximum HC, CO, and NO_x, respectively.

6. J.M. Pierrard, R.D. Snee, and J. Zelson, "A New Approach to Setting Vehicle Emission Standards," 66th Annual Meeting of APCA, June 24, 1973.

7. R.I. Larsen, *A Mathematical Model for Relating Air Quality Measurements to Air Quality Standards,* U.S. EPA Air Programs Publ. No. AP-89.

8. *Ibid.*

9. Critique, "EPA's Position on the Health Effects of Airborne Lead," Texaco, Inc., March 6, 1973. Included as Enclosure 2 of supplementary information to the Subcommittee.

10. "The Feasibility and Costs of Using Lead Traps as an Alternative to Removing Lead from Gasoline," E.I. duPont Report, November 30, 1972; "An Assessment of the Effects of Lead Additives in Gasoline on Emission Control Systems Which Might Be Used to Meet the 1975-76 Motor Vehicle Emission Standards," Aerospace Corporation Report, November 15, 1971, No. TOR-0172 (2787)-2; "The Reduction of Vehicle Lead Emissions by Simple Catchment," Associated Octel Co., Ltd., October 1971, Attached.

11. See E.I. duPont Report, 1972; and Associated Octel Co. Report, 1971.

12. Bonner and Moore Associates to EPA, "An Economic Analysis of Proposed Schedules for Removal of Lead Additives from Gasoline," Document PB 201 133, U.S. Dept. of Commerce, June 25, 1971; Bonner

and Moore Associates, "No-Lead Cost to Consumer Put at 5.5-7 ¢ Gal,"
Oil and Gas Journal, October 11, 1971, p. 55; Bonner and Moore
Associates, "An Economic Analysis of Proposed Regulations for
Removal of Lead Additives from Gasoline," March 15, 1972; and Bruce
S. Bailey, "Gasoline-Motor Engineering," *Journal of the Washington
Academy of Sciences,* Vol. 61, No. 2, June 1971.

13. E.I. duPont Report, 1972.

14. *Ibid.*

15. W.J. Coppoc *et al.,* "A Stratified Charge Multifuel Engine Meets 1976
U.S. Standards," Presented to API Division of Refining, Philadelphia,
May 14-17, 1973.

16. *Federal Register,* Vol. 58, No. 120, Part 11, June 22, 1973.

17. *Federal Register,* Vol. 36, 8186, 1971.

18. R.R. Beard and G.A. Wertheim, *American Journal of Public Health,* Vol.
57, 1967, p. 2012.

19. NAS Report, "Effects of Chronic Exposures to Low Levels of CO on
Human Health, Behavior and Performance," Washington, 1969; R.D.
Steward, J.E. Petersen, E.D. Baretta, R.T. Bachard, M.J. Hasko, and A.P.
Hermann, *Arch. Environm. Health,* 21, 154 (1970) and letter R.D.
Stewart to EPA, March 5, 1971, commenting on CO stand.; P. Mikulka,
R. O'Donnell, P. Heinig, and J. Theodore, *Toxicol. Appl. Pharmacol.,* 18,
593 (1971); J. Theodore, R. O'Donnell, and K.C. Back, *J. Occupational
Med.,* 13, 242 (1971); CRC APRAC Symposium, Washington Hilton
Hotel, Washington, D.C., March 7-9, 1973:

    a. R.D. Stewart, "Determination of Carboxyhemoglobin in Vari-
ous Segments of the Population"

    b. R.A. McFarland, "Effects of Low Levels of Carbon Monoxide
Upon Humans Performing Driving Tasks"

    c. E.P. Radford, "Effects of Carbon Monoxide Exposures Upon
Myocardial Infarction Fatality Rates"

    d. R.D. Steward, "Effects of Carbon Monoxide on Human Behav-
ior"

    e. D.A. DeBias, "Effects of Chronic Exposure to Low Levels of
Carbon Monoxide on the Cardiovascular System"

20. C.M. Shy, J.P. Creason, M.E. Pearlman, K.E. McClain, F.B. Benson, and M.M. Young, *JAPCA*, 20, 539 (1970); C.M. Shy, J.P. Creason, M.E. Pearlman, K.E. McClain, F.B. Benson, and M.M. Young, *Imid*, 20, 582 (1970); M.E. Pearlman, J.F. Finklea, J.P. Creason, C.M. Shy, M.M. Young, and R.J.M. Horton, *Pediatrics*, 47, 391 (1971).

21. J.M. Heuss, G.I. Nebel, and J.M. Colucci, *JAPCA*, 21, p. 535 (1971).

22. *Air Quality Criteria for Hydrocarbons*, AP-64, U.S. Department of Health, Education and Welfare, Washington, D.C.

23. *Ibid.*

24. Heuss *et al.*, *JAPCA*, 1971.

25. CRC-APRAC, CAPA-11, *Interim Technical Report*, Washington State University, July 1973.

26. *Air Criteria for Photochemical Oxidants*, AP-63, U.S. Department of Health, Education and Welfare, Washington, D.C.

27. C.E. Schoettlin, and E. Landau, *Public Health Report*, 76, 545 (1961).

28. W.S. Wayne, P.F. Wehrle, and R.E. Carroll, *J. Amer. Med. Assoc.*, 199, 901 (1967).

29. R. Hauskenecht, "Air Pollution Effects Reported by California Residents," California Dept. of Public Health, Berkeley, 1960.

30. Heuss *et al.*, *JAPCA*, 1971. (see Notes 21).

31. *Air Criteria for Photochemical Oxidants* (Note 26)

32. *Ibid.*

33. Not all available to U.S.

34. "Data Report, Aerometric Network, Winter Season, December 1971-February 1972," The City of New York, Environmental Protection Administration, Department of Air Resources.

Case 7
Some Experiences with Guaranteed Incomes and Lump Sum Payments: The Case of the Klamath Indians*

DAVID BUNTING[†] and W.T. TRULOVE[†]

INTRODUCTION

There appears to be fairly widespread agreeement that existing poverty programs suffer significant defects.[1] Yet a goodly amount of conjecture surrounds current proposals for reforms or new programs. On the one hand, these proposals are viewed as a means whereby recipients can cast off the shackles of their current circumstances and begin to make their own way in a competitive society. On the other hand, they are viewed as devices which ultimately expand welfare rolls at prohibitive expense. Since these proposals are virtually untested, this conjecture serves both to continue the status quo and to justify visionary schemes.

A number of proposals have focused on some type of basic allowance (either a cash grant or income guarantee) which eligible individuals or families may claim subject to a variety of qualifications.[2] While usually involving increased public monies, most of these proposals seem more concerned with administrative changes to increase the efficiency and effectiveness of current poverty expenditures. If implemented, these suggestions would probably do

*Based on a paper presented at the 137th meeting of the American Association for the Advancement of Science, session for contributed papers of The National Institute of Social and Behavioral Science, Chicago Room, Sheridan-Blackstone Hotel, Chicago, December 26, 1970.

This paper, part of a wider study of the economic impact of the Klamath Indian Reservation termination, is supported by a grant from the Louis W. and Maud Hill Family Foundation, Saint Paul, Minnesota. The views expressed herein are solely those of the authors and not necessarily those of the Hill Family Foundation.

[†]Eastern Washington State College

much to improve the existing system but, nevertheless, they may be less comprehensive than their proponents claim.

Essentially, these basic allowance proposals are short-run measures which do not remedy the underlying "causes" of poverty. Since cash incomes may be the most immediate need for those classified as poor, many proposals suggest procedures to change the 100 percent earnings tax or "don't work" aspect of the current poverty system. Unquestionably, this tax is a serious disincentive to seeking economic independence, but other disincentives associated with work/leisure choices may be equally important.[3] This failure to consider education, employment information, retraining, civil rights, and other basic needs may produce rather disappointing results in the long run.

Virtually none of the proposals has been tested. Since programs of this type usually involve increased public spending, they face slim chance of political acceptance and implementation without information to evaluate their probable consequences. To overcome this difficulty, a few test programs have been initiated. Several demonstration projects involving a small number of families in New Jersey, Pennsylvania, Iowa, and North Carolina are currently being supported by the Office of Economic Opportunity.[4] Two experiments with model neighborhoods of Seattle and Gary are in progress under the sponsorship of the Department of Health, Education and Welfare.[5] The former project is attempting to test various negative income tax plans, while the latter is investigating family assistance schemes. A major objective in these projects is to determine the effects of various basic allowances on work incentives. Research design calls for the sample population to be divided into several groups, each of which will receive varying allowances, subject to different offsetting taxes on earnings. By comparing responses with control groups, it is hoped that the effects of various programs on work incentives, family well-being, and family stability can be traced.

While a necessary first step, these experiments may not produce entirely convincing results. First, the limited time period encompassed (three to four years) may not be long enough to evaluate possible short-run effects, and is certainly not long enough to consider the long-run impact of such programs. Second a "Hawthorne effect" may lead to atypical family behavior.[6] Individuals involved know that they are part of an experiment with a definite time limit and subject to close observation. This knowledge may introduce significant bias into spending, saving, indebtedness, and work patterns resulting in behavior unlikely to occur in the long run. Third, there is some evidence that changes in existing welfare rules may have adversely affected some experimental results.[7] Finally, even if the tests successfully generate some data, they are rather limited. In sum, we are left with the need for additional information as to the probable consequences of proposed basic allowance schemes. Nearly ideal would be tests based on long-term experiences which were not contrived in an experimental setting.

SOME EXPERIENCES WITH GUARANTEED INCOMES
AND LUMP SUM PAYMENTS

The Klamath Indians of Southern Oregon have experienced situations which are analogous to two current basic allowance proposals. First, for about 40 years tribal income was distributed to tribal members in a manner which approximated a guaranteed income. Second, after terminaton of federal supervision, they received a large cash lump sum payment from the liquidation of their reservation assets. In both situations, there was little attempt at social manipulation. The Klamath received their guaranteed incomes as a consequence of timber cutting on their reservation. While subject to the variation of market conditions, timber revenue was distributed on a per capita basis, with few restrictions, to every adult tribal member. Equal amounts due minors were either paid to parents without restrictions or placed in escrow for maintenance and education. Under similar restrictions, monies amounting to about $43,000 per person were distributed following partial liquidation of the Klamath Reservation in 1961.

In the following pages we consider the experiences of the Klamath under these programs.[8] Briefly, we examine the effects of quasi-guaranteed incomes on Klamath incentives for employment, education, and other modes of self-improvement. We then examine the impact on Klamath economic circumstances after the large lump sum cash payment. While our data are imperfect and impressionistic, we nevertheless believe this examination provides insight into the probable consequences of guaranteed incomes and lump sum payments as well as reducing somewhat the conjecture surrounding current proposals of a similar nature. Furthermore, we believe our study has some advantage over current demonstration projects in that the Klamath received their payments over a long period, unhampered by continous close observation.

The history of the Klamath Indians after their 1864 peace treaty with the United States is essentially a history of response to various federal Indian policies. At first, this policy sought to "individualize" through the elimination of tribal subgroups, encouragement of independent activities, and education in dominating ideologies.[9] Under the paternalistic umbrella of the Agency Superintendent and his staff, the Klamath quickly lost their native customs, social organization, language, and religion. By 1890, "a large number . . . were productively engaged in work of 'civilized' character . . . material wants had come to approximate those of . . . white neighbors. Many were conversant . . . in English . . . numbers were increasing steadily."[10] Stripped of social constraints, "individualism flourished . . . the field (was) free for the burgeoning of narrow self-interest."[11] As a consequence, the Klamath "became increasingly unresponsive to political control vested in an alien administration, when the Agency later became aware of the need to limit the growth of rampant individualism, it no longer was heeded."[12]

The reservation itself contained valuable resources. Nearly 80 percent of it (645,000 acres) was covered by commercial timber stands consisting primarily of Ponderosa pine.[13] Within its boundaries were found "approximately one-fourth of the total commercial forest land in the Klamath Basin."[14] As other timber reserves were depleted, this resource appreciated in value. With the completion of rail facilities in 1911, previous modest exploitation greatly accelerated.[15] This timber was extremely valuable and sale of cutting rights quickly became the primary source of reservation income. By 1927, the Klamath, in terms of tribal assets, were the richest Indian group in the United States.[16] By 1954, enough timber had been harvested to house the entire population of San Francisco, Portland, and Seattle.[17]

Opening of the Klamath Reservation to timber exploitation created a "boom" atmosphere which attracted outsiders with less than missionary inclinations. By 1929, there were more Whites on the reservation than Indians;[18] by 1938, only one-quarter of the population was Klamath.[19] Chiloquin, the major reservation town, became known as "Little Chicago."[20] "From the relative quiet of the outlying . . . farms, the Indians were sucked into this environment of rough and fast living."[21] Ambiguous legal status freed the Klamath from prosecution for all but . . . major crimes.[22] As the distribution of tribal timber income rose to substantial levels, the Klamath had for their model of White behavior the often drunken, lawless, promiscuous antics of loggers and related timber "beasts." "I do not believe," the Agency Superintendent reports, "that the moral condition is much, if any, worse among the Indians than it is among the same class of white people on and near the reservation."[23]

Because tribal lands were involved, each Klamath was legally eligible to participate in the distribution of reservation timber income. The actual distribution of the income was conducted semi-annually on a per capita basis with payments due minors disbursed to parents or individually as necessity demanded.[24] With the exception of minors and a few incompetents, these nontaxable payments were made without restrictions. While Agency personnel were free to encourage certain forms of spending behavior, they had little control over how the funds were actually spent. Creation of the timber income required little Klamath participation since the Agency undertook various forestry management obligations while leasing agreements were subject to federal regulations and Department of Interior approval.[25] In effect, the per capitas were unearned; they arose without Klamath effort and were distributed on the basis of legal status rather than need.

Since per capita payments continued for more than 40 years, we shall examine their effects on Klamath economic and social behavior as if they were a form of guaranteed income. This assumption is consistent with the Klamath treatment of these payments. As per capitas continued year after year, various commentators indicate that the Klamath began to assume that they would continue indefinitely to meet their current needs.[26] With the exception of the Depression years of 1932-36, this assumption was essentially sound.

Per capita payments made each year during the period 1923-1954 are listed in Table 7.1. Although payments were made earlier, 1923 marks the first year for which continuous data can currently be found. The series ends with 1954 because in that year the Klamath were terminated by federal legislation, thereby throwing reservation affairs into a morass not yet resolved.[27] Table 7.1 also shows each per capita payment as a percent of U.S. per capita personal disposable income and, for the years available, as a percent of Oregon per capita personal income.[28]

If a poverty line is drawn at 50 percent of U.S. personal per capita disposable income,[29] the Klamath received per capita payments large enough in 18 to 32 years to be above that line. Applying the same criterion to Oregon per capita personal income, they were above that line in ten of 26 years. Therefore, on an individual basis, the Klamath were fairly well off; their yearly unearned income was generally sufficient to keep them from the depths of extreme poverty. Further, if they earned an amount equal to their per capita payments, they would in every year but 1934 be excluded from America's poor.

Family income statistics, shown in Table 7.2, are even more impressive. For every year in which data are available (except 1947 when calculated as a percent of mean U.S. family disposable income), a Klamath family of five[30] would not be classified as "poor" under the criterion adopted above. As a percent of U.S. median white family income and U.S. median non-white family income, a Klamath family was always above the poverty line. This relative affluence is especially apparent when non-white median incomes are examined. Finally, 63 percent and 49 percent of all American families in 1950 and 1954, respectively, had incomes lower than Klamath families.[31]

Therefore, in most years (as indicated by one commonly accepted standard of poverty) Klamath individuals and families were not "poor." Yet the system of guaranteed income under which they lived was harshly criticized by all who were familiar with its operation. This criticism centered on three basic points. First, per capitas produced yearly incomes at levels which nearly extinguished incentives for gainful economic activities. Second, per capitas destroyed family organization by placing each family member in a financially independent position. Finally, per capitas reduced educational incentives by eliminating any apparent need to acquire employable skills. These points will now be examined in some detail.

However, this examination should not be viewed as pontifical criticism of individual Klamath behavior; rather, it is a description of what appears to be reasonable responses to various existing economic incentives. It quickly became apparent that this guaranteed income system was defective and not beneficial to the long-run welfare of the Klamath. Therefore, the per capita system itself is criticized as well as those public officials and private citizens who were aware of these defects but did little to remedy the situation.[32]

Table 7.1. Klamath Per Capita Payments as Percent of U.S. Per Capita
Personal Income and Oregon Per Capita Personal Income, 1923-1954

YEAR	(A) Klamath Per Capita Payment	(B) (A) as % of U.S. Per Capita Personal Disposable Income	(C) (A) as % of Oregon Per Capita Personal Income
	$	%	%
1923	50	8	—
1924	225	37	—
1925	200	31	—
1926	500	77	—
1927	550	85	—
1928	600	92	—
1929	600	88	88
1930	700	116	113
1931	550	107	107
1932	350	90	91
1933	225	62	62
1934	100	24	23
1935	100	22	22
1936	175	34	32
1937	325	59	58
1938	375	74	69
1939	300	56	52
1940	300	52	48
1941	320	46	38
1942	350	40	31
1943	400	41	29
1944	400	39	28
1945	400	37	29
1946	400	35	29
1947	325	28	21
1948	400	31	25
1949	800	63	52
1950	800	59	51
1951	850	58	49
1952	800	53	44
1953	800	51	44
1954	850	54	47

Sources: A. *Annual Narrative* (various years), Zakoji, *Termination . . .*, p. 28,
and various documents in Record Group 75, The National Archives,
Suitland, Maryland.

B. *Tax Foundation, Facts and Figures*, 12th Ed., 1962-1963, p. 60.

C. U.S. Dept. Comm., *Personal Income by States Since 1929*, pp. 142-143.

Table 7.2. Klamath Five-Member Family Income from Per Capita Payments
as Percent of U.S. Mean Family Disposable Income, U.S. Median
White Family Income, and U.S. Median Non-white Family Income,
Selected Years

Year	(A) Klamath five- Member Family Income From Per Capitas $	(B) (A) As % Of Mean U.S. Family Dispos- able Income %	(C) (A) As % Of Median White Family Income %	(D) (A) As % Of Median Non- White Family Income %
1929	3000	129	—	—
1936	875	54	—	—
1941	1600	76	—	—
1944	2000	63	—	—
1946	2000	56	—	—
1947	1625	44	52	101
1948	2000	50	61	113
1949	4000	104	124	242
1950	4000	98	116	214
1951	4250	97	111	209
1952	4000	88	97	171
1953	4000	83	91	163
1954	4250	88	98	176

Sources:

A. Table 1. Note: For comparative purposes, 1936 is average of 1935 and
   1936 family incomes.
B. U.S. Bureau of Census, *Income Distribution in the United States*, by
   Herman P. Miller; a 1960 census monograph (Washington, D.C.; G.P.O.,
   1966), p. 9.
C. *Economic Almanac*, 1967-68, p. 373.
D. Same as C.

Available statistics on the economic effect of the Klamath guaranteed income scheme indicate a reduction in economic activity as experience with per capitas was gained. Before World War II, in response to a Bureau of Indian Affairs questionnaire, the Agency Superintendent was required to submit an *Annual Statistical Report.* Data in these reports for 1923, near the beginning of the per capita system, and 1930, after per capitas had become firmly established, show the impact of this sytem on gainful employment.[33] Table 7.3 contains some questions asked and the Superintendent's estimates.

By 1944, the Superintendent indicated tribal income from timber sales was $850,000, while individual income from all other sources (labor and rentals) was about 11 percent of this amount.[34] During hearings in 1955 before an Oregon Legislative Committee, Agency personnel presented estimates of Klamath family income, which are shown in Table 7.4.

Observational comments are consistent with these data. Per capitas are ". . . practically enough to keep a family with very little effort on their part. This condition takes away the necessity of work and always leads to idleness, lawlessness, and discontent. The Indians are no different from white people in this respect."[35] As this unearned income continued, various Indians disposed of their cattle and sold their grazing allotments. "It is my opinion that they went out of the stock business because they wanted the money for other purposes and the income from the tribal fund did not make it necessary for them to work as in former years. . . . I am convinced that these payments are of no real value and assistance to many of the able-bodied adult Indians who should be supporting themselves without the assistance of per capita payments."[36] The development of timber created numerous new jobs. "With all these opportunities for employment, there is no reasonable excuse for any able-bodied Indian being out of work and unable to support himself and family in a satisfactory manner . . . Unfortunately, the annual income is sufficient to remove, to a considerable extent, the necessity of work."[37] "Generally speaking, the Klamaths live much above the average of other Indians in the United States [in 1944] and, to some degree, better than their white neighbors. . . . (Their) unearned income is much greater than (their) earned income."[38] In 1958, an Oregon Legislative Committee concluded: "For 40 years now, tribal income has been derived, almost completely, from timber sales, with some additional amounts accruing from leases on tribal farms and grazing lands."[39]

The effects of this guaranteed income on economic incentives were apparent when payments were reduced as a consequence of the Great Depression. After 1931, as per capitas fell, the Klamath attempted to increase their economic activity. Many began to seek employment, usually with federal public works or conservation projects.[40] Others sought to return to farming, ranching, or to enter into other economic pursuits. The Agency Superintendent concluded: this response ". . . shows very clearly that if large per capita payments will even again be made to these Indians that they will again be content to live without work."[41] After World War II, when per

Table 7.3. Extent of Self-support Among Able-bodied Klamath Adults, 1923 and 1930

	1923		1930	
Question	Number	Percent	Number	Percent
1. Number of able-bodied adult Indians under your jurisdiction who support themselves by their own industry and thrift	450	80%	134	20%
2. Number of able-bodied adult Indians other than above who make an effort at self-support but are not entirely self-supporting through their own industry and thrift	75	13%	383	57%
a. Number who receive sufficient Indian moneys or annuities to make up their deficiency	50	—	383	—
3. Number of able-bodied adult Indians who make no effort at self-support . . .	40	7%	150	22%
a. Number who receive Indian moneys or annuities sufficient for their support	25	—	150	—
Total	565	100%	656	100%

Source: Questions 51, 52, 52a, 53, and 53a, *Annual Statistical*, 1923 and 1930.

Table 7.4. Estimate of Klamath Family Dependence Upon Per Capita Payments

Able to or making a living without per capita payments	35%
Needing some assistance from per capita payments	20%
Depending almost entirely on per capita payments	45%
Total	100%

Source: Klamath Indian Agency, *Statistical Information Pertaining to Klamath Tribe: People and Income,* (Klamath Falls, Oregon, October 14, 1955), unnumbered page 4. (Found in General Services Administration Records Center, Seattle, Washington. BIA Klamath Agency, file 14137, box 2.)

capitas again became large, this prophesy was fulfilled as the Klamath again began to withdraw from the labor market.[42]

Economic incentives were damaged further by credit practices related to the regularity of per capitas. Numerous Klamath borrowed against future income (most often in the form of successive small credit purchases from local stores), the debt to be repaid from forthcoming per capitas. This practice increased reliance on the per capita system by creating a situation of continuous mortgaging of future expected payments.

While this guaranteed income stifled economic incentive, it also was not conductive to cohesive family relationships.[43] Since per capitas were the major source of income, "parents are practically independent of each other, the father is not compelled to support the wife and children and the mother, not being dependent upon him, can leave and seek other company any time she wishes."[44] Further, per capitas due minors were held in trust, to be disbursed as needed. If a parent was absent from a given family, the Agency would generally increase these disbursements. Hence, a parent could leave the family environs with little concern about its future financial status.[45] While this situation did not arise in the majority of families, it did occur with enough frequency for the Superintendent to comment on is existence.[46] Finally, minors could gain access to their per capitas by leaving their family residence, thus giving them financial independence from their parents and the power to substantially reduce family income by leaving. Parental controls were decreased and the influence of children in family affairs increased. In some cases, this resulted in disintegration of family life.

While this form of guaranteed income reduced economic incentives and induced family instability, it also adversely influenced educational propensities. Although it is difficult to distinguish between the inpact of environment and per capitas, various commentators have indicated the effects of these payments. "The schools . . . offered little incentive to children who were convinced that a ceaseless flow of per capita dividends gave them an assured income for life."[47] This ". . . knowledge that a certain income is assured without effort on their part makes (the youth) careless and indifferent."[48]

Wright generally summarized the situation:

> . . . the younger generation has always lived on an unearned income. Statistics indicate that these reservation people, generally speaking, have not sought employment nor have they seen the need of getting an education. The court records show that an alarming juvenile delinquency problem exists on the reservation which is attributed to idleness and easy money under the parentalism of Uncle Sam.[49]

As a consequence, this guaranteed income tended, over time, to increase dependency on its existence, decrease economic activity, foster family instability, and create a future based on its continuation.

In conclusion, it must be remembered that per capitas were paid out of tribal funds arising from the exploitation of tribal assets. Moreover, it was quickly realized that this form of distributing tribal wealth had adverse effects on Klamath economic and social life. Yet, in the absence of viable alternatives and unified tribal leadership, this system continued for 40 years. The underlying paradox is obvious:

> To withhold the tribal funds always leads to the criticism that the Indians cannot develop industrially on account of the lack of moneys and to many like complaints. To give the Indians large and frequent payments always leads to the criticism that they are being demoralized and debauched. It is a case of choosing the lesser of two evils.[50]

Unfortunately, little effort was made to resolve the paradox. The Tribal Council, while voicing concern, continued to vote per capitas. The Agency, apparently unable to influence Washington policy, assented. The Klamath responded to existing incentives as might be expected.

We turn now to a brief discussion of the impact of large cash lump sum payments. In 1954 Congress, by approving Public Law 587,[51] terminated federal control over the Klamath Indians. This law, defective in many respects, was finally promulgated in 1961 after considerable controversy, patchwork legislation, and incredible administrative difficulties. It is not our purpose here to discuss the faulty philosophical and factual premises underlying this legislation nor its substantial cost to American taxpayers. Instead, we shall focus on its economic impact on a small number of Klamaths.

Predominant in implementing P.L. 587 was the disposition of tribal assets, ultimately valued at approximately $90,000,000.[52] By vote, 78 percent (1660) of the Klamath chose to "withdraw" from the tribe and receive their pro rata share of tribal assets in cash. The other 22 percent (473) chose to "remain" and receive their pro rata shares in tribal lands which were to be administered under a management plan approved by the Secretary of the Interior.

In order to pay the withdrawing members, a variety of lands, mostly in timber, representing 78 percent of tribal assets, were offered for sale, subject to various qualifications including sustained yield forestry practices. Since these restrictions discouraged private buyers, the Federal Government as buyer of last resort purchased these lands for about $68 million. In 1961, this money was distributed to various withdrawing Indians as their pro rata share of tribal assets. Approximating $43,000 each, these non-taxable shares were paid to adults without restriction or placed under various legal controls according to individual preference or finding of incompetence. Shares payable to minors were placed under various legal restrictions which continued until majority or marriage to an adult.

In response to Congressional inquiry, the Portland Office of the Bureau of Indian Affairs conducted a one in ten interview survey to determine the overall impact of this termination legislation.[53] Of 213 individuals randomly selected, 33 were deceased; those living were interviewed during August 1965. From this sample, by cross-tabulation, we were able to identify 45 adults who received their pro rata shares in cash, without restriction. Since women included in this subsample generally indicated no response (NR) or not applicable (NA) to questions concerning income and employment, we differentiated our sample by sex. The mean age in our sample is 45 for males and 47 for females.

At best, our data are only generally indicative of the impact of these pro rata shares. First, the survey itself was conceived and conducted in great haste.[54] Second, our analysis depends upon the veracity and memory of various respondents. In some instances, we have found internal inconsistencies and apparent erroneous responses.[55] Finally, our sample is small and, for that reason, we have limited our tabular presentation to absolute distributions. However, interviews with various public officials, Klamath Basin businessmen, and local private citizens as well as an examination of related public documents lead us to believe that our findings are representative of the approximately 525 Klamath who received their shares without restrictions in 1960.[56]

Economic conditions experienced on the Reservation from 1954 to 1961 were rather severe. By 1958, P.L. 587 ended further sale or cutting of tribal timber while, at the same time, effectively prohibiting any discounting or prior sale of individual pro rata rights. Consequently, per capita payments sharply declined, thereby eliminating a large fraction of the Klamaths' cash income. Circumstances ultimately became so desperate that small advances were made to withdrawing members and a loan fund, with very restrictive conditions, was established.[57] However, these measures did not greatly improve conditions.

Given these economic circumstances, it might be expected that the Klamath would purchase items reflecting their immediate domestic needs and desires. Unfortunately, respondents were not requested to indicate amounts spent. Thus, Table 7.5 shows only the frequency of expenditure for various items. Generally, this table shows that pro rata shares were most commonly used for domestic needs such as living and medical expenses, automobiles, home improvements, household furnishings, and housing. Less frequently, funds were "invested" in education, business, and related agricultural activities. It is also apparent that shares were many times partially saved or invested.

It is difficult to determine the degree of "riotous spending" which followed pro rata distribution. Popular opinion in the Klamath Basin is permeated with stories of reckless splurges, wild parties, and similar sensational activities. Unquestionably, spending in this style did transpire, but

Table 7.5. Frequency of Responses Concerning Use of Pro Rata Shares

Did you use your share for any of these items?	Male		Female	
Item (in order asked)	Yes	No	Yes	No
Capital Investments:				
Livestock	3	20	6	16
Land	11	12	6	16
Farm Buildings	2	21	3	19
Farm Equipment	1	22	4	18
Business	4	19	4	18
Housing	16	7	10	12
Home Improvement	11	12	9	13
Home Furnishings	14	9	15	7
Other	3	20	2	20
Other Expenditures:				
Self-Education	5	18	2	20
Family Education	6	17	4	18
Living Expenses	21	2	16	6
Investment or Savings	17	6	16	6
Medical Expenses	18	5	15	7
Automobiles	16	7	11	11

Source: BIA Survey Data.

Note: Since multiple responses were possible, columns cannot be totaled. This table also follows the BIA classification of items.

its magnitude is unknown. However, the BIA did request respondents to estimate the balance remaining (presumably cash and savings) of their pro rata shares as of September 1,1965. In Table 7.6, two fairly distinct patterns are found. One group (remaining balance from $0 to $10,000) apparently utilized their funds relatively rapidly for diverse current expenditures and various household items. The other group (balances of over $10,000) probably purchased fewer items and invested more of their funds. This interpretation of Table 6 is consistent with opinions expressed by various public officials and regional businessmen during interviews. While the same stories of squandering were continually repeated, these individuals were of the opinion that a minority extravagantly spent large fractions of their shares. This extravagance naturally attracted wide public attention and quickly passed into basin folklore as representative of all Klamath spending behavior.

Table 7.6. Remaining Balance of Pro Rata Shares
(as of September 1, 1965)

Amount	Male	Female
NONE	10	7
L.T. $5000	2	—
$5000 to $10,000	3	4
$10,000 to $20,000	5	4
$20,000 to $30,000	—	2
G.T. $30,000	3	4
NA, NR	—	1
Total	23	22

Source: BIA Survey Data.

Amount and sources of earned income, as found in Table 7.7, remained virtually unchanged from 1960 to 1964.[58] As Table 7.8 shows, unearned income also changed slightly during the same period. However, the sources of unearned income, reflecting the end of tribal sources and the beginning of private sources, changed dramatically.

Table 7.7. Amount and Source of Earned Income
1960 and 1964

Amount	Male 60	Male 64	Female 60	Female 64	Primary Source	Male 60	Male 64	Female 60	Female 64
None	4	5	7	8	Salaries	2	3	1	—
L.T. $2000	6	6	—	1	Wages	8	8	—	2
$2000-3500	3	4	1	1	Private Bus.	5	6	—	1
$3600-5000	4	2	2	2	Farm/Ranch	2	1	2	2
$5100-6500	1	2	—	—	NA, NR	6	5	19	17
$6600-8000	2	4	—	—					
NA, NR	3	—	12	10					
Total	23	23	22	22	Total	23	23	22	22

Source: BIA Survey Data.

Table 7.8.   Amount and Sources of Unearned Income
             1960 and 1964

Amount	Male 60	Male 64	Female 60	Female 64	Primary Source	Male 60	Male 64	Female 60	Female 64
None	4	6	4	5	Investments	1	11	2	9
L.T. $1000	11	5	4	2	All Trusts	15	2	14	3
$1000-2000	5	5	7	6	Pensions	1	1	—	—
$2100-3000	1	4	1	1	Other	1	5	1	1
G.T. $3000	—	—	1	2	NA, NR	5	4	5	9
Don't Know	1	3	4	3					
NA, NR	1	—	1	2					
Total	23	23	22	22		23	23	22	22

Source: BIA Survey Data.

Employment patterns, found in Table 7.9, with the exception of self-employed women, similarly exhibited little change from 1960 to 1965.[59] Also, the large number of no-responses or not-applicable responses by females probably indicates their status as housewives.

Table 7.9.   Employment—1960 and 1965

Type	Male 60	Male 64	Female 60	Female 64
Wage:				
Full-Time	6	7	—	1
Part-Time	3	4	1	—
Self-Employed:				
Full-Time	4	4	1	4
Part-Time	3	3	—	—
Full-Time Waged:				
Self-Employed	—	1	1	—
Unemployed	4	2	3	2
NA, NR	3	2	16	15
Total	23	23	22	22

Source: BIA Survey Data.

However, time in present job as shown in Table 7.10 indicates an increasing tendency among males to gain some sort of permanent employment status. That is, seven of 20 respondents indicated in 1965 that they had worked in their present job from one to four years. This would seem to imply that after final termination various males began to realize that some substitute for the per capita system was required. Hence, permanent employment was sought.

Table 7.10. Length of Time in Present Employment

Time	Male	Female
3 months	3	—
6 months	1	—
1 year	1	—
2 years	1	—
3 years	3	1
4 years	2	—
5 years	2	—
5 years +	5	2
unemployed	2	1
NA, NR	3	16
Total	23	22

Source: BIA Survey Data.

Finally, analysis of other variables shows few changes in Klamath social and economic patterns. Some attempted various forms of education but few completed their studies. No change in residence patterns was found. Participation in local civic activities did not increase nor did the Klamath begin to rely on welfare.

Generally, the large cash lump sum payments had little impact on adult income and employment patterns from 1960 to 1965. Some change was beginning but until present research is completed, we do not know how profound it will be. Therefore, we agree with the findings of the BIA survey.

> Termination as yet has not brought about great economic or social change. Indian ways and outlooks are persistent and still meaningful. They reflect the preference of many individuals to retain identification with their racial and cultural heritages. This attitude may be expected to slow the process of full assimilation. . . . However, the

period of time since termination is far too short to assess (its) ... long term effects ... upon either the withdrawing or the remaining members of the tribe.[60]

Overall, we find the guaranteed income/per capita scheme of little benefit to the Klamath. Instead of encouraging viable, meaningful activities, it fostered dependent, indolent behavior. Further, all indications are that the large cash lump sums have been of little permanent benefit. Instead, these funds have been utilized for current needs until exhausted.

Very obvious economic incentives explain these findings. Per capitas generated a yearly income which provided an acceptable standard of living requiring little work. Continuance of these payments created the illusion of a lifetime guaranteed income. Therefore, the Klamath adjusted their style of life downward in order to exist under this income. Education and employable skills became unimportant or unnecessary. Consequently, the ability to assimilate into an industrialized society decreased while dependency on this guaranteed income increased.

Similar incentives existed for the Klamath to utilize their lump sum payments for current consumption and durable purchases. Since skills and work habits were underdeveloped, most were forced to seek and accept monotonous and menial employment. Therefore, entrance into the labor market was both difficult and discouraging while the existence of pro rata funds rationalized both postponement and exit. Further, these funds permitted participation in the cornucopia of conveniences offered by the dominant society. For the first time, many were able to purchase nearly anything desired. Consequently, these lump sums appear to have been used for current needs as the Klamath adjusted their style of life, but not their incomes, upward.

Needless to say, these conclusions do not apply to all of the Klamath. For young children, per capitas provided necessary maintenance and education and for the elderly, a much needed income. Some individuals were not affected by the per capita system. A few became successful ranchers or teachers while others became regular employees of local businesses. Similarly, pro rata shares were utilized by some to purchase stocks, bonds, and durable assets. But, for the majority, we believe that the per capita/guaranteed income system and the pro rata/lump sum payments generated few lasting benefits.

IMPLICATIONS FOR CURRENT PROPOSALS

Before discussing some implications of our study, two points must be considered but not belabored. First, we realize that certain biases underlie our analysis. Bluntly, we have analyzed from the perspective of the Protestant

Work Ethic, Middle Class Mentality, or some such similar "Capitalistic" orientation. If this perspective is incorrect, if some other research attitude is superior, then our analysis necessarily suffers. Second, we do not know how general our results are. We have presented various historical materials so that those familiar with the circumstances of ghetto dwellers, the rural poor, and similar groups for whom basic allowance proposals are designed, can decide. Needless to say, we believe that our investigation does provide insights into the probable behavior of other groups under similar programs.

Based on the experiences of most Klamath, guaranteed incomes and lump sum payments are not enough. It is naive to maintain that groups lacking education, employment opportunities, civil rights, job information, expert advice, and "correct" incentives, will suddenly—upon notification of their guaranteed income or payment of their lump sum—change their social and economic propensities. Moreover, basic allowance schemes such as these present strong incentives not to change basic propensities. Why should a person, now facing a secure future, seek education, employment, and so forth? Why shouldn't a person, now suddenly enriched, purchase items the dominant society drums into his head to desire?

The Klamath were clearly victims of their own economic calculations. They weighed the alternatives—painful education for unknown uses, hard work with uncertain returns, and self-reliance with limited applications versus early retirement on a secure income. Similarly, lump sums presented nice opportunities for accumulating wealth, sharpening skills, or acquiring talent, but in the absence of basic necessities, sufficient income, and minimal skills, these opportunities were sacrificed to an acceptable standard of living.

In conclusion, it is obvious that for the aged, young, and infirm, guaranteed incomes or similar schemes would be more beneficial and more efficient than present methods. For these groups, the Klamath experience has little relevance. However, the Klamath case does suggest that basic allowance schemes should be applied very cautiously to those who are potentially productive members of society. By slightly miscalculating the incentives involved, such schemes may reinforce nonproductive behavior rather than fostering economic independence. If the ultimate welfare policy goal is to make guaranteed incomes and lump sum payments unnecessary, then much more than these simple programs is required. If a choice must be made, we think most funds ought to be channeled toward the creation of "meaningful" employment opportunities and the establishment of "viable" labor market skills. But this slow, painful, and costly process may not be very popular. Yet, in the long run, success depends upon self-reliance, and self-reliance can be fostered only in very special cases through basic allowance schemes.

NOTES–CASE 7

1. See, generally, Committee for Economic Development (CED), Research and Policy Committee, *Improving the Public Welfare System*, New York, April 1970; and the President's Commission on Income Maintenance Programs, *Poverty Amid Plenty: The American Paradox*, Washington, D.C., GPO, 1969.

2. See Sar A. Levitan, *Programs in Aid of the Poor for the 1970's*, Baltimore, Johns Hopkins Press, 1969; Frank Riessman, *Strategies Against Poverty*, New York, Random House, 1969.

3. The level of support may result in the substitution of leisure for work. See Christopher Green, "Negative Taxes and Monetary Incentives to Work: The Static Theory," *Journal of Human Resources*, Vol. III, Summer 1968, pp. 280-288. Non-economic factors such as job agreeability, satisfaction, companionship, and so forth are among incentives influencing the decision to work.

4. Harold W. Watts, "Graduated Work Incentives: An Experiment in Negative Taxation," *American Economic Review*, Vol. LIX, May 1969, pp. 463-472. Preliminary findings are becoming available. See, for example, Office of Economic Opportunity, *Preliminary Results of the New Jersey Graduated Work Incentive Experiment*, Washington, D.C., February 1970, Mimeo.

5. Helen Nicol, "The Economist and Aspects of Social Welfare Research," *Welfare in Review*, Vol. 8 No. 2 March/April 1970, pp. 7-9.

6. Guy H. Orcutt and Alice G. Orcutt, "Incentive and Disincentive Experimentation for Income Maintenance Policy Purposes," *American Economic Review*, Vol. LVIII, September 1968, pp. 759-761.

7. For example, liberalized welfare rules appear to have interfered with OEO's New Jersey Experiment. See "Can Handouts Make Better Wage Earners?" *Business Week*, February 20, 1970, p. 82.

8. NOTE ON SOURCES: The standard account of the Klamath is Theodore Stern, *The Klamath Tribe*, Seattle, University of Washington Press, 1966. Office (later Bureau) of Indian Affairs records containing various Agency reports exist on microfilm at the University of Oregon Special Collections under U.S. Bureau of Indian Affairs. Klamath Agency, Oregon, *Annual Narrative Report 1910-1921, 1924, 1926-30, 1932, 1934-36; Annual Statistical Report 1920-1935*, pt. 1; and *Reservation Planning:*

Klamath Reservation Program, March 1, 1944. These records, hereafter cited as *ANNUAL NARRATIVE, ANNUAL STATISTICAL,* and *1944 PLANNING PROGRAM,* respectively, compose part of Record Group 75, General Services Administration. The National Archives, *Records of the Office of Indian Affairs, Annual Narrative Report, Klamath Reservation, Oregon,* Washington, D.C. (Available as microfilm No. 66-67, 1950, at the university of Oregon, Special Collections.)

9. Stern, *The Klamath Tribe,* pp. 119-121. This policy, found early to be defective, continued until the 1930s when changes were attempted through the Indian Reorganization Act. "The chief defect, we believe, in the carrying out of the Government's Indian policy has been caused by the preponderance of attention which has been given to material things, with the result that the real good of the individual man and woman has become a subordinate matter. For a generation the emphasis has been placed on the property rights of the Indians . . . The enormous resources belonging to the red man should be conserved in every possible way and be protected till such a time as he is able to stand alone. But in doing this the human side of the involved problem must not be minimized or the job is less than half done." U.S. Department of the Interior, Board of Indian Commissioners, *Fifty-Fourth Annual Report, 1923,* Washington, D.C., GPO, 1923, p. 9.

10. Stern, *The Klamath Tribe,* p. 119. Population for selected years: 1201 in 1923, 1284 in 1930, 1412 in 1936, 1532 in 1944, and 2133 in 1954. *ANNUAL STATISTICAL,* various years; *1944 PLANNING PROGRAM,* p. 17; *Federal Register,* Vol. 22, No. 226 (November 21, 1957), p. 9303.

11. Stern, *The Klamath Tribe,* p. 120.

12. *Ibid.,* p. 121.

13. Hiroto Zakoji, (Compiler), *Termination and the Klamath Indian Education Program 1955-1961,* Salem, Oregon, State Department of Education, n.d., p. 29.

14. *Ibid.*

15. Stern, *The Klamath Tribe,* p. 153.

16. Lewis Meriam, *The Problem of Indian Administration,* Baltimore, Johns Hopkins Press, 1928, p. 443.

17. Harvey A. Wright (compiler), *Data on Termination of Federal Supervision Over the Klamath Indian Reservation,* Salem, Oregon, State Department of Education, 1956, p. 17.

18. *1929 ANNUAL NARRATIVE,* p. 10.

19. *1938 ANNUAL NARRATIVE,* p. I-b-3.

20. Hiroto Zakoji, *Klamath Culture Change,* Eugene, Oregon, University of Oregon, Unpublished Masters Thesis, 1953, p. 117.

21. *Ibid.*

22. Crimes not covered: most "vices," delinquency, and "all of the misdemeanors as defined by the state statutes," *1929 ANNUAL NARRATIVE,* p. 9.

23. *Ibid.,* p. 42.

24. "Needs" were in fact ambiguous. Parents could use these funds for a variety of purposes (home purchases, industrial development, land acquisition, etc.) in addition to maintaining their children. Since the needs of children were intermixed with the needs of their parents, it appears parents had ready access to these funds. Sometime after 1936 the per capitas of minors were paid directly to parents, without restriction. See *1928 ANNUAL NARRATIVE,* pp. 45, 124; Oregon Legislative Assembly, Interim Committee on Indian Affairs, *A Reintroduction to the Indians of Oregon,* Salem, Oregon, October 1958, p. 59; *1935 ANNUAL NARRATIVE,* n.p.

25. As one local merchant observed: ". . . the Great White Father, no matter what his other faults, was very zealous in protecting his children's wealth." Claudia Spink Lorenz, "The Time of My Life," *Klamath County Museum Research Papers, No. 4,* Klamath Falls, Oregon, Klamath County Museum, 1969, p. 90.

26. Zakoji, *Klamath Culture Change,* (see Note 20), pp. 110, 113. See also, generally, Stern, *The Klamath Tribe,* Chapter 13; and *ANNUAL NARRATIVE,* various years.

27. Research is currently underway to untangle some of these affairs. See Keith Mobley, *The Klamath Indians: Federal Trusteeship 1864-1954,* 1970, Mimeo; and W.T. Trulove and David Bunting, *The Liquidation of a Southern Oregon Indian Reservation: A Study of the Economic Impact of Windfall Payments,* Paper presented at the Western Economic Association annual meeting in Davis, California, August 26, 1970, Mimeo.

28. A series on Oregon per capita personal disposable income is apparently not available. Note that disposable income equals personal income minus personal taxes plus transfers, and thereby is less than personal income.

29. Lines such as this are commonly drawn although subject to a variety of difficulties. For a general discussion, see Victor R. Fuchs, "Redefining Poverty and Redistributing Income," *The Public Interest*, No. 8, Summer 1967, pp. 88-95. Thurow (Lester C. Thurow, *Poverty and Discrimination*, Washington, D.C., Brookings Institution, 1969, p. 21) dismisses objections: ". . . the search for a single poverty line is utopian at best." Also, the Klamath, living in a rural environment, could hunt and fish at will and thereby supplement their food needs. Further, the Tribal Council and BIA provided some required social services. Therefore, lines based on national or state statistics probably overstate poverty conditions on the reservation.

30. Other discussions also assume Klamath family size to be five. See *1944 PLANNING PROGRAM*, p. 23; and Wright, *Data on Termination of Federal Supervision* (see Note 17), p. 2.

31. U.S. Bureau of Census, *Current Population Reports*, P-60, No. 51, "Income in 1965 of Families and Persons in the United States," Washington, D.C., GPO, 1967, Table 14, p. 29.

32. In 1928 the Board of Indian Commissioners passed a resolution opposing per capita payments because ". . . if the capital fund is frittered away by small per capita payments the main purpose of holding the fund intact will be lost. Per capita distribution from tribal funds should be available only for productive purposes. Too often they are authorized by Congress on the plea that all the tribespeople are in dire need, when the facts are the needy represent but a small proportion of the tribe. The anticipation of per capita payments tends to hinder economic progress, for the prospect of receiving money without having to perform any labor for it quite naturally encourages indolence and thriftlessness. This state of affairs has been observed by members of the Board and other disinterested friends of the Indian people. It is not a desirable condition, and we believe no sound reason can be advanced for its encouragement." U.S. Department of the Interior, Board of Indian Commissioners, *1928 Annual Report*, p. 14. Since per capita payments still continued, it is apparent these board members and "disinterested friends" were unable to propose viable substitutes for the practice.

33. Because of the timber boom and Indian preference clauses in timber contracts, jobs in and near the reservation were plentiful. See *1926 ANNUAL NARRATIVE*, p. 55; *1930 ANNUAL NARRATIVE*, p. 50.

34. *1944 PLANNING PROGRAM*, pp. 13, 17.

35. *1926 ANNUAL NARRATIVE*, p. 78.

36. *1928 ANNUAL NARRATIVE*, pp. 75, 126.

37. *1930 ANNUAL NARRATIVE*, pp. 116, 132.

38. *1944 PLANNING PROGRAM*, pp. 17, 18.

39. Oregon Legislative Assembly, *A Reintroduction to the Indians of Oregon* (see Note 24), p. 19.

40. *1932 ANNUAL NARRATIVE*, p. 2; *1934 ANNUAL NARRATIVE*, p. 4; *1936 ANNUAL NARRATIVE*, p. 5.

41. *1932 ANNUAL NARRATIVE*, p. 3.

42. Stern, *The Klamath Tribe*, pp. 190-191.

43. *1932 ANNUAL NARRATIVE*, p. 4.

44. *1934 ANNUAL NARRATIVE*, p. 7.

45. Zakoji, *Klamath Culture Change*, p. 156.

46. *1934 ANNUAL NARRATIVE*, p. 7.

47. Stern, *The Klamath Tribe*, p. 210.

48. U.S. Department of the Interior, Board of Indian Comissioners, *1930 Annual Report*, p. 29.

49. Wright, *Data on Termination of Federal Supervision* (see Note 17), p. 2.

50. *1926 ANNUAL NARRATIVE*, p. 79.

51. P.L. 83-587, 67 Stat. 718, ch. 732 (1954)

52. Zakoji, *Termination and the Klamath Indian Education Program 1955-1961* (see Note 13), pp. 52-67.

53. U.S. House of Representatives, Subcommittee on Indian Affairs, *Colville Termination*, Serial 89-23, Washington, D.C., GPO, 1966, p. 328. This document also includes the BIA's study *Report on the Effects of Withdrawal of Federal Supervision of the Klamath Indians Tribes*, pp. 327-339.

54. The survey was requested August 19, 1965, and introduced during hearings held on November 5, 1965, although its transmittal letter is dated February 14, 1966. *Ibid.,* pp. 30. Incidentally, it is the only published economic evaluation of the Klamath termination we have found. Our research in progress will hopefully correct this deficiency.

55. For example, we believe respondents overstated their education.

56. At the time of termination, 970 withdrew under restrictions, 437 remained in the tribe, and about 200 were deceased. *Supra* fn 53, p. 328.

57. Advances made: $370 in December 1958, $1300 in June 1960, and $485 in October 1960. See Trulove and Bunting, *The Liquidation of a Southern Oregon Indian Reservation* (see Note 27), p. 10. Conditions for loans are outlined in a memorandum *Loans to Withdrawing Members of the Klamath Tribes* (n.p., January 16, 1959), found in the Management Specialists file, Special Collections, University of Oregon Library.

58. Respondents were requested to estimate their income as of December 1960 and December 1964; U.S.H.R., *Colville Termination* (see Note 53), pp. 329, 335.

59. As of December 1960 and September 1, 1965, *ibid.,* p. 329.

60. *Ibid.,* pp. 338-339.

Case 8
Annual Reporting by Municipal Governments: An Extension of the Corporate Annual Report

ARIE Y. LEWIN* and GERALD A. CAHILL*

The concept of and the need for requiring municipal governments to publish an annual report to their residents similar to the annual report published by corporations for their stockholders was presented by Lewin and Blanning.[1] This case analyzes primarily the accounting feasibility of requiring municipalities to publish such a report analogous to the corporate report.

Although the corporation is a relatively old form of business organization, the concept of reporting to stockholders is a 20th-century phenomenon which gained impetus from the Securities Acts of 1933 and 1934. The objective of this landmark legislation and that of subsequent legislation was to require corporate managements to disclose to stockholders, annually, the results of operations and to have the reports certified by independent auditors. The hope was to make managements more accountable to their stockholders and to provide a means for evaluating the performance of management.

At the start of the 20th century, the typical American business was either run by owner-managers or controlled by a comparatively few wealthy individuals. It has been estimated by Hellinger[2] that in 1900 no corporation had more than 60,000 stockholders; A.T.&T. had approximately 7,500 and U.S. steel approximately 54,000. "The average stockholder received short shrift in 1900. The favored few resisted all attempts to secure information regarding corporate activities, including those made by the government. Mr. Vanderbilt's 'public-be-damned' attitude was still in the saddle."[3]

However, as ownership of securities became more widespread, interest in more accurate and uniform reporting grew. William C. Redfield (first Secretary of Commerce) discussed the problem with Federal Reserve officials

*Duke University

and in 1917 the Board published "Approved Methods for the Preparation of Balance Sheet Statements." In 1920, Haney commented that a major problem with the corporate form of business organization was "the difficulty of securing in practice adequate responsibility of officers and directors for their fraudulent acts." Responding to criticism of this nature, the New York Stock Exchange, during the 1920s, began a campaign to get corporations to provide more financial information. In 1926, in order to provide more effective surveillance of financial reporting by listed companies, the NYSE named J.B. Horsey to the new, full-time position of Executive Assistant to the Committee on Stock List.[4]

In 1933, for the first time, the NYSE threatened a listed company (Allied Chemical) with delisting unless it improved the quality of its financial disclosures. In that same year, the Exchange announced that henceforth it would require independent audits. For the first time, during the 1933-1936 period, corporations in general began mailing information to stockholders.[5] Many corporations did not welcome stockholder disclosure, and in 1934 Standard Oil of New Jersey demonstrated its attitude by holding its annual meeting in a room above a filling station in Newark, New Jersey.

Livingston[6] describes the gradual change in corporate attitudes toward disclosure. For example, the General Electric Company's original listing application contained neither a consolidated balance nor earnings figures. In a 1900 application, the company submitted a consolidated balance sheet and a profit and loss statement for the preceding seven months but it contained no annual earnings figures. In 1929, however, an income statement in modern format was included and in 1956 an application to list debentures included a prospectus filed with the SEC.

Probably the two major factors leading to greater disclosure were the Securities Act of 1933, which required "full and fair disclosure" in registration statements, and the 1934 Securities Exchange Act, which required the filing of periodic reports by companies whose stock is listed on national securities exchanges. Only in 1964, however, was this act amended to include over-the-counter companies, and even then it exempted smaller (under $1 million of assets) companies.

Detailed annual reports, of the kind quite familiar today, were uncommon enough in 1939 for *The New York Times* to editorially compliment General Mills for the clarity and completeness of its annual report. The report, according to Wright,[7] contained:

a)   a consolidated balance sheet,
b)   a consolidated income statement,
c)   a consolidated surplus account,
d)   condensed comparative consolidated balance sheets,
e)   comparative income data,
f)   a statement of earnings and dividends per share by years,

g)   a list of principal products,
h)   a list of the divisions and trade names of General Mills,
i)   a list of the company's principal manufacturing and grain storage facilities,
j)   a list of principal sales offices,
k)   graphs illustrating certain financial data, and
l)   a President's letter.

In 1963-64, the Accounting Principles Board issued Opinion No. 3, which recommended that funds statements "be presented as supplementary information in financial reports." Afterwards, the NYSE sent copies of the Opinion to the presidents of all listed companies, and strongly urged that, on a comparative basis, they be included in annual reports to stockholders. In 1964, the SEC amended proxy rule 14a-3 to require that any material differences in the application of accounting principles between reports filed with the SEC and reports to stockholders must be reconciled or explained to the latter. As a result, the SEC asserts indirect surveillance over annual reports to stockholders issued by companies under its jurisdiction.

As recently as 1969, the NYSE announced that banks and insurance companies would no longer be exempt from submitting audited financial statements in listing applications, and in 1971, in ASR No. 121, the SEC deleted the exemption from certification enjoyed by banks.

In summary, then, at the turn of the century, the typical large American corporation provided its stockholders with little or no information. As the number of stockholders grew during the first 30 years of the century, corporations gradually disclosed more information, but essentially remained the judge of what should be revealed. The financial collapse of 1929 followed by the Securities Acts of 1933 and 1934 provided a major impetus for greater and more timely disclosure, and, subsequent to that date, considerable effort has been spent in clarifying and defining acceptable accounting principles in order to ensure greater uniformity in reporting. Thus the intent of the Securities Acts of 1933, 1934, and 1964, and the regulations issued by the Securities and Exchange Commission was to explicitly disclose the financial consequences of company operations so that investors could more readily evaluate management performance for themselves and to make managements more accountable to their shareholders.

Lewin and Blanning[8] note that a similar situation of nonaccountability by city government and inability of residents to evaluate the performance of city government exists in a city.

> The public, through its exercise of the ballot, is called upon to evaluate the performance of the mayor and the city council and to decide whether to keep them in office or to replace them. Unlike the investing public, citizens of a city do not presently receive from the "city executives" a report similar to the corporate annual report to

aid them in evaluating the performance of the city administration. Because of the size of many city governments, the tendency of the bureaucracy to insulate itself from the public, the complexity of functions and services performed for city residents, and the relative importance of municipal demand for resources in a city economy, it is almost impossible for citizens to evaluate the performance of their government.

In a sense, citizens face a dilemma similar to that which confronted the investor in 1929. Their inability to perform an objective evaluation of municipal performance and to influence the city administration's goals and programs has contributed to apathy and a lack of confidence in municipal government.[9]

THE USERS OF THE CORPORATE ANNUAL REPORT

The annual report represents the official communication from corporate management to the stockholders informing them about the previous year's operations. The report, including the financial statements contained therein, are quite clearly the responsibility of management. "The responsibility for the reliability of an enterprise's financial statements rests with its management. This responsibility is discharged by applying generally accepted accounting principles that are appropriate to the enterprise's circumstances by maintaining effective systems of accounts and internal control, and by preparing adequate financial statements."[10]

The principal users of corporate reports are investors, creditors, and governmental regulatory agencies. Regulatory agencies generally require certain specific information and have the authority to require the corporation to deliver it. Similarly, creditors such as bond-rating agencies normally can derive little of the information they require from annual reports sent to stockholders.

For example, they may wish to examine the trust indenture contract between the issues and the bond holder. This information will be derived from sources other than the company's report to shareholders. Hence, in preparing the annual report, management will normally orient the report to the needs of its stockholders.

The annual report usually has a number of distinct sections and typically will include

    a)   a review of the year's operations,
    b)   a financial review,
    c)   financial statements,
    d)   an auditor's report,

e) a ten-year financial summary,
f) special items, which may appear anywhere in the report, and
g) the auditor's report.

CONTENTS OF FINANCIAL STATEMENTS

The Accounting Principles Board has stated that the basic purpose of financial statements is "to provide quantitative financial information about a business enterprise that is useful to statement users, particularly owners and creditors, in making economic decisions. This purpose includes providing information that can be used in evaluating management's effectiveness in fulfilling its stewardship and other managerial responsibilities." To provide guidance in achieving this purpose, accounting theory has developed a series of general objectives and a series of qualitative objectives.[11]

General objectives are those that help determine the appropriate content of financial information, specifically they

a) provide reliable financial information about economic resources and obligations of a business enterprise,
b) provide reliable information about changes in net resources of an enterprise that result from its profit-directed activities,
c) provide financial information that assists in estimating the earning potential of the enterprise,
d) provide other needed information about changes in economic resources and obligations, and
e) disclose, to the extent possible, other information related to the financial statements that is relevant to the statements users' need.

Underlying these general objectives is the recognition that decisions of financial statement users involve the process of choosing among alternative courses of action.

Qualitative objectives are those characteristics that make financial information useful:

a. *Relevance*. Relevant financial accounting information bears on the economic decisions for which it is used.
b. *Understandability*. Understandable financial accounting information presents data that can be understood by users of the information and is expressed in a form and with terminology adapted to the users' range of understanding.
c. *Verifiability*. Verifiable financial accounting information provides results that would be substantially duplicated by independent measures using the same measurement methods.

d. *Neutrality.* Neutral financial accounting information is directed toward the common needs of users and is independent of presumptions about particular needs and desires of specific users of the information.
e. *Timeliness.* Timely financial accounting information is communicated early enough to be used for the economic decisions which it might include and to avoid delays in making those decisions.
f. *Comparability.* Comparable financial accounting information presents similarities and differences that arise from basic similarities and differences in the enterprises and their transactions and not merely from differences in financial accounting treatments.
g. *Completeness.* Complete financial accounting information includes all financial accounting data that reasonably fulfills the requirements of the other qualitative objectives.

The audited financial statements contained in the report to the shareholders must meet the qualitative standard of fair presentation in conformity with generally accepted accounting principles.[12] This standard is met if

a) generally accepted accounting principles applicable in the circumstances have been applied in accumulating and processing the financial accounting information,
b) changes from period to period in generally accepted accounting principles have been appropriately disclosed,
c) the information in the underlying records is properly reflected and described in the financial statements in conformity with generally accepted accounting principles,
d) a proper balance has been achieved between the conflicting needs to disclose important aspects of financial position and results of operations in accordance with conventional concepts and to summarize the voluminous underlying data into a limited number of financial statement captions and supporting notes.

Twelve principles guide the reporting of financial accounting information:

1. *Basic financial statements.* A balance sheet, a statement of income, a statement of changes in retained earnings, a statement of changes in other categories of stockholders' equity, and related notes comprise the minimum presentation required.

2. *Complete balance sheet.* The balance sheet should include and properly describe all assets, liabilities, and classes of owners equity as defined by generally accepted accounting principles.

3. *Complete income statement.* The income statement of a period should

include and properly describe all revenue and expenses as defined by generally accepted accounting principles.

4. *Complete statement of changes in financial position.* The statement of changes in financial position of a period should include and properly describe all important aspects of the company's financing and investing activities.

5. *Accounting period.* The basic time period for which statements are presented in one year.

6. *Consolidated financial statements.* Consolidated financial statements are presumed to be more meaningful than the separate statements of the component legal entities. Consolidated statments are usually necessary for fair presentation in conformity with generally accepted accounting principles if one of the enterprises in a group directly or indirectly owns over 50 percent of the outstanding voting stock of the enterprises.

7. *Equity basis.* Unconsolidated subsidiaries and investments in 50 percent or less of the voting stock of companies in which the investors have the ability to exercise significant influence over investees should be presented on the equity basis.

8. *Translation of foreign balance.* Financial information about the foreign operations of U.S. enterprises should be "translated" into U.S. dollars by the use of conventional translation procedures that involve foreign exchange rates.

9. *Classification and segregation.* Segregate disclosure of the important components of the financial statements is presumed to make the information more useful. Examples in the income statement are sales or other sources of revenue, cost of sales, depreciation, selling and administrative expenses, interest expense, and income taxes. Examples in the balance sheet are cash, receivables, inventories, plant and equipment, payables, and categories of owners' equity.

10. *Other disclosures.* In addition to informative classifications and segregation of data, financial statements should disclose all additional information that is necessary for fair presentation in conformity with generally accepted accounting principles. Notes that are necessary for adequate disclosure are an integral part of financial statements.

11. *Form of financial statement presentation.* No particular form of financial statements is presumed better than all others for all purposes, and several forms are used.

12. *Earnings per share.* Earnings-per-share information is most useful when furnished in conjunction with net income and its components and should be disclosed on the face of the income statement.

THE USERS OF THE MUNICIPAL ANNUAL REPORT

The corporate annual report was intended to disclose financial information to stockholders to facilitate their evaluation of management performance and to aid them in their investment decisions. The municipal annual report should, similarly, facilitate the evaluation of municipal performance by its residents and other groups having a need to do so. In contrast to the corporate situation, where the report is primarily intended for stockholders, the municipal report would be used by various individuals and groups with an interest in city government.

These individuals and groups can be identified as the residents who live, work, vote, and/or pay taxes in the city, special interest groups, city council legislators, the state government, the federal government, public media, and city officials.

Although this classification is not exhaustive, each of these groups has an interest in obtaining a performance evaluation of city government. Although residents of a city may be viewed as diffused and politically disorganized, they do have an impact on city government through their exercise of the ballot in the elections for mayor, member of the city council, and other elected officials. Special interest groups and their constituencies have specific social, economic, or political goals, the attainment of which depends on city government. Political civic action groups in particular have an interest in evaluating city government performance on issues of importance to them.

The city legislator as the elected representative of his constituents on the city council has review power over the executive. In particular the city council has the power to approve the city budget proposed by the mayor. However, although city legislators have these powers they typically do not have access to the detailed information available to the city executives. In addition they are hampered by the lack of staff resources to evaluate information when it is presented. Yet it is clear that city legislators have the duty to evaluate the performance of city government.

State and federal agencies have specific needs to evaluate the performance of city government in specific instances. These are generally mandated by legislation where state and/or federal agencies participate in the funding of city projects and programs. Public media (e.g., journalists) have a deep interest in the performance of city government and historically have served the function of the independent investigative arm of the public.

It is clear that all of the above-described participants have an interest in monitoring and evaluating the performance of city government even though they have conflicting objectives and motivations for doing so. It is therefore important that the annual report present an objective and fair statement of city government performance and that it be subject to independent evaluation and interpretation by the various users. Also it is obvious that the report would have to be prepared by the city management—the mayor and his cabinet.

MUNICIPAL REPORTING PRACTICES

Municipal reporting in the United States may be called a jungle through which run only a few trails, and some of those are little used. . .

Everyone concedes that some reports are indispensable; but few consider what the reports should contain, for whom they should be prepared, in what form they should be presented, how they might most advantageously be circulated, how their content and form might be improved. But few have had the inclination and the leisure to consider carefully and systematically the analyses and syntheses of data which are the prerequisite of specific improvement in the situation. No field is more important to the electors who seek information on the working of their government, to administrators within and without the particular city, and to special students of the science of municipal government.[13]

This section reviews the manner in which municipalities adopt budgets and the reporting practices of a number of municipalities. The reporting practices of several authorities and similar quasi-governmental agencies are also summarized to provide a broader frame of reference. An understanding of existing practices provides a useful starting point for improvement in the reporting procedure.

Municipal Appropriation Procedures

The exact manner by which municipalities adopt budgets and authorize expenditures varies considerably from municipality to municipality, due to differences in charter provisions, local customs, and state law. The following procedure, however, is representative:

1. *Requests and forms for budget information.* The chief fiscal officer requests each department to provide estimates on its requirements for the coming fiscal year.

2. *Collecting and revising the requests.* The budget requests are received and summarized. The fiscal officer and the mayor conduct informal hearings

and reduce the requests until a balanced financial program is reached. At this point, a proposed budget is normally printed. This material is available for public inspection.

3. *Submission to the council.* The budget is submitted to the city council for approval and modification. In some areas the council can only reduce, but not increase, the recommended expenditures. The council will generally hold public hearings on the proposals and representatives of interested organizations will normally attend.

4. *Form and itemization of budget.* Ordinances and resolutions are adopted to put the budget into effect.

5. *Reporting of the finance officer.* Following the end of the fiscal year, the finance officer of the municipality will normally prepare an annual financial report to show the financial condition of the municipality and its financial operations. This report is generally not widely disseminated, although it is public information.

Annual Financial Report

The National Committee on Governmental Accounting categorizes financial reports as *technical* if prepared for use by accountants, financial administrators, investors, and others professionally trained in accounting and finance, or *popular* if prepared for use by the general public. The report of the finance officer is of the former type. The Committee suggests that the report be organized in three major sections:

(1) Introductory
(2) Financial, consisting of a minimum of four combined statements and three combined schedules:
   (a) combined balance sheet—all funds
   (b) combined statement of revenue—estimated and actual, general and special revenue funds
   (c) combined statement of general governmental expenditures compared with authorizations—general and special revenue funds
   (d) combined statement of cash receipts and disbursements—all funds
   (e) combined schedule of delinquent taxes receivable by funds
   (f) combined schedule of bonds payable by funds
   (g) combined schedule of investments by funds
(3) Statistical Section—the data contained herein will sometimes cover a period up to ten years in length. Another feature is that some of the data, economic and social in character, will be derived from sources

other than the accounts maintained by the governmental unit. The following are suggested for inclusion:

(a) general governmental expenditures by function—last ten fiscal years
(b) general revenues by source—last ten fiscal years
(c) tax revenues by source—last ten fiscal years
(d) property tax levies and collection—last ten fiscal years
(e) assessed and actual value of taxable property—last ten fiscal years
(f) property tax rates and tax levies—last ten fiscal years
(g) special assessment collections—last ten fiscal years
(h) ratio of net general bonded debt to assessed value—last ten fiscal years
(i) computation of legal debt margin
(j) computation of direct and overlapping debt
(k) ratio of annual debt service expenditures for general bonded debt to total general expenditures
(l) schedule of revenue bond coverage—last ten fiscal years
(m) debt service requirements to maturity
(n) summary of debt service charges to maturity
(o) schedule of insurance in force
(p) salaries and surety bonds of principal officers
(q) miscellaneous data

An analysis of the annual financial reports of a number of cities indicates that, with some deviations, they tend to follow the format suggested by the National Committee on Governmental Accounting. The result is an impressive document with a great number of schedules and tables.

Several cities have modified the Annual Financial Report and include it as part of the mayor's budget request. The 1972 budget request, submitted by the Mayor of Pittsburgh on December 6, 1971, contains comparative statements showing estimated 1972 expenditures, estimated (based on actual for a portion of the year) 1971 expenditures, and actual 1970. The document is approximately 240 pages long and includes over 200 tables. Allentown follows a similar practice of combining its annual financial report with its proposed budget for the next year. This procedure appears to have the definite advantage of making the financial information available when most useful—i.e., at the time decisions are being made on future appropriations. It appears, however, that a limited number of cities make use of this approach.

Although the annual financial reports reviewed are impressive documents and would be a useful starting point for any student of municipal finance, they do not appear to be a practical or effective means of reporting to the electorate at large, nor are they intended for this purpose. Specifically, (1) they are highly complex and technical. They are intended to present the financial condition and operations of each fund and to demonstrate compliance with legal provisions. By themselves, they do not provide any measure of the stewardship of the public officials. In a letter to this author dated November 13, 1972, Mayor Bill McCormick of Topeka stated, "It is my observation that the annual report of the City of Topeka is of very little value so far as planning is concerned, inasmuch as it consists of a plethora of atomized funds which make it very difficult to digest; and secondly, it is published only after the succeeding year's budget has been adopted." This statement would seem to apply to most annual financial reports observed by this author. (2) Distribution is limited. The reports, while public documents and generally available upon request, are not widely distributed. For example, the City of Cleveland distributes 500 copies to libraries and financial institutions. The City of Huntsville disseminates its report to local news media, with copies available to the public upon request. Nashville's report is issued to the mayor and council, with additional copies distributed to the Chamber of Commerce, libraries, and other governmental units and interested citizens as long as the supply lasts. Tuscaloosa distributes its reports primarily to municipal bond purchasers during a proposed bond sale or upon request.

Post Audit

The final stage of the municipal budget cycle is the post audit: the examination of the financial records and statements by an auditor who is independent of the executive branch of government. The post audit may be performed, depending on state legislation and local customs, by[14]

1) an independent auditor who is an official of the governmental unit being audited, but generally elected and independent of the executive,
2) a state audit agency, or
3) an independent CPA (this procedure is least common).[15]

The purpose of the audit is to establish fidelity and compliance with legal provisions,[16] specifically:

1) to ascertain whether, in the auditor's opinion, the statements presented fairly the financial position and results of operations of the organization;
2) to determine the adequacy of accounting records and procedures and to suggest improvements thereof which will promote effective administration;
3) to serve as a control device to help prevent the loss of public funds through fraud or inefficiency. To verify the stewardship of those responsible for the organization's financial operations;
4) to determine compliance with legal provisions relating to reports.

The budgetary and audit cycle just described is generally prescribed by state and municipal law. In some respects, it is analogous to the reporting procedures prescribed for corporations by the SEC. However, in the case of corporations, the SEC has established rules regarding the solicitation of proxies, which have the indirect effect of requiring that an annual report be distributed to each stockholder. Municipalities are not subject to similar suasion, hence the main thrust of this section will concern the type and contents of municipal reports prepared for distribution to the electorate at large.

MUNICIPAL ACCOUNTING PRACTICES

Basic to an understanding of the reporting problems and practices of municipalities is some understanding of the procedures of municipal accounting. The following discussion is based on material prepared by the National Committee on Governmental Accounting.

Governmental and commercial accounting utilize many of the same accounting concepts and conventions. Among these are a double-entry system of accounts; broad, generally-accepted concepts such as consistency, objectivity, cost, full disclosure materiality and conservatism; and the nature of the entire accounting process—i.e., beginning with the recognition and analysis of primary transactions and documents through the process of journalizing to the preparation of financial statements.

Although the foregoing similarities exist between commercial and governmental accounting, there are also significant differences which give rise to a group of accounting principles and concepts that have distinct applicability for governmental entities. These principles recognize the facts that most governmental operations are not profit-oriented and that their accounting systems must comply with legal requirements applicable to them. Moreover, the accounting system must produce data and information which indicate the extent to which the financial operations carried out by all agencies comply with applicable law and legal regulations.

Following are the basic principles underlying governmental accounting operations:

1. *Legal compliance and financial operations.* A governmental accounting system must make it possible
   a. to show that all applicable legal provisions have been complied with, and
   b. to determine fairly and with full disclosure the financial position and results of financial operations of the constituent funds and self-balancing account groups of the governmental unit.

2. *Conflicts between accounting principles and legal provisions.* If there is a

conflict between legal provisions and generally accepted accounting principles applicable to governmental units, legal provisions must take precedence. Insofar as possible, however, the governmental accounting system should make possible the full disclosure and fair presentation of financial position and operating results in accordance with generally accepted principles of accounting applicable to governmental units.

3. *The budget and budgetary accounting.* An annual budget should be adopted by every governmental unit, whether required by law or not, and the accounting system should provide budgetary control over general governmental revenues and expenditures.

4. *Fund accounting.* Governmental accounting systems should be organized and operated on a fund basis. A fund is defined as an independent fiscal and accounting entity with a self-balancing set of accounts recording each and/or other resources together with all related liabilities, obligations, reserves, and equities which are segregated for the purpose of carrying on specific activities or attaining certain objectives in accordance with special regulations, restrictions, or limitations.

5. *Types of Funds.* The following types of funds are recognized and should be used:
   a. general fund
   b. special revenue funds
   c. debt service funds
   d. capital projects funds
   e. enterprise funds
   f. trust and agency funds
   g. intragovernmental service funds
   h. special assessment funds

6. *Number of funds.* Every governmental unit should establish and maintain those funds required by law and sound financial administration. Only the minimum number of funds consistent with legal and operating requirements should be established.

7. *Fund accounts.* A complete self-balancing group of accounts should be established and maintained for each fund.

8. *Valuation of fixed assets.* Fixed assets should be recorded on the basis of original cost.

9. *Depreciation.* Depreciation charges on general fixed assets should not be recorded in the general accounting records.

10. *Basis of accounting.* The accrual basis of accounting is recommended for enterprise, trust, capital projects, special assessment and intragovernmental service funds. For the general, special reserve, and debt service funds, the modified accrual basis of accounting is recommended.

11. *Classification of accounts.* Governmental revenues should be classified by fund and source. Expenditures should be classified by fund, function, organization unit, activity, character, and principal classes of objects in accordance with standard recognized classification.

12. *Common terminology and classification.* A common terminology and classification should be used consistently throughout the budget, the accounts, and the financial reports.

13. Financial statements and reports showing the current condition of budgetary and proprietary accounts should be prepared periodically to control financial operations. At the close of each fiscal year, a comprehensive annual financial report covering all funds and financial operations of the governmental unit should be prepared and published.

MUNICIPAL REPORTING TO THE PUBLIC

This section discusses the manner in which municipalities report the results of the year's activities to their public. It is based on a survey of 50 municipalities listed in Table 8.1.

A number of different procedures are used by municipalities in reporting. Those identified in this study are:

1. *Popular annual report.* Preparation by the municipality of an annual report somewhat similar to a corporate annual report. This report will normally be given wide distribution either through the mail or some other form of door-to-door delivery.

2. *Newspaper supplement.* Publication in a local newspaper of an annual report similar in content to that of the printed annual report.

3. *Report to Council.* A formal annual report to the city council by the mayor or city manager on the "State-of-the-City." The report will be printed for public distribution, generally on request, and will be reported by the local news media.

4. *Departmental reports.* Preparation by each individual department of a municipality of an annual report covering that department's activities.

Table 8.1. Municipalities Included in Study

City	Population	City	Population
Los Angeles, Calif.	2,816,000	Huntsville, Ala.	137,000
Philadelphia, Pa.	1,950,000	Montgomery, Ala.	133,000
Cleveland, Ohio	750,000	Topeka, Kan.	125,000
Indianapolis, Ind.	745,000	Las Vegas, Nev.	125,000
San Francisco, Calif.	715,000	Chattanooga, Tenn.	119,000
San Diego, Calif.	696,000	Columbia, S.C.	113,000
St. Louis, Mo.	622,000	Allentown, Pa.	109,000
Jacksonville, Fla.	528,000	Waterbury, Conn.	108,000
Pittsburgh, Pa.	520,000	Stockton, Calif.	107,000
Buffalo, N.Y.	426,000	Trenton, N.J.	104,000
Nashville, Tenn.	447,000	Ann Arbor, Mich.	99,000
Minneapolis, Minn.	434,000	Pueblo, Colo.	97,000
Oklahoma City, Okla.	368,000	Wichita Falls, Tex.	96,000
El Paso, Tex.	322,000	Durham, N.C.	95,000
Norfolk, Va.	307,000	Brockton, Mass.	89,000
Wichita, Kan.	276,000	Eugene, Ore.	78,000
Austin, Tex.	251,000	Sioux Falls, S.D.	72,000
Richmond, Va.	249,000	Oxnard, Calif.	71,000
Syracuse, N.Y.	197,000	Charleston, W.Va.	71,000
Providence, R.I.	179,000	Santa Barbara, Calif.	70,000
Madison, Wis.	172,000	Tuscaloosa, Ala.	65,000
Spokane, Wash.	170,000	Gainesville, Fla.	64,000
Baton Rouge, La.	165,000	Greenville, S.C.	61,000
Jackson, Miss.	153,000	Meriden, Conn.	61,000
Greensboro, N.C.	144,000	Fayetteville, N.C.	53,000

Distribution is generally upon request and no consolidated report is prepared.

5. *Film and slide presentation.* A visual report, prepared to be shown before civic groups, high school classes, and local television stations.

6. *Newspaper Legal Notice.* This category includes those municipalities which prepare annual financial reports, as required by law, but make only limited distribution thereof.

Table 8.2 includes a summary of the frequency of usage of each approach found by the study.

Table 8.2. Relative Frequency of Reporting Methods*

Method	Frequency
1. Popular annual report	9
2. Newspaper supplement	5
3. Report to council	5
4. Departmental reports	5
5. Film or slide presentation	3
6. Newspaper legal notice	5
7. No popular annual report**	21

*Total adds to more than 50. Some municipalities reported more than one method.

**Includes several municipalities which indicated that they discontinued the issuance of annual reports for financial reasons.

Of the seven reporting methods employed by the municipalities in the study, three have the potential of reaching a large audience of local citizens— specifically they are popular annual reports, newspaper supplements, and film or slide presentations. The remaining four approaches will receive only limited attention from the public at large as they are either too technical or receive only limited distribution. As the major thrust of the dissertation involves the development of a report intended for wide distribution, emphasis will be placed in that area. Film and slide presentations also appear to be outside the major area of interest.

Report Contents

Both the popular annual reports and newspaper supplements examined were similar in content, and an analysis of one applies equally to the other. Primarily, the annual report represents the official communication from municipal management to the electorate, informing them about the preceding year's operations. The report usually has a number of distinct sections. A typical format might be as follows:

1. Introductory letter from the mayor and/or city manager.

2. Picture of the council and/or key municipal managers.

3. Departmental descriptions or reports.

4. Summary of financial information, often through the use of two

pie-shaped charts or bar graphs, depicting sources of revenues and purpose of expenditures.

5. Filler information, such as organization charts or key telephone numbers.

6. Special items, which may appear anywhere in the report.

An analysis of the reports suggests that they satisfy one or more of the following objectives:

1. To present the results of financial operations for the year. The financial presentation serves this purpose, although little detail or explanatory notes are generally included.

2. To describe departments and their operations and accomplishments. By far the greatest amount of space in the typical report is devoted to this purpose. Generally, there is a separate section for each municipal department, such as public safety, health and welfare, etc., which describes the department's functions and enumerates accomplishments of the past year.

3. To develop loyalty and amity toward the city on the part of local citizens and other readers. Generally, the style of writing and the points of emphasis lead the reader to the view that the city is dynamic and progressive—a good place to live and a good place for industry.

4. To give recognition to municipal officials, especially upon retirement.

5. To provide citizens with an understanding of the organization of their municipal government.

Limitations of Present Reports

In terms of a concept of accountability, the existing popular annual report suffers from severe limitations. First, some of the purposes listed work against achievement of accountability. It appears basically impossible to produce an annual report which presents the city as a dynamic and progressive municipality and at the same time presents a complete and unbiased presentation of the major decisions, policies, and activities, including a fair evaluation of their results. Second, there are no standards as to what the report should contain. What appears is essentially the choice of those responsible for its preparation and approval. As a result, the detail contained and emphasis provided vary greatly from report to report. Without generally accepted standards as to content, political expediency will quite often triumph over objectivity. Third, financial content is generally minimal, does not lend itself to analysis, and, since it is unaudited, the reader does not know if the material is accurate, complete, and fairly presented.

MODEL FOR FINANCIAL STATEMENTS
OF THE MUNICIPAL ANNUAL REPORT

This section of the report will consist of financial statements intended to show the municipality's financial position and the results of operations for the year then ended. Since the underlying purpose of the report is to provide information useful to an informed citizen in evaluating management's stewardship, consolidated statements should be provided.

The use of consolidated statements represents a departure from normal usage in municipal reporting; customary usage is to provide separate statements for each fund. The major reasons underlying this are:

1. Municipal accounting practice developed with its major aim being to facilitate and ensure compliance with law. Consequently, it is oriented toward facilitating review of the executive's compliance with legislative appropriations. It is not oriented toward providing information necessary for an evaluation of management's stewardship.

2. The assets of each fund are, legally, often not transferable to another fund. Thus, the presentation of a consolidated statement may not fairly reflect the position of each fund consolidated therein. This problem, however, may easily be handled by footnote disclosure.

In preparing a consolidated statement, the problem arises as to which funds should be consolidated. It is possible that certain funds are administered by authorities either wholly or in part independent of the municipality's management. Commercial financial accounting has encountered a similar problem with the question of consolidated of subsidiaries. The approach recently accepted in the commercial area provides some guidance for us. Basically, it provides that

1. a corporation owning 50 percent or more of another corporation should consolidate that subsidiary in its financial statements,

2. a corporation owning 20 percent or more (but less than 50 percent) of another corporation should use the equity method of reporting the results of its subsidiary, and

3. a corporation owning less than 20 percent of another corporation may use either the equity method or carry its ownership position as an investment.

Furthermore, even if a parent owns less than 20 percent, but is in a position of control (such as by domination of the Board of Directors), it should also use the equity method.

In our situation, of course, each fund is owned ultimately by the citizens of the community. Since our purpose, however, is to provide a measure of the stewardship of municipal management, it appears that the question of control is key. If management controls the operation of a fund, either directly or indirectly (such as through appointment of the controlling parties), then that fund should be consolidated. If no control is exerted (such as where the administrators of a fund are elected directly and are not under the operational authority of the mayor), it should be excluded.

COST ANALYSIS BY TYPE OF EXPENSE

This section is intended to provide a breakdown of the type of expenses incurred by a municipal department (or function) and by the municipality as a whole. By providing the information on a comparative basis, unfavorable changes in such items as overhead rate and G&A rate become apparent.

The financial statements were prepared on a pro forma basis, to reflect the financial position following accepted accounting standards. However, in view of the difficulty that would be involved in attempting to make pro forma adjustments on a departmental basis, the information contained herein should conform to the municipality's records, without such adjustment.

It is also quite possible that the municipality's records do not provide a breakdown of expenses by type, as is common in industry. Initially, this problem should be handled by certain assumptions based on the facts of the situation. For example, a police department should know the number of patrolmen assigned to its precincts. If one patrolman at each precinct is always required in the precinct to operate the switchboard, the number of men on patrol—i.e., direct labor—can be derived. Other assumptions such as all sergeants and lieutenants are overhead, and all inspectors and above are G&A could also be made. Ultimately, the municipality's accounting system might be geared to provide this information.

The following exhibits reflect the proposed format of the required financial statements. Specifically, they would consist of:

Exhibit 1—Pro Forma Consolidated Balance Sheet

Exhibit 2—Pro Forma Consolidated Statement of Revenue and Expense

Exhibit 3—Pro Forma Consolidated Statement of Cash Receipts and Disbursements

Exhibit 4—Notes to Consolidated Financial Statements

The exhibits are intended to reflect a typical situation. It is apparent that the line items contained in each statement will vary with the peculiar requirements of a specific municipality. The important thing is that the statements reflect fairly the results of operations for the year ended, on a basis consistent with that used for the preceding year, and the financial position of the municipality at the end of the fiscal year, again on a basis consistent with that used for the preceding year.

The Notes to the Consolidated Financial Statements will be particularly important in this instance, due to the number of pro forma adjustments that may be required. Just as in the corporate area, where some corporations may elect a conservative approach to accounting and other corporations a more liberal approach (both approaches being justified by accounting principles), municipalities will have similar options. Because of the impact on the statements of the pro forma adjustments, it is not unreasonable to expect extreme examples of "creative" accounting. Consequently, the user of the statements must look to the Notes for an explanation of the accounting approach taken. Given full and accurate disclosure, he may make his own assessment of the appropriateness of the techniques employed.

It is interesting to speculate that, at some future date, newspapers may editorialize over the accounting principles employed by a municipality, and mayoralty candidates may debate the merits of conservative vs. liberal accounting practices.

ILLUSTRATIVE PRO FORMA CONSOLIDATED BALANCE SHEET
CITY OF _____
DECEMBER 31, 1973 AND 1972

Assets	1973	1972
Current Assets:		
Cash	$XXX	$XXX
Investments	XXX	XXX
Accounts Receivable (net)	XXX	XXX
Taxes Receivable:		
Current (net)	XXX	XXX
Deferred	XXX	XXX
Due from other Governmental Units	XXX	XXX
Material & Supplies Inventory	XXX	XXX
Prepaid Expenses	XXX	XXX
Total Current Assets	$XXXX	$XXXX

Fixed Assets (Note 2):

Land	$XXX	$XXX
Building & Structure	XXX	XXX
Public Improvements	XXX	XXX
Equipment	XXX	XXX
	$XXXX	$XXXX
Less: Reserve for Depreciation	XXX	XXX
	$XXXX	$XXXX
	$XXXXX	$XXXXX

Liabilities

Current Liabilities:	1973	1972
Accrued Salaries Payable	$XXX	$XXX
Accounts Payable	XXX	XXX
Workmen's Compensation Claims	XXX	XXX
Refundable Deposits	XXX	XXX
Taxes Payable	XXX	XXX
Due to other Governmental Units	XXX	XXX
Accrued Liabilities	XXX	XXX
Bonds, Notes, & Interest Payable	XXX	XXX
Other Current	XXX	XXX
Total Current Liabilities	$XXXX	$XXXX

Long-Term Liabilities:

Long-Term Debt	$XXX	$XXX
Accrued Pension Liabilities (Note 3)	XXX	XXX
	$XXXX	$XXXX
Fund Balance	XXXX	XXXX
Total Liabilities and Fund Balance	$XXXXX	$XXXXX

The accompanying notes are an integral part of this statement.

ILLUSTRATIVE PRO FORMA CONSOLIDATED STATEMENT
OF REVENUE AND EXPENSE
CITY OF _____
YEARS ENDING DECEMBER 31, 1973 AND 1972

Revenues	1973	1972
Taxes	$XXX	$XXX
Assessments	XXX	XXX
Licenses and Permits	XXX	XXX
Intergovernmental	XXX	XXX
Charges for Services	XXX	XXX
Fines and Forfeits	XXX	XXX
Miscellaneous	XXX	XXX
Total Revenues	$XXXX	$XXXX
Expenses		
General Government	$XXX	$XXX
Debt Service	XXX	XXX
Depreciation (Note 2)	XXX	XXX
Accrued Liabilities (net)	XXX	XXX
Miscellaneous	XXX	XXX
Total Expenses	$XXXX	$XXXX
Total Surplus or Deficit (Note 4)	$XXXXX	$XXXXX

The accompanying notes are an integral part of this statement.

ILLUSTRATIVE PRO FORMA CONSOLIDATED STATEMENT
OF CASH RECEIPTS AND DISBURSEMENTS
CITY OF _____
YEARS ENDING DECEMBER 31, 1973 AND 1972

Sources of Cash Receipts	1973	1972
Total Surplus (Deficit) from Operations	$XXX	$XXX
Changes to Operations not requiring		
Cash Expenditure		
Depreciation	XXX	XXX
Accrued Liabilities	XXX	XXX
Proceeds from Borrowings	XXX	XXX
Other	XXX	XXX
	$XXXX	$XXXX

Applications of Cash Expenditures		
Additions to Property, Plant & Equipment	$XXX	$XXX
Repayment of Debt	XXX	XXX
Payment of Prior Period Accruals	XXX	XXX
Other	XXX	XXX
	$XXXX	$XXXX
Increase (Decrease) in Cash	$XXX	$XXX

The accompanying notes are an integral part of this statement.

Notes to Consolidated Financial Statements

Note 1—Principles of Consolidation

The consolidated financial statements include the accounts of the general fund, special assessment fund, special revenue fund, debt service fund, and permanent improvement fund. The educational fund has not been consolidated, as the trustees of that fund are elected separately and are therefore deemed to be independent of municipal management.

Note 2—Fixed Assets

Provision for depreciation of property, plant, and equipment has been made on the straight-line method based on the following useful lives:

Building and Structures—40 years

Public Improvements—20 to 50 years

Equipment—3 to 10 years

The accounts of the individual funds reflect neither the value of these assets nor the associated depreciation charges. Consequently, the amounts shown represent pro forma adjustments.

Note 3—Accrued Pension Liabilities

This amount consists principally of liabilities accrued in connection with municipal pension programs. These liabilities are not funded as incurred, but are paid out of current revenues when due. The municipality and the funds consolidated have several pension plans covering substantially all of their employees. The total pension expense for the year was $, which includes, as to certain of the plans, amortization of prior service cost over periods ranging from 25 to 40 years. The actuarially computed value of vested benefits for all plans, as of December 31, 1973, exceeded the total of the balance sheet accruals by $

As discussed above, the municipality pays pension expenses when due and has not established a vested pension fund. Consequently, the accrued pension liability figure represents a pro forma adjustment.

Note 4—Total Surplus (Deficit)

The amount shown includes the effects of a number of pro forma adjustments. The following adjustments have been reflected herein and have had the following effect on expenses:

Items Increasing Expense:

Accrual of Pension Liabilities	$XXX
Depreciation Charges	XXX
Other	XXX
Total	$XXXX

Items Decreasing Expense:

Capitalization of Fixed Assets	$XXX
Other	XXX
Total	$XXXX

Note 5—Debt Obligations

During the year ending December 31, 1973, the municipality increased its long-term debt through the sale of $XXX of bonds, paying interest at the rate of   %, due in 1998. The municipality retired bonds in the face amount of $XXX, bearing interest at the rate of   %, which matured during the year. Debt outstanding at December 31, 1973, was:

Amount	Coupon Rate	Issue Date	Maturity Date

Note 6—Subsequent Events

Subsequent to December 31, 1973, the municipality entered into a two-year contract with Local _____ of the United Federation of Teachers, effective January 1, 1974, which provides for a general wage increase of $1,000/year for each of two years. This contract will increase salary expense in 1974 by approximately $ _____ . In addition, the contract allows retirement at age 60, rather than age 65, as previous. This will increase unfunded prior service pension liabilities by $ _____ , which amount is not reflected in the statements.

Changes in the method of disbursement of revenue-sharing funds by the United States Government is expected to increase the amounts received in 1974 by approximately 20 percent from that received in 1973.

Note 7—Summary of Required Expenditures to be
Incurred in Subsequent Periods

The following summary presents expenditures to which the municipality is obligated and which will be incurred in future periods. These items must be provided for in future budgets, and hence represent a claim against the municipality's resources. The expenditures may be made over approximately 50 years.

Item	Balance at Year End	
	1973	1972
Interest on Outstanding Debt	$XXX	$XXX
Redemption of Outstanding Debt	XXX	XXX
Contractual Construction Commitments	XXX	XXX
Actuarially Computed Liabilities under Existing Plans	XXX	XXX
Salary Payments under Tenure Agreements	XXX	XXX
	$XXXX	$XXXX

MODEL FOR PERFORMANCE EVALUATION STATISTICS OF THE MUNICIPAL ANNUAL REPORT

This section of the report will consist of financial and statistical data intended to provide the reader with sufficient information to assist in evaluating management's performance when taken in conjunction with the financial statements.

Definition of Municipal Functions

The performance evaluation statistics will relate to a number of municipal functions or departments to be reported upon. In some instances, a municipality may elect to report upon each department separately, while in other instances, municipalities may choose to group several departments into a common function and to report upon the function. The choice, within the bounds of reasonableness, should be left to the reporting municipality. However, the municipality should first be required to clearly define the function or activity being reported upon. In addition, as previously discussed, the definition should be consistent from year to year. Changes should not be made without good reason, and the reason should be disclosed when a change is made. In addition, disclosure should be made of the results that would have been achieved under the old reporting basis. The following are illustrative definitions of municipal function which also served as the basis for the actual application developed for this case.

Community Development
This function reflects those activities intended to improve the physical, economic, and social condition of the city. Included are activities carried on by city agencies directed toward planning for physical growth, improving general physical attractiveness, eliminating blight, increasing the number of habitable housing units, preventing decline of residential neighborhood, and improving the economic well-being of the city. Included herein are the activities of:

    a. Municipal Planning Commission
    b. Community Improvement Commission
    c. Building Inspection Department
    d. Property Acquisition and Management Bureau
    e. City Engineer
    f. Model Cities Program

Environmental Health and Protection
This function reflects those activities intended to promote environmental health and protection through the collection and disposal of solid wastes and the provision of treated water. Included are those activities related to collecting and disposing of garbage, cleaning streets, and supplying quality water. Specifically included are the activities of:

    a. Refuse and trash collection and disposal
    b. Street cleaning
    c. Water supply and treatment
    d. Sewerage treatment

   e. Pollution monitoring and control
   f. Environmental planning

Public Safety

This function reflects those activities intended to protect persons and property from external harm and to maintain an atmosphere of personal security from external events. Included are those activites related to preventing and controlling crime, reducing fire loss, controlling animals, preparing for natural disasters, and providing ambulance services. Specifically included are the activities of:

   a. Police Department
   b. Fire Department
   c. Animal Control and License Bureau
   d. Civil Defense
   e. Ambulance Service

Transportation

This function reflects those activities intended to move people and goods safely and economically. Included are activities directed toward designing street and highway systems, controlling traffic, maintaining existing streets, and providing adequate street lighting. Specifically included are:

   a. Traffic engineering
   b. Traffic control
   c. Street maintenance
   d. Street lighting

Parks, Recreation, and Cultural Affairs

This function reflects those activities intended to provide year-round use of leisure time. Included are activities intended to provide recreation and athletic programs, care and maintenance of parks, and cultural enrichment experiences. Specifically included are:

   a. Parks and Recreation
   b. Civic Center Authority
   c. Library Board

Policy Formulation and Administration

This function reflects those activities intended to formulate city policy and assure its implementation through management and support activities. Included are those activities directed toward policy determination, management leadership, legal, public information, budget, purchasing, financial, personnel, and data processing. Specifically included are:

a. Mayor and City Council
b. Legal Services
c. Comptroller's Office
d. Purchasing/Printing
e. Finance
f. Personnel
g. Data Processing

Figures of Merit

This section is intended to provide a series of performance indices for each department or function. The purpose of the index is to measure the effectiveness of each department or function being evaluated. The definitions developed earlier in this chapter should be used in conjunction with the following discussion.

Community Development

The community development function involved a number of factors, both tangible and intangible. For example, among the activities included herein is "improving general physical attractiveness." Intangible factors of this nature will be excluded from the computation of any performance index in view of the subjective nature of measurement.

In evaluating the community development function, the following factors are taken as being keys to its performance.

a. Assessed value of residential housing. The activities of the community development function are devoted to improving the physical, economic, and social condition of the city. While assessed value is different from market value, the relationship is, in most communities, a proportional, and a real property assessment ratio is well established. Hence, changes in assessed value may be used to derive changes in market value. The market value of the residential real estate available in a community may be taken as a measure of the quantity and quality of housing available to the citizens of the community.

b. Number of habitable housing units. The number of habitable housing units available in the community is a measure of the community development agency's ability to generate housing starts for the community. While it is a measurement somewhat related to assessed value it does provide a measure of the community's ability to provide basic housing needs for its population. It would be possible for assessed value to increase while the supply of habitable housing decreases. This situation could occur through increased selling prices for homes and/or the construction of a relatively small number of high-value homes.

c. Assessed value of commerical and industrial property. This statistic should serve as a measure of the economic health of the community. The function of the community development department is, of course, to improve the economic strength.

Credit Rating

The credit rating assigned by Moody's or Standard & Poor's to the debt obligations of a municipality provide significant information on a municipality and its management. As previously discussed, the rating agencies do not disclose the means by which they arrive at a rating; however, we do know that they consider economic, governmental, financial, and debt factors. In brief, they are attempting to assess the ability of a municipality to honor its obligations. The rating which they assign may save, or cost, the municipality a substantial amount of interest.

A citizen, evaluating the management of his municipality, should be aware of the rating given for it reflects the supposedly objective view of an expert, and, if a change is involved, it will have an impact over many years. For example, suppose a mayor strengthens the finances of a city and hence achieves an upgraded rating. The resultant saving in interest expense associated with new debt will be spread over perhaps 40 years, and will be reaped by subsequent mayors, but credit properly belongs to the administration that achieved the change.

Environmental Health and Protection

This function is principally involved in the collection and disposal of wastes and the provision of potable water. Consequently, this activity lends itself more than most to the quantitative evaluation of performance. It is obviously much easier to measure gallons of water treated per year than the success of a community development agency in promoting general economic well-being.

In evaluating the environmental health and protection function, the following factors are taken as being the keys to its performance.

a. Refuse and trash collected. The number of tons of trash and refuse collected during the year is a key measure of the volume of work handled.

b. Refuse disposal. Tons of refuse disposed of in a safe and sanitary manner, either through landfill operations or processing facilities is also a key measure of the volume of work handled.

c. Street cleaning. The total number of miles of streets cleaned and flushed during the year within the municipality.

d. Water supply and treatment. Number of gallons of potable water supplied to the municipality during the year.

e. Sewerage treatment and disposal. Number of gallons of raw sewerage treated and disposed of within the municipality, in accordance with city, state, and federal regulations.

Public Safety

The public safety function is intended to protect persons and property from external harm and to maintain an atmosphere of personal security from external events. The principal activities of this function are carried on through the police and fire departments, although animal control, civil defense, and ambulance service units also contribute.

In evaluating the activities within this function, care should be taken not to confuse other valid but lower level measures of performance with the basic function. That is, the true measure of performance is the ability of the municipality to protect persons and property from external harm. Consequently, a homicide should be viewed as a negative statistic; the ability of the police to speedily apprehend and collect evidence for conviction is not an adequate offset. One must assume that a municipality with an efficient police department will enjoy a lower crime rate than one with an inefficient department (either because the criminal is more quickly removed from society by the efficient department or because the knowledge that a high probability of arrest exists deters some potential criminals). Hence, the measure of performance is the protection offered, not the ability to take corrective action.

In evaluating the public safety function, the following factors are being taken as keys to its performance.

a. Number of felonies involving attacks on individuals. Included in this category are all reported homicides, assaults (felonious), robberies, and rapes. This is a key measure of the ability of an individual to enjoy protection from external harm.

b. All other felonies. Included in this category are burglaries, arson (not involving injury to humans), embezzlement, narcotics violations, and other felonies as defined by the state penal code and not involving an attack on an individual. This is a measure of an individual's ability to enjoy protection of property from external harm.

c. Traffic accidents. Number of traffic accidents reported within the municipality involving damage in excess of $100, personal injury, or death. This statistic would be a measure of the police department's enforcement of traffic regulations, as well as other more intangible factors such as highway design and placement of regulatory signs and lights. This is another measure of an individual's ability to enjoy protection of life and property from external harm.

d. Deaths and injuries caused by fire. Included in this category are all deaths resulting from fires and injuries requiring medical attention. Excluded, however, are indirect deaths—i.e., a heart attack or exhaustion from a fire. This is another measure of an individual's ability to enjoy protection from external harm.

e. Property damage caused by fire. Included in this category are estimates of the dollar value of damage done by fire in the municipality during the year.

In view of the fact that animal control, civil defense, and ambulance service activities account for a nominal percentage of expenditures for public safety, no specific performance measurements for these areas will be included.

Transportation

This function is devoted to those activities intended to move goods quickly, safely, and economically. In general, it encompasses the functions of street maintenance and traffic control and engineering. In evaluating this function, the following factors will be considered as key to the evaluation of its performance.

a. Miles of street resurfaced. This is a measure of the volume of work performed on a regular basis in the maintenance of streets.

b. Square yards of repair performed. This is a measure of the square yards of potholes, etc. repaired during the year.

c. Sign and signals replaced or installed. The number of traffic control signs and signals replaced or installed during the year is a measure of the activity of the traffic control function.

Parks, Recreation, and Cultural Affairs

This function is devoted to those activities providing opportunities for pleasurable and constructive use of leisure time. In general, it includes those activities carried on by city agencies providing recreation and athletic programs, care and maintenance of parks, and cultural enrichment activities. In evaluating this function, the following factors will be considered as key to the evaluation of its performance.

a. Acres of municipal parks. This is a measure of the total amount of park land provided by the city for the use of its citizens.

b. Attendance at workshops and classes. During the course of a year, municipalities will normally offer courses in swimming, golf, arts and crafts, and other activities. Total attendance by citizens is a measure of the number of courses offered and the interest aroused.

c. Attendance at concerts and similar events. This is a measure of the number of concerts and the interest aroused.

Policy Formulation and Administration

This function reflects those activities intended to formulate city policy and assure its implementation through management and support activities. Since this function is essentially an administrative one, no performance statistics will be presented. Rather, see the exhibit entitled Comparative Consolidating Analysis of Type of Expense, on page 410. The G&A rate (total) should be the key measure of the efficiency of this function.

Supplementary Departmental Report

Since each function defined in the report will generally consist of more than one department, and since a department is generally the basic unit for budgetary purposes, it is suggested than an additional departmental report be included. This material might either immediately follow the particular function discussed or could be included as an appendix to the report.

The material presented on each department should allow the reader to determine the resources devoted to the department, the allocation of resources among the various programs for which the department has responsibility, and the relative success achieved with each program. In view of the number of departments, it appears more practical, for purposes of this paper, to present a typical format for one department. All others would follow somewhat similar formats.

ILLUSTRATIVE DEPARTMENTAL REPORT
FIRE DEPARTMENT
CITY OF _____
DEFINITION OF PROGRAMS

The Fire Department has as its general objective: Reduce the incidence and severity of fires and minimize danger to life and property.

In order to achieve this objective, the Department has implemented the following programs with their associated objectives:

1. Fire Prevention and Investigation. Prevent fires through education, engineering and enforcement programs and investigate fires of unknown origin.
2. Fire Control. Maintain manpower and equipment ready to suppress and control fires on an emergency basis.
3. Fire Training. Improve fire-fighting capability of fire personnel through recruit, inservice, and special training.
4. Fire Communications. Provide a reliable system for reporting fires and dispatching manpower to the scene.
5. Fire Equipment Maintenance. Assure availability of fire apparatus when required to fight fires.
6. Fire Administration. Provide leadership and coordination of other programs, and perform clerical and inventory functions.

ILLUSTRATIVE DEPARTMENTAL REPORT
FIRE DEPARTMENT
CITY OF _____
ANALYSIS OF PROGRAM ACTIVITY

	1973 $	1973 Manpower	1972 $	1972 Manpower
A. Resource Allocation				
Fire Prevention	X	a	y	b
Fire Control	X	a	y	b
Fire Training	X	a	y	b
Fire Communications	X	a	y	b
Fire Equip. Maint.	X	a	y	b
Fire Administration	X	a	y	b
B. Program Effectiveness				
1. Fire Prevention				
No. of Fires		m		n
Inspections Completed		m		n
Fires Investigated		m		n
2. Fire Control				
Fire Deaths		m		n
Fire Injuries		m		n
Fire Losses		$m		$n
3. Fire Training				
Recruits Trained		m		n
Man-hours of Other Training		m		n

4. Fire Communications
   Alarms Received   m   n
   Alarm Boxes Operated   m   n

5. Fire Equipment and
   Maintenance
   Vehicles Maintained   m   n
   Equipment Availability   %   %
   Administration
   Personnel in Department

ILLUSTRATIVE DEPARTMENTAL REPORT
FIRE DEPARTMENT
CITY OF _____
ANALYSIS OF EXPENSES

Item	1973	1972
Salaries	$XXX	$yyy
Utilities	—	—
Telephone	XX	yy
Electricity	XX	yy
Water	XX	yy
Fuel	XX	yy
Office Supplies	XX	yy
Building Maintenance	XX	yy
Automotive Supplies	—	—
Gas & Oil	XX	yy
Tires	XX	yy
Repairs	XX	yy
Operating Expenses	XX	yy
Miscellaneous	XX	yy
Equipment Purchase	XXX	yyy
Total	$XXXX	$yyyy

CITY OF PROVIDENCE, RHODE ISLAND
JUNE 30, 1972 AND 1971
PRO FORMA CONSOLIDATED BALANCE SHEET

Assets (Note A)	1972	1971
Cash	$ 7,932,829	$ 9,298,038
Receivables	14,642,138	19,851,879
Supplies	197,670	147,273
Investment (Note B)	64,251,743	68,523,100
Property, Plant & Improvements (Note C)	76,169,748	84,087,675
(Net of Amortization & Depreciation)		
Unexpended Balances	7,626,252	1,954,325
Funds Available	22,392,000	14,892,000
Miscellaneous Equipment	621,787	788,172
Real Estate (Held in Trust)	2,972,886	2,978,220
Total Assets	$196,807,055	$202,520,682

CITY OF PROVIDENCE, RHODE ISLAND
JUNE 30, 1972 AND 1971
PRO FORMA CONSOLIDATED BALANCE SHEET

Liabilities	1972	1971
Accounts Payable	$ 3,303,891	$ 4,561,907
Accrued Liabilities	961,673	1,803,230
Interfund Liabilities	107,169	439,316
Matured Bonds & Interest	164,010	938,757
Notes Payable	5,308,000	15,808,000
	$ 9,844,743	$ 2,551,210
Long-Term Debt (Including current portion)	78,488,000	70,234,000
Other	10,958,767	16,060,794
Accrued Pension Liabilities (Note B)	150,000,000	150,000,000
	$249,291,210	$259,846,004
Equity (Note D)	($ 52,484,155)	($ 57,325,322)
	$196,807,055	$206,520,682

APPLICATION TO A MUNICIPALITY

This section utilizes actual data to construct (for illustrative purposes) a municipal annual report of the type proposed in this study. It also demonstrates the feasibility of the approach taken.

The ideal approach would have been to enlist the cooperation of a municipality and to construct the report utilizing data from that municipality. This, however, was not feasible. Therefore, the example utilizes published data of several municipalities since no single municipality reviewed publishes all of the requisite data. In several instances, requisite material was completely unavailable, and this necessitated either omission of the related performance evaluation statistics or the use of certain reasonable assumptions to allow their computation. For example, the actuarial determination of accrued pension liabilities would require detailed data on age and sex of the employee population. Not only is this information unavailable, but its use would add little to the illustrative purposes of this section.

Financial Statements

The following statements are included:

1. Pro Forma Consolidated Balance Sheet.
2. Pro Forma Consolidated Statement of Revenue and Expense.
3. Pro Forma Consolidated Statement of Cash Receipts and Expenditures.

The data for the statements were taken from the annual reports of Providence, Rhode Island, and Fair Lawn, New Jersey, for the years in question. Two municipalities were used, as neither annual report contained the necessary data for the preparation of all three statements included.

Several assumptions were necessarily made in the preparation of the statements. The most material was the estimate made as to the actuarially computed value of vested pension benefits for the City of Providence. It should be pointed out, however, that, given the necessary data as to employees' age distribution, benefits, etc., a trained actuary could easily arrive at an adequate estimate.

NOTES TO CONSOLIDATED BALANCE SHEET

City of Providence

Note A—Principles of Consolidation

The consolidated financial statements include the accounts of the General Fund, School Fund, Capital Fund, Sinking Fund, Trust and Special Funds, Revolving Fund and Federal Programs Fund.

Note B—Investments

At June 30, 1972 and 1971, investments included $50,353,235 and $47,297,242, respectively, held in trust for the Employees Retirement System. The actuarially computed value of vested benefits of all pension plans exceeded the total of balance sheet accruals by approximately $150,000,000 on both June 30, 1972 and 1971. This accrued pension liability figure is included as a pro forma adjustment to the Balance Sheet.

Note C—Property, Plant and Improvements

Carried at cost less amortization, depreciation, and miscellaneous write-offs. Available records do not permit reconstruction of all past write-offs; however, carrying costs reasonably approximate Assessors' Valuation of $76,340,011 and $70,603,185 in 1972 and 1971, respectively.

Note D—Equity

The amount shown reflects the effect of a number of pro forma adjustments. The principal adjustment involved the recognition of an un-funded pension liability (see Note B) of approximately $150,000,000.

Note E—Debt Obligations

Long-term debt, $78,488,000 and $70,234,000 at June 30, 1972 and 1971, respectively, consisted of 79 and 81 bond issues, respectively, bearing interest at various rates between 2 percent and 6.60 percent with various maturities between 1/1/73 and 6/1/01 in 1972 and 7/1/71 and 6/1/01 in 1971.

BOROUGH OF FAIR LAWN, NEW JERSEY
YEARS ENDING DECEMBER 31, 1971 and 1970
PRO FORMA CONSOLIDATED STATEMENT OF REVENUE AND EXPENSE

Revenues (Note A)	1971	1970
Licenses and Fees	$1,609,635	$1,554,379
Receipts from Delinquent Taxes	111,390	99,320
Local Taxes for Municipal Purposes	3,073,022	2,704,295
Total Revenues	$4,794,047	$4,357,994

Expenses

General Government	$3,110,407	$2,894,996
Interest Expense	80,407	85,389
Statutory Expenditures	515,703	540,577
Miscellaneous Accruals	218,673	144,990
Depreciation (Note B)	150,000	135,000
	$4,075,190	$3,800,952
Total Surplus	$ 718,857	$ 557,042

BOROUGH OF FAIR LAWN, NEW JERSEY
YEARS ENDING DECEMBER 31, 1971 and 1970
PRO FORMA CONSOLIDATED STATEMENT
OF CASH RECEIPTS AND EXPENDITURES

Sources of Cash Receipts	1971	1970
Total Surplus from Operations	$718,857	$557,042
Charges Not Requiring Cash Expenditures		
Depreciation	150,000	135,000
Net Income in Miscellaneous Accruals	73,683	25,752
Proceeds from Borrowings	0	0
	$942,540	$717,794

Applications of Cash Expenditures

Capital Expenditures	$300,867	$ 96,087
Repayment of Debt	113,000	88,000
	$413,867	$184,087
Increase in Cash	$528,673	$633,707

Notes to Consolidated Financial Statements
Borough of Fair Lawn, New Jersey

Note A—Principles of Consolidation
   The consolidated financial statements include the accounts of the General
Fund and the Capital Fund. The School Fund is not included, as it is

separately administered. However, the category Statutory Expenditures includes $350,000 in each of 1971 and 1970 for transfer to the local school board.

Note B—Amounts for depreciation represent a pro forma adjustment, as depreciation is not charged. The amounts used are estimates, as precise information is not available. Capital expenditures, which are included in the published financial statements, have been removed from the accounts as a pro forma adjustment.

Performance Evaluation Statistics

The following section contains performance evaluation statistics, as they might appear in the proposed municipal annual report. Data from several municipalities are included, as no one municipality investigated published sufficient data to permit development of the section in its entirety.

PERFORMANCE EVALUATION STATISTICS
CITY OF NASHUA, NEW HAMPSHIRE
REPORT FOR THE YEAR ENDING DECEMBER 31, 1971
DEFINITIONS OF FUNCTIONS REPORTED UPON

In preparing the Performance Evaluation Statistics it was necessary to define the municipal function to be evaluated. Each function encompasses one or more municipal departments, which was assumed to represent the most typical grouping of municipal responsibilities.

Community Development. This function reflects those activities intended to improve the physical, economic, and social condition of the City. Included are activities directed toward planning for physical growth, improving general physical attractiveness, eliminating blight, and increasing the economic well-being of the City. Included herein are the activities of:

	1971 Budget (Excluding Capital Appropriations)
a. Code Enforcement	$31,391
b. Zoning Board	2,920
c. City Planning Board	49,248

Environmental Health and Protection. This function includes those activities intended to promote environmental health and protection through the collection and disposal of solid wastes and the provision of treated water.

Included are those activities related to collection and disposal of garbage, cleaning streets, and supplying quality water. Specifically included are the activities of:

	1971 Budget (Excluding Capital Appropriations)
a. Water Supply	$276,063
b. Board of Plumbers	200
c. Board of Health	147,230

Public Safety. This function reflects those activities intended to protect persons and property from external harm and to maintain an atmosphere of personal security from external events. Included are those activities related to controlling crime, reducing fire loss, controlling animals, and preparing for natural disasters. Specifically included are:

	1971 Budget (Excluding Capital Appropriations)
a. Weights and Measures	$ 7,082
b. Dog Officer	15,957
c. Police Department	1,142,117
d. Fire Department	877,881
e. Civil Defense	21,948

Transportation. This function reflects those activities intended to move people and goods safely and economically. Included are activities directed toward designing street and highway systems, controlling traffic, maintaining existing streets, and providing adequate street lighting. Specifically included are:

	1971 Budget (Excluding Capital Appropriations)
a. Board of Public Works	$1,699,030
b. Street Lighting	212,106
c. Aeronautical Fund	67,197

Parks, Recreation and Cultural Affairs. This function reflects those activities intended to provide year-round use of leisure time. Included are activities intended to provide recreation and athletic programs, care and maintenance of parks, and cultural enrichment experiences. Specifically included are:

	1971 Budget (Excluding Capital Appropriations)
a. Public Libraries	$ 322,648
b. Parks & Recreation	313,031

Education and Welfare. This function reflects those activities intended to provide for the education and welfare of the populace. Included are activities intended to educate, including vocational training, medical assistance, and support payments to indigents. Specifically included are:

	1971 Budget (Excluding Capital Appropriations)
a. Old Age Assistance	$ 125,000
b. General Welfare	68,249
c. Edgewood Cemetery	46,721
d. Suburban Cemeteries	9,590
e. Woodlawn Cemetery	56,052
f. School Department	7,325,171
g. School Activities	110,287

Policy Formulation and Administration. This function reflects those activities intended to formulate city policy and assure its implementation through management and support activities. Included are those activities directed toward policy determination, management leadership, legal, public information, purchasing, financial, personnel, and data processing. Specifically included are:

	1971 Budget (Excluding Capital Appropriations)
a. Mayor's Office	$ 30,434
b. City Treasurer	63,817
c. City Clerk	90,648
d. District Court	59,532
e. Legal	10,200
f. Finance Officer	0

g.	Alderman	15,350
h.	Community Services (Misc.)	8,022
i.	Wards & Elections	13,967
j.	Board of Registrars	15,475
k.	City Hall	49,437
l.	Pension Fund	620,926
m.	Insurance	237,408
n.	Board of Assessors	66,746
o.	Interest	679,013

In connection with the Analysis of Type of Expense, the following classifications of expenses were made:

Community Development
1. Code of Enforcement
   a. Payroll Account—salaries of director and secretary classified as G&A. Salaries of inspectors classified as Direct Labor. Longevity pay as Overhead.
   b. Utilities—all G&A.
   c. Office Supplies and Services—all G&A.
   d. Other—Overhead.
2. Zoning Board—all G&A
3. City Planning Board
   a. Payroll—Director and secretary classified as G&A. Planners as Direct Labor.
   b. Utilities—G&A.
   c. Office Supplies and Services—G&A.
   d. Building &Equipment Expense—Overhead.
   e. Miscellaneous—Overhead.
   f. Outside Services—Overhead.

Environmental Health & Protection
1. Water Supply—all as direct material as entire budget is for purchase of water from private utility
2. Board of Plumbers—all G&A
3. Board of Health
   a. Payroll—salaries of Board Members, Director and Secretary—G&A. Health Officers, nurses, pollution control officer, and technicians classified as Direct Labor. Other payroll (principally office clerical and maintenance) as Overhead.
   b. Utilities—all G&A.

CITY OF NASHUA, NEW HAMPSHIRE
YEARS ENDING DECEMBER 31, 1971 AND 1970
COMPARATIVE CONSOLIDATING ANALYSIS OF TYPE OF EXPENSE

Type of Expense	Community Development		Environmental Health		Public Safety		Transportation	
	1971	1970	1971	1970	1971	1970	1971	1970
Direct Labor	$ 29,174	$23,492	$ 64,731	$ 51,792	$1,121,236	$ 979,344	$ 675,724	$ 679,640
Direct Material	0	0	280,313	271,683	0	0	639,756	463,690
Overhead	14,298	19,260	49,624	43,188	845,614	793,294	523,393	768,612
Total Direct	$ 43,472	$42,752	$394,668	$366,663	$1,966,850	$1,772,638	$1,838,873	$1,911,942
G&A**	40,087	34,589	28,825	20,062	98,135	101,907	139,460	136,457
Total Expense	$ 83,559	$77,341	$423,493	$386,725	$2,064,985	$1,874,545	$1,978,333	$2,048,399
Capital	30,000	0	15,680	81,971	33,000	154,400	557,467	495,881
Total Expenditures*	$113,559	$77,341	$439,173	$468,696	$2,097,985	$2,028,945	$2,535,800	$2,544,280
Overhead Rate	49%	82%	76%	83%	76%	81%	71%	113%
G&A Rate	92%	81%	7%	6%	5%	6%	7%	6%

*Excludes repayment of bonded indebtedness.

Type of Expense	Parks and Recreation		Education and Welfare		Policy Formulation		Total	
	1971	1970	1971	1970	1971	1970	1971	1970
Direct Labor	$253,320	$207,632	$4,821,286	$4,023,359	$ 0	$ 0	$6,965,471	$5,965,259
Direct Material	60,710	55,180	485,042	404,725	0	0	1,465,821	1,195,278
Overhead	292,885	270,294	2,089,157	1,684,378	0	0	3,814,971	2,579,026
Total Direct	$606,915	$533,106	$7,395,485	$6,112,462	$ 0	$ 0	$12,246,263	$10,739,563
G&A**	28,764	23,879	345,585	275,720	1,960,975	1,740,450	2,641,831	2,333,064
Total Expense	$635,679	$556,985	$7,741,070	$6,388,182	$1,960,975	$1,740,450	$14,888,094	$13,072,627
Capital	220,728	235,799	0	15,000	141,671	254,482	998,546	1,237,538
Total Expenditures	$856,407	$792,784	$7,741,070	$6,403,182	$2,102,646	$1,994,932	$15,886,640	$14,310,165
Overhead Rate	112%	130%	43%	42%	N/A	N/A	55%	60%
G&A Rate	4%	4%	5%	4%	N/A	N/A	22%	22%

**Includes miscellaneous and contingency funds.

   c. Office Supplies—all G&A.
   d. Health Services & Supplies—classified as direct material, vaccines, and pesticides. All other as Overhead.
   e. Automotive—Overhead.
   f. Building & Equipment—Overhead.
   g. Outside Services—Overhead.
   h. Other & Miscellaneous Equipment—Overhead.

Public Safety

1. Weights & Measures—Sealer of Weights—Direct Labor. All other— Overhead
2. Dog Officer—Salary—Direct Labor. All other—Overhead
3. Police Department
   a. Payroll—Commissioners, Commission Clerk, Chief and Deputy Chief —G&A. Captains, lieutenants and sergeants—Overhead. Patrolmen, Special Officers, Meter Maids, and School Crossing Guards—Direct labor. All other (principally office clerks)—Overhead.
   b. Communications—All overhead.
   c. Insurance—Liability and Equipment—G&A; Medical provided personnel—Overhead.
   d. Uniform Allowance—all Overhead.
   e. Supplies—Overhead.
   f. Automotive—Overhead.
   g. Medical (principally care of prisoners)—Overhead.
   h. Other and Miscellaneous—all Overhead.
4. Fire Department
   a. Payroll—Commissioners, Commission Clerks, Chief, Assistant Chiefs and Chaplain—G&A. Firemen—Direct Labor. All others (principally fire officers)—Overhead.
   b. Overtime, longevity, and holiday pay—Overhead.
   c. Utilities—Overhead.
   d. Supplies—Overhead.
   e. Building Supplies—Overhead.
   f. Automotive—Overhead.
   g. Operating Supplies—Overhead.
   h. Miscellaneous & Equipment—all G&A.

Transportation

1. Board of Public Works
   a. Payroll—administrative personnel classified as G&A. Engineering personnel, superintendents and foreman as Overhead. Laborers and equipment operators as Direct Labor.
   b. Overtime, longevity, and holiday—Overhead.
   c. Utilities—G&A.
   d. Miscellaneous—Overhead.

    e. Equipment Maintenance—Overhead.

    f. Supplies—Overhead.

    g. Construction Supplies (asphalt, tar, top, etc.)—Direct material.

    h. Equipment Rental (includes rental of such items as trucks) —Overhead.

2. Parks

    a. Payroll—Commissioners and Clerk—G&A. Superintendent, directors, and foremen—Overhead. Remainder of Payroll (principally men lifeguards and athletic instructors)—Direct Labor.

    b. Utilities—Overhead.

    c. Equipment Supplies—Overhead.

    d. General Supplies (principally athletic equipment)—Overhead.

    e. Equipment—Overhead.

    f. Athletic Equipment & Programs—Overhead.

    g. Miscellaneous—Overhead.

Education and Welfare

1. Old Age Assistance—Total Budget consists of grants. Treated as Direct Material

2. General Welfare

    a. Payroll—salary of Welfare Investigator and Clerk treated as Direct Labor.

    b. Utilities—Overhead.

    c. Supplies—Overhead.

    d. Welfare Services—expense consists principally of provision of groceries, fuel, rent, etc. to welfare recipients. Treated as Direct Material.

    e. Other—Overhead.

3. Edgewood Cemetery

    a. Payroll—Superintendent, Foreman, Overtime and Longevity— Overhead. Laborers—Direct Labor.

    b. All else (principally supplies)—Overhead.

4. Suburban Cemeteries—same as Edgewood

5. Woodlawn Cemetery—same as Edgewood

6. School Department

    a. Payroll—Administrators—G&A. Teachers & Substitutes—Direct Labor. All others (principally superintendents and clerical) —Overhead.

    b. Utilities—Overhead.

    c. Supplies—Overhead.

d. Educational Supplies (principally textbooks)—Direct Material.
e. Other—Overhead.
f. Maintenance—Overhead.
g. Miscellaneous—Overhead.
7. School Athletics
a. Payroll—Direct Labor.
b. Athletic Activities—Direct Material.
c. Other—Overhead.

CITY OF NASHUA, NEW HAMPSHIRE
RATING ASSIGNED TO MUNICIPAL OBLIGATIONS
DECEMBER 31, 1971 AND DECEMBER 31, 1970

Rating Agency	Rating	
	December 31, 1971	December 31, 1970

Moody's

During 1971 the City sold $3,540,000 of School Bonds, maturing in 1991, at an interest rate of 5.50 percent. During 1970 the City sold $600,000 of Bridge Bonds, maturing in 1985, at an interest rate of 6.20 percent and $400,000 of School Bonds, maturing in 1974, at an interest rate of 5.20 percent.

COMMUNITY DEVELOPMENT
DETAILED ANALYSIS BY TYPE OF EXPENSE

Nature of Expense	Direct Labor	Direct Material	1971 Overhead	General and Administrative	Direct Labor	Direct Material	1970 Overhead	General and Administrative
Code Enforcement								
Payroll	$14,060		$ 100	$14,346	$13,396		$ 100	$13,663
Utilities				185				185
Office Supplies				1,225				1,102
Other			1,475				1,525	
Zoning Board-All				2,920				3,120
City Planning Board								
Payroll	$15,114			$19,211	10,106			$14,288
Utilities				1,000				995
Office Supplies				1,200				1,235
Bldg. & Equip.			1,650				4,105	
Miscellaneous			1,900				3,330	
Outside Services			9,173				10,200	
	$29,174	0	$14,298	$40,087	$23,492	0	$19,260	$34,589
1971 Total	$83,559							
1970 Total						$77,341		

415

ENVIRONMENTAL HEALTH & PROTECTION
SUPPLEMENTAL INFORMATION

	DL	1971 DM	OH	G&A
Water Supply (All)		$276,063		
Board of Plumbers (All)				$ 200
Board of Health				
Payroll	$64,731		$18,579	21,325
Utilities				4,750
Office Supplies				2,550
Health Services		4,250	25,320	
Automotive			2,075	
Bldg. & Equip. Exp.			1,600	
Outside Services			500	
Other & Equipment			1,550	
	$64,731	$280,313	$49,624	$28,825
				$423,493

ENVIRONMENTAL HEALTH & PROTECTION
SUPPLEMENTAL INFORMATION (Cont'd.)

	DL	1970 DM	OH	G&A	
Water Supply (All)					
Board of Plumbers (All)		$266,962			
Board of Health				$ 200	
Payroll	$51,792		$11,689	16,427	
Utilities				850	
Office Supplies				2,585	
Health Services		4,721	20,495		
Automotive			696		
Bldg. & Equip. Exp.			0		
Outside Services			3,250		
Other & Equipment			7,064		
	$51,792	$271,683	$43,188	$20,062	$386,725

PUBLIC SAFETY
CITY OF NASHUA, NEW HAMPSHIRE
SUPPLEMENTAL INFORMATION

1971

	DL	DM	OH	G&A	
Weights & Measures	$ 5,782		$ 1,300		
Dog Officer	4,992		10,965		
Police Department					
Payroll	577,300		381,430	$29,885	
Communications			12,096		
Insurance			1,691	4,450	
Uniforms			79,650		
Supplies			22,000		
Automotive			33,890		
Medical			5,160		
Other			54,565		
Fire Department					
Payroll	533,162		174,864	41,852	
Overtime			75,643		
Utilities			10,630		
Supplies			2,455		
Bldg. Supplies			7,000		
Automotive			7,900		
Operating			17,500		
Miscellaneous			6,875		
Civil Defense			21,948		
	$1,121,236	0	$345,614	$98,135	$2,064,985

PUBLIC SAFETY
CITY OF NASHUA, NEW HAMPSHIRE
SUPPLEMENTAL INFORMATION

1970

	DL	DM	OH	G&A
Weights & Measures	$ 5,512		$ 1,550	
Dog Officer	6,000		10,700	
Police Department				
Payroll	511,612		339,427	$ 33,269
Communications			10,498	
Insurance			17,990	4,079
Uniforms			15,750	
Supplies			21,923	
Automotive			30,490	
Medical			5,068	
Other			31,410	
Fire Department				
Payroll	456,220		165,368	39,895
Overtime			70,270	
Utilities			10,530	
Supplies			955	
Bldg. Supplies			9,800	
Automotive			9,115	
Operating			17,250	
Miscellaneous			25,200	
Civil Defense				24,664
	$979,344	0	$793,294	$101,907

$1,974,545

TRANSPORTATION
SUPPLEMENTAL INFORMATION

1971

	DL	DM	OH	G&A	
Board of Publishers					
Payroll	$675,724		$245,853	$ 51,138	
Overtime			103,740		
Utilities				21,125	
Miscellaneous			8,600		
Maintenance			113,200		
Supplies			11,000		
General Supplies			22,500		
Construction Supplies		$375,950			
Other Cons. Supplies		52,700			
Equipment Rental			18,500		
Street Lighting		212,106			
Aeronautical Fund				67,197	
	$675,724	$639,756	$523,393	$139,460	$1,978,333

TRANSPORTATION
SUPPLEMENTAL INFORMATION

1970

	DL	DM	OH	G&A	
Board of Publishers					
Payroll	$679,640		$219,862	$ 59,072	
Overtime			102,120		
Utilities				22,635	
Miscellaneous			12,100		
Maintenance			118,050		
Supplies			17,000		
General Supplies			22,500		
Construction Supplies		$403,990			
Other Cons. Supplies		59,700			
Equipment Rental			68,300		
Street Lighting			208,680		
Aeronautical Fund				54,750	
	$679,640	$463,690	$768,612	$136,457	$2,048,399

PARKS, RECREATION & CULTURE
SUPPLEMENTAL INFORMATION

1971

	DL	DM	OH	G&A
Public Libraries				
Payroll	$129,970		$ 75,752	$27,164
Utilities			11,900	
Office Supplies			11,252	
Building Maintenance		$60,710	2,600	
Library Service				
Other			3,300	
Park & Recreation				
Payroll	123,350		82,200	1,600
Utilities			15,000	
Equipment Supplies			7,690	
General Supplies			36,106	
Equipment			8,300	
Athletic Equipment			19,950	
Miscellaneous			78,830	
	$253,320	$60,710	$292,885	$28,764

$635,679

PARKS, RECREATION & CULTURE
SUPPLEMENTAL INFORMATION

1970

	DL	DM	OH	G&A	
Public Libraries					
Payroll	$ 96,546		$ 76,144	$22,279	
Utilities			6,777		
Office Supplies			12,678		
Building Maintenance			3,550		
Library Service		$55,180			
Other			3,541		
Parks & Recreation					
Payroll	111,086		65,933	1,600	
Utilities			15,400		
Equipment Supplies			6,950		
General Supplies			33,100		
Equipment			11,211		
Athletic Equipment			14,300		
Miscellaneous			20,710		
	$207,632	$55,180	$270,294	$23,879	$556,985

EDUCATION & WELFARE
SUPPLEMENTAL INFORMATION

1971

	DL	DM	OH	G&A
Old Age Assistance		$125,000		
General Welfare				
Payroll	$ 9,774			
Utilities			$ 350	
Office Supplies			300	
Service		53,700		
Other			4,125	
Edgewood Cemetery				
Payroll	14,859		15,336	
Other			16,526	
Woodlawn Cemetery				
Payroll	23,387		20,595	
Other			12,070	
Suburban Cemetery				
Payroll	3,500		4,675	
Other			1,415	
School Department				
Payroll	4,741,106		1,174,620	$345,585
Utilities			148,245	
Supplies			173,940	
Ed. Supplies		228,955		
Other			9,300	
Maintenance			109,000	
Miscellaneous			394,420	
School Athletics				
Payroll	28,660			
Activities		77,387		
Other			4,240	

EDUCATION & WELFARE
SUPPLEMENTAL INFORMATION

	DL	DM	OH	G&A	
		1970			
Old Age Assistance		$ 90,553			
General Welfare					
Payroll	$ 5,948				
Utilities			$ 300		
Office Supplies			300		
Services		37,317			
Other			3,925		
Edgewood Cemetery					
Payroll	16,713		14,787		
Other			14,920		
Woodlawn Cemetery					
Payroll	22,273		20,802		
Other			12,120		
Suburban Cemetery					
Payroll	3,500		4,029		
Other			1,505		
School Department					
Payroll	3,945,665		894,890	$275,720	
Utilities			136,875		
Supplies			161,420		
Ed. Supplies		201,855			
Other			10,350		
Maintenance			114,503		
Miscellaneous			291,410		
School Athletics					
Payroll	29,260	75,000			
Activities			4,240		
Other					
	$4,023,359	$404,725	$1,684,378	$275,720	$6,388,182

POLICY FORMULATION
ALL G & A
SUPPLEMENTAL INFORMATION

	1971	1970
Mayor's Office	$ 30,434	$ 28,649
City Treasurer	63,817	57,150
City Clerk	90,648	95,672
District Court	59,532	39,838
Legal & Prof.	10,200	7,425
Finance Officer	0	6,853
Alderman	15,350	19,750
Community Services	8,022	6,860
Wards & Elections	13,967	20,633
Board of Registrars	15,475	5,500
City Hall	49,437	47,323
Pension Fund	620,926	588,128
Insurance	237,402	111,975
Board of Assessors	66,746	50,886
Interest	679,013	653,808
	$1,960,975	$1,740,450

Figures of Merit

The material contained in this section is based upon the annual reports published by the City of Ann Arbor, Michigan. Each municipal department prepares an annual activity report for submission to the City Administrator. Copies of the reports are distributed to libraries, city officials, and news media. As the reports generally are activity-oriented rather than financial, the Performance Statistics presented do not contain financial information.

An actual report would contain summary financial data such as that contained in the earlier part of this chapter.

Summary and Conclusions

The ideal approach to determining the feasibility of producing the proposed municipal annual report would have been to generate the report for a convenient municipality. In practice, however, this proved to be impossible. As an alternative, therefore, published data was used to generate an actual sample report. As no single municipality investigated had published all of the necessary data, published data from several municipalities were used.

A Pro Forma Consolidated Balance Sheet was prepared using data from the City of Providence, Rhode Island. In constructing this Balance Sheet several assumptions were necessarily made. The principal one involved the amount of unfunded pension liabilities to be accrued. In actual practice,

CITY OF ANN ARBOR, MICHIGAN
COMMUNITY DEVELOPMENT FUNCTION*
FISCAL YEAR ENDED JUNE 30,1971

Factor	% Change	1969-70	1970-71
Permits Issued	+ 2%	$ 7,400	$ 7,593
Inspections Made	+ 3%	13,822	14,156
New Construction ($ Value)	+24%	30,515,790	37,945,034

*Includes the following Municipal Departments:
1. Department of Building and Safety Engineering
2. Planning
3. Housing Commission
4. Model Cities
5. Code Enforcement

CITY OF ANN ARBOR, MICHIGAN
ENVIRONMENTAL HEALTH AND PROTECTION FUNCTION*
PERFORMANCE STATISTICS
FISCAL YEAR ENDED JUNE 30, 1971

Factor	% Change	1969-70	1970-71
Waste Water Treated	+ 4%	5,171 million gallons	5,396 million gallons
Refuse Collected	+ 7%	134,783 cu yds	143,174 cu yds
Street Lights in System	+ 2%	3,929	4,026
New Streets Paved (by City)	+ 7%	20,012 L.F.	21,415 L.F.
Sanitary Sewers Installed (by City)	-51%	6,082 L.F.	2,973 L.F.
Delivered Water	- 4%	5,516 M.G.	5,291 M.G.
Public Health Home Visits	+ 1%	13,530	13,650
Laboratory Tests	-23%	1,575	1,212

*Includes the following Municipal Departments:
1. Department of Public Works
2. Utility Department
3. Health Department

CITY OF ANN ARBOR, MICHIGAN
PUBLIC SAFETY FUNCTION*
PERFORMANCE STATISTICS

Function	% Change	1969-70	1970-71
Criminal Homicides	–75%	4	1
Other Felonies Involving Attacks	+12%	363	406
Other Class I Offenses	+22%	7,695	9,355
Other Class II Offenses	+29%	4,621	5,986
Property Value Stolen	+14%	$1,295,963	$1,482,143
Property Value Recovered	–24%	$ 373,690	$ 284,605
Persons Killed in Traffic Accidents	+33%	3	4
Personal Injury Accidents	– 6%	913	852
Property Damage Accidents	+ 3%	921	960
Tickets Issued	+ 2%	294,367	310,855
Estimated Property Valuation	+ 6%	$914,967,000	$985,393,000
Persons Killed by Fires	– 0%	2	2
Persons Injured by Fires	+ 6%	15	16
Total Estimated $ Loss	–52%	$ 968,434	$ 465,554
Total Inspections	+23%	3,874	4,868

*Includes the following Municipal Departments:
   1. Police Department
   2. Fire Department

CITY OF ANN ARBOR, MICHIGAN
TRANSPORTATION FUNCTION*
PERFORMANCE STATISTICS

Function	% Change	1969-70	1970-71
Street & Traffic Signs Installed	+105%	2,162	4,428
Average Bus Passengers	+ 19%	40,752	45,173
Aviation Fuel Sales	+ 10%	$238,776	$260,886

*Includes the following Municipal Departments:
  1. Traffic Engineering and Transportation
  2. Airport Department
  3. Transportation Authority

CITY OF ANN ARBOR, MICHIGAN
PARKS, RECREATION AND CULTURAL AFFAIRS FUNCTION*
PERFORMANCE STATISTICS

Factor	% Change	1969-70	1970-71
Acres of Developed Parks	+ 1%	550	553 acres
Undeveloped Parks	0%	1,480	1,480 acres
Golf Courses	0%	350	350 acres
Natural Ice Rinks	N/A	N/A	6
Pools	0%	3	3
Ice Rink Income	− 1%	$46,876	$46,033
Swimming Income	+60%	$48,434	$76,899

*Includes the following Municipal Departments:
  1. Parks and Recreation

however, this amount could be reasonably well estimated by a skilled actuary. Consequently, in an actual situation, the determination of this amount, while probably involving tedious computations, involves well-known techniques and does not represent significant problems.

The Municipal Finance Officers Association, in conjunction with the National Committee on Governmental Accounting, has published certain principles and standards for public financial reporting. Municipalities publishing annual reports in conformity with these standards will have little problems in producing the pro forma consolidated balance sheet, as the bulk of the necessary data is already included in their published statements and need only be rearranged and adjusted.

A Pro Forma Consolidated Statement of Revenue and Expense and a Pro Forma Consolidated Statement of Cash Receipts and Disbursements is included based on data from the Borough of Fair Lawn, New Jersey. In preparing these statements, an assumption as to depreciation included was made. However, little problem was encountered in preparing the statements.

Most municipalities reviewed have a number of departments included as line items in their budget. Little difficulty was encountered in slotting them into general municipal functions, i.e.:

a. Community Development
b. Environmental Health and Protection
c. Public Safety
d. Transportation
e. Parks, Recreation, and Cultural Affairs
f. Education and Welfare
g. Policy Formulation

It is clear, however, that other functions could be defined, based on the unique requirements of a municipality.

Data from the City of Nashua, New Hampshire, was used in the construction of the Comparative Consolidating Analysis of Type of Expense. It is apparent, however, that at the time of budget preparation, it would not be difficult to categorize expenses. The use of overhead and G&A rates has long been considered an important measure of efficiency by private industry. Its extension to the public sector seems natural. Because of differences in classification between municipalities, it would initially appear to be a more useful tool for detecting trends in a given municipality rather than as a comparative indicator.

Data from the City of Ann Arbor, Michigan, was used in the preparation of the Comparative Performance Statistics. Of the municipalities reviewed, Ann Arbor appears to publish the most complete performance statistics. It appears, however, that the City does not attach great importance to their publication. As of July 1973, the Administrative Annual Report for the year ending June 30, 1972, had not yet been finalized.

It appears that essentially all of the information required for the proposed municipal annual report is available, in some form, for some municipalities. This is encouraging, as it demonstrates that it is feasible to collect the necessary data for the report.

FEASIBILITY OF ATTESTATION

This section discusses the feasibility of requiring attestation by an independent auditor of the municipal annual report. This attestation would be limited to the financial statements and performance evaluation statistics contained therein, and would not encompass informational material in other parts of the report. The independent audit function could be performed by an independent firm of certified public accountants or by a state audit agency or similar legally established group.

Audit Standards and Procedures

Over a number of years, the American Institute of Certified Public Accountants has developed a set of audit standards and procedures.[17] These represent the result of many years of collective experience in the audit of financial statements. Consequently, they provide a framework against which to measure the feasibility of attestation of the municipal annual report. Additional guidance in the area of audit standards, closely parallelling those of the AICPA but emphasizing governmental activities, is provided by the Comptroller General.[18] Auditing standards fall into three sections. These are:

1) general standards,
2) field work standards, and
3) reporting standards.

The general standards relate to the scope of the audit and the qualifications of the personnel employed by the audit firm to perform the various phases of the audit.

The field work standards set out those aspects of the audit process which are necessary to provide an audit. These standards concern such phases of the audit as preplanning of the audit, evaluation of the system of internal control by which the information presented is prepared, and evaluation of the evidential matter which provides the support for the information presented in the statements.

The reporting standards deal with the consistency of reporting, the adequacy of disclosure, the form of the auditor's opinion, and reporting on subsequent events.

Our investigation into the feasibility of attestation must address two questions with respect to these audit standards:

1. Can each of these standards be extended to the Municipal Annual Report?

2. Is the extension of these standards sufficient to provide a complete set of audit standards for the entire report?

Discussion of General Standards

The following discussion investigates the applicability of the general standards to the proposed Municipal Annual Report.

Qualifications

"The examination is to be performed by a person or persons having adequate technical training and proficiency as an auditor."[19]

This standard imposes upon the auditor the responsibility for ensuring that the audit is conducted by personnel who collectively have the skills necessary for the type of audit that is to be performed. At the present time, since municipalities are generally subjected to audit and the preparation of pro forma financial statements is not uncommon, this standard raises no problem with respect to the financial statement portion of the proposed municipal annual report.

Performance statistics, as proposed, are not now commonly reported upon; consequently, no training ground for that type of audit is presently available. Also, it is apparent that the auditor will be required to make judgments concerning statements which are outside the field of knowledge represented by financial statements. For example, the auditor must consider the reasonableness of the definitions of functions being reported upon by the municipality. His judgments may encompass such diverse fields as economics, sociology, traffic engineering, and other areas.

This problem may be readily solved by including in the audit team members having expertise in any requisite area. These skills may be possessed by staff members or by consultants to the staff. As a practical matter, most of the large accounting firms today provide their clients with management advisory services, and hence are likely to already have personnel in their employ with the requisite skills. In addition, experienced auditors normally become quite knowledgeable about industries in which they work, so much so that it is quite common for a firm to hire an auditor for a key management position. Consequently, the requirement for adequate training does not appear to offer any obstacle to the audit of the proposed municipal annual report.

Independence

"In all matters relating to the assignment an independence of mental attitude is to be maintained by the auditor."[20]

Audits of most municipalities are presently performed by independent auditors, either by certified public accountants or governmental agencies. Extension of the scope of the audit to include the proposed municipal annual report should have no effect upon the independence of the auditor.

The Comptroller General's statement on Standards discusses the problem of independence. The statement considers impairments to the auditor's independence to fall into three categories:

1. *Personal Impairments.* Circumstances in which an auditor cannot be impartial because of his views or his personal situation. Included are:
   a. Relationships of an official, professional, and/or personal nature that might affect his inquiry in any way.
   b. Preconceived ideas.
   c. Previous involvement in a decision-making capacity in the governmental entity being audited.
   d. Biases or prejudices, including those resulting from political or social convictions.
   e. Actual or potential restrictive influences.
   f. Financial interest, direct or indirect, in an organization benefiting from an audited program.

2. *External Impairments.* Those factors which can restrict the audit or impair the auditor's ability to form independent and objective opinions and conclusions. Examples are:
   a. Interference or other influence that improperly restricts or modifies the the scope of the audit.
   b. Interference with the selection or application of audit procedures.
   c. Denial of access to sources of information.
   d. Interference in the assignment of personnel.
   e. Retaliatory restrictions placed on funds or other resources dedicated to the audit operation.
   f. Activity to overrule or significantly influence the auditor's judgment.
   g. Influences that place the auditor's continued employment in jeopardy.
   h. Unreasonable restrictions on the time allowed to competently complete an audit assignment.

3. *Organization Impairments.* The auditor's independence can be affected by his place in the organizational structure of state or local government. The auditor should also be sufficiently removed from political pressures to insure objectivity.

Due Professional Care

"Due professional care is to be exercised in the performance of the examination and the preparation of the report."[21]

... Due care imposes a responsibility upon each person within an independent auditor's organization to observe the standards of field work and reporting. Exercise of due care requires critical review at every level of supervision of the work done and the judgment exercised by those assisting in the examination. . . .

The matter of due care concerns what the independent auditor does and how well he does it. For example, due care in the matter of working papers requires that their content be sufficient to support the auditor's opinion and his representation as to compliance with auditing standards.

There is nothing in the content of the proposed municipal annual report which would alter the above. The requirement for "Due Professional Care" will apply equally and without change.

Discussion of Field Work Standards

Planning
This field work standard involves adequate planning and supervision of the audit. Although this standard is important, no problem appears to exist in extending it to the proposed municipal annual report.

Internal Control
"There is to be a proper study and evaluation of the existing internal control as a basis for reliance thereon and for the determination of the resultant extent of the tests to which auditing procedures are to be restricted."[22]

The traditional role of the system of internal control is two-fold. First, it is designed to safeguard the assets of a business. Second, it is designed to check the accuracy of accounting data. Beyond these functions, however, Statement 33 extends the concept to the promotion of operational efficiency and the ensuring of adherence to prescribed managerial policies.

With respect to the proposed municipal annual report, the concept of internal control is critical to the auditability of the report. To the extent that portions of the annual report rely on accounting data, the accounting system of internal control is relevant. However, since most municipalities are presently subject to an audit of their financial records, there appears to be no problem with this portion of the report.

Portions of the proposed municipal annual report rely on data derived outside of the accounting records. Examples of this type of data are such items as Tons of Trash Collected, Felonies Involving Attacks, and Miles of Street Resurfaced. This information must be derived from the records of the municipal department performing the function being reported upon. If an adequate system of internal control exists, the auditor can have a relatively high degree of confidence in the accuracy of the data, once being satisfied that the system is functioning properly.

However, if the auditor concludes that the system of internal control is not adequate or is not functioning properly, he must significantly enlarge his tests of the records to ensure the fairness of the data used.

The definition of accounting control comprehends reasonable, but not absolute, assurance that the objectives expressed in it will be accomplished by the system."[23] The auditor may enlarge this concept of reasonable assurance to the evaluation of the fairness of the data used in the performance evaluation statistics. He must observe the systems of internal control established within the municipality's different organizations to determine the reliance he can place upon them.

Evidential Matter

"Sufficient competent evidential matter is to be obtained through inspection, observation, inquiries, and confirmations to afford a reasonable basis for an opinion regarding the financial statements under examination."[24]

For our purposes, this standard may also be applied to the non-financial data used in the computation of the performance evaluation statistics. It will be the responsibility of the auditor to satisfy himself as to the adequacy of the evidential matter which he examines. This may require that he review police blotters, quantities of asphalt and other road surfacing material purchased, water bills sent out by the city, (i.e., to verify quantities of water delivered), and other evidential material. "The amount and kinds of evidential matter required to support an informed opinion are matters for the auditor to determine in the exercise of his professional judgment after a careful study of the circumstances in the particular case."[25]

Although in some instances sufficient or competent evidential matter may not exist, there is nothing in this standard which would, in general, preclude an audit of the proposed municipal annual report. Also, as in financial reporting, the auditor would be expected to prepare and preserve adequate working papers.

Discussion of Reporting Standards

Adherence to Generally Accepted Accounting Principles

"The report shall state whether the financial statements are presented in accordance with generally accepted principles of accounting."[26]

This standard of reporting imposes upon the auditor the obligation of judging agreement with generally accepted principles of accounting. In the case of the proposed municipal annual report, initially there will be no generally accepted principles directly applicable. It appears, however, that this need not present a serious obstacle to auditability for two reasons.

First, in the initial years of implementation of this type of report, the auditor would have great flexibility in determining adherence to generally accepted principles. Since no generally accepted principles exist, he need determine only that the statements presented are logically consistent and based on some reasonable rationale.

Second, as time progresses, just as has happened in accounting, one may assume that a series of principles will become generally accepted. At this time, the auditor should be prepared to examine the statements in the light of these principles and evaluate their adherence thereto.

Consistency of Application

"The Report shall state whether such principles have been consistently observed in the current period in relation to the preceding period."[27]

This statement imposes upon the auditor the obligation to assure consistency of presentation between two consecutive years. Strict adherence to this standard is essential to avoid manipulation of the proposed municipal annual report for political purposes.

While this standard was developed with financial statements in mind, there is nothing in the proposed municipal annual report that would preclude its application or provide the auditor with unusual difficulties. The scope of his examination would be broader, as he would now be reviewing such non-financial items as definitions of the functions reported upon and the performance evaluation statistics. However, the underlying principle would remain unchanged.

Adequacy of Informative Disclosure

"Informative disclosures in the financial statements are to be regarded as reasonably adequate unless otherwise stated in the report."[28]

This standard imposes upon the auditor the obligation of reviewing the statements for the adequacy of disclosures involving material matters. This standard applies equally as well to an audit of the proposed municipal annual report.

In the course of audit, it may be that the auditor may conclude that the performance evaluation statistics presented are not relevant to the function reported upon. Assume, for example, that an auditor determines that, for a specific function, the activities reported upon account for only ten percent of the expenditures for that function, and that no statistics are presented with respect to the remaining 90 percent. Although the statistics presented may be completely accurate, he could reasonably conclude that additional or alternate statistics are required to satisfy disclosure requirements.

Should a municipality refuse disclosure of a matter the auditor considers to be material, the matter should be included in his report and he should appropriately qualify his opinion.

Reporting

"The report shall either contain an expression of opinion regarding the financial statements, taken as a whole, or an assertion to the effect that an opinion cannot be expressed. When an overall opinion cannot be expressed, the reasons therefore should be stated. In all cases where an auditor's name is associated with financial statements the report should contain a clear-cut indication of the character of the auditor's examination, if any, and the degree of responsibility he is taking."[2][9]

Basically, this statement would apply equally well to an auditor undertaking the examination of the proposed municipal annual report. The auditor must be prepared to express his opinion on the statements and performance evaluation statistics taken as a whole.

Subsequent Events

The independent auditor's obligation to report on subsequent events relates to the auditor's previously discussed obligation with respect to the adequacy of disclosure. The independent auditor is required to consider the subsequent event and require action necessary to proper interpretation of the statements being presented. This requirement should apply to our proposed municipal annual report. The auditor should require disclosure of material items occurring subsequent to the period of the report.

Summary and Conclusions

Over a number of years, the public accounting profession has developed a number of standards for the audit of financial statements. These standards, when used in conjunction with generally accepted accounting principles, provide the auditor with guidance and a basis for evaluation of financial statements. Basically, they represent the collective wisdom of the accounting profession.

If we examine the proposed municipal annual report, we see that it consists of three types of information:

1) pro forma financial statements,
2) definitions of municipal function, and
3) performance statistics.

With the exception of the definitions, the material is all quantitative in nature. Insofar as the pro forma financial statements are concerned, the auditor is operating in a relatively familiar area. The bulk of the information is taken directly from the books and accounts of the municipality, and hence introduces no complexities beyond those inherent in any normal audit. The pro forma adjustments do add a complexity not normally found in an audit. However, pro forma statements of a different nature may often be found in Corporate Registration Statements (S-1 Form) and other published financial data. Hence, while the nature of the adjustments may be somewhat different, the auditor is familiar and experienced with the approach. There appears to be no problem, then, with respect to attestation of the pro forma financial statements.

When the auditor examines the definitions of municipal functions, he is operating with non-quantitative information. However, the scope of the audit does not require that he determine that the functions defined are the most logical set of functions that could be defined. Rather, he is auditing only their reasonableness, in a broad sense, the consistency of definition from period to period, and the completeness of the definitions. Consequently, this area does not appear to present a problem with respect to attestation.

The performance statistics present the auditor with two problems: first, he must satisfy himself that the information contained in the various statements is accurate; second, that they are reasonably relevant to the function being reported upon.

The first problem (accuracy) is a familiar one to the auditor. In this instance, he must investigate the source documents from which the statistics are derived. This may be from various departmental reports, conversations with employees and managers, the mailing of confirmations, etc. While the subject matter under investigation may be unfamiliar ground to the auditor, it is quantified data, and the techniques for verifying the accuracy of quantifiable data are well known to the auditor.

The second problem presents more difficulties if the auditor is to determine that the performance statistics are relevant to the fucntion being measured. However, this problem may be handled simply in the auditor's report with a statement as to the scope of the audit. The auditor is expressing an opinion as to the accuracy of the statistics, not as to whether the proper statistics are being presented. This should be made clear in the content of his report. In some instances, the auditor may conclude that the statistics are so unrelated or irrelevant to the function being reported upon that they are misleading. In this instance, his report should contain an appropriate disclaimer. However, this situation should be rare.

It appears, therefore, that an auditor, using conventional auditing standards that have been modified in some minor ways, could conduct an audit of the proposed municipal annual report and express his opinion thereon. It would appear that the requirement for independent audit would reduce the opportunity for political manipulation of the report and lend greater credence to the information contained therein. Thus, a requirement for audit should be established.

NOTES–CASE 8

1. A.Y. Lewin and R.W. Blanning, "Urban Government Annual Report," in D. Rogers and W.D. Hawley (Eds.), *Improving the Quality of Urban Management,* Beverly Hills, California, Sage, 1974.

2. Herman Hellinger, *Financial Public Relations for the Business Corporation,* New York, Harper, 1954, p. 183.

3. *Ibid.*

4. See discussion in Alfred Rappaport and Lawrence Revsine (Eds.), *Corporate Financial Reporting,* Chicago, Commerce Clearing House, 1972, p. 219.

5. See Rhodes Henderer, *A Comparative Study of the Public Relations Practices in Six Industrial Corporations,* Pittsburgh, University of Pittsburgh Press, 1956, p. 5.

6. J.A. Livingston, *The American Stockholder,* New York, Lippincott, 1958, p. 194.

7. Milton Wright, *Public Relations for Business,* New York, McGraw-Hill, 1939, p. 265.

8. Lewin and Blanning, "Urban Government Annual Report" (see Note 1).

9. *Ibid.*, p. 66.

10. American Institute of Certified Public Accountants (AICPA), Accounting Principles Board Statement No. 4, *Basic Concepts and Accounting Principles Underlying Financial Statements of Business Enterprises,* Chapter 4, 1970, p. 107.

11. AICPA, *APB Accounting Principles,* Chicago, Commerce Clearing House, 1971, pp. 221-232.

12. AICPA, *APB Accounting Principles: Current Text,* Chicago, Commerce Clearing House, 1971, pp. 357-363.

13. Charles E. Merriam, "Preface," in Herman C. Boyle, *Governmental Reporting in Chicago,* Chicago, University of Chicago Press, 1928, p. ix.

14. See Irving Tenner, *Municipal and Government Accounting,* Englewood Cliffs, New Jersey, Prentice-Hall, 1955, p. 305.

15. See Eric L. Kohler and Howard W. Wright, *Accounting in the Federal Government,* Englewood Cliffs, New Jersey, Prentice-Hall, 1956, p. 68.

16. See Irving Tenner and Edward S. Lynn, *Municipal and Governmental Accounting,* Englewood Cliffs, New Jersey, Prentice-Hall, 1960, p. 391.

17. AICPA, *Auditing Standards and Procedure,* New York, 1963.

18. Comptroller General of the United States, *Standards for Audit of Governmental Organizations, Programs, Activities & Functions,* Washington, D.C., GPO, 1972.

19. AICPA, *Statement No. 33,* (see Note 17) p. 18.

20. *Ibid.,* p. 15.

21. *Ibid.,* p. 18.

22. AICPA, *Statement on Auditing Standards,* New York, 1973, p. 13.

23. *Ibid.,* p. 21.

24. *Ibid.,* p. 55.

25. *Ibid.,* p. 57.

26. *Ibid.,* p. 71.

27. *Ibid.,* p. 72.

28. *Ibid.,* p. 78.

29. *Ibid.,* p. 80.

Case 9
The Politics of Manpower Delivery Systems*

DAVID ROGERS†

The 1960s witnessed a vast proliferation of manpower training programs. Though the funds were limited relative to need, they probably could have been used much more effectively than they were. One big obstacle to that taking place was the *style of policy making* by which they were developed. New manpower programs in the '60s constituted a series of discrete pieces of legislation, developed in an incremental, *ad hoc* way, with too little attention paid to problems of *implementation*. A prevailing point of view in Washington which made sense at the time, especially in view of the tremendous ghetto unrest, was to get the programs developed fast, get the money out to the cities, and somehow muddle through the rest. This resulted in little planning, no coherence on fundamental policies, and inadequate central control and guidance. And we now know that the many problems of implementation that this style created do not take care of themselves.[1]

Recognizing this problem, manpower policy makers have shifted their attention in recent years from better *programs* alone to better *delivery*

*Presented under the title Organizing Manpower Delivery Systems in Big Cities" at the Seminar Series on Manpower Planning sponsored by the Manpower Research Program of the New York State School of Industrial and Labor Relations, Cornell University, Spring 1972. The papers from this series originally appeared in Robert Aronson (Ed.), *The Localization of Federal Manpower Planning,* New York State School of Industrial and Labor Relations, Cornell University, 1973. This paper is a partial summary of a larger report on the author's three-year study of the politics and management of inner-city manpower programs. For the full report, see David Rogers, "Inter-Organizational Relations and Inner City Manpower Programs," Report submitted to the Director, Office of Research and Development, Manpower Administration, U.S. Department of Labor, October 1971. Reprinted by permission.

†New York University

systems as well. Three strategies have been widely discussed: (1) *decentralization* to the states and localities on the theory that federal agencies were increasingly unable to manage this growing and fragmented set of programs; (2) *decategorization* and *block grants* to improve flexibility and encourage local planning, initiative, and accountability; and (3) greater *local coordination* and *agency linkages* to minimize the inefficiency and political conflict that so often result from the fragmented, duplicative, and competing programs the federal government has funded.

All these changes are being recommended, however, without any systematic knowledge of state and city agencies, particularly of their capabilities and commitments. Many states and cities are not ready to receive block grants and become prime sponsors for manpower programs.[2] Furthermore, even for those that are, little thought has been given to what the respective roles of federal, state, city, and neighborhood agencies might be, to what kinds of prior planning and technical assistance might be set up, and to how a whole transition strategy might be developed. Hopefully, the mistake of applying a single "made in Washington" model will not be made.

One way to avoid that mistake and develop the "locality-relevant" strategy that is required is to study intensively the politics and interorganizational relations of manpower agencies at the site of delivery, especially in the big cities where most of the programs are located. This should aid policy makers in developing a more effective decentralization strategy by indicating what some of the problems of implementation will be and how they may be overcome.

This paper reports some findings from a three-year field study on interorganizational relations of manpower agencies in Cleveland, Philadelphia, and New York City—a study done with that policy issue in mind. All were selected as "strategic research sites" because of their particular characteristics.[3] *New York City* is significant because its size, scale, diversity, and consequent political fragmentation make the task of developing a local manpower delivery system especially difficult. It is perhaps the most extreme case of fragmentation among big cities, and the constraints that this places on coordination efforts are more dramatic and visible there than elsewhere, allowing one to study them in greater depth. *Philadelphia* was selected because of the close linkages in the past of its business elite with ghetto manpower agencies and City Hall. Also considered was the fact that its last two mayors (Tate and Rizzo) had a more traditional style (machine politics) than New York's, and one that political scientists suggest may lead to less fragmentation as City Hall controls patronage and the brokerage of power among various interest groups and organizations. Finally, *Cleveland* was selected because it was the first big city to have elected a black mayor, who became for a while a key integrative force there. He had been successful in increasing the participation of business in civic development (including manpower) activities.

The main questions of the study included: (1) How was the city doing in developing a coordinated manpower delivery system, if it was doing anything at all, and how might it move faster in that direction? (2) What were particularly productive and unproductive relations between agencies from which one could derive some lessons for future strategy? (3) How did actions by state and federal agencies affect local coordination? (4) How did organizational and partisan politics affect coordination? I assumed that just by looking at the manpower coordination process in big cities in terms of these basic questions one could learn a lot that would be helpful in the future as guides in setting up effective local manpower delivery systems.

It soon became clear that all cities, regardless of differences, have a number of common problems, including agency fragmentation, duplication, baronialism, conflict, and how to achieve greater collaboration. Viewed more generically, they all face both *political* and *organizational design* problems. The political ones relate to who will control the programs and how one resolves conflicts between various parties—the city and state, the city and counties, new and old-line agencies, commissioners and directors who actually administer programs—and among various client groups with competing claims for services. The organizational design issues, in turn, include who should do what, how centralized or decentralized should various components of the manpower system be (policy, planning, operations), and what administrative, research, and programmatic services should be provided.

At the same time, there have to be local variations in the strategies to take into account local politics, labor markets, and agency commitments and capabilities.[4] This does not mean that the federal government needs a completely different strategy for every city. That would be most inefficient and unproductive. It is more likely that there is a limited range of *types* of inner cities, each of which merits a somewhat different federal strategy. Three such broad types are suggested here from my research in Cleveland, Philadelphia, and New York City.

COORDINATION IN THREE INNER CITIES

Cleveland

Of all the big cities in the nation, Cleveland is probably one of the farthest along in putting together a local manpower delivery system; and it bears looking at as a generic case, if only for that reason.[5] It is not that Cleveland has been so much more successful than other cities in developing jobs, which depends at least as much on national economic policies as on local actions. Nor is it that Cleveland is without serious political conflicts, as Mayor Stokes found out after two trying terms. Despite the usual problems, however, Cleveland has established many productive linkages among manpower agencies. It has learned some of the basic lessons that every big city will have to learn about agency coordination, and it is important to know how and why that came about.

There is a coordinated manpower delivery system in Cleveland called the Metropolitan Cleveland Jobs Council. It is one kind of *model* for cities, the *non-profit, private corporation model,* with private employers in key leadership position. The Council came out of several streams of coordination activity, including those of City Hall, employers, the state, and the Board of Education—four of the most powerful participants in manpower programs in every city.

This is how the Council came into being. When Mayor Stokes was elected in 1967, manpower programs in Cleveland were like they were everywhere else—duplicating, fragmented, and with much mutual distrust among agencies. Stokes imported, with some modifications, the *superagency model* from New York City. A Department of Human Resources and Economic Development was established that pulled together under a single administrative umbrella many federally funded programs. It developed an information system, in-service training for manpower administrators, and it got the agencies to specialize and link their resources more than before.

A second significant coordination effort was among private employers. Cleveland had a cohesive business leadership which had done much coordinating work on manpower through a series of employer councils. They developed many common understandings about the difficult problems of job development and hiring and upgrading minority group employees. They were much more successful at the design stage than at implementation and to some degree replicated the old National Alliance of Business pattern of generating many pledges for jobs and then not delivering. But they did at least build up some valuable experience at coordination, at analyzing the gaps in the city's manpower programs, and at trying to fill them.

There were two other significant participants, both of them traditional, mainstream agencies. One was the Ohio Bureau of Employment Security (OBES), which had extraordinary linkages with Cleveland manpower agencies. Much has been written about the extreme conflicts between these state agencies and city ones, especially local community action agencies. Cleveland developed an almost spectacularly collaborative relationship between the Employment Service and the city that constitutes one of the few examples of such successful collaboration in the country.

There was the same sharp city-state conflict between the Ohio governor (Rhodes, a Republican) and the Cleveland mayor (Stokes, a Democrat) that often exists, but the manpower agencies worked out a positive relationship. The Cleveland area manager of OBES had been working for many years on plans for a comprehensive manpower agency for the city, as part of a bigger state structure, and he shared those plans with City Hall and private employers when they were putting together the Jobs Council. There were two main reasons for this close linkage. One was the progressive, city-orientation of the area manager. The other was his strong political base locally, especially among Republican business leaders. He could use that base as leverage in deflecting the state's demands for control over the city structure. The critical group in Cleveland, then, was the Republican business leaders, especially a younger progressive group. Fearing racial unrest in Cleveland, as well as continued loss of control over the local economy (because many city-based firms were becoming absorbed in larger conglomerates elsewhere), they worked hard for a strong city manpower agency. Indeed, they supported the efforts of a Democratic mayor against those of a Republican governor for state control over manpower, indicating how far they were willing to go to establish a city structure, even against their partisan interests.

The fourth party was the Board of Education, and its participation was also critical. It was deeply involved in vocational education and manpower training programs with employers and the Employment Service. It supplied a huge facility—a converted old high school near downtown Cleveland—for much of the Jobs Council's training and job development. Equipped with much industrial machinery donated by employers, this site was the headquarters office of the Jobs Council. It was also the place where most manpower agencies had out-stationed their job developers to pool resources.

In brief, the four main institutional participants in manpower were working together at a common site and on common problems to develop a city manpower system. Relative to what other cities had done, this was an extraordinary achievement.

Limitations of space preclude an extended discussion of this coalition's performance. It has developed numerous skills training programs. It has designed a metropolitan area-wide manpower delivery system, hoping to become the prime sponsor. It has established groups of key manpower officials in town, each working on a particularly critical program component of the system—e.g., job development, skills training, outreach, supportive services, and so on. And it has provided more technical assistance to companies with manpower training contracts than they had before, and moved ahead on a much more aggressive job development effort.

Though this manpower delivery system has shown promise, there is not complete consensus in Cleveland that it should be the prime sponsor for city manpower programs. Indeed, there remains continued conflict between City Hall and the Jobs Council (on which the mayor is represented) as to which of them should take charge. The conflict was unresolved as of early 1972 and is likely to remain that way for some time.

My view is to lean toward this non-profit private corporation model, though it should be required to perform even better by producing more jobs, before being actually designated the prime sponsor. The political structure of Cleveland seems to preclude making City Hall the prime sponsor. Cleveland has a weak mayoral system, with the mayor having only a two-year term; it has a strong, ward-based city council, representing local neighborhood ethnic interests, that makes constant demands on the mayor for patronage and prevents city-wide planning; there are continuing conflicts within both political parties, between city and county organizations making metropolitan area-wide collaboration difficult; and there has been little sign since early in Mayor Stokes' first term that Cleveland mayors have given manpower that high a priority.

This recommendation runs counter to the view of most manpower policy makers in Washington who argue, for political accountability reasons, that the mayors should be designated as prime sponsors.[6] But some big cities, and Cleveland is a prototypic case, should not adopt that model. Its mayor has no political base and no leverage. Furthermore, since the labor market there is a metropolitan one, it requires the active participation of suburban mayors and county commissioners. Given the tremendous city-county conflicts in Cleveland, it would be unproductive to design a manpower system with the Cleveland mayor in charge. He would have great difficulty in getting the suburbs and counties in.

The big problem with the model I have suggested is, of course, its limited political accountability, and there is no easy solution to that. The Department of Labor and other involved agencies would have to monitor the Council's performance very closely. Despite that difficulty, however, Cleveland constitutes a receptive political setting for interagency linkages. It has more of a *problem-solving* than a *political power-oriented climate.*

Philadelphia

In sharp contrast to Cleveland, Philadelphia is a prototype of what practitioners often refer to as a "manpower jungle." There is marked political conflict among agencies and interest groups, with a highly personalized politics of distrust pervading the city.

This can best be explained in terms of the city's politics and power structure. There are *three loosely joined coalitions* or *centers of power* in Philadelphia—the Democratic Party machine, the old reform coalition, and the blacks—each with its own peak associations and constituencies. City Hall patronage extends to poor and lower middle-class white ethnic groups, blacks, many craft and civil service unions, real estate developers, and contractors.

The second group includes moderates and reformers of both parties, the business and civic elite, middle and upper middle-class white liberals, the ADA, some unions, and various good government groups. This is the old reform coalition from the late '40s, '50s, and very early '60s—Philadelphia's great period of renewal and development.

These coalitions reflect fundamental religious, ethnic, and class cleavages in Philadelphia that are similar to those in other municipalities. They pit non-college educated, lower middle-class white ethnic groups, especially Irish and Italian Catholics, against upper middle and upper class, college-educated Protestants and Jews. The former endorse old-style machine politics, while the latter are, if not supporters of radical, new style politics (participatory democracy, community control), at least reformers.

Such a power structure perspective is important because Philadelphia's manpower agencies constitute clusters of programs that reflect these political forces. Take the City Hall-based coalition, for example. Philadelphia has many manpower programs and coordinating councils that are run and controlled by the mayor, including its Concentrated Employment Program, its city manpower commission, the city CAMPS (Cooperative Area Manpower System), and many others. These programs are part of the mayor's machine and constitute a straight patronage operation. This has profound delivery system implications. One might assume that they are positive. The conventional wisdom of political scientists about the big city machine, in contrast to that of middle-class reformers, is that it is often the cement that holds things together.[7] Thus, Chicago's Mayor Daley is often depicted as coalescing all the main interest groups and institutions and arranging the trade-offs to make the town run—for some, relatively efficiently.[8]

It doesn't work that way at all in Philadelphia, if in fact it does in Chicago. The non-planning, particularistic, and patronage style of Philadelphia's last two mayors has been very divisive and fragmenting. City Hall was so baronial and protective of the machine that it activated and reinforced considerable distrust from other manpower agencies. Its political style was that of having city manpower programs run as one-man operations by loyal political lieutenants who put party and patronage needs first and other needs only later. Sharp lines were drawn between agencies loyal to the mayor and those considered "outsiders." Most were placed in the latter group and their officials given little opportunity to participate in policy and program decisions. The resulting polarization between City Hall and all other agencies became so pronounced that many of the multiagency manpower programs faced continued revolts and dissatisfaction by the other member organizations. Even when there weren't such revolts, each agency was forced to spend its limited resources in offensive and defensive reactions to City Hall efforts at exclusive control. A *political power-seeking* rather than *problem-solving* style (such as Cleveland's) thus pervaded the city's manpower politics. The playing out of that style involved each agency pressing its baronial interests to the hilt, substituting competition and institutional isolation for collaboration and bringing into play a highly personalized politics of distrust.

This was reinforced by the second coalition, including as one of its most prominent groups the city's business leaders. They contributed to this political conflict by their own strong partisanship and by a status consciousness that was reflected in invidious comparisons they made between Mayor Tate with his populist lifestyle (an Irish machine politician) and his two upper-class WASP predecessors, Joseph Clark and Richardson Dilworth. The business leaders decided, partly for these political reasons, to do their own thing in manpower. They publicly criticized the city's programs, rarely came to key meetings (and sent lower level executives when they did), made end runs to Harrisburg (when Republican governors Scranton and Shaffer were there) and to Washington (after President Nixon was elected) for funding to set up their own highly separate programs. They ran these programs through various peak associations—e.g., the Chamber of Commerce, the Urban Coalition, as well as particular federally funded agencies like the local NAB (National Alliance of Business) and Philco-Ford.

By and large, Philadelphia's business leaders were a progressive group, having already participated actively in urban reform programs under liberal Democratic mayors.[9] They developed many close relations with neighborhood-based black manpower agencies. One of many reasons for those close relations was to broaden their coalition to unseat the mayor and his machine. Unfortunately, it led to much duplication, fragmentation, and political in-fighting, hampering the delivery of manpower services in the city. On many programs, for example, the city had to subcontract to an employer program for a particular component, or vice versa. The delivery in these cases was invariably poor, precisely because of the political climate and the mutual distrust that existed.

The third center of power in Philadelphia manpower was black community agencies, and mainly OIC (Opportunities Industrialization Center). It is by far the largest black self-help organization in the nation, now located in over 60 cities. Philadelphia is the home of OIC, and that agency has tremendous power there. Indeed, it has become the new manpower center in Philadelphia, typifying what happens to local neighborhood agencies when they get big and institutionalized. They begin to look like the old Establishment agencies they berate—with large administrative overhead, little accountability, and limited outreach to the hard-core poor. One doesn't coordinate OIC with anybody in Philadelphia; and yet it got into all kinds of manpower activity for which it was not equipped and refused to enter into larger multiagency structures unless it ran them.

The result, then of this politics was considerable manpower agency fragmentation and little positive effort to establish a broad-based delivery system. The situation was not completely negative, however. Philadelphia has many excellent public and private manpower agencies whose top officials are able to move among the warring coalitions. One is the State Employment Service, which, like its counterpart in Cleveland, has done well in linking up with other manpower agencies, including City Hall and black community groups. Another is the Board of Education, which has an excellent skills training center. In addition, Philadelphia has several small social agencies with good programs and ties to various political coalitions.[10] Each was nonpartisan and was able to maintain working relationships with the big manpower agencies because it had a specialized skill that no other agency did and it did not therefore constitute any threat. This set of agencies, along with business, constitutes the leadership group from which future efforts at developing a manpower delivery system in Philadelphia might begin.

That may be a long way off, however. If one looks at how far coordination has really gone there, with the exception of the agencies just mentioned, it hasn't really begun. Nobody locally is taking the leadership, as was at least tried in Cleveland. Most manpower officials are busy being political, acting and reacting in the negative climate created by the conflict between City Hall and the reformers to such an extent that they do not have resources or trust available for collaboration.

Yet, one has to develop a strategy for dealing with that situation, especially since it is prevalent in so many big cities. The best that can be done at this time may be to develop a *live and let live model* that lets each coalition of agencies do what it can do best. This might mean that City Hall be given the major role on public employment, since patronage is their way of life and they can negotiate productive agreements with civil service unions to let minority groups in. Employers and other manpower agencies might then work on private sector programs, and OIC might be maintained at its present size, while perhaps encouraged to concentrate more on what it does best—prevocational, work orientation, and basic education programs.

There are at least some positive elements in the Philadelphia situation. Large employers are civically minded and close to black agencies, reflecting a reform tradition that many big cities, including New York, have not had from within their big business community. The Employment Service and state agencies have been quite progressive in Philadelphia, working collaboratively with City Hall and neighborhood black groups. And there are some excellent small agencies with expertise and capability for forming a nucleus, along with one or two of the superpowers, of an effective manpower system.

New York City

The tremendous size, scale, diversity, and turbulence of my third case, New York City, almost defy any attempt at a brief analysis of its manpower politics as was done for the other cities. Rather than go through the maze of manpower agencies and coalitions piece by piece (and it is even difficult to get a consensus on the makeup of the coalitions and the history of what happened), I have drawn from New York's experience the model or strategy that was followed there and evaluated it. I will refer to it as the *superagency, subcontracting, broker model.*

New York was the first inner city in the nation to establish its own city-funded and managed manpower agency, the Manpower Career and Development Agency (MCDA), under the administration of the first anti-poverty superagency, the Human Resources Agency (HRA). It was also the first to set up the beginnings of a comprehensive manpower system with a network of regional training and outreach centers throughout the city.

HRA and MCDA constitute one test of Mayor Lindsay's strategy to reform New York City government by setting up a series of superagencies. The bureaucracies had gotten way out of control of the mayor as well as the citizenry in New York City in recent decades; and Lindsay's advisors suggested to him through a series of task force reports in 1965 and 1966 that it was impossible to get significant reforms or even simple improvements in efficiency unless he got more control over the bureaucracies.[11]

MCDA began in 1966 with one of these task forces which produced the Sviridoff Report, named after Mitchell Sviridoff, its chairman and the first HRA administrator. The report suggested that in manpower perhaps more than in any other area of social services, there were unrelated pieces of programs, serious gaps, and little orderly progression and follow through. It diagnosed the problem, then, as lack of coordination and gaps in services and created a city manpower agency to begin correcting that.[12] When MCDA was first established, for example, city officials estimated that there were more than 65 different manpower programs operating in the Bedford-Stuyvesant ghetto in Brooklyn, all separately funded and administered, with no way of coordinating their resources or consolidating information on how they were doing.

The actual design of MCDA was an elaborate *subcontracting arrangement,* with MCDA playing the role of activating and linking all available manpower resources in the city into a single, multiagency system. A central headquarters was created for planning, program and job development, monitoring, and other management functions, but the delivery of services was decentralized to 11 Regional Manpower Centers in poverty areas and a network of outreach centers.[13]

Agencies opposed to this system have often asserted that MCDA created a needlessly duplicative agency, that it was into operations, and for this reason could not also play an effective role as manager and broker.[14] In fact, very little of MCDA's system was duplicative, and it tried hard to keep out of operations, subcontracting instead to outside agencies. Before MCDA, for example, there was no outreach of significance, no coherent manpower system in the city, and absolutely no way to get coherent planning or consolidated information on what was happening.

MCDA tried to subcontract the main program components of a city manpower system—outreach, basic education, English as a Second Language, high school equivalency, skills training, supportive services, and job development. There were many agencies involved, including the City University of New York (CUNY) for basic education and skills training, the Board of Education for skills training, the New York State Division of Employment (Employment Service) for counseling, testing, and placement, the N.Y. State Department of Vocational Rehabilitation, OIC, and many others.

There were other parts to this unique manpower delivery system besides conventional manpower programs. One was a *minority economic development strategy* that got played out through MCDA's use of minority contractors, management consulting firms, and maintenance and security staff to improve the workings of the system. It also placed special deposits of MCDA funds in minority banks, and it had an active program to train minority people as staff and administrators in the agency.

Another significant feature of the system was MCDA's explicit attempt to develop a *management system* to enable it to effectively run this complex agency. MCDA was one of the first agencies in New York City to begin to establish its own management information system. This system was computerized, including intake and other data to trace the flow of clients through the agency and to assess the performance of staff; and it generated weekly output and budget control reports that could be used in program planning.

Anybody who knows much about the complexities of setting up a management information system, especially in highly volatile and politicized agencies like manpower, understands the problems involved. MCDA had many of them. Getting the computer to work, training staff to use it and feed in information, and minimizing their fears as to how the information would be used all hampered the operation. But this agency at least began to set up such an information system. As is well known, good information is a major requirement for effectiveness in any big institution, and certainly in the public sector.

The New York City experience has strategic significance for the many cities and states that will undoubtedly adopt such a subcontracting model. At the least, they will be setting up multiagency delivery systems that will face many of the problems MCDA did. In assessing the implications of the MCDA experience for future manpower delivery system efforts, it is useful to look at the positive and negative lessons.

There were several things MCDA did well. One of its early achievements was to establish close linkage to poverty area communities through a *strong outreach agency*. When MCDA was first established in 1966, many of the local community action agencies in New York had their own separate manpower training programs. They all wanted a "piece of the action" and to hold on to what they had. Yet, the Sviridoff Report correctly indicated that fragmentation contributed to much inefficiency in the delivery of manpower services and it recommended that a single agency, MCDA, should coordinate and be in control of all manpower training. The aspirations of community action agency officials for community control were so great that it takes little imagination to grasp the fundamental conflict that this recommendation raised. It is to the credit of MCDA and its top officials that through prolonged negotiation they got the community agencies out of training and gave them a critical role as the outreach agency (recruiting clients, doing preliminary testing, orientation and assessment, and referral to jobs or training) for which they were much better suited. The fact that top MCDA administrators were former community action agency officials themselves undoubtedly helped in this effort.

Another success of MCDA was its *regionalization* (decentralization) of manpower training in the city. The problems of delivering manpower services in New York are very complex, given the numerous local ethnic and racial groups and different local economies in the city. It was an important achievement that a regional system was established that took account of such local community and economy variations. Furthermore, the regional manpower training centers that were set up on a decentralized basis provided a wide variety of comprehensive manpower services. This decentralized, multi-service center model is one that is likely to be adopted in many cities in the future; they will have much to learn from the New York City experience. Of particular importance were the close links that MCDA had with the poverty area communities, on the supply side of the labor market. At a time when neighborhood government is seen as an important direction for big city delivery systems, MCDA's regional manpower system was an important early example.

MCDA also provided *other important linkages*. It was perhaps the first city agency in the nation to build a large university (the City University of New York—CUNY) into its manpower delivery system. Though the relationship did not endure, the concept of working with CUNY and its elaborate community college system, its many paraprofessional programs, and the prospects of state matching funds was a good one. MCDA brought the N.Y. State Department of Vocational Rehabilitation into the system, because one of MCDA's target populations is the unemployed and underemployed handicapped. The two agencies worked well together in many manpower centers with a minimum of friction.

On the negative side, there were several major problems with the system that suggest lessons for the future, both for New York City and for other cities, counties, and states that will soon be developing manpower delivery systems. First, if one establishes such a multiagency delivery system, it is necessary to develop *performance contracts* with the many participating agencies and to enforce them. This was not done for the first few years in New York, and it produced enormous problems. Managers of MCDA's regional training centers referred to their agency as a multiheaded monster. MCDA was legitimately held accountable for the performance of these many subcontractors, but it had no authority and control over them. It is no simple matter, of course, to establish such controls, since the agencies all fear they will lose their autonomy. Indeed, one could argue that if MCDA had originally established such administrative controls through performance contracts, many agencies that became part of its manpower delivery system would have stayed out. Such a system has to be pulled together now, however, with strong central controls and accountability, or it will never function effectively.

Not only are performance contracts essential, but *adequate information* is also needed for MCDA to be informed about how its subcontractors are doing. This would enable it to move in early when programs are not going well, diagnose problems quickly, and help the subcontractors begin to correct things. Yet MCDA's system was slow in developing. The main reason for this was that MCDA did not thoroughly establish a situation of understanding among its own staff and the subcontractor agencies as to what the system was to do. They were resistant initially to providing the information the system required and they remained so. The lesson to be learned from this experience is that massive resources have to be allocated for orienting and training personnel when such an information system is first established, so that the staff will understand its uses and be supportive of it, rather than be threatened and resist its implementation. A corollary to this is that the agency responsible for the delivery system, in this case MCDA, should use the information system in a nonpunitive, supportive way itself.

Another lesson from the New York experience has to do with the *strategy MCDA followed in first designing the manpower system.* Initially, it designed the system in isolation, with no participation from other agencies, especially those that had been in manpower for many years, like the New York State Division of Employment (Employment Service) and the Board of Education. After the whole system was designed, MCDA announced it in the press, indicating that it would have an advisory board that included all the key agencies, but with MCDA making the final decisions. None of the old-line agencies had been consulted or informed beforehand about the design or the board, and they responded with strong opposition.

Actually, MCDA was in a "no win" situation, regardless of what strategy it adopted. Had it consulted the mainstream agencies at the design stage, their vested interests would have been activated, and they would probably have never developed any design at all. On the other hand, the strategy it followed of not consulting them also led to great resistance.

Given where it is now, MCDA would do well to reach out to a wider network of agencies to establish a broader political base. Large employers, unions with an interest in public employment and upgrading programs, and traditional manpower and education agencies like the Employment Service and the Board of Education are the most significant.

One of the great administrative weaknesses of MCDA, over and beyond any linkages it failed to establish, was *its central bureaucracy.* MCDA had all the negative and few of the positive features of centralization. The paper did not flow; critical inquiries from operations staff in the field were not answered; and planning went on in an ivory-tower atmosphere, far removed from conditions and problems in the outreach and manpower training centers. Thus, there was a central job development unit that did not link well with employers and did not provide adequate information about changing employment patterns to the training centers; and there was a central program planning unit that invited very little input from operations staff, did not provide the research required to develop training programs relevant to the New York City economy, and did not relate productively to operational problems. MCDA's central management staff was thus quite isolated from its own operations, from the New York City economy, and from outside manpower expertise. Based on this experience, a recommendation for MCDA and like agencies elsewhere is to place many headquarters staff in actual outreach and training centers, retaining only a small core of central staff for technical assistance to operations.

A further weakness of MCDA, reflecting a common one among manpower agencies nationally, was that it paid *much more attention to the supply than the demand side.* It developed many training programs without adequate linkages with employers or input from them on what would be the most relevant curriculum. Any future training, both in the public and private sectors, will have to be tied in much more closely to the demand side. Otherwise, placement rates are liable to be low, and manpower training may be reduced to a revolving-door experience, where clients go from one program to another without getting jobs.

A final weakness of this structure relates to the *heavy MCDA emphasis on institutional skills training.* MCDA sunk the $30-40 million of the city funds it received every year into costly building renovations and heavy machinery for its regional training centers. Much legitimate concern has been expressed in New York, even within the city administration itself, that this investment has limited the agency's flexibility and efficiency by tying up valuable funds in some unproductive skills training programs that may be only marginally related to the city's economy. Any effective manpower agency has to have the flexibility to move quickly in and out of particular occupational skills training programs, as the economy changes and as information becomes available on those changes. One future direction for MCDA, then, might be to phase out some of its skills training and subcontract that out to private trade schools, to give precisely the flexibility lacking before. The city training centers might then be used for supportive services and other prevocational programs. Numerous safeguards, of course, have to be taken. Many private trade schools have not dealt with the hard core poor in the past. Many have few supportive services; and they would have to be closely monitored by MCDA, the public agency, which would continue to be held accountable for the entire program. A particularly important linkage that was effectively established in the other two cities but not in New York is between the New York State Employment Service and the city. The chronic baronialism of that agency, however, in conjunction with abrasive relations between Albany and New York City, exacerbated, in turn, by the personal hostilities between Governor Rockefeller and Mayor Lindsay, limit the prospects for such collaboration. Skilled mediation efforts by powerful public officials who have close ties to both sides (for example, Senator Javits) may help.[15]

SOME NORMATIVE GUIDELINES FOR DEVELOPING LOCAL MANPOWER DELIVERY SYSTEMS

There are many general lessons in political strategy and organizational design that the experiences of these cities suggest. To place this discussion in a broader perspective, effective local manpower planning involves three major questions—*who* is it for, *what* is its substance, and *how* will it be done?[16] To be more specific: The "who" question refers to selecting the target populations one wants to serve and establishing priorities based on that. There is then the "what" or the program question of the appropriate packaging, mix, and sequence of services one wants to provide to these populations. Finally, there is the "how" or the delivery system question. It is important to deal with all three in any rational planning effort. For too long, as indicated initially, we have dealt with the first two, but without any consideration of the third. There is the danger as well, however, of becoming so involved with it that one does not pay enough attention to the first two. The trick is to effectively orchestrate all three considerations—no easy task. The following are some preliminary lessons from our experience that suggest what should be done:

1. In setting up a delivery system, it is better to *take the existing manpower agencies and try to work from there* than to develop an entirely new, superordinate structure. Cleveland did this through employer councils, the National Alliance of Business, the city administration's human resources agency, and the Employment Service, and was somewhat successful because of that. New York City established a new manpower system that included most established agencies, but was a separate administrative body under the city's control, and it faced strong and continued resistance as a result. Despite the fact that the delivery system was not that duplicative, many critics from among the traditional agencies always labeled it as such, especially those that felt bypassed in the initial planning and design. MCDA was also tarnished with the image of community action by ·being part of the city's anti-poverty social services agency, having many minority managers, and being tied in so closely to poverty area communities. One must have a broader political base than that to survive and to gain the legitimacy necessary for bringing in established agencies.

2. *No single agency should develop the design alone,* without input from many others. The relative success of Cleveland resulted from its having convened the top officials from the main agencies at the start. New York, by contrast, suffered from MCDA's initial strategy of developing the design itself and then inviting other agencies in for comments. They were relegated to advisory status only and resented what they regarded as MCDA's unilateral and monopolistic style. No amount of later compromises, overtures, and invitations by MCDA to participate seemed to soften their resistance.

3. After program priorities have been set, a concerted attempt must be made to *develop some consensus about appropriate agency specializations.* This is extremely difficult, since most agencies don't want to give up their authority and independent funding arrangements with state and federal agencies. Though no single model should be imposed on all cities, some general patterns of agency specialization and expertise make sense. *City Hall* should take the main responsibility for public sector jobs; an *employer association or consortium* (NAB, Urban Coalition, Chamber of Commerce) should develop and train for private sector jobs. The *Employment Service* should provide counseling, testing, placement, and labor market analysis, including its computerized job bank (job matching system). *Community action agencies* are best for outreach, intake, initial counseling, testing,

orientation, and assessment. *Board of Education MDT programs, vocational schools, and skills centers* should do much of the occupational training, along with private trade schools. *Traditional social agencies* like settlement and neighborhood houses should provide supportive services; *newer community agencies like OIC* should provide work orientation, basic education, and related prevocational services. *Universities* should be used for research, program planning, staff training, curriculum development, and management assistance; they may also be used for skills training and to provide continuing education opportunities. *Community colleges* are an especially important resource in this regard. Finally, *labor unions* and the *AFL-CIO's community service agency, the Human Resources Development Institute (HRDI)* are often an important resource for apprenticeship training assistance, negotiating with craft unions for minority group entry, and even in some cases for upgrading programs.

The problem is not so much to list each agency's expertise, but rather to provide incentives and arrange the necessary trade-offs so that they will be willing to specialize and collaborate. One major obstacle is that many new style manpower agencies, community-based and minority controlled, are quick to become as baronial as the traditional agencies they were set up to displace. Their desire for political power, control, and expansion lead them to take on all manpower services, often at great cost to the very minority clients they want to serve better. The role of OIC in Philadelphia is a good example. Many problems of duplication, inefficiency, nonaccountability, and distrust in Philadelphia are exacerbated by OIC's separatism.

4. The big issue in facilitating such agency specializations and coordination is the *political trade-offs* that can be arranged. If each agency (or set of agencies) is given major responsibility for a particular manpower function, relatively untrammeled by competitors, this sometimes helps. It is often difficult to arrange, however. One way to do this is to continue the agency's level of funding, thereby increasing substantially the scale and scope of those manpower activities it does best. The incentive may be that the agency will then have the opportunity to develop its expertise where its performance is already good, enhancing its reputation by continued improvement in that area.

5. The local manpower system should have a *central administrative and program unit* which would engage in several key activities: training manpower administrators, distributing information about programs and about what is going on nationally in manpower, doing evaluations of programs (evaluations which are accurate, not fabricated to meet agency interests), developing a standardized information system to help in evaluation and monitoring, doing good research on labor market trends and occupational analysis within firms, developing curriculum, training manpower staff, and providing organizational development and management consultation services. Much of this may be contracted out to manpower experts in these fields, in universities, or in other

private sector organizations. All these functions, however, are essential in coordinating city manpower programs and services.

6. *Various phasing strategies should be followed with initially modest goals,* in establishing a local manpower delivery system. Limited linkages of agencies involved in the same programs and manpower activities should be established, building later from there, rather than trying to set up the entire delivery system at one time. Furthermore, the same modesty applies as well to the geographic scope of the delivery system. Though the labor market may well be a metropolitan one, the inner city should get its own house in order first, before entering into a larger compact with outlying counties or suburbs. Otherwise, a metro-wide manpower authority will involve so much factionalism that it will founder on that order of internal consensus-building. Metropolitan area-wide manpower planning should begin instead with particular programs (e.g., transportation of ghetto residents out to suburban jobs), later moving on to more extended contacts and a delivery system.

7. Many new and traditional agencies will have to change if local manpower systems are to be effective, but the one perhaps most in need of major changes is the *State Employment Service.* It should be decentralized as much as possible, so that the local area manager has the autonomy and flexibility required to fit his agency's operations into the city manpower situation. Effective state-city linkages should not have to depend mainly on the personalities and political skills of the area managers, as seemed to be the case in Cleveland and Philadelphia. Furthermore, it should encourage big city area managers to accept the desires of community and city agency officials to maintain local over state control. Recruiting and training progressive, city-oriented area managers to head Employment Service operations in inner cities would help, as would changes in salary scales, examinations, and civil service promotional procedures. The agency might then attract more competent staff, maintain their morale, keep them, and provide a setting in which they would be encouraged to innovate. Many able manpower specialists are discouraged from working for the Employment Service because salaries are often low relative to those in city or community agencies. Beyond that, the traditional and cumbersome testing and recruitment procedures further discourage able people from the Employment Service. And the slow promotional pattern and automatic tenure encourage a bureaucratic, non-innovative outlook.

If the Employment Service could, in addition, relax its rigid bureaucratic procedures and record-keeping, it would make a more significant contribution to local manpower delivery systems than it does now. It must have greater flexibility in working under the forms and information systems of city agenices. Otherwise, there will never be effective collaboration that includes it. That would be most unfortunate, since the Employment Service does have some expertise that other agencies don't readily have—for example, testing, counseling, placement, and job matching.

8. *Considerable responsibility for these reforms rests with the Department of Labor.* Specifically, it should single out effective area managers and other staff in the Employment Service and use them in training others. Beyond that, it should withhold federal funds from those localities that don't make tangible progress toward coordination. Without such federal leadership, cities will be much slower in establishing local manpower delivery systems than they should be.

The Department of Labor should also continue its own internal reorganization to support the trend toward decentralization and local integration. In this regard, its regional offices should be given a major role in promoting local agency linkages, rather than just enforcing national guidelines on a program-by-program basis. Regional officials of the Department of Labor should be given more authority and flexibility to provide such leadership, and they should have ready access to high level Department of Labor officials in Washington to bring that agency's full resources to bear in promoting local coordination.

Further, the Department of Labor should maintain in each regional office and for each large city and metropolitan area a cadre of manpower experts and social scientists who are highly knowledgeable on matters of organizational design and politics as they relate to establishing manpower delivery systems. These problems are often defined as too complex and intractable for systematic study and action, and decisions are then drifted into. That is obviously not a rational way to deal with the issue. The Department of Labor should therefore not just passively respond to crises in the cities as the latter attempt to establish manpower delivery systems. Nor should it just make a series of *ad hoc* decisions without any knowledge of local politics and administration. Maintaining a permanent task force to help set up, monitor, and provide technical assistance for local manpower systems would thus be a move in the right direction.

Finally, the Department of Labor should tailor its policies to conditions in the localities, including the local labor market, agency capabilities, and politics. Part of such a locality-relevant strategy would be the recognition by the Department of Labor that there is much variation among states, counties, and cities in manpower capabilities and in commitments to establish a delivery system. This does not mean, then, that the federal government should provide block grants indiscriminately if the necessary legislation is passed. Some cities and states may merit such autonomy and some will not. Despite strong political pressure for equal treatment, the Department of Labor should try to develop some criteria by which the capability and commitments of cities can be assessed; and it should then try to act on such assessments.

CONCLUSIONS

Much of the analysis of this paper dealt with the micro-, local politics of manpower agencies at the point of delivery—in the inner cities. The main argument was that the local power structure and politics place upper and lower limits on the implementation strategy and organizational design that get adopted. Other contextual or independent variables are important—for example, the labor market, extent of unemployment and underemployment, and agency capabilities, but the political-institutional constraints (the concern of this research) are critical.

Cities will not be able to develop effective local manpower delivery systems, however, without leadership from Washington. The common condition of duplicative, competitive agencies, leading to distrust, inefficiency, and poor local planning is a direct result of the pattern of federal funding. Unless Washington stops proliferating numerous categorical programs and begins to show leadership in decategorizing, increasing coordination of administration at the federal level, and in decentralizing, there will be little the cities can do. It is an indication of their interest and initiative that some, like Cleveland and New York City, have gone as far as they have in trying to establish better agency and program linkages despite the major roadblocks that the federal government has perpetuated. If the federal government were to show some leadership in reversing that condition, through the passage of legislation that mandated some of these reforms, it is most likely that the cities will move ahead much more rapidly in that task.

There has been much discussion in recent years, a lot of it rhetoric, about a "new" and "creative" federalism. Manpower training programs are one area of government where we will have the opportunity to see if the rhetoric can be translated into reality. The research reported on in this paper is an attempt to assist in that effort.

NOTES–CASE 9

1. For good analyses of these developments, see Stanley H. Ruttenberg and Jocelyn Gutchess, *Manpower Challenge of the 1970s' Institutions and Social Changes: Policy Studies in Employment and Welfare,* 2, Baltimore and London, Johns Hopkins Press, 1970; and National Manpower Policy Task Force, *Improving the Nation's Manpower Efforts,* a position paper, February 12, 1970.

2. The limited capabilities of state manpower agencies are perceptively discussed by Curtis Aller and Samuel Bernstein, "Falling Down on the Job: The United States Employment Services and the Disadvantaged," in R. Thayne Robson and Garth Mangum (Eds.), *Manpower Planning,* Proceedings of National Conference on State and Local Manpower Planning, Human Resources Institute, University of Utah, April 1971. See also Stanley H. Ruttenberg and Jocelyn Gutchess, *The Federal-State Employment Service: A Critique,* Baltimore, Johns Hopkins Press, 1970; and The National Urban Coalition and the Lawyers' Committee for Civil Rights Under Law, *Falling Down on the Job: The United States Employment Service and the Disadvantaged,* June 1971.

3. For an analysis of the power structure of these cities as it affects their capacity to implement social programs, see David Rogers, *The Management of Big Cities,* Beverly Hills, California, Sage, 1971.

4. As Kenneth C. Olson, State Planning Coordinator for the Utah State Manpower Planning Council, wrote in the context of federal-state relations: "Yet, in spite of this diversity the federal government now writes one set of regulations embodying one pattern of relationships with all states being treated as though they were the same. The result is much like the mail order suit built for the average man. It fits no one precisely." In Robson and Mangum, *Manpower Planning* (see Note 2).

5. See David Hill, "Local Manpower Planning and Administration Case Study; Cleveland," in Robson and Mangum, *Manpower Planning,* pp. 133-138. Hill and Krauskopf were Mayor Stokes' two top anti-poverty and manpower officials. Also see Rogers, *The Management of Big Cities* (see Note 3).

6. An early statement of this view appears in *Improving the Nation's Manpower Efforts* (see Note 1).

7. See David Greenstone and Paul F. Peterson, "Reformers, Machines and The War on Poverty," in James Q. Wilson (Ed.), *City Politics and Public Policy,* New York, Wiley, 1968.

8. An analysis of the Chicago machine appears in Edward Banfield, *Political Influence,* New York, Free Press, 1961.

9. For a good history of the reform movement in Philadelphia, see Jeanne Lowe, *Cities in a Race with Time,* New York, Random House, 1968.

10. The main agencies include the Jewish Employment Vocational Service, which has developed a culture-free work sample test that is used nationally; the Crime Prevention Association, very skilled at working with street gangs; the Urban League, which has some good job and white-collar programs; and the Human Resources Development Institute of the AFL-CIO, which does a lot in apprenticeship training and in negotiating with craft unions for more positions for minorities.

11. The main task force reports included *Developing New York City's Human Resources,* Institute of Public Administration (Sviridoff Report), June 1966; *Report of Housing and Urban Renewal Task Force* (Abrams Report), January 1966; *Let There be Commitment,* A Housing Planning Development Program for New York City, 1966, Institute of Public Administration (Logue Report), 1966; and *The Mayor's Task Force on Reorganization of New York City Government* (Graco Report), December 1966.

12. As the Sviridoff Report indicated: "Nowhere in our studies have we found as many unrelated pieces, gaps, and as much duplication and overlap as in the field of manpower and employment . . . One thing that is sorely lacking in the city is orderly progression and follow through . . . The trouble is lack of coordination and the absence of ties between different parts of the system" (p. 22).

13. The design and rationale for this system were originally stated in *Opportunity Centers System,* Manpower and Career Development Agency, Human Resources Administration, City of New York, 1968, Vol. 1-3.

14. From interviews with Department of Labor, New York State Division of Employment, and Board of Education officials.

15. Sen. Javits testified at a recent hearing of Governor Rockefeller's Scott Commission to investigate the management of NYC government that this conflict between the city and the state had probably cost both a lot of federal monies. He indicated that federal officials were reluctant to get involved in such a "hornet's nest" of local political conflict and often did not fund state and local programs for that reason. One of his main recommendations was that the Rockefeller Commission investigating the

city and the Lindsay Commission investigating city-state relations be merged. City officials embraced this proposal, though the state did not. Increased pressure from Washington, going beyond just making speeches and recommendations, is now required.

16. I am indebted to my colleague, Professor S.M. Miller, for this conception. See also, the excellent piece by Thayne Robson on local manpower planning in Robson and Mangum, *Manpower Planning* (see Note 2).

References

Ackoff, R.L. (1970) *A Guide to Corporate Planning,* New York, Wiley.

Ackoff, R.L., and Emery, F.E. (1972) *On Purposeful Systems,* Chicago, Aldine-Atherton.

Ashby, W.R. (1956) *An Introduction to Cybernetics,* New York, Wiley.

Baier, K., and Rescher, N. (1969) *Values and the Future,* New York, The Free Press.

Bonjean, Charles M., and Olson, David M. (1964) "Community Leadership: Directions of Reseach," *Administrative Science Quarterly,* Vol. 9, December, 278-300.

Bright, James R. (1968) *Technological Forecasting for Industry and Government,* New Jersey, Prentice Hall.

Bright, James R. (1972) *A Brief Introduction to Technology Forecasting,* Austin, Texas, James R. Bright.

Buchanan, J.M., and Stubblebine, W.C. (1962) "Externality," *Economica,* N.S. 29, 371-384.

Clarkson, Geoffrey P.E. (1962) *Portfolio Selection: A Stimulation of Trust Investment,* Englewood Cliffs, N.J., Prentice-Hall.

Clarkson, Geoffrey P.E. (1968) "Decision Making in Small Groups: A Simulation Study," *Behavioral Science,* Vol. 13, July, 288-307.

Clarkson, Geoffrey P.E., and Tuggle, Francis (1966) "Toward a Theory of Group-Decision Behavior," *Behavioral Science,* Vol. 11, January, 33-42.

Coddington, A. (1968) *Theories of the Bargaining Process,* Chicago, Aldine.

Crecine, John P. (1967) "A Computer Simulation Model of Municipal Budgeting," *Management Science,* July, 768-815.

Crecine, John P. (1969) *Governmental Problem Solving: A Computer Simulation of Municipal Budgeting,* Chicago, Rand-McNally.

Cyert, Richard M., and March, James G. (1963) *A Behavioral Theory of the Firm,* Englewood Cliffs, N.J., Prentice-Hall.

Dantzig, G.B. (1963) *Linear Programming and Extensions,* Princeton, Princeton University Press.

Davis, O.A., and Rueter, F.H. (1972) "A Simulation of Municipal Zoning Decision," *Management Science,* Vol. 19, Vol. 4, Part II, December 1972, 39-77.

Davis, Otto A., Dempster, M.A. H., and Wildavsky, A. (1966) "On the Process of Budgeting: An Empirical Study of Congressional Appropriations," in G. Tullock, (Ed.), *Papers on Non-Market Decision Making,* Charlottesville, Virginia, Thomas Jefferson Center for Political Economy.

Dror, Y. (1970) "Prolegomena to Policy Sciences," *Policy Sciences,* Vol. 1, No. 1, 135-151.

Dror, Y. (1971) *Design for Policy Sciences,* New York, American Elsevier.

Eckstein, Otto, and Wilson, Thomas A. (1962) "The Determination of Money Wages in American Industry," *The Quarterly Journal of Economics,* Vol. LXXVI, August, 379-414.

Emery, F.E. (Ed.) (1969) *Systems Thinking,* Hammondsworth, England, Penguin Books, Ltd.

Feigenbaum, Edward A. (1963) "The Simulation of Verbal Learning Behavior" in E.A. Feigenbaum and Julian Feldman (Eds.), *Computers and Thoughts,* New York, McGraw-Hill.

Galbraith, Jay (1973) *Designing Complex Organizations,* Reading, Mass., Addison Wesley.

Gerwin, Donald (1969a) *Budgeting Public Funds: The Decision Process in an Urban School District,* Madison, University of Wisconsin Press.

Gerwin, Donald (1969b) "Towards a Theory of Public Budgetary Decision Making," *Administrative Science Quarterly,* Vol. 14, March, 33-46.

Gerwin, Donald (1971) "An Information Processing Model of Salary Determination in a Contour of Suburban School Districts," School of Business Administration Working Paper, University of Wisconsin-Milwaukee, October.

Gerwin, Donald (forthcoming) "Formulation Salary Policy in Suburban School Districts," *Education and Urban Society.*

Guetzkow, H., Kotler, P., and Schultz, R.L. (1972) *Simulation in Social and Administrative Science,* Englewood Cliffs, New Jersey, Prentice-Hall.

Hillier, F.S., and Lieberman, G.J. (1967) *Introduction to Operations Research,* San Francisco, Holden-Day.

Jantsch, E. (1972) *Technological Planning and Social Futures,* New York, Wiley.

Jantsch, E. (1973) "Forecasting and Systems Approach: A Frame of Reference," *Management Science,* Vol. 19, No. 12, August.

Katz, D., and Kahn, R.L. (1966) *The Social Psychology of Organization,* New York, Wiley.

Kuhn, Thomas S. (1970) *The Structure of Scientific Revolutions* (2nd ed.), Chicago, University of Chicago Press.

Laszlo, E. (1973) "A Systems Philosophy of Human Values," *Behavioral Science,* Vol. 18, No. 4, July.

Lawrence, Paul, and Lorsch, J. (1967) *Organization and Environment,* Boston, Division of Research, Harvard Business School.

Learner, D., and Laswell, H.D. (Eds.) (1951) *The Policy Sciences: Recent Developments in Scope and Methods,* Stanford, Stanford University Press.

Leavitt, H.J. (1965) "Applied Organizational Change in Industry: Structural Technological and Humanistic Approaches," in J.G. March, *Handbook of Organizations,* Chicago, Rand McNally.

Levinson, Harold M. (1966) *Determining Forces in Collective Wage Bargaining,* New York, Wiley.

Lewin, A.Y., and Blanning, R.W. (1974) "Urban Government Annual Report," in D. Rogers and W.D. Hawley (Eds.), *Improving the Quality of Urban Management,* Beverly Hills, California, Sage.

Lewin, A.Y., and Shakun, M.F. (1971) "Situational Normativism and Teaching of Policy Sciences," *Policy Sciences,* No. 2, 59-66.

March, J.G., and Simon, H.A. (1958) *Organizations,* New York, Wiley.

Mason, R.O. (1969) "A Dialectical Approach to Strategic Planning," *Management Science,* Vol. 15, No. 8, 403-415.

Meier, Newell, and Pazor (1969) *Simulation in Business and Economics,* Englewood Cliffs, N.J., Prentice-Hall.

Mesarovic, M., and Pestel, E. (1974) *Mankind at the Turning Point,* New York, Dutton.

Mintzberg, H. (1973) *The Nature of Managerial Work,* New York, Harper and Row.

Naylor, T.H., Balintfy, J.L. *et al.* (1966) *Computer Simulation Techniques,* New York, Wiley.

Newell, Allen, and Simon, Herbert A. (1972) *Human Problem Solving,* Englewood Cliffs, N.J., Prentice-Hall.

Popper, Karl R. (1965) *The Logic of Scientific Discovery,* New York, Harper Row.

Rao, A.G., and Shakun, M.F. (1974) "A Normative Model for Negotiations," *Management Science,* Vol. 20, No. 10, June.

Rogers, David (1971) *The Management of Big Cities,* Beverly Hills, California, Sage.

Selznick, P. (1949) *TVA and the Grass Roots,* Harper Torch book edition 1966. Originally published by the University of California Press, Berkeley and Los Angeles.

Shakun, M.F. (1960) "Statistical Quality Control—The Cybernetic Approach to Business Operations," *Industrial Quality Control,* Vol. XVII, No. 3, September.

Shakun, M.F. (1966) "Summary of the Session on Comparative Operations Research" in Hertz, D.B. and Melese, J. (Eds.), *The Proceedings of the Fourth International Conference on Operations Research,* New York, Wiley, pp. 1069-1073.

Shakun, M.F. (1972) "Management Science and Management: Implementing Management Science Via Situational Normativism," *Management Science,* Vol. 18, No. 8, April.

Shakun, M.F. (1975) "Policy Making Under Discontinuous Change: The Situational Normativism Approach," *Management Science,* Vol. 22, No. 2, 1975.

Simon, H.A. (1964) "On the Concept of Organizational Goal," *Administrative Science Quarterly*, June, 1-22.

Soelberg, P. (1967) "Unprogrammed Decision Making," *Industrial Management Review*, Spring, 19-29.

Vickers, G. (1973a) "Values, Norms and Policies," *Policy Sciences*, Vol. 4, No. 1, March.

Vickers, G. (1973b) "Motivation Theory—A Cybernetic Contribution," *Behavioral Sciences*, Vol. 18, No. 4, July.

Waterman, D.A., and Newell, A. (1971) "Protocol Analysis as a Task for Artificial Intelligence," *Artificial Intelligence*, Vol. 2, 285-318.

Watson, James D. (1968) *The Double Helix*, New York, New American Library.

Weber, C.E. (1965) "Intraorganizational Decision Processes Influencing the EDP Staff Budget," *Management Science*, Vol. 12, No. 4, B69-94.

Weber, C.E., and Peters, G. (1969) *Management Action: Models of Administrative Decisions*, Scranton, Pennsylvania, International Textbook.

Whitehead, C.T. (1967) *Use and Limitations of Systems Analysis*, Unpublished Ph.D. Dissertation, Sloan School of Management, MIT.

Wildavsky, A. (1964) *The Politics of the Budgetary Process*, Boston, Little, Brown.

Zangwill, W.I. (1969) *Nonlinear Programming*, Englewood Cliffs, N.J., Prentice-Hall.

Selected Bibliography

I. INTRODUCTION TO POLICY SCIENCES

Adams, H., "On Economic Value in Policy Sciences," *Policy Sciences,* Vol. 1, No. 2, Summer 1971.

Archibald, K.A., "Three Views of the Expert's Role in Policymaking," *Policy Sciences,* Vol. 1, No. 1, Spring 1970.

Bouland, H.D., "Systems Analysis and the Community," *Public Administration,* Vol. XXX, 1970.

Dror, Y., *Public Policymaking Reexamined,* San Francisco, Chandler, 1968.

Dror, Y., "Teaching of Policy Sciences: Design for a University Doctorate Program," *Social Sciences Information,* Vol. 9, No. 2, 1970.

Dror, Y., "A Policy Sciences View of Future Studies: Alternative Futures and Present Action," RAND paper P-4305, Santa Monica, California, The RAND Corporation, February 1970.

Dror, Y., "Prolegomena to Policy Sciences," *Policy Sciences,* Vol. 1, No. 1, Spring 1970.

Dror, Y., *Design for Policy Sciences,* New York, American Elsevier, 1971.

Dror, Y., *Ventures in Policy Sciences,* New York, American Elsevier, 1971.

Hoos, I.R., *Systems Analysis in Social Policy,* London, Institute of Economic Affairs, 1959.

Laswell, H.D., "The Emerging Conception of Policy Sciences," *Policy Sciences,* Vol. 1, No. 1, Spring 1970.

Laswell, H.D., *A Pre-view of Policy Sciences,* New York, American Elsevier, 1971.

Leanner, D., and Laswell, H.D. (Eds.), *The Policy Sciences: Recent Developments in Scope and Methods,* Stanford, Stanford University Press, 1951.

Lepawsky, A., "Graduate Education in Public Policy," *Policy Sciences,* Vol. 1, No. 4, Dec. 1970.

Lindbloom, C.E., *The Policy Making Process,* Englewood Cliffs, N.J., Prentice-Hall, 1968.

Moran, W., "A Model of Business—Society," *Management Science*, Vol. 16, No. 6, Feb. 1970.

Moynihan, D., "Urban Conditions: General," *The Annals*, Vol. 371, May 1967.

Simon, H.A. *The New Science of Management Decision*, New York, Harper and Row, 1960.

II. FUNDAMENTALS FOR POLICY ANALYSIS

A. The Individual Decision Maker

Costello, T.W., and Zalkind, S.S., *Psychology in Administration*, Englewood Cliffs, N.J., Prentice-Hall, 1963.

Davidson, D., McKinsey, J.C.C., and Suppes, P., "Outlines of a Formal Theory of Value," *Philosophy of Science* 1955, pp. 140-160.

Fishburn, P.C., *Decision and Value Theory*, New York, Wiley, 1964.

Marschak, J., "Probabilities and the Norms of Behavior," P. Lazarfeld (Editor), *Mathematical Thinking in the Social Sciences*, Distributed by Macmillan, N.Y., The Free Press, 1954, pp. 166-187.

Marschak, J., "Toward a Preference Scale of Decision Making," M. Schubik (Ed.), *Game Theory and Related Approaches to Social Behavior*, New York, Wiley, 1964, pp. 95-109.

Newell, A., Simon, H.A., and Shaw, J.C., "Elements of a Theory of Human Problem Solving," *Psychology Review*, 1958, pp. 151-166.

Shackle, G.L.S., *Expectation in Economics*, Second Edition, New York, Cambridge University, 1952.

Shubik, M. (Ed.), *Game Theory and Related Approaches to Social Behavior*, New York, Wiley, 1964.

Simon, H.A., *Administrative Behavior*, Second Edition, New York, Macmillan, 1961, Chapter 5.

B. Organizational Decision Making

Ackoff, R.L., "Structural Conflicts Within Organizations," J.R. Lawrence (Ed.), Operations Research and the Social Sciences, London, Tavistock Publications, 1966.

Ackoff, R.L., "Choice Communication & Conflict: A Systems Approach to the Study of Human Behavior," Philadelphia, University of Pennsylvania, 1967.

Ackoff, R.L., *et al.*, "Toward a Quantitative Theory of the Dynamics of Conflict," (ACDA/ST-127), *Management Science Center*, Philadelphia, University of Pennsylvania, Feb. 1968.

Alexis, M., and Wilson, C.Z., *Organizational Decision Making*, Englewood Cliffs, N.J., Prentice-Hall, 1967.

Charnes, A., Clower, R.W., Kortanek, K.O., "Effective Control Through Coherent Decentralization with Preemptive Goals," *Econo.*, April 1967.

Cyert, R.M., and March, J.G., *A Behavioral Theory of the Firm*, Englewood Cliffs, N.J., Prentice-Hall, 1963, Chapters 2, 3, 4, (pp. 44-47), 5, 6.

Evan, W.M., "Toward a Theory of Interorganizational Relations," *Management Science,* August 1965.

Evan, W.M., and MacDougall, J.A., "Interorganizational Conflict: A Management Programming Experiment," *Journal of Conflict Resolution,* Dec. 1967.

Gore, W., *Administrative Decision Making,* New York, Wiley, 1964, Chap. 2.

Hill, W.A., and Egan, D.M., *Readings in Organization Theory A Behavioral Approach,* Boston, Allyn and Bacon, 1967.

Hurwicz, L., "Information Requirements for Joint Decision Making," presented at Northwestern University Conference on Interorganization Decision Making, 1969.

March, J.G., and Simon, H., *Organizations,* New York, Wiley, 1958.

Marschak, J., "Elements for a Theory of Teams," *Management Science,* Jan. 1955, pp. 127-137.

Marschak, J., "Efficient and Viable Organizational Forms," M. Haire (Ed.), *Modern Organization Theory,* New York, Wiley, 1959, pp. 151-166.

Radner, R., "Team Decision Problems," *Annals of Mathematical Statistics,* Sept. 1952, pp. 857-881.

Radner, R., "Mathematical Specifications of Goals for Decision Problems," in M.W. Shelly and G.L. Bryan (Eds.), *Human Judgments and Optimality,* New York, Wiley, 1961.

Rapaport, A., and Chammah, A.M., *Prisoner's Dilemma,* Ann Arbor, University of Michigan Press, 1965.

Rapaport, Anatol, and Orwant, C., "Laboratory Studies of Conflict and Cooperation," J.R. Lawrence (Ed.), *Operation Research and the Social Sciences,* London, Tavistock Publications, 1966.

Schelling, T.C., *The Strategy of Conflict,* Washington, D.C., Howard University Press, 1960.

Shubik, M., "Incentives, Decentralized Control, The Assignment of Joint Costs and Internal Pricing," C.O. Bonini, R.K. Jaedicke and H.M. Wagner (Eds.), *Management Controls: New Direction in Basic Research,* New York, McGraw Hill, 1964. (This is a slight revision of the paper, *Management Science,* Vol. 8, No. 3, April 1962.)

Simon, H.A., *Models of Man,* New York, Wiley, 1957.

Simon, H.A., "On the Concept of Organizational Goal," *Administrative Science Quarterly,* June 1964, pp. 1-22.

Stedry, A.C., and Charnes, A., "The Attainment of Organization Goals Through Appropriate Selection of Sub-Unit Goals," J.R. Lawrence (Ed.), *Operational Research in Social Sciences,* London, Tavistock Publications, 1966.

Thompson, J.D., *Organizations in Action,* New York, McGraw-Hill, 1967.

Tuite, M., Chesholm R., and Radnor M., *Interorganizational Decision Making,* Chicago, Aldine, 1972.

Vroom, V., *Work and Motivation,* New York, Wiley, 1964.

Walton, R.E. and McKensie, R.B., "Behavioral Dilemmas in Mixed Motive Decision Making," *Behavioral Science,* Sept. 1965.

Walton, R.E., "Interpersonal Confrontation and Basic Third Party Functions: A Case Study," *Journal of Applied Behavioral Science,* Vol. 4, No. 3., 1968.

Walton, R.E., "Structural and Behavioral Requirements for Joint Decision Making," Northwestern University Conference on Interorganizational Decision Making, Feb. 1969.

Weber, C.E., and Peters, J., *Management Action: Models of Administrative Decision,* Scranton, International Textbook, 1969.

Weill, R.L., "The N-Persona Prisoner's Dilemma," *Behavioral Science,* Vol. 11, No. 3, May 1966.

Whinston, A., "Price Guides in Decentralized Organizations," W.W. Cooper, H.J. Leavitt, and N.W. Shelly (Eds.), *New Perspectives in Organizational Research,* New York, Wiley, 1964.

Whinston, A., "Theoretical and Computational Problems in Organizational Decision-Making," *Operational Research,* London, Tavistock Publications, 1966.

Williamson, O.E. *Corporate Control and Business Behavior,* Englewood Cliffs, N.J., Prentice-Hall, 1970.

C. Decision Analysis and Game Theory

Aumann, R.J., Harsanyi, J.C., *et al.,* "The Indirect Measurement of Utility" (ASDA/ST-143), Vol. 1 and 2 prepared for U.S. Arms Control and Disarmament Agency by *Mathematica,* Princeton, N.J. and Bethesda, Maryland, Nov. 1968.

Bean, B.V., "Application of Operations Research to Managerial Decision Making," *Administration Science Quarterly,* 1953, pp. 412-428.

Harsanyi, J.C., *A General Theory of Rational Behavior in Game Situations, Econometria,* 34, p. 613.

Harsanyi, J.C., A Generalized Nash Solution for Two-Person Cooperative Games with Incomplete Information *Models of Gradual Reduction of Arms,* Vol. II, Final Report to Arms Control and Disarmament Agency, Washington, D.C. under contract ACDA/ST-116 prepared by *Mathematica,* Princeton, New Jersey.

Harsanyi, J.C., Games with Incomplete Information Played by Bayesian Players, Parts I-III, *Management Science,* pp. 14, 159, 320, 436.

Howard, R.A., "Decision Analysis: Applied Decision Theory," *Proceedings of the Fourth International Conference on Operational Research,* Boston, 1966.

Luce, R.D., and Raiffa, H., *Games and Decision,* New York, Wiley, 1957.

Nash, J.F., "Two Person Cooperative Games," *Econometrica* Vol. 21, No. 128, 1953.

Owen, G., *Game Theory,* Philadelphia, Saunders, 1968.

Pratt, J.W., Raiffa, H., and Schlaifer, R., *Introduction to Statistical Decision Theory,* New York, McGraw-Hill, 1965.

Raiffa, H., *Decision Analysis,* Reading, Mass., Addison-Wesley, 1968.

Raiffa, H., and Schlaifer, R., *Applied Statistical Decision Theory*, Graduate School of Business Administration, Boston, Harvard University, 1961.

Rapaport, A., and Mowshowitz, A., "Experiemental Studies of Stochastic Models for Prisoner's Dilemma," *Behavioral Science*, Vol. 11, No. 6, Nove. 1966.

Savage, J.J., *Statistics: Uncertainty & Behavior*, Boston, Houghton Mifflin, 1968.

Savage, J.J., *The Foundations of Statistics*, New York, Wiley, 1954, Chap. 1-5.

Schelling, T.C., "Game Theory and the Study of Ethical Systems," *Journal of Conflict Resolution*, March 1968.

III. METHODOLOGY

A. Situational Normativism

Lewin, A.Y. and Shakun, M.F., "Situational Normativism: A Discriptive Normative Approach to Decision Making and Policy Sciences," *Policy Sciences*, Vol. 7, No. 1, March 1976.

Lewin, A.Y. and Shakun, M.F., "Situational Normativism and Teaching of Policy Sciences," *Policy Sciences*, Vol. 1, No. 2, pp. 59-66, 1971.

Shakun, M.F., "Management Science and Management: Implementing Management Science Via Situational Normativism," *Management Science*, Vol. 18, No. 8, April 1974.

Shakun, M.F., "Policy Making Under Discontinuous Change: The Situational Normativism Approach," *Management Science*, Vol. 22, No. 2, Oct. 1975.

B. Descriptive and Decision Process Models

Bartee, E.M., "On the Methodology of Solution Synthesis," *Management Science*, Vol. 17, No. 6, Feb. 1971.

Bellman, R., and Zadek, L.A., "Decision Making in a Fuzzy Environment," *Management Science*, Vol. 17, No. 4, Dec. 1971.

Bright, J.R. *An Introduction to Technology Forecasting*, Austin, Texas, James R. Bright, 1972.

Churchman, C.W., "On Rational Decision Making," *Management Technology*, Dec. 1962.

Churchman, C.W., *Prediction and Optimal Decisions*, Englewood Cliffs, N.J., Prentice-Hall, 1963.

Clarkson, G.P.E., *Portfolio Selection: A Simulation of Trust Investment*, Englewood Cliffs, N.J., Prentice-Hall, 1962.

Crecine, J.P., "A Computer Simulation Model of Municipal Budgeting," *Management Science*, Vol. 13, No. 11, July 1967.

Cyert, R.M., Simon, H.A., and Trow, D., "Observation of a Business Decision," *Journal of Business*, 1956, pp. 237-248.

Davis, O.A., Dempster, M.A.H., and Wildavsky A., "A Theory of the Budgeting Process," *American Political Science Review*, Vol. 60, No. 3, September 1966.

Dewey, J., *How We Think*, Lexington, Mass., Heath and Co., 1933.

Dill, W.R., "Decision Making," *63rd Yearbook of the National Society for Study of Education*, Part II, 1964, Chap. 9 also C.I.T. reprint #158.

Gerwin, D., "Towards a Theory of Public Budgeting Decision Making," *Administrative Science Quarterly*, Vol. 14, No. 1, 1969.

Gerwin, D., "A Process Model of Budgeting in a Public School System," *Management Science*, Vol. 15, No. 7, March 1969.

Grayson, J., *Decisions Under Uncertainty: Drilling Decisions by Oil Operators*, Cambridge, Mass., Harvard University, 1961.

Ikle, F., *How Nations Negotiate*, New York, Praeger, 1967.

Kapoor, A., *International Business Negotiations: A Study in India*, New York, New York University Press, 1970.

Paige, G.D., *The Korean Decision*, New York, The Free Press, 1968.

Pill, J.P., "The Delphi Method: Substance, Context, A Critique and an Annotated Bibliography, *Socio-Economic Planning Sciences*, Vol. 5, No. 1.

Quade, B.S., "Methods & Procedures," E.S. Zuade (Ed.), *Analysis for Military Decisions*, New York, Rand McNally, 1964.

Williamson, O., *The Economics of Discretionary Behavior: Managerial Objectives in the Firm*, Englewood Cliffs, N.J., Prentice-Hall, 1964.

Williamson, O., *Corporate Control and Business Behavior*, Englewood Cliffs, N.J., Prentice-Hall, 1970.

C. Normative Mathematical Models

Babrow, D., "Computers and the Normative Model of Policy Process," *Policy Sciences*, Vol. 1, No. 1, p. 123.

Bryan, S.E., "TFX—A Case in Policy Level Decision Making," *Academy of Management Journal*, March 1964, pp. 54-70.

Cooper, W.W. (Ed.), "Urban Issues," *Management Science*, Vol. 16, No. 12, August 1970.

Cooper, W.W. (Ed.), "Urban Issues II," *Management Science*, Vol. 19, No. 4, December 1972.

Dean, A., *Test Ban and Disarmament-The Path of Negotiations*, New York, Harper and Row, 1968.

Dickson, G., "A Generalized Model of Administrative Decisions," *Management Science*, Vol. 17, No. 1, Sept. 1970.

Drake, A.W., Kenney, R.L., and Morse, P.M., *Analysis of Public Systems*, Cambridge, Mass., The MIT Press, 1972.

Emshoff, J.R., and Ackoff, R.L., "Explanatory Models of Choice Behavior," *Management Science Center*, University of Pennsylvania, Oct. 1968.

Joyner, R., "Computer Augmented Organizational Problem Solving," *Management Science*, Vol. 17, No. 4, Dec. 1970.

Kapur, K., "Mathematical Methods of Optimization for Multi-Objective

Transportation Systems," *Socio-Econ. Planning Sciences,* Vol. 4, No. 4, Dec. 1970.

Moller, D.W., and Starr, M.K., *Executive Decisions and Operations Research,* Englewood Cliffs, N.J., Prentice-Hall, 1961.

Rao, A.G., and Shakun, M.F., "A Normative Model for Negotiations," *Management Science,* Vol. 20, No. 10, June 1974.

Revelle, C., "An Analysis of Private & Public Sector Location Models," *Management Science,* Vol. 16, No. 11.

Ruefli, T.W., "A Generalized Goal Decomposition Model," *Management Science,* Vol. 17, No. 8, April 1971.

Shakun, M.F., "Competitive Organizational Structures in Coupled Markets," *Management Science,* Vol. 14, No. 12, August 1968.

Shakun, M.F., "International Joint Ventures: A Decision Analysis–Game Theory Approach," J.R. Lawrence (Ed.), *Proceedings of Fifth International Conference on Operational Research,* London, Tavistock Publications, 1970.

Shakun, M.F. (Ed.), "Game Theory and Gaming," special issue of *Management Science,* Vol. 18, No. 5, January 1972, Part II.

Stimson, D.H., "Utility Measurement in Public Health Decision Making," *Management Sciences,* Vol. 16, No. 2, Oct. 1969.

D. Simulation and Gaming

Amstutz, A.E., *Computer Simulation of Competitive Market Response,* Cambridge, Mass., The M.I.T. Press, 1967.

Friedmann, J., "An Information Model of Urbanization," *Urban Affairs Quaterly,* Vol. IV.

Forrester, J.W., *Urban Dynamics,* Cambridge, Mass., M.I.T. Press, 1969.

Forrester, J.W., *Systems Analysis as a Tool for Urban Planning,* IEEE Transaction on Systems Science and Cybernetics, Vol. SSC-6, No. 4, October 1970.

Forrester, J.W., "Urban Dynamics: A Critical Examination," *Policy Sciences,* Vol. 1, No. 3, Fall 1970.

Guetzkow, C.F., *Simulation in International Relations,* Englewood Cliffs, N.J., Prentice-Hall, 1963.

Guetzkow, H., Kotler, P., and Schultz, R., *Simulation in Social and Administrative Behavior,* Englewood Cliffs, N.J., Prentice-Hall, 1972.

Shubik, M., "Experimental Gaming and Some Aspects of Competitive Behavior," W.W. Cooper, H.J. Leavitt, M.W. Shelly (Eds.), *New Perspectives in Organizational Research,* New York, Wiley, 1964.

Sorenson, E., "A Simulation for Harvest Operations Under Stochastic Conditions," *Management Science,* Vol. 16, No. 8, April 1970.

Taylor, J., and Maddison, R., "A Land Use Gaming Simulation," *Urban Affairs Quarterly,* Vol. III, No. 4.

Van Horn, R., "Validation of Simulation Results," *Management Science,* Vol. 17, No. 5, Jan. 1971.

IV. APPLICATIONS

A. Social Responsibility of Business and Consumerism

Assael, H., "Constructive Role of Interorganizational Conflict," *Administrative Science Quarterly,* Vol. 14, No. 4, 1957, pp. 464-483.

Assael, H., "The Political Role of Trade Association in Conflict Resolution," *Journal of Marketing,* May 1968.

Barnard, C.E., *The Functions of the Executive,* Washington, D.C., Howard University, 1938.

Bowen, H., *Social Responsibility of the Businessman,* New York, Harper, 1953.

Chamberlain, N.W., *Social Responsibility and Strikes,* New York, Harper, 1953.

Fitch, J.A., *Social Responsibilities of Organized Labor,* New York, Harper, 1957.

Foregen, J.H., "Social Responsibility for Unions Too," *Management Psychl. Quarterly,* Vol. 8, No. 4, 1969, pp. 28-33.

Leys, W., "Ethics in American Business & Gov't.," *The Annals,* Vol. 373, July 1968, p. 34.

Nash, J.F., The Bargaining Problem, *Econometrica,* Vol. 18, No. 155, 1950.

Sawyer, J., and Guetzkow, A., "Bargaining and Negotiation in International Relations," in H.C. Leman (Ed.), *International Behavior A Social-Psychological Analysis,* New York, Holt, Rinehart and Winston, 1965.

Walton, R.E., and McKensie, R.B., *A Behavioral Theory of Labor Negotiations: An Analysis of a Social Interaction System,* New York, McGraw Hill, 1965.

B. Social Accountability

Cassidy, R.G., Kirby, M.J.L., and Raike, W.W., "Efficient Distribution of Resources Through Three Levels of Gov't.," *Management Science,* Vol. 17, No. 8, April 1971.

Moran, W., "A Model of Business-Society," *Management Science,* Vol. 16, No. 6, Feb. 1970.

Patcher, M., "Decision Theory in the Study of National Action Problems and a Proposal," *Journal of Conflict Resolution,* Vol. 9, No. 2, 1965.

Reynolds, H.N. Jr. (Ed.), "Intergovernmental Relations in the U.S.," *The Annals,* Vol. 359, May 1965.

Robinson, J., "Decision Making in the House Rules Committee," *Admin. Science Quarterly,* June 1953, pp. 73-86.

Rogers, D., *110 Livingston Street: Politics and Bureaucracy in the New York City Schools,* New York, Random House, 1968.

Young, K., *Negotiating with the Chinese Communists: The United States Experience 1953-67,* New York, McGraw Hill, 1968.

C. Social Policies

Bessiere, F., "The Investment 85 Model of Electricité de France," *Management Science,* Vol. 17, No. 4, Dec. 1970.

Conrad, John P. (Ed.), "The Future of Corrections," *The Annals,* Vol. 381, Jan. 1969.

Cunningham, L., "Educational Governance and Policy Making in Large Cities," *Public Administration,* Vol. XXX, 1970.

Ferman, Louis A. (Ed.), "Evaluating the War on Poverty," *The Annals,* Vol. 385, Sept. 1969.

L. Fitch & Associates, *Urban Transportation and Public Policy,* San Francisco, Chander, 1964.

Haveman, R.H., and Margolis, J. (Eds.), *Public Expenditures and Policy Analysis,* Chicago, Markham, 1970.

Klausner, Samuel Z. (Ed.), "Society and its Physical Environment," *The Annals,* Vol. 389, May, 1970.

Krieger, M., "Six Propositions on the Poor and Pollution," *Policy Sciences,* Vol. 1, No. 3, Fall 1970.

Meyer, J.R., Kain, J.F., and Wohl, M., *The Urban Transportation Problem,* Cambridge, Mass., Harvard University Press, 1966.

Ohlin, Lloyd E., and Ruth, Henry S. Jr. (Eds.), "Combatting Crime," *The Annals,* Vol. 374, Nov. 1967.

Roseman, C., "Rationality in Urban Problem Solving: Transportation," *Urban Affairs Quarterly,* Vol. III, No. 2.

Tri-State Transportation Commission, *Managing the Natural Environment: a Regional Plan,* New York, 1970.

Wolfgang, Marvin E. (Ed.), "Patterns of Violence," *The Annals,* Vol. 364, March 1966.

D. Social Indicators

Bauer, Raymond (Ed.), *Social Indicators,* Cambridge, Mass., MIT Press, 1966.

Boskin, Joseph, and Rosenstone, Robert A. (Ed.), "Protest in the Sixties," *The Annals,* Vol. 382, March 1969.

Carr, F.J., "Urban Statistics & Their Treatment and Use for Decision Makers," *Management Science,* Vol. 16, No. 12, Aug. 1970.

Charlesworth, James C. (Ed.), "Ethics in America," *The Annals,* Jan. 1966.

Enstment, Charles, "A New Approach: To an Urban Information Process," *Management Science,* Vol. 16, No. 12, Aug. 1970.

Etzioni, A., "Some Dangers in Valid Social Measurement," *The Annals,* Vol. 373, Sept. 1967.

Mackay, F., "A Statement Concerning the Evaluation Function in Government," *Management Science,* Vol. 16, No. 4, Dec. 1969.

Olsen, M., "An Analytic Framework for Social Reporting and Policy Analysis," *The Annals,* Vol. 388, March 1970.

Springer, M., "Social Indicators, Reports & Accounts: Toward Management of Society," *The Annals,* Vol. 388, March 1970.

Stagner, R., "An Approach to Urban Indicators," *The Annals,* Vol. 388, March 1970.

Terleckyj, N., "Measuring Progress Towards Social Goals," *Management Science,* Vol. 16, No. 12, Aug. 1970.

E. Urban Management

Buehler, Alfred G. (Ed.), "Financing Democracy," *The Annals,* Vol. 379, Sept. 1968.

Davis, M., and Weinbaum, M., *Metropolitan Decision Processes, An Analysis of Case Studies,* Chicago, McNally, 1969.

Greene, Lee S. (Ed.), "City Bosses & Political Machines," *The Annals,* Vol. 353, May 1964.

Grundstein, N.D., "Urban Information Systems & Urban Management Decision and Control," *Urban Affairs Quarterly,* Vol. 1, No. 3, pp. 20-32.

Mack, Raymond, "Urban Social Differentiation," *The Annals,* Vol. 352, March 1964.

McKelvey, B., *The Emergence of Metropolitan American (1915-1966),* Brunswick, N.J., Rutgers Press, 1968.

Mitchell, Robert B. (Ed.), "Urban Revival: Goals & Standards," *The Annals,* Vol. 352, March 1964.

Schmandt, H., "Metropolitan America: A Mixed Bag of Problems," *Public Administration,* Vol. XXX, p. 188.

Socio-Economic Planning Sciences (July 1968), Vol. 1, No. 3. Issue devoted to "Applications of Computers to Problems in Urban Society."

Socio-Economic Planning Sciences (Oct. 1968-April 1969), Vol. 2; Volume devoted to the "Educational Process and Planning."

Socio-Economic Planning Sciences (March 1970), Vol. 4, No. 1; Issue devoted to "Applications of Computers to Problems in Urban Society."

Stuart, D., "Urban Improvement Programming Models," *Socio-Econ. Plan. Sci.,* Vol. 4, No. 2, June 1970.

F. Developing Countries

Ballon, R.J. (Ed.), *Joint Ventures and Japan,* (Sophia University, Tokyo with Charles E. Tuttle, Company, Rutland, Vermont) 1967.

Charlesworth, James C. (Ed.), "American Civilization: Its Influence on Our Foreign Policy," *The Annals,* Vol. 366, July 1966.

Charlesworth, James C. (Ed.), "Latin America Tomorrow," *The Annals,* Vol. 360, July 1965.

Kapoor, A., *International Business Negotiations: A Study in India,* New York, New York University Press, 1970.

Parmer, T. Norman (Ed.), "The Peace Corps," *The Annals,* Vol. 365, May 1966.

Von Vorys, Karl (Ed.), "New Nations: The Problem of Political Development," *The Annals,* Vol. 358, March 1965.

G. Planning and Adaptive System Design

Ackoff, R.L., "Some Ideas on Education in the Management Sciences," *Management Sciences,* Oct. 1970.

Ackoff, R.L., *A Concept of Corporate Planning,* New York, Wiley, 1970.

Ackoff, R.L., "Towards a System of Systems Concepts," *Management Sciences,* July 1971.

Ackoff, R.L., and Emery, F.E., *On Purposeful Systems,* Chicago, Aldine-Atherton, 1972.

Beer, S., *Decision and Control,* New York, Wiley, 1966.

Beer, S., and Ackoff, R.L., "In Conclusion: Some Beginnings," Aronofsky, J.S. (Ed.), *Progress in Operations Research,* Vol. III, New York, Wiley, 1966.

Branch, M., "Simulation, Mathematical Models & Comprehensive City Planning," *Urban Affairs Quarterly,* Vol. 1, No. 3, pp. 15-38.

The Brookings Institute, "Organizing the U.S. Social & Economic Development," *Public Administration,* Vol. XXX, 1970.

Chadwick, G., *A System View of Planning,* Oxford, England, Pergamon Press, 1971.

Churchman, C.W., *The Design of Inquiring Systems,* New York, Basic Books, 1971.

Cooper, W.W., "An Introduction to Some Papers on Urban Planning, Information, Goals & Implementation," *Management Science,* Vol. 16, No. 12, Aug. 1970.

Emery, F.E. (Ed.), *Systems Thinking,* New York, Penguin, 1969.

Emshoff, J.R., *Analysis of Behavioral Systems,* New York, Macmillan, 1971.

Galbraith, J., "Organization Design: An Information Processing View," *European Institute for Advanced Studies in Management,* Nov. 1972.

Harris, B., and Ackoff, R.L., "Strategies for Operations Research in Urban Metropolitan Planning," D.B. Hertz and J. Melese (Eds.). *The Proceedings of the Fourth International Conference on Operational Research,* New York, Wiley, 1966.

Richfield, J., and Copi, I.M., "Deciding and Predicting," *Philosophy of Science,* Jan. 1961, pp. 47-51.

Stuart, D.G., "Rational Urban Planning: Problems & Prospects," *Urban Affairs Quarterly,* Vol. V.

V. IMPLEMENTATION

Bennis, W.G., Benne, K.D., and Chen, R., *The Planning of Change,* Second Edition, New York, Holt, Rinehart and Winston, 1969.

Biderman, A., "Information, Intelligence, Enlightened Public Policy: Societal Feedback," *Policy Sciences,* Vol. 1, No. 2.

Chik, P.A., *Action Research and Organizational Change,* London, Harper & Row, 1972.

Cooper, W.W., "An Introduction to Some Papers on Urban Planning,

Information, Goals, & Implementation," *Management Science,* Vol. 16, No. 12, August 1970.

Frederickson, H.G., "Exploring Urban Priorities: The Case of Syracuse," *Urban Affairs Quarterly,* Vol. V.

Friend, J.K., and Jessup, W.N., *Local Government and Strategies Choice,* London, Tavistock Publications, 1960.

Gross, Bertram M. and Springer, Michael (Eds.), "Political Intelligence for America's Future," *The Annals,* Vol. 338, March 1970.

Huysmans, J.H.B.M., *The Implementation of Operations Research,* New York, Wiley, 1970.

Leavitt, H.J., "Applied Organizational Change in Industry: Structural, Technological and Humanistic Approaches, J.G. March (Ed.), *Handbook of Organizations,* Chicago, Rand McNally, 1965.

Neal, R.D., and Radnor, M., "The Relations between Formal Procedures for Pursuing OR/MS Activities and OR/MS Group Success," *Operations Research,* Vol. 21, No. 2. March-April 1973.

Radnor, M., and Neal, R.D., "The Progress of Management Science Activities in Large U.S. Industrial Corporations" *Operations Research,* Vol. 21, No. 2, March-April 1973.

Whiteleather, Melvin K. (Ed.), "Seven Polarizing Issues in America Today," *The Annals,* Vol. 397, Sept. 1971.

Wildavsky, A., *The Politics of the Budgetary Process,* Boston, Little Brown, 1964.

Williams, W., *Social Policy Research and Analysis,* New York, American Elsevier, 1971.

Williams, W., and Evans, J.W., "The Politics of Evaluation: The Case of Head Start," *The Annals of the American Academy of Political and Social Science,* September 1969.

VI. PHYSICAL ENVIRONMENT

Accounting for Environmental Pollution, The Committee on Accounting and Auditing Procedure, "The New York Certified Public Accountant," August 1970, pp. 657-661.

Act # 222, Session of 1970 (Pennsylvania Legislature) Article IV, *Other Pollutions and Potential Pollution.*

Air Pollution . . . Where We're At!, "National Safety News," November 1970, pp. 48-52.

Allegheny County Health Department, Rules and Regulations, Article XVII, *Air Pollution Control.*

The Business of Pollution: The Stick and the Carrot, "Columbia Journal of World Business," January-February 1971, pp. 35-41.

"A Blueprint for Survival" (entire issue), *The Ecologist,* January 1972, (British periodical).

Brubaker, Sterling, *To Live on Earth,* Baltimore, Johns Hopkins Press, 1972.

Bylinsky, G., *"The Mounting Bill for Pollution Control,* "Fortune," July 1971, pp. 86-89, 130-132.

California Task Force Calls for Cooperation, "Solid Wastes Management," April 1970, pp. 14-15, 44.

Chamberlain, Neil W., *Enterprise and Environment, Long Range Planning in an Expanding Economy,* (AMA).

Charnes, A., Cooper, W.W., and Kozmetsky, G. (Eds.), "Management Science Ecology and The Quality of Life," *Management Science,* Vol. 19, No. 10, June 1973.

Corporate Responsibility and the Environment, "The Conference Board Record," April 1971, pp. 42-47.

Council on Economic Priorities, Paper Profits: Pollution in the Pulp and Paper Industry, "Economic Priorities Report," Vol. 1, No. 6, December-January, 1971.

C.E.P., *Campaigns for Corporate Responsibility: Commonwealth Edison Challenged Over Air Pollution,* "Economic Priorities Report," Vol. 1, No. 1, April 1970, pp. 13-14.

Dahmen, E., *Problems of Environmental Policy in Relation to General Economic Policy,* Economic Commission for Europe Conference on Problems Relating to Environment, May 1971.

Dales, J.H., *Pollution, Property and Prices,* "An Essay in Policy-Making and Economics," University of Toronto Press, Toronto, 1968.

Davies, J.C., *Pollution: Developing a Public Policy, Management Review,* May 1970, pp. 16-21.

DeBell, Garrett (Ed.), *The Environmental Handbook,* New York, Ballantine Books, 1970.

Dole, Hollis M., "Economic Needs Must Not be Abandoned for Environment's Sake," *American Banker,* New York, October 18, 1971, pp. 48-51.

Ehrlich, P., *The Population Bomb,* New York, Ballantine Books.

The Environment Monthly, the Environment League, Inc., New York, April 1971.

Ford, Henry, "Controlling Environmental Pollution," A Progress Report, Ford Motor Company, December 10, 1970.

Friedman, Milton, *Capitalism and Freedom,* Chicago, University of Chicago Press, 1962.

Goldman, Marshall I. (Ed.), *Controlling Pollution: The Economics of a Cleaner America,* Englewood Cliffs, N.J., Prentice-Hall, 1967.

"Growing Industrial Expenditures for Pollution Control," *The Conference Board Record,* February 1970.

"A Guide to Industrial Pollution Control: Section IV: Air Pollution Control," *Chemical Engineering,* April 27, 1970.

Hickel, Walter J., *Who Owns America?,* New York, Paperback Library, 1972.

Jarrett, H., *Environmental Quality,* Baltimore, Johns Hopkins Press, 1966.

Jesser, B., "Natural Resources Management," *Mechanical Engineering,* March 1969, pp. 25-28.

Kolb, W.J., "Chrysler Plant Offers Pollution Solution," *The Iron Age*, May 2, 1968.

Kelso, Louis O., and Hetter, Patricia, *Two-Factor Theory: The Economics of Reality*, New York, Random House, Vintage paperback, V482, 1968.

Kneese, Allen V., *The Economics of Regional Water Quality Management*, Baltimore, Johns Hopkins Press, 1964.

Lund, L., "Industry's Current Pollution Control Costs," *The Conference Board Record*, April 1971, pp. 39-41.

McClanahan, R., "More Money for Pollution Control," *The Conference Board Record*, Vol. v, No. 9, September 1968, pp. 26-29.

Moody's Stock Survey, "Pollution: A Soaring Cost of Industrialization," Special Report, Vol. 61, No. 41, October 13, 1969, pp. 417-433.

Moranian, Thomas *et al.* (Eds.), *Business Policy and Its Environment*, New York, Holt, Rinehart and Winston, 1965.

National Wildlife Federation, *Conservation Directory*, Washington, D.C., undated.

National Wildlife Federation, *EQ Reference Guide*, Washington, D.C., NWF Series #49647 KG, no date.

"1971 EQ Index," *National Wildlife*, October-November, 1971.

Revelle, Roger, and Landsberg, Hans I., *America's Changing Environment*, Boston, Massachusetts, Houghton Mifflin, 1970.

Ridgeway, James, *The Politics of Pollution*, New York, Dutton, 1970.

"The Economics of Environmental Quality," *Fortune*, February, 1970, pp. 120-123, 184-186.

Sierra Club Handbook for Environmental Activists, *Ecotactics*, New York, Pocket Books, 1970.

Slomich, S.J., *The American Nightmare*, New York, Macmillan, 1971.

Smith, F., "To Win the War on Water Pollution: A New Approach to the Disposal of Liquid Waste," *The Conference Board Record*, April 1970, pp. 13-17.

"Society and its Physical Environment," *The Annals*, Vol. 389, May 1970.

"Studies Outline Pollution Economics," *Engineering News Record*, March 21, 1968.

Survey Pegs Pollution Control Needs in the $35-Billion Range," *Engineering News-Record*, July 16, 1970.

U.S. Dept. of Interior, "Cost of Clean Water," Vol. 1, Summary Report.

U.S. Senate, "Summary and Analysis of Legislation Pending before the Subcommittee on Air and Water Pollution of the Committee on Public Works," March 1971.

Votaw, D., and Sethi, P., "Do We Need a New Corporate Response to a Changing Social Environment?" *California Management Review*, 1969, No. 1, Vol. 12, No. 1, pp. 3-31.

Wolozin, Harold (Ed.), *The Economics of Air Pollution: A Symposium*, New York, Norton, 1966.

VII. COMMUNITY & EDUCATION

American Management Association, "The President's Involvement in Urban Problems," Frank Doeringer, *The President's Association, Inc.*, January-February 1969.

American Society of Corporate Secretaries, *Corporate Contributions Report*, 3rd Edition, New York, March 1965.

Barr, John A., "Seven Guides to Better Community Relations," *Management Review*, June 1957, Vol. 46, No. 6, pp. 44-46.

Baumol, William J., "Enlightened Self-Interest and Corporate Philanthropy," *A New Rationale for Corporate Social Policy*, Committee for Economic Development, Supplementary Paper Number 31, New York, 1970.

Berg, Ivar E., *Education and Jobs: The Great Training Robbery*, Center for Urban Education, New York, Praeger, 1970.

Cohn, J. "Is Business Meeting the Challenge of Urban Affairs?" *Harvard Business Review*, March/April, 1970, pp. 68-82.

Commoner, Barry, *The Closing Circle*, New York, Knopf, 1971.

Commission on Foundations and Private Philantrophy, "Foundations Private Giving, and Public Policy," Chicago Press, University of Chicago, Standard Book Number: 0-226-66286-1.

Committee for Economic Development, "Paying for Better Public Schools," and "Raising Low Incomes Through Improved Education," New York, 1959 and 1965, respectively.

Council for Financial Aid to Education, Inc., "1968 Survey of Corporation Support of Higher Education," New York, November 1969.

Council for Financial Aid to Education, Inc., "Aid-To-Education Programs of Some Leading Business Concerns," December 1970.

Davis, K., and Blomstrom, R.L., *Business, Society, and Environment: Social Power and Social Response*, New York, McGraw-Hill, 1971.

Eells, Richard, *The Meaning of Modern Business*, New York, Columbia University Press, 1960.

Eells, Richard, "A Philosophy for Corporate Giving," *The Conference Board Record*, Vol. V, No. 1, January 1968, pp. 14-18.

Fielden, J., "Today the Campuses, Tomorrow the Corporations," *Business Horizons*, Vol. 13, No. 3, 1970, pp. 13-30.

Fisher, Barton R., and Withey, Stephen B., *Big Business as the People See It*, Ann Arbor, Michigan, University of Michigan Survey Research Center, 1951.

Freedman, Marcia, "Business and Education," Ivar Berg (Ed.), *The Business of America*, New York, Harcourt, Brace & World, 1968.

"IBM and the Community: What a Corporation Can Do," *Think*, December 1971, pp. 34-40.

Kimball, L., "Business as Usual with the Foundations, or a New Partnership with Business?" *The Conference Board Record*, October 1970, pp. 45-49.

"Making Company Contributions More Effective," *The Conference Board Record*, Vol. VI, No. 2, February 1969.

Mintz, Morton, and Cohen, Jerry S., *America Inc.*, New York, Dial Press, 1971.

Myrdal, Gunnar, *Beyond the Welfare State*, New York, Bantam Books, 1960.

NICB, "Philanthropy and the Corporation," *The Conference Board Record*, Vol. V, No. 1, January 1968.

NICB, "Business Amid Urban Crisis: Private-Sector Approaches to City Problems," 1968.

NICB, "Mayors Evaluate Business Action on Urban Problems," New York, Grace J. Finley, 1968.

NICB, "The Urban Dilemma: Seven Steps Toward Resolution," No. 7, 1969.

NICB, "Report on Company Contributions for 1968," New York, 1969.

NICB, "20 Company-Sponsored Foundations, Programs and Policies," No. 6, 1970, pp. 9-70.

Odiorne, G., *Green Power: The Corporation and the Urban Crisis*, New York, Pitman, 1969.

Walton, C., *Corporate Social Responsibilities*, Belmont, California, Wadsworth, 1967.

Ward, Barbara, *The Lopsided World*, New York, Norton, 1968; *Spaceship Earth*, New York, Columbia University Press, 1966.

Watson, John H., "Corporate Contributions Policy," *The Conference Board Record*, Vol. IV, No. 6, June 1967.

VIII. MANPOWER (EMPLOYEES)

Blum, Fred H., "Social Audit of the Enterprise," *Harvard Business Review*, March/April 1958, Vol. 36, No. 2, pp. 77-86.

Brooks, G., "Ethical Responsibilities of Labor," *Stanford Business Bulletin*, 1963.

Ginsburg, Eli, *The American Worker in the 20th Century*, New York, (Macmillan), Free Press of Glencoe, 1963.

Ginsburg, Eli, *The Development of Human Resources*, New York, McGraw Hill, 1966.

Ginsburg, Eli, *Manpower Strategy for the Metropolitis*, Conservation of Human Resources Staff, New York, Columbia University Press, 1968.

Ginsburg, Eli, *Manpower Agenda for America, Essays*, New York, McGraw Hill, 1968.

Jay, A., *Management and Machiavelli: An Inquiry Into the Politics of Corporate Life*, New York, Holt, Rinehart and Winston, 1968.

Kaufmann, Carl B., *Man Incorporate: The Individual and His Work in an Organized Society*, New York, Doubleday, 1967.

Likert, Rensis. *The Human Organization: Its Management and Value*, New York, McGraw-Hill, 1967.

McGregor, Douglas, "The Human Side of Enterprise," 1957, in Leavitt, H.J., and Pondy, L.R., *Readings in Managerial Psychology,* 1964, Chicago, University of Chicago press, pp. 267-279.

Pyle, William, C., "Human Resources Accounting," *Financial Analysts Journal,* September-October 1970, Vol. 26, No. 5, pp. 69-78.

Ruttenberg, Stanley H., and Gutchess, Jocelyn, *Manpower Challenge of the 1970's: Institutions and Social Change,* Baltimore, Johns Hopkins Press, 1970.

Sayles, Leonard R., *Behavior of Industrial Work Groups: Prediction and Control,* New York, Wiley, 1958.

Sayles, L.R., *et al., The Measure of Management, Designing Organizations for Human Effectiveness,* New York, Macmillan, 1961.

Sayles, Leonard R., *Human Behavior in Organizations,* Englewood Cliffs, N.J., Prentice-Hall, 1966.

Sayles, L.R., and Strauss, George, *Personnel: The Human Problems of Management,* Englewood Cliffs, N.J., Prentice-Hall, 1967.

Schoen, Donald R., "Human Relations: Boon or Boggle?" *Harvard Business Review,* November/December 1957, Vol. 35, No. 6, pp. 41-47.

Shepard, Paul, and McKinley, Daniel (Eds.), *The Subversive Science, Essays Toward an Ecology of Man,* Boston, Mass., Houghton Mifflin, 1969.

Theobald, Robert, *Free Men and Free Markets,* New York, Potter, 1963.

Whyte, William H., Jr., *The Organization Man,* New York, Simon and Schuster, 1956.

IX. CONSUMERISM

Aaker, D., and Day, G., *Consumerism: Search for The Consumer Interest,* New York, Free Press, 1971.

Caplovitz, D., "Consumer Credit in the Affluent Society," *Law and Contemporary Problems,* 1968, Vol. 33, No. 4, pp. 641-55.

Cordtz, Dar, "City Hall Discovers Productivity," *Fortune,* October 1971, pp. 92.

Cravens, D., and Hills, G., "Consumerism: A Perspective for Business," *Business Horizons,* 1970, Vol. 13, No. 4, pp. 21-28.

Grether, Ewald T., *Marketing and Public Policy,* Englewood Cliffs, N.J., Prentice-Hall, 1966.

Lavidge, Robert J., and Holloway, Robert J. (Eds.), *Marketing and Society, the Challenge,* Homewood, Illinois: Irwin, 1969.

Levitt, T., "The Morality of Advertising," *Harvard Business Review,* 1970, Vol. 48, No. 4, pp. 84-92.

Magnuson, Sen. R., *The Dark Side of the Marketplace,* Englewood Cliffs, N.J., Prentice-Hall.

Nader, Ralph, *Unsafe at Any Speed,* New York, Grossman, 1965.

Nelson, J. Russell, and Strickland, Aubrey (Eds.), *Ethics and Marketing,* Minneapolis, Minn., University of Minnesota, 1966.

Packard, Vance, *The Hidden Persuaders,* New York, McKay, 1957, Pocket Books, 1958.

Preston, Lee E. (Ed.), *Social Issues in Marketing,* Glenview, Ill., Scott, Foresman, 1968.

Public Law 90-321 May 29, 1968, *Consumer Credit Protection Act,* Title I, Consumer Credit Cost Disclosure.

Quinn, Francis X., S.J. (Ed.), *Ethics, Advertising, and Responsibility,* Canterbury, Westminster, Maryland, 1963.

Stevens, William D., *The Social Responsibilities of Marketing,* Proceedings of the Winter Conference, December 27-29, 1961, Chicago AMA, 1962.

Turner, James S., *The Chemical Feast,* New York, Grossman, 1970.

X. POLITICS & GOVERNMENT

Baran, Paul A., *The Political Economy of Growth,* New York, Monthly Review, 1957.

Committee for Economic Development, *Social Responsibilities of Business Corporations,* A Statement by the Research and Policy Committee, June 1971.

Cheit, Earl F. (Ed.), *The Business Establishment,* New York, Wiley, 1964.

Council on Economic Priorities, *Efficiency in Death,* New York, Harper and Row, 1971.

Drucker, Peter, *The New Society: The Anatomy of the Social Order,* New York, Harper, 1950.

Drucker, Peter, *The Age of Discontinuity,* New York, Harper and Row, 1969.

Epstein, Edwin M., *The Corporation in American Politics,* Englewood Cliffs, N.J., Prentice-Hall, 1969.

"Financing Democracy," *The Annals,* Vol. 379, September 1968.

Friedmann, W., "Corporate Power, Government by Private Groups, and the Law," *Columbia Law Review,* 1957, Vol 57, No. 2, pp. 155-186.

Hacker, Andrew, *The Corporation Takeover,* Garden City, New York, Anchor Books, 1965.

Heilbroner, Robert L., *Between Capitalism and Socialism, Essays in Political Economics,* New York, Vintage Books, 1970.

Osborne, Philip B., *The War That Business Must Win,* New York, McGraw-Hill, 1970.

Sheldon, Horace, E., "Businessmen Must Get Into Politics," *Harvard Business Review,* March/April 1959, Vol. 37, No. 2, pp. 37-47.

Steiner, George, *Government's Role in Economic Life,* New York, McGraw-Hill, 1953.

Index